The Furies of Marjorie Bowen

Marjorie Bowen, 1930

The Furies of Marjorie Bowen

JOHN C. TIBBETTS

Foreword by Michael Dirda

McFarland & Company, Inc., Publishers
Jefferson, North Carolina

Also by John C. Tibbetts:
The Gothic Worlds of Peter Straub (McFarland, 2016)

Note on the cover painting: William-Adolphe Bouguereau's *Orestes Pursued by the Furies*," dates from 1862. It is reproduced with permission from the Chrysler Museum, Norfolk, Virginia (gift of Walter P. Chrysler, Jr. 71.623). The painting illustrates a moment in the *Oresteia*, the second play from Aeschylus's *Oresteian Trilogy*, from the 5th century BCE, when Orestes is assaulted by the vengeful Furies after murdering his mother, Clytemnestra.
Orestes cries out: "Look, see them, there! Like Gorgons, with grey cloaks and snakes coiled swarming around their bodies! I know them—avenging hounds incensed by a mother's blood. And see—their dreadful eyes dripping with bloody pus! I know you do not see these beings, but I see them. I am lashed and driven! I can't bear it!"

All drawings in this book are by John C. Tibbetts

Unless otherwise designated, all photographs
are courtesy of the Marjorie Bowen Estate

LIBRARY OF CONGRESS CATALOGUING-IN-PUBLICATION DATA

Names: Tibbetts, John C., author. | Dirda, Michael, writer of foreword.
Title: The furies of Marjorie Bowen / John C. Tibbetts ;
foreword by Michael Dirda.
Description: Jefferson, North Carolina : McFarland & Company, Inc.,
Publishers, 2020 | Includes bibliographical references and index.
Identifiers: LCCN 2019046387 | ISBN 9781476677163 (paperback ; acid-free paper) ∞
ISBN 9781476638164 (ebook)
Subjects: LCSH: Bowen, Marjorie, 1888–1952--Criticism and interpretation.
Classification: LCC PR6003.O676 Z87 2020 | DDC 823/.912--dc23
LC record available at https://lccn.loc.gov/2019046387

BRITISH LIBRARY CATALOGUING DATA ARE AVAILABLE

ISBN (print) 978-1-4766-7716-3
ISBN (ebook) 978-1-4766-3816-4

© 2019 John C. Tibbetts. All rights reserved

No part of this book may be reproduced or transmitted in any form or by any means, electronic or mechanical, including photocopying or recording, or by any information storage and retrieval system, without permission in writing from the publisher.

Printed in the United States of America

McFarland & Company, Inc., Publishers
Box 611, Jefferson, North Carolina 28640
www.mcfarlandpub.com

To the Enchanter and Muse of my life,
Ms. Mary Lou Pagano

Table of Contents

Acknowledgments — ix
Foreword by Michael Dirda — 1
Introduction: "Music at Midnight" — 5

ONE • "The Music on the Hill": Pagans and Christians — 13
TWO • "Painting History": The Historical Romances — 53
THREE • "We Human Beings Cannot Endure Too Much Reality": The Ghost Stories — 97
FOUR • "Curious Happenings": The Short Stories — 119
FIVE • "Angels of the Darker Drink": The True-Crime Stories of Joseph Shearing — 157
SIX • Marjorie Bowen: A Life Within — 183

Appendix I: Biographical Timeline — 193
Appendix II: "Too Much Posturing": Media Adaptations — 195
Chapter Notes — 207
Bibliography — 218
Index — 221

Acknowledgments

Above all, I wish to thank Sharon Eden and the Estate of Gabrielle Long for permissions to quote from the many writings cited in this book. Ms. Eden has been a constant companion, by mail and email, always responsive to my many questions and unfailingly generous in sharing materials and enthusiasms. This association has proven to be one of my happiest experiences in preparing this book. Also, my appreciation to Moira Fitzgerald of the Beinecke Rare Book and Manuscript Library at Yale University for the two days I spent examining the Marjorie Bowen Papers. Thanks to Nicholas Diak and Michele Brittany, who invited me to speak about Marjorie Bowen at the Ann Radcliffe Academic Conference, held in Providence, Rhode Island, as part of the 2018 StokerCon. My gratitude goes also to Natalie Foreman of McFarland for her patience and encouragement, Jessica Amanda Salmonson, who shared with me her views on Bowen. Many friends and colleagues read and commented on portions of the manuscript, including Jon Lellenberg, T.E.D. Klein, Michael Dirda, Jason and Sunni Brock, William F. Nolan, Harry Haskell, and Dan Nastali. My colleagues in the Department of Film and Media Studies at the University of Kansas have been very supportive, and I want to acknowledge my Chair in the Department of Film and Media Studies, Professor Michael Baskett, and Professors Matt Jacobson, Kevin Willmott (congratulations on your Oscar!), Catherine Preston, Brian Faucette, Josh and Stephanie Wille. My Department Executive Secretary, Karla Conrad, and University Administrative Assistant, Pam LeRow ably assisted me in the preparation and formatting of the manuscript. I hope I have not

Sharon and Mike Eden of the Bowen Estate (courtesy Bowen Estate).

exhausted the patience of personal friends who gave of their time to read portions of the manuscript, including Professors Baerbel Goebel Stolz of Coventry University and Cindy Miller of Emerson College. And, of course, my love and thanks to my Muse and Enchanter, Mary Lou Pagano, whose wise counsel, patience, and encouragement have seen me through more than a few doubts, hesitations, and obstacles encountered along the way.

All that being said, any errors in the book are mine alone.

Author John C. Tibbetts at Beinecke Library, Yale (courtesy Harry Haskell).

"I am Fantasy, day-dreaming and the unattainable. I beckon just round the corner where no one has been yet. I reside in those violet horizons which no man has reached. I am all you missed in the past and will evade you in the future. I am all that is incredible yet pursued, all that is never credited, yet longed for. Those who do not know me are no better than blind worms, but those who do know me are always tormented by unsatisfied desires."
—Marjorie Bowen, "Homage to the Unknown"

Foreword
by Michael Dirda

To discover—or rediscover—an important but neglected writer is nearly every scholar's dream. How is it that authors such as Jean Toomer and Dawn Powell or novels as beloved as John Williams's *Stoner* once came close to being forgotten? It seems impossible. Yet such—until now—has been the fate of Marjorie Bowen. Happily, this neglect should soon be over. John C. Tibbetts's *The Furies of Marjorie Bowen* provides so knowledgeable and enthusiastic an introduction to this astonishing woman of letters that it will almost certainly send readers to bookshops, libraries and internet sites, eagerly searching for her fiction and nonfiction.

Much of it, alas, is still hard to find. I acquired my copy of *"Five Winds"*—one of the supernaturally inflected novels that Tibbetts raves about—from a bookdealer in Sweden who didn't do any international business. So a Swedish friend bought the novel for me. Since he in his turn didn't trust Paypal, he asked me to send him a parcel of my own books in lieu of cash. A little later, on a business trip to London, my wife picked up a copy of the fragile paperback issue of *The Devil Snar'd* from the wonderful Any Amount of Books.

More recently, amidst a raucous visit to my oldest son and his family in Portland, Oregon, I escaped one afternoon to Powell's "City of Books" where I found the short-story collections *Bagatelle* and *The Knot Garden*. And so it goes. Just yesterday, after finishing *The Furies of Marjorie Bowen*, I went online to snag one of the few copies then available of *The Courtly Charlatan*, Bowen's account oft the 18th-century magus, the Comte de Saint-Germain. Given Tibbetts' description of its pleasures, you would do the same.

The hunt is obviously part of the fun in book-collecting, but I'm sure some savvy publisher will soon reprint many of the above titles. As it is, my copy of *The Poisoners*—which Tibbetts likens to John Dickson Carr's eerie masterpiece, *The Burning Court*—is a handsome, readily available contemporary paperback. Several well-chosen selections from Bowen's ghost stories and "twilight tales" are also relatively easy to find. The Arkham House *Kecksies* assembles such anthology favorites as "The Crown Derby Plate," "Scoured Silk" and "The Avenging of Ann Leete" while the Ash-Tree Press compilation *Twilight* adds a dozen others, including "The Fair Hair of Ambrosine" and that bewitching and chilling short novel, *Julia Roseingrave*. What's more, that volume features a superb essay on Bowen by Jessica Amanda Salmonson.

Still, Tibbetts—author of *The Gothic Imagination*, among many other excellent studies—is now our go-to authority on this splendid writer. Not only does he know the work better than anyone now alive, but he's also earned the enthusiastic support of the Bowen estate, which generously granted him full access to the writer's archives. As a result, once you've read Tibbetts's wide-ranging overview of Bowen's career, you will wonder how she could have ever fallen into relative obscurity. I suspect that her early success, her avoidance of simple happy endings, and the sheer range and volume of her writing have worked against her, as it sometimes seems to have done for our own era's comparably brilliant and versatile Joyce Carol Oates.

As you will learn in the coming pages, Margaret Gabrielle Vere Campbell, born in 1885, began work on her first novel—a Machiavellian swashbuckler set in the Renaissance—around the age of 16. When *The Viper of Milan* appeared in 1906, she was all of 21. This first success was quickly followed by two further blood-soaked historical romances, *The Glen O'Weeping*—wisely retitled *The Master of Stair* for its American edition—and *The Sword Decides*. By then, the young Bowen had earned the admiration of such literary eminences as Mark Twain and Arthur Conan Doyle. Graham Greene would later join them in praising her work. In his essay "The Lost Childhood," he specifically pointed to his adolescent discovery of *The Viper of Milan* as a primal moment in the evolution of his imagination.

In 1974 Dennis Wheatley—author of the occult classic *The Devil Rides Out*—included Bowen's *Black Magic* in a reprint series he oversaw devoted to supernatural classics. He concluded his introduction by calling the final chapters of this 1909 "Tale of the Rise and Fall of the Antichrist" nothing less than a "*tour de force* in describing the terrific battle between the powers of Good and Evil."

By the time of her death in 1952, Bowen had written over 150 books and at least that many short stories. Though publishing most often as Marjorie Bowen, she also used the pennames George Preedy and Joseph Shearing, the first for numerous historical romances and the second for noirish novels based on celebrated crimes, often poisoning, and usually featuring abused or desperate women. Several books were turned into successful movies and Tibbetts—who teaches film at the University of Kansas—provides an insightful filmography.

Since Bowen supported herself and three sons by her pen, she needed to work fast, scribbling or sometimes dictating a steady series of novels, biographies, plays, *contes cruels* and historical studies. Whatever the project, she could always count on her natural gifts as a storyteller to carry her through, most notably a flair for evocative description and an ability to enter into the inner selves of ruthless and clever men and women who typically view themselves as "beyond good and evil." Such amoral overreachers, however, seldom come to happy ends. Georgette Heyer's Regency romances could conclude, after 250 pages of stormy action and witty repartee, with the ringing of joyous wedding bells—not so Bowen's much more sinister, albeit equally accomplished excursions into history. As Shearing, in particular, she dealt in unhappy marriages, sordid adulteries and murderous spouses. Whether beautiful or brainy, her Nietzschean heroes and heroines discover, in Jim Morrison's words, that "No one here gets out alive." The rock singer's signature phrase might well sum up Bowen's clear-eyed philosophy of both fiction and life.

Let me stress, though, that one finds throughout her writing a welcome thread of wry humor, often the kind of ironic wit expected of suave rogues and sly villains. Still, the book you hold in your hands isn't called *The Furies of Marjorie Bowen* for nothing. Just take a look at that Bouguereau cover painting. Bowen's thrillingly told stories will leave anyone shaken and stirred, shocked and exalted. As John C. Tibbetts demonstrates again and again, her stunning work deserves rediscovery and reprinting, but also something more: the attention of readers like you.

Michael Dirda is a Pulitzer Prize–winning critic for *The Washington Post*. He is the author of several books about books, most recently the essay collection *Browsings* and the Edgar Award–winning *On Conan Doyle*.

Introduction: "Music at Midnight"

There they were, handwritten, a few lines on a scrap of paper:

> My life was not set in pleasant places
> In the jostle of the hundreds I always stood alone.
> I saw the devil look through many laughing faces
> And often felt his likeness rising in my own.
> —Marjorie Bowen.[1]

While researching a book that has come to be called *The Furies of Marjorie Bowen*, I had already spent two days going through the Marjorie Bowen Papers at Yale's Beinecke Library, when I ran across these lines, written in her own hand on ruled paper in a little black notebook. It was tucked away in a folder along with pages and pages of handwritten notes, publisher's contracts, and photographs. Those lines leaped off the page and waggled their dark fingers at me. They inspired my search but have continued to rebuke my attempts to understand the mysteries of the life, work, and contradictions of this most elusive of twentieth-century British writers.

Born Gabrielle Margaret Vere Campbell (1885–1952), the woman the literary world came to know as "Marjorie Bowen" quietly and industriously produced in a lifetime of struggle and stress more than 150 published novels and biographies, dozens of sharply etched social commentaries, and more than two hundred short stories of an incredible variety.

I could never have anticipated what I was getting in to when I first considered tackling the subject three years ago. I couldn't yet know what I didn't know. Which is to say, now that I know what I know, I can only offer the reader, at best, a work in progress. Locating and reading the staggering number of her writings demands superhuman industry, and I am a mere mortal. Tracing the course of her life invites a measure of speculation, even empathy, and I am no seer. And attempting to walk in her footsteps requires a long stride, and I have stubbed my toe on reality.

Marjorie Bowen, 1920

STARING AT ASHES, RECALLING THE FLAMES

How do we explain the current obscurity of a writer once celebrated in her own lifetime? How did she transmute a lonely, neglected, and untutored childhood into a career writing fiction and nonfiction of considerable range and erudition? Who did she know; what did she read; and how did she write? How did she maintain her career while enduring a wretched childhood, supporting two troubled marriages, surviving two world wars, and shouldering the responsibilities as the sole breadwinner for her family? And how did she feel about her status as woman in a mostly male-dominated literary community? At hand are just two autobiographical memoirs, a cache of papers at Yale, a handful of available newspaper and magazine accounts, and a few essays by her admirers.[2] That construct called "Marjorie Bowen" floats out there, like Lewis Carroll's Cheshire Cat, itself a fiction, insubstantial, faintly mocking, always beckoning...

How to begin? She herself provides a hint in her whimsical Introduction to a volume of stories called *Shadows of Yesterday* (1916), in which she rambles through a museum of historical artifacts. The biographer, she says, is like an archaeologist on a dig, sifting through the fossil remains, or a detective on a case, considering the clues:

> If one could look back—beyond the dust, beyond the years to the time when all these dead things were fresh—when the originals of those portraits moved and worked and laughed, when beer was really brewed in those jugs and tea drunk from those cups, when those cards were dashed on to the playing table, when that sword graced some gallant's thigh, that paste necklace some woman's neck.... If one could look back to those times, might not one find curious stories, sad stories, and gay stories attached to these old worthless objects?—as staring at ashes one may recall the flames [5].

Maybe there's only scant evidence to work with. A measure of empathy is needed. In her short story, "Ann Mellor's Lover," from *Seeing Life*, only a piece of paper bearing a penciled portrait is at hand: "I knew that it was a clue that I was bound to follow through the labyrinth of the past. The feeling was that I knew all about it—the whole story but could not for the moment remember it...." Soon, the crude drawing assumes in his mind "a warm-coloured human face; she lived before my inner eye, a complete creature," *yet one that was a "dark, troubled creature about whom I felt such excitement."* italics added] (92–93).

This, to me is Marjorie Bowen. There is a certain seductiveness about her. Be warned: As you turn these pages, you may find yourself likewise happily entangled in her riddles and mysteries.

"THEIR WORKS SHALL FOLLOW THEM"

We must turn to her writings. Gladly. In the face of a scanty biographical record, Marjorie Bowen demands that we read her works. They help connect the dots to suggest the Figure in the Carpet that was her life. I unabashedly subscribe to the words of Walter Benjamin. I put them in italics: *"The traces of the Storyteller cling to the story the way the handprints of the potter cling to the clay vessel."*[3]

I believe wholeheartedly in that. Despite what textual critics, among others, may say, I am convinced that writers may run, but they cannot hide. The problem here is that Bowen ran *fast*, as if the very Furies hounded and drove her. Perhaps, as the title of this book implies, perhaps they did. And she was so damned *prolific*, as if prescient of the unexpected demise that awaited her. Moreover, we might reasonably expect that a body of work of such abundance and variety could not possibly be the work of just one writer. Indeed, to the confusion of readers and critics of her day and even now, the books are published under the names "Joseph Shearing," "George R. Preedy," "Robert Paye," "John Winch," "Margaret Campbell," and, yes, "Marjorie Bowen." They all belong to one woman, born in 1885 in Hayling Island, Hampshire. Her autobiography, *The Debate Continues* (1939), rather compounds this name game. It was published under the authorship "Margaret Campbell," but subtitled as "Being the Autobiography of Marjorie Bowen"! Sometimes it is written in the first person; at others, in the third. Subjective and objective voices intermingle, or, as may be, are at odds. There are even instances when she attached the name "Long," carried over from her second husband, Arthur L. Long. "I have used many names for business purposes," Bowen declared, rather disingenuously in another memoir, "Myself When Young" (1938), "but they were none of them of my own choosing and seemed rather to be fastened on me like a series of masks." She adds, mysteriously, "I did not greatly care for any of them, nor does my other name—legally mine—appear to belong to me."[4]

And so, it is best if I simply group all these personae under the sobriquet by which she is best known, "Marjorie Bowen."[5] And that is the name under which she published in 1906 her first novel, *The Viper of Milan,* begun when she was just sixteen. This colorful melodrama of Renaissance violence and intrigue drew raves from *The New York Times* and so impressed Mark Twain that he sought an interview with her. Other writers soon in her thrall included Rebecca West and Arthur Conan Doyle.[6] It so dazzled the young Graham Greene that, as he recalled later, "One could not read her without believing that to write was to live and to enjoy, and before one had discovered one's mistake it was too late.... Anyway, she had given me my pattern—religion might later explain it to me in other terms, but the pattern was already there—perfect evil walking the world where perfect good can never walk again."[7] And "Marjorie Bowen" is the name attached to her last novel, *The Man with the Scales,* posthumously published in 1954, two years after her death. By contrast to *Viper,* it crowns her career with a narrative so complex, so elusive, that it has baffled readers then and now. It qualifies as a postmodernist experiment long before the term was coined.

In between, what do have?

Of the more than 150 books and two hundred short stories, barely a handful of her weird tales are read today. But, to quote James Cagney, they are "*cherse.*" Bowen enthusiast, and herself an acclaimed author of fantasy and the supernatural, Jessica Amanda Salmonson, has argued: "I declare her supernatural romances not merely among the best ever composed, but more than that, they deliver evidence that even at our lowest and meanest, there is something of merit and beauty in the transience and suffering of human existence."[8] And in his recent assessment of weird fiction by women, including Elizabeth Gaskell, Vernon Lee, and Edith Wharton, Pulitzer Prize–winning critic Michael Dirda declares Bowen the finest British woman writer of the uncanny of the last century.[9]

But what about the *other* short stories? These are stories of piquant social commentary, roaring adventure, and historical anecdote scattered among many volumes published under her name in her lifetime. Together, they constitute a major body of work that, although unheralded today, I argue constitutes a formidable contribution to the art of the short story in the first half of the twentieth century.

The many historical novels and true-crime dramatizations, which enjoyed a measure of popularity and critical respect in her day, are now almost forgotten. While sharing the themes and subjects of the short stories, they are more leisurely, detailed, and complex in character and incident. They constitute an *oeuvre* whose sheer variety of subjects and narrative complexities challenge and delight. In her day they were highly praised. "She has handled fact in the manner of a novelist," wrote cultural critic Edward Wagenknecht; "she has used her imagination to explain what life left unexplained."[10] Reading them is no mere lazy afternoon's entertainment. They demand attention and concentration. The rewards are immense.

As to the many other volumes, the essays on religion and philosophy and progressive social commentary, and the biographies of historical figures, male and female—including William of Orange, George Washington, Charlotte Corday, Mary Wollstonecraft, William Hogarth, William Cobbett—where are they? They are totally unknown. Yet they all bear the stamp of Bowen's academic rigor, narrative drive, and sharply observed detail. They cry out for our attention.

A FEMALE GOTHIC?

Any consideration of Bowen must estimate her place in the tradition of what has come to be known as the Female Gothic. Once dubbed "an enchanting brewer of dread,"[11] Bowen follows in the literary footsteps of Ann Radcliffe, Mary Shelley, the Brontës, George Eliot, Charlotte Perkins Gilman, Edith Wharton, and other women who, since the late eighteenth century, have demonstrated a profound insight into the darker aspects of the human experience, particularly the tangled mysteries of female identity. Ellen Moers famously described the "Female Gothic" as a construction wherein women are "examined with a woman's eye, woman as girl, as sister, as mother, as self." More broadly, she continues, it is a genre to which women impart a feminine perspective on patriarchal societies that thrive on the marginalization and outright repression of women.[12] This has produced nothing less, declares Patricia Murphy in *The New Woman Gothic*, than a recent reinvigoration of Gothic studies in general.[13]

But while many of Bowen's novels and stories—particularly *Stinging Nettles, Moss Rose, Golden Violet, Blanche Fury, For Her to Keep, Airing in a Closed Carriage*—are, underneath their intense and near-hallucinatory surfaces, devastating indictments of the stifling conventions of society and gender that impede women's struggle against male authority and the loss of civil identity, their women depart somewhat from the passive stereotypes. They are rarely helpless. They give as good as they get. They are creatures of *agency*. More often monstrous aggressors than helpless victims, they inherit the mantle of those women generally described as "mad women in the attic," in the classic volume of that name by Sandra M. Gilbert and Susan Gubar.[14]

For example... A special subset of this topic will be referenced frequently in these pages and gives it name to the title of this book. Bowen herself acknowledged as her muses the Furies of Greek and Roman mythology. As we shall see, their murderous intensity and poisonous practices inspired and fueled many of her female characters. Thus, Bowen, while happily not a poisoner herself—but perhaps under a "chtonian cloud" of her own at times—may be regarded as herself an agent of the Furies.[15]

"THERE'S A LONG, LONG TRAIL A-WINDING"

Every time I locate and read yet another Marjorie Bowen novel, one more story collection, another hard-to-find essay, I come away, alarmed—*how could I have done without this?* For example, just a few days before this writing, a full-length play of which I had known nothing came to my attention. Now, I know this book cannot do without it. My lament is also a discovery. It's like one of those camera tricks in Alfred Hitchcock's *Vertigo,* where a camera's forward dolly move is accompanied—and countered—by a reverse zoom: So near, but how far... How we all can relate to the words of Michael Dirda, who says the scholar's "malady" lies in its "perfidiousness": "Its sufferers can never fully finish their research. Always, like the elusive blue flower of the German romantics, there beckons yet one more important text to peruse, just a few more documents to consult ... [and] the sense that somewhere the key work awaits, that single reference that will turn the lock and open a new era."[16]

Amen.

Marjorie Bowen's own assessment of her worth can be found in the concluding pages of her memoir, *The Debate Continues*. This unvarnished account surely belongs with the best autobiographies of any writer, past or present. Looking back on her identity as a female writer working in a man's world, she refers to herself in the third person and declares, "She cultivated her mind as far as her powers enabled her.... Rationalism attracted and convinced her mind, but the heart has reasons that the mind knows not of, and she delighted in the mystics" (293).

As you turn the pages of *The Furies of Marjorie Bowen*, relish her contradictions. Read the stories. Thrill to the noble pages of adventure, flinch under the cruel indictments of social injustice, and succumb to the nightmares of horror and dread. "If I be a devil, I go whence I came," she once wrote; "I have known Love, conquered it and by it have been vanquished. Whatsoever I am, I perish on the heights, but I do not descend from them."[17] Indeed, there is a "voice" here, a personality that is vivid, generous, humorous and humane, sometimes cranky, occasionally grim, always passionate, always wise. An hour in her company is a stimulant to the soul. You may come to share the wonder and admiration I have for the remarkable woman who calls herself "Marjorie Bowen." And perhaps we can all bear testament to "the music at midnight," i.e., what she defines as "the courage to find beauty in dark places." She explains, it's "a vision of beauty all my own." And it illumines her pages.[18]

"New Canterbury Tales": An Invitation

> Looking on alle oure revelryes and warres
> Short joys, sade loves and weary hates,
> Peace for alle; after most stormy daye
> Cometh Peace which lasteth for alwaye.[19]

Tucked away among Marjorie Bowen's earliest short stories is a whimsical little thing called "An Initial Letter." It chronicles a blooming June day in the late fourteenth century in Merrie Olde England. A curious procession passes outside the window of the scribe, Master Humphrey. The names of the travelers are familiar—John of Gaunt, his wife the Duchesse Blanche, his mistress Katherine Swynford, and assorted soldiers, clerics, and jesters. At their head is a youth named Jeffray. He's a jaunty lad—

> tall and slender; his hair was a soft brown, his lips red, his eyes very brightly gray: he wore a clear-green doublet, one red hose and one white, a hood of blue satin, and a cloak of cramoisy [sic]. One hand he held on his hip, where a little dagger hung; he walked daintily, careful of his pointed shoes, and his manner was most joyous [663].

Jaffray, too, is honored by history. He is none other than Geoffrey Chaucer (1343–1400), future author of *The Canterbury Tales*, a collection of—

> People of all kinds that had chanced to fall
> In fellowship, and they were pilgrims all...
> It seems to me no more than reasonable
> That I should speak of each of them and tell
> Their characters, as these appeared to me,
> And who they were, and what was their degree,
> And something likewise of their costumes write...[20]

This is not the Chaucer familiar to us today as a stolid, corpulent, elderly gentleman; rather, his description matches the image envisaged in a biographical sketch by G.K. Chesterton, of a youth "light on his feet, who knew fighting and foreign travel, yet had already what was called his elvish face and the pleasant shyness that covered so much sharpness."[21]

Jeffray pauses, peeks in at Master Humphrey's open window, and chides him for the portentous lines the scribe is putting to paper. "Ich am tyred of Hercules and Lysander," Jaffray says (in perfect Middle English, of course!), "I would like to write tales well enough—but differently. Come out into the fields; thou art so bemused with chant royal, couplet, 'rime couée,' thou canst not see there is a better poem than ever thou stained vellum with in that fresh hawthorn facing thee!" (664).

Obediently, Master Humphrey puts aside the page and gazes out the window. His ears ring to the shouts of the pilgrims: *"The whole world goes to the field today"* (665).

Perhaps Marjorie Bowen thought little of this charming story, little more than a vignette, since she did not reprint it in any of her published volumes of short stories. Yet, it immediately commands our attention. It issues an invitation. Written in the springtime of Bowen's career, it reveals her "Chaucerian pastime of the telling of tales"[22]—*new* Canterbury Tales; and her characters make their own pilgrimage to a New Canterbury—a place full of the Blaze of History and the Thunder of the Supernatural:

> Like Chaucer's Knight's Tale, here are tales of blood and battle ...
> Like the Wife of Bath, here are portraits of women, in and out of love and marriage ...
> Like the tales by the Friar and the Summoner, here are stories of religious deceit and churchly corruption ...
> Like the Reeve's tale, here are farcical carnal mixups ...
> Like the Monk's tale, here are morals drawn from the rise and fall of figures of power, Biblical, classical, and historical ...
> And, like the Pardoner's tale, here are stories wicked and cruel, wry and treacherous, driven by the poisonous energies of the Furies ...
> Let us go then.
> Marjorie Bowen, Master Humphrey and Jeffray are beckoning us to follow.
> Turn the page ...

A Note on Bowen Page References

For the ease and convenience of the reader (and not to clutter up this book with more chapter notes than is absolutely necessary), this book provides page numbers parenthetically inserted within the text from the Bowen novels and short story collections that are listed in the Bibliography. All other sources are included in the chapter notes.

Gods and Goddesses

ONE

"The Music on the Hill": Pagans and Christians

"We have entered a world of fantasy, let us play our parts with spirit."—Marjorie Bowen

In Marjorie Bowen's *The Haunted Vintage*, a Christian monastery and vineyard in Bavaria are under assault. Primal Nature is beating at its doors. The unholy Harvest is a fine Pagan frenzy of "all the crude wildness, the black melancholy, the morbid glooms, the religious terrors, of Gothic fancy." Here are "glimpses of the age of the Pagan gods before monk and nun, ghost and demon, robber knight came to dwell on the banks of the Rhine" (59–60).[1]

Indeed, the Pipes of Pan are blowing through the Victorian and Edwardian worlds of Marjorie Bowen. Pagan gods are everywhere. "They say Pan has left his ruined temple," she writes, "to enter Christian churches and laugh in the face of the marble Christ."[2]

A fickle bunch, according to their mood, these Pagan gods are as destructive in their energies as intoxicating in their enchantments. They challenge and transcend the strict social conventions and religious orthodoxies of the age. Ecstasy erases the stern contours of Reason and Virtue. Spiritualism, Theosophy, and other Occult Sciences lure the spirit world to domestic drawing rooms and parlors.[3] New evolutionary theories and philosophies usurp conventional social, political, and gender roles. As people starved for a spiritual life in a desacralized age turn to cultic Paganism, reality, truth, and morality are no longer absolutes but variable propositions.[4] "[England] is peopled with nymphs and dryads," wryly observes Virginia Woolf in 1918, "and Pan, far from being dead, is at his pranks in all the villages of England [and] a group of writers who have the sense of the unseen ... may bring visions of fairies or phantoms."[5]

In sum, as Derek Jarrett reports in *The Sleep of Reason*, "the nineteenth century saw the opening up of many new channels of knowledge that led to the partial understanding of what religion is, what mysticism is, what produces trances, visions, 'voices,' and other manifestations hitherto believed to be of divine origin."[6]

Indeed, poets, composers, and painters are attending to sounds and fancies beyond their senses. They are *listening*. Listening to the "music on the Hill," as Saki put it[7]— music that seemed to *have been heard before*, music from beyond space and time. As essayist Charles Lamb observed, it is a "music" already within us, within and without the body, that afford "a peep at least into the shadowland of pre-existence."[8] And so, to listen is to be transformed. No longer autonomous creators, artists become vessels, mere reeds, through which the gods force their breath. As Elizabeth Barrett Browning wrote in 1860, in "The Musical Instrument": "Half a beast is the Great God Pan," who blows through his reed, *"making a poet out of a man"* [italics added].

This transformative consequence is an important point. Artists attend to the music on the hill and, in effect, find their own Pagan within. Throughout the nineteenth and early twentieth centuries, John Keats is listening to the "wild ecstasy" of the "unheard melodies" of "pipes and timbrels"; Hawthorne, Coleridge, and Thoreau are discovering the "music" of nature; Robert Browning's Pied Piper and James M. Barrie's Peter Pan are piping children to an unknown Never Land; Charles Baudelaire, inspired by E.T.A. Hoffmann, is sailing to "a planet pale" on "unearthly music"[9]; Algernon Swinburne is inhaling the "daily breath" of those "Ladies of Pain," the goddesses "Dolores" and "Proserpina" ("cruel as love or life, and lovely as death")[10]; Adolphe-William Bouguereau and the Pre-Raphaelite painters are lost in Fairyland; and composers Claude Debussy, Gustav Mahler, and Igor Stravinsky, are tugging at the restraints of western tonality in their supersensual evocations of pagan rituals and lusty songs of the earth—respectively, *The Afternoon of a Faun,* the "Pan" Symphony (No. 3), *The Rite of Spring.* (Robert Schumann goes them one better: As if responding to John Keats's lines, "Heard melodies are sweet but those unheard are sweeter," he writes music inscribed on a third stave on the page but with instructions to the performer *not to play them.*[11])

Immediate contemporaries of Marjorie Bowen, modern masters of dark fiction, such as Arthur Machen, Vernon Lee, Algernon Blackwood, are recognizing the unearthly sources of this "music on the hill"—entities that, in the words of Vernon Lee, are "moulded out of cloud and sunlight and darkness, forever changing, fluctuating between a human or animal shape." Here is "the vitality of the myths of paganism, from the scorching and pestilence-bearing gods of India to the divinities shaped out of tempest and snowdrift of Scandinavia."[12]

Herself a member of this Dark Company, we must ask, what "music on the hill" is Marjorie Bowen hearing? *To whom—or what—is she listening?* Are they the screams of Dionysian Pagan Furies, or the more seductive pipings of Apollonian gods? Or both? How do they *transform* her? Witness her admission, uttered in the story, "Homage to the Unknown," from *Bagatelle*: "I beckon just round the corner where no one has been yet.... I am all that is incredible yet pursued, all that is never credited, yet longed for.... Those who know me are always tormented by unsatisfied desires."[13] We begin to wonder, if Bowen, in a deep and personal way, is not a Pagan herself?

What has happened? Explanations are complicated. Her childhood was surrounded by angry gods, moving in a most "exalted sphere" whose "Jovian shafts" were dangers to be dodged, whose "actions were not to be questioned nor their judgment resisted?" In reality, they were "the grownups in charge of me"—her own parents. They presided over the emotional abuse and fear she felt as a child, which led to her feelings of a "fall" from grace, that she was "an outcast" from her own family.[14] Religious teachings from her mother only made matters worse. "[My mother] added unwittingly to my misfortunes by teaching me something about religion." If young Marjorie grew up confused about Heaven, she learned very well to imagine "torment, loneliness, unhappiness and pain—in other words, Hell."[15]

In her book, *The Church and Social Progress*, Bowen outlines a belief system wholly at variance with her mother's teachings, what she calls a "mingled pantheism and genuine mysticism."[16] Bowen says she has little understanding of metaphysics "in the fullest implication of the term," or "what is meant by pantheism and mysticism"; but she goes on to describe the formation of what she describes as an "active" mysticism, a sense of God."[17] As Alan Watts, of the Society for Comparative Philosophy, argues, this is a pantheism in its broadest sense, of seeing the world as a body, "as a vast pattern of intelligent energy that has a new relationship to us. We are not in it as subjects of a king, or as victims of a blind process. We are not *in* it at all. We *are* it." This is a moral imperative, "that every individual in this organic myth of the world must look upon himself as responsible for the world."[18]

Haunted Vintage book jacket.

Everyone is responsible, Bowen declares, for "finding for himself and without compulsion from Churches, or priests, or any other authoritarian source, the God or 'spirit' or ideal he wishes to worship or follow…:

> Unless we can attain this freedom; unless the Churches are deposed from the position where they can use their missionary zeal, their wealth, their remaining prestige, and their monopoly of many means of propaganda to rivet their dogmas on the minds of old and young, we have not the liberty of which we boast and for which so many of our forebears suffered and died…

"As a consequence," she continues,

> It is the duty of all who enjoy the mental freedom gained by martyrs under the Christian dispensation to resist to the full any attempt of official Christianity to regain power. However gently and plausibly this attempt may begin, it must, if permitted to succeed, lead to a revival of the worst form of tyranny that ever enslaved the mind of man.[19]

"How much better," she observed in her memoir, "Myself when Young," "to delight in yet another iteration of the word 'mysticism': "I did not find it at all difficult to believe that God was in everything and that it was possible to feel in direct communion with Him."[20]

A JOURNEY TO CYTHERA

And so it is that Marjorie Bowen is "listening" to provocative literary influences, Apollonian and Dionysian by turns. The former included the seventeenth-century clergyman-poet, George Herbert and the nineteenth-century clergyman who abjured his post as a Congregationalist minister, George MacDonald. She is sympathetic to Herbert's love of Nature and his ambivalence about matters of faith and doubt. In MacDonald, she suffers nothing less than an epiphanic induction into Fairyland: "The Lovely art of George MacDonald is full of the delicate beauty with which this sensitive writer endued everything that he touched."[21] As Elizabeth Browning had written, Bowen suffers that transformation from the "man" [sic] to the "poet"; in effect, as poet Edward Young writes, her soul listens to the "phantastic measures trod/O'er Fairy Fields."[22]

Herbert is frequently acknowledged in her works. One of her earliest published short stories, for example, "The Holy Mr. Herbert" (1910), refers to one of George Herbert's best-known works, *The Priest to the Temple* (1652), the priest and poet's "practical" guide to matters of faith and daily living. And she is sympathetic to the quiet, existentialist resignation of his poem, "I made a Posie."[23] "I can still hear," she writes in her autobiography, "Herbert's lovely phrase, 'music at midnight,' that I interpret as the courage to find beauty in dark places. That courage and that beauty are my own."[24] Bowen's story was later cited in Frances M. Malpezzi's article, "The Parson Fictionalized: A Reprise," in *The George Herbert Journal*.[25]

George MacDonald's remarkable and complex allegory, *Phantastes* (1858) was a book for which Bowen had a special fondness all her life. She recalls keeping its consoling presence by her side during early years of great stress, while caring for her terminally ill first husband and mourning the death of her first child. She admits she knows it by heart and that was a "good friend" to her "when there was nothing else."[26] There are many references to it in her harrowing semi-autobiographical novel, *Stinging Nettles*. She included its "Magic Mirror" chapter in her edited anthology, *Great Tales of Horror* (1933). It was to her, what it was for her contemporaries G.K. Chesterton and C.S. Lewis, an invocation of the interface of Pagan and Christian worlds.[27] An enchanted music reaches the ears of the protagonist, Anodos, while lying beneath the trees, a "sweet, inarticulate music" of the leaves overhead; moreover, "by and by, the sound seemed to begin to take shape, and to be gradually molding itself into words; till, at last, I seemed able to distinguish these, half-dissolved in a little ocean of circumfluent tones."[28] A tiny fairy creature issues to Anodos—and, in effect, to Bowen herself—an invitation: "You shall find the way into Fairy-land.... Now look into my eyes." Anodos is engulfed by them: "They filled me with an unknown longing.... I looked deeper and deeper, till they spread around me like seas, and I sank in their waters."[29] After many bizarre adventures, by turns erotic and dangerous, including his own death, he finally reawakens to the "real" world, confused, transformed. The man has become a poet: "I have a strange feeling, sometimes, that I am a ghost, sent back into the world to minister to my fellow-men."[30] How effectively that admission captures the elegiac tone of wisdom, sacrifice, and compassion that illumines so much of Bowen's own work.

Both Enchantress and Enchanted, Bowen is embarking on her own "Journey to Cythera." That procession of capering figures in Jean-Antoine Watteau's famous painting by that name is cited in her aforementioned story, "Homage to the Unknown." Dancing to the music of the Mezzetin's guitar (and do we not also hear Debussy's *L'Isle Joyeuse*?) and surrounded by a profusion of exotic flowers, she joins the goddess Venus and the pairs of lovers as they frolic on the lawn in pagan abandonment during their journey to the Island of Love. Are they going, or are they returning? (If they are returning, are they not poetically transformed?) Surely Bowen loves the ambiguity.[31] What they find there is a world depicted in the vast frescoes and canvases of the eighteenth-century painter

Giambattista Tiepolo. Her story, "Capriccio," in *Bagatelle,* evokes Tiepolo's bizarre, extravagant world, "a crazy, motley universe," where all is "air, light, beauty, love," with "lilac parasols, diamond cuirasses, palaces upside down, leopards entangled in mantles of rose brocade, peacocks plucking at grapes made of emerald"; and where "a unicorn with a coral horn blows a gold trumpet" (61).[32] There is music, of course, such as Handel's "Heathen Chorus," from *Theodora,* which she talks about in her story, "The Proud Pomfret," from *Seeing Life!*:

> Venus laughing from the skies,
> Will applaud her votaries.
> While seizing the treasure
> We revel in pleasure,
> Revenge sweet love supplies [181].

The spirit of Fairyland pervades many of her stories, evoking the Pagan myths of England, Ireland, Scotland, Scandinavia, India, and Greece. A few brief examples are in order:

In the short-story collection, *Fond Fancy,* "Beltarbet's Darlin" is saturated with Irish folklore. There is a magical moment when Beltarbet and his horse, Diarmuid, have come to the site of an ancient battlefield near Malahide, the land of the pagan shee. Beltarbet has an epiphany:

> Might not here, on this tragic and enchanted ground ... would come Firvanna, the King of the Shee himself, and guide him and the lovely horse to Faeryland? Might not here, in this consolation of loneliness, one feel free of the foreigner, the alien, the usurper, the conqueror? Here, where the invader had been driven back after the sands were piled deep with dead.... The horse snorted and tossed his small, noble head on the delicate arched neck as if he scented the gallant company of his peers, and trod carefully as though he made his way among a gathering of phantom warriors ... as if he knew that he passed over ground rich with Irish blood and bones [259].

Beltarbet muses further, "We'll gallop into the sea, Diarmuid, my darling, where the Danish ravens went down, and as the surf goes over us, perhaps Firvanna himself will catch your bridle and lead us to the company of the Shee. We'll then possess the land, my darling, and ride over it day and night with the English never seeing us" (259).[33]

Another story, "He Made a Woman—," in *Seeing Life!,* takes us to the haunted forests of Welsh mythology. When writer Edmund Charnock travels through Feryllwg, or the Forest of Dean—among "hills haunted by many a mysterious legend" (214)—to visit his former mentor, the scientist Blantyre, he finds himself immersed in a strange world. Blantyre fancies himself the incarnation of the magician Gwydion ap Don, "an older and more mighty magician than Merlin" (215), explains Blantyre, and he is presently conducting some "old experiments," and he chants some lines about Gwydion:

> Gwydion, the son of Don, of toil serene,
> He made a woman [Blodewwedd] out of flowers
> Blossoms of broom, of oak, of meadowsweet.

Charnock interrupts. He cries out. Blodewwedd is before him, and he reaches out— "He caught in a frantic grasp the green silver robe of Blodewwedd. She vanished; there was a heavy coil of perfume in the air, and Charnock's thin hand grasped a spray of oak flower, a twig of broom, a cluster of meadowsweet" (220).[34]

Hinduism is introduced into contemporary Roman settings in the novel, *The Presence and the Power.* The sinister Dr. Francesco Michelozzi, who may be a magician, inducts the restless and troubled protagonist, Raulyn Dyppre, into the doctrines of the god Shiva. "[He is] the deity who symbolizes destruction," Michelozzi explains. "In one hand he holds fire, in the other, a drum ... destruction followed by transformation, destruction that is a recreation, the shaking together of new forms" (162). From his drum beats "the great vibration of the universal spirit, shaking old forms into new ones.... It quivers to the throb of ceaseless life" (193). Michelozze perceives no distinction between destruction and creation, beauty and ugliness: "Ugliness and horror are the last delusions of intelligence," he says, "—the last superstition of our civilization" (193).[35]

Pagan gods linger in the forests and fields of Scotland and England. In the novel, *Lindley Waters*, a young woman, Grace Morrison, with ambitions to become a witch, has her eyes and ears cocked to the fantastic creatures that haunt the Scottish forests and glens:

> In the early morning, when the light strikes athwart the glen and the eagle hovers in the silver mist, one may see perhaps wraiths crossing lonely fords, one may behold the spirit of the water kelpie waiting with his flowing white mane to catch the unwary traveler ... hobgoblins lurk in the granaries of the lonely farmhouses, and it is possible when passing through some lonely ravine to behold on a distant slope phantom armies [47].

In "A Princess of Kent," from the story collection, *The Pleasant Husband*, a medieval English knight, Valerian, rides to Canterbury on a mission to destroy false gods and convert the land to Christianity. But the young lady he meets in the enchanted wood declares she is loyal to the pagan gods: "They are very gracious to me—I will be true to them" (252). To his protest that the old gods are dead, that she should embrace the "true faith," she replies, "The old gods neither die nor sleep" (254). The long night approaches and Valerian, half suspecting she is a goddess herself, softens his attitude toward her and guards her sleep. Comes the dawn and her father, the King of Kent, comes to retrieve her. She leaves Valerian a kiss. As she rides away, Valerian continues on his way to Canterbury. But now he sings a pagan song:

> What hope have I of heaven.
> Myrra—when virtues are few.
> Myrra—when sins are seven.
> And the sweetest sin is you—is you! [260].

Two novels, *The Sacked City* and *Nightcap and Plume*, conclude this brief survey. Both are fraught with many allusions to pre–Christian Norse and Scandinavian mythology. In the first, the ageing Klara Linderoth recounts some of the legends of the island— "old stories repeated very often and always a little differently according to the mood of the teller of the tale":

> The island was very old. The gods lived and died here before the coming of Christ.... The gods had come there one day a long time ago. Dreadful histories were told of the Eastern coast, now deserted. Not a blade of grass grew there, constantly swept by winds, and covered by scrub, it was uninhabitable. A dangerous marsh separated it from the past of the island that bloomed with lilacs, roses, and beautiful meadows and pastures. Shocking creatures, that Christianity had never been able to reach, flitted over those swamps and this blighted shore. This island is very, very old, the gods lived and died here before the coming of Christ [46–50].

Further, explains Klara:

> On the other coast you may meet the ghostly huntsman. There are many tales about him; prayers have driven him out of the forest and now he rides across the sands. There, also, is Huldra, the wood-wife, who is sometimes beautiful and sometimes hideous, but always hollow, with no heart or spirit, you

understand, as with Jane Gifford and perhaps Aurora Edstrom, If you go into the forests you must be careful about the wood-wives.... Here grew Yggdrasil, the ash that held the universe, the uttermost boughs touching the rainbow bridge into Asgard, its roots clasping the rock, oceans and earth [52].[36]

In the second, *Nightcap and Plume*, a novel about the last four years in the life of Gustaf III of Sweden, Norse mythology is blended with Greek mythology. Gustaf's production in 1773 of Sweden's first opera, *Thetis and Peleus,* blends them both in a tour-de-force of storytelling. The Greek story of the marriage between the mortal Peleus and the immortal, shape-shifting sea goddess Thetis is transformed into a celebration of Swedish folklore: "Thetis is a 'nereid,'" Gustaf explains, "a daughter of the most kindly of deities, Nereus, who reigns so placidly over the sea nymphs and those who guard coasts, lakes, mariners and islands—the titular goddesses of Sweden" (73). After Thetis captures the goddess disporting on the back of a dolphin, a marriage is arranged. But when the Apple of Discord disrupts the marriage ceremony, disaster follows: "Was it not at the marriage of Peleus and Thetis," continues Gustaf, "that Discord threw the apple so disastrously disputed. Such fruit is tossed at most feasts" (71). Thus, Gustaf's *Thetis and Peleus* is not only a national festival but a prophecy of the corruption that will overtake the House of Vasa. The staging of the opera, moreover, is one of the great scenes in all of Bowen's novels. Painted sets and costumed players give way to fantastic scenes and gods and goddesses. Is this a performance enacted on a stage or only the product of Gustav's imagination? Indeed, it is a spectacle that "seemed more the realization of a dream than a cunning human contrivance, the troupe of singers more like a band of the native spirits of Sweden than men and women playing parts" (72).

Dreadful Conjurings

On the other hand, during her *Journey to Cythera*, Bowen is also "listening" to a music darker, more Dionysian than the sweet notes plucked from Mezzetin's guitar. It is a cacophony fraught with discords. They don't drift down from the clouds but emanate from under the earth.[37] She describes these influences in different ways. In a memoir, she remembers first falling under the spell of an "all-pervading Power of which I am part—of Descarte's Daemon beside me." The teachings, Lucretius and Giordano Bruno, "come nearest to satisfying me."[38] Elsewhere, she writes of hearing the wild chthonic screams and groans of the Dionysian Greek Furies. The ground has given way under her feet, and she falls away from the perfumed beauties of gods and goddesses to the infernal practices of witchcraft, the Occult, and Satanism.

Marjorie Bowen's fascination with historical accounts of witchcraft and necromancy was lifelong. An important book in her oeuvre, albeit one not generally known, is *The Courtly Charlatan* [as by George R. Preedy], a semi-fictional account of the notorious, enigmatic magician/ alchemist/storyteller, the Comte de St. Germain.[39] This witty tome is nothing less than a *divertissement*, an abundance of anecdotes and testimonies regarding Germain's alchemical exploits—many told by Germain himself (of course)—at the court of Louis XV. The infernal practices of other historical magicians, such as Albertus Magnus, Roger Bacon, and Paracelsus are cited. Shape-shifters, ghosts, and a medley of Pagan spirits abound. Germain himself maintains an essential ambivalence about his practices, frequently disavowing them with a wink. *The Courtly Charlatan* is an amiable companion to other books presently discussed in these pages.

Dark Fantasies

Among other scholarly works, Bowen carefully researched *Wrestling Jacob*, on the life and preachments of John Wesley, whose Methodism was supposed at the time to be "not of the god but of the Devil." Further, "It was well known that John Wesley believed in witchcraft, and some of his lay preachers ... lived in perpetual fear of ghosts and were ready to credit any wild tale of the supernatural." In the popular mind his ministry involved "all manner of witchcraft, sorcery, satanic possession, and all the phantasmagoria that arises from the dark recesses of the mind and trespasses on the borderland of religions" (244–245). Indeed, John and his many siblings had grown up in an atmosphere of their parents' rants about Hellfire. Thus, it was not surprising that the parsonage at Epworth, Lincolnshire was purportedly assaulted by poltergeists for several days, beginning on 1 December 1719:

> The Rectory was haunted by creatures not of this world, either imps of Hell or the phantoms of departed sinner; these reports formed the least of the parents' troubles; they were quite equal to Satan or the souls of the lost, but [John] found a fearful pleasure in speculating on the nature of these invisible inhabitants of their dark and ancient home [18].

Moreover, she published several articles in *The Occult Review* in 1932–1933, at the same time that she was researching and publishing her historical novel, *I Dwelt in High Places*, a dramatization of the occult and alchemical practices of Queen Elizabeth's court astrologer, John Dee and his assistant, the diabolical Edward Kelley. "The *Daemonologia* of Edward Fairfax, 1621" examines Fairfax's account of his attempts to prosecute six neighbors for bewitching his children. They were acquitted, but his *Daemonologia* was his attempt to vindicate himself. A second article is a review of the historical record about "Dr. John Dee, M.A., Astrologer and Alchemist." The third article, "Suspicion," cautions against the outright dismissal of witchcraft:

> Who shall decide whether the explicable comes from the powers of Good or the powers of Evil? Many a saint has been destroyed as a wizard; many a disciple of Hecate has sat in Holy Places.... Genius has never despised superstition, but used it with the finest effect and for the noblest purpose ... the disclosures of the laboratory and the observatory do not eliminate the causes of awe and terror that still haunt the most complex and sophisticated of evils, actions. Believe? Perhaps the word should be "hope," since it is natural to bring even a fearful delusion, if it go hand in hand with the ecstatic promise...[40]

As a romancer, easily the rival of the Comte de St. Germain himself, Marjorie Bowen's many novels and short stories are fraught with spells, conjurings, and other occult rituals: The aforementioned *The Courtly Charlatan* contains several stand-alone stories and anecdotes, including a memorable account of a Spectral Bride and a Mechanical Man. In the story cycle, "Seven Deadly Sins," contained in *Crimes of Old London* (1919), are sardonic accounts of the doings of a gallery of sorcerers, alchemists, witches, and devils. The Devil's appearance to two witches in "Wrath," for example, is grotesque and amusing:

> He was as tall as a cathedral; he had a tail that lashed over the house-tops, and his long hair shook in the sky like banners. So he puts one hoof in the market-place and glances down with his red eyes; then he takes up the two witches as a man might take up two hens and tucks them under each arm; and off he goes over the houses—stride, stride, stride—and disappears with another clap of thunder [287].

The witty "Sheep's-Head and Babylon," from the collection of that name, tells of a clergyman's interest in a volume of witchcraft. After several trance visions and enticements by a mysterious, beautiful woman, he meets his death. As a local villager says (in Scots dialect), "It's nae wonder that the douce man should gang queer in the head wi' a' that book..." (15).

"They Found My Grave," from *Orange Blossoms* (1938), is a cautionary tale about the disastrous consequences of séances that overtakes an insatiably curious young woman (although the apparition raised is not nearly as monstrous as that raised in a séance in the novel, *The Spectral Bride*).

"One Remained Behind," from *Kecksies* (1976), is a feast of dark conjurings that leads a greedy young student of witchcraft—despite his elaborately protective paraphernalia of spells and rituals—to his doom at the hands—or claws—of those Satanic spirits Astaroth, Beelzebub, Belial, and Beleth.

"The Extraordinary Story of Grace Endicott," from *Exits and Farewells*, recounts in archaic prose the fate of the titular character, who has abjured the Christian God. An admitted witch, her arm bears a "purple hoof-print on the flesh that was known for the particular mark and sign of Hell" (150). At her execution, she voices this remarkable confession:

> Powerful is evil and hard to escape, and wise are those who step aside from the world which is set with springes [sic] into one of which I fell.... I had a warning and beheld Hell in its flames and saw that Love was but the Devil and so let go his hand.... Yet was the Devil busy and pursued me and set his hounds on my soul, and his traps for my feet ... and having the seal of the Devil on me I slew my father and saw him die in the night [152].

Grace Morrison, in the aforementioned novel, *Lindley Waters*, has grown to believe she possesses infernal powers: "She knew how to play many tricks ... those spells and incantations which she believed … would some time or other bring her fortune.… She believed that strange results had occurred, but these were always confused in her memory" (199). But her attempts to seize control of her husband's estates, despite her sorceries, womanly guile, and duplicities, fails miserably and leaves her abandoned by her lover. "[Magic] is for old wives and children," he tells her scornfully. "It amused us when we had nothing better to do.… I neither believe nor disbelieve; I do not know" (168). She dies, alone and rejected, her corpse found on a lonely road with the tools of her magic strewn about her—"the wooden mannequin, a few sticks, a few soaked packets of what had been powders, a few lengths of chalk … [her] paraphernalia for obtaining an entry into paradise" (252–252). Critic Edward Wagenknecht has noted that Grace's confusion in the matter is the main theme of the book: "If Grace is not a witch, she still tries her best to be one, and the book comes close to being a study of the effect of a deceptive belief in the supernatural upon a weak mind and of the fatality that follows upon disillusionment" (165).

"Julia Roseingrave," was originally published in 1933 and reprinted in the story collection, *Twilight*. As one of Bowen's finest, most subtle stories, it deserves a more extended examination. It presents another of Bowen's witches who may or may not be the real thing. A meeting with the handsome Sir William Notley might be Julia's ticket out of the rustic village, where she leads a blunted existence with her imbecile sister and sickly mother. Gifted with great beauty and a seductive manner, she recruits two magician-accomplices in her scheme to seduce Sir William: Dr. Gowland is an alchemist, "whose mind and spirit dwelt much in other worlds.… He was more used to the stars than to the earth, more at home in space than on solid ground" (226); and old Goody Cloke, the local crone, is a reputed witch who lives in a cottage down on the marshlands.

The plot thickens and Sir William is lured down to the stream where, he has been told, "a nymph or fairy or goddess walks there and bathes in the deep pool underneath the willow trees" (213). He visits the enchanted spot and is struck by the "nymph's" beauty, "but in his fascination was an awareness of something *wrong*" (217). A warning voice in his head urges: "Fly, you are in more danger now than you ever were in your life!" (222). At length, he learns the identity of this nymph is Julia Roseingrave. But by spurning his romantic advances, she withholds sex on condition of marriage. He succumbs to her "spell," all right, but it's a love that threatens to curdle into revulsion, even hate. Julia must move quickly. With the aid of her accomplices, she concocts a deadly potion which she persuades Sir William to administer to his wife, who has inconveniently just now arrived in the village. Julia's voice is enticing—and deadly:

> We have made our bargain and resolved to put it through.… And it can be done so easily. The body can be disposed of down in the marshes: Afterwards, when the rain comes, all will be hidden, and the lilies will grow again and no one will ever go searching near there, for the place is supposed to be haunted. Could she have a better end? It is pleasanter for her this way than to live married to you [247].

He considers, then, "with half-insane cunning," that the time will come when her spell will break—"And I shall loathe you." Maybe he can obtain for himself the secret of the potion and, after satisfying himself after the wedding journey, administer it to her (247) …

But at the last minute, Dr. Gowland double-crosses Julia. Because he has carnal designs on her himself, he applies his own dark artistry to reunite Sir William with his wife.

Defeated, Julia is condemned to return to her poor cottage, where she will spend her days with her imbecile sister.

The simplicity of the plot is enhanced and supercharged with Julia's erotic allure. Her body is both a Dionysian lure and an Apollonian ideal of grace and beauty. Sir William is unable to resist her sexual enticements. Implications of witchcraft aside, her deceptions, her seductions, and her murderous intention are entirely her own.

I cannot leave this marvelous story without quoting the magical moment in the twilight when Julia first appears as a "nymph" to the startled Sir William:

> He waited but five minutes or so as he judged ... when she appeared on the other side of the clearing. She was naked and held a long twist of black hair in her hand as she came lightly over the ground towards the pool.... He stared, his heart panting, thick and frightening, believing he looked on something unearthly.... She dipped her long limbs, and then sank beneath the water and began swimming across so that only her head and the black hair floating like a weed, showed.... The young man stayed his impetuous movement and stared down through the leafage on to the pool where her face floated like a water lily and her hair like a dark leaf; and looking down into that face, which remained still for a moment on the surface of the water with closed eyes and slightly parted lips and all the light of the moon turning the flesh to an unearthly look of silver, he knew himself lost ... [She] stepped out into the sheer moonlight which clothed her from head to foot as modestly as a veil. He saw her blurred by this radiance; he could observe only that she was tall and curved and very slender and surely unearthly after all ... [215–216].

THE FURIES

Perhaps we can trace an affinity between the fictional Julia Roseingrave and Marjorie Bowen herself. Roseingrave embodies both the Apollonian sweetness and the Dionysian Furies that are the wellsprings of Bowen's art. Her capacities for rendering beautifully tender and sensitive stories about music, poetry, loss, and compassion are matched by stories bluntly and horribly graphic, written with that "ink of bile" as Salmonson so memorably put it.[41]

Eventually, as we will see in detail in the later chapter on "Joseph Shearing," we come face to (screaming) face with those Dionysian Furies. In the noir-esque *For Her to See* a character declares: "I might term myself the Messenger of Tisiphone, the third Fury, who was the avenger of blood" (219). Indeed, Tisiphone was the third of the "Erinyes" of Greek mythology, who exists, as Camille Paglia has explained in her book, *Sexual Personae*, "under the chthonian cloud" and administers to her male victims a fatal poison extracted from the froth of the mouth of Cerberus."[42] And it is immediately apparent to even the most casual exposure to Bowen's work how prevalent these destructive female agencies are. These include those Fury-inspired poisoners, the eponymous women in *The Crime of Laura Sarelle* and *Blanche Fury*; and the characters of Madame de Montespan and Catherine Montvoisin in the court of Louis XIV in *The Poisoners*. We learn in many of stories like these, in almost clinical detail, about the many varieties of arsenic poison administered—"arsenic everywhere—packets of arsenic in a chocolate box, arsenic in solutions in a scent bottle, traces of arsenic on aprons, handkerchiefs, and dressing gowns."[43] Other women, if not directly driven by supernatural agencies, respond just as violently to the more prosaic "furies" of the social and personal repressions women face in a patriarchal society. Angelica Cowley, Olivia Sacret, May Beale, and Belle Adair in, respectively, *The Golden Violet*, *For Her to See*, *Airing in a Closed Carriage*, and *Moss Rose*, all voice their personal acts of vengeance as poisoners and blackmailers.

Malevolent, yet proud, terrible, yet vulnerable, together they voice what surely is a testament of Bowen herself: "If I be a devil, I go whence I came.... I have known Love, conquered it and by it have been vanquished. Whatsoever I am, I perish on the heights, but I do not descend from them."[44]

Novels of Christians and Pagans

And now we come to the fatally discordant "music on the hill" in some of Marjorie Bowen's most important, and darkest novels—*The Carnival of Florence, Black Magic, The Haunted Vintage, The Abode of Love, Circle in the Water, Nightcap and Plume, I Dwelt in High Places, The Poisoners, God and the Wedding Dress,* and, lastly, *"Five Winds."* They constitute, along with *The Courtly Charlatan*, Bowen's most extended and detailed examinations of sorcery and alchemy. In effect, whenever we find a Christian theology, a temple, a church, a priest, there will also be the emergent threat of an underlying Pagan practice. And whenever we encounter a séance or a Satanic ritual we suspect chicanery and fraud. *Carnival of Florence* leads off and establishes this template: The priest Savonarola's Christian usurpation of the Epicurean philosophy of the Medicis in late fifteenth-century Florence is countered by his death at the stake and the subsequent re-emergence of the Medicis. *Black Magic, The Haunted Vintage, The Abode of Love* are outright assaults by Pagan gods on citadels of Christian worship. In the first, practices of witchcraft and demon worship threaten to topple the Papacy itself. In the second, primordial gods usurp a monastery. And in the third, the false prophet of a putative Christian cult is overthrown by his own susceptibility to Pagan practices. As for the others, *The Circle in the Water* and *Nightcap and Plume* place legends of witchcraft and the Black Mass within the political contexts of seventeenth and eighteenth-century politics; *I Dwelt in High Places* dramatizes the historical record of the occult practices of Queen Elizabeth's court astrologer, John Dee, and his assistant, or "skryer," the notorious Edward Kelley; *The Poisoners* is a wild blend of history and black magic practiced by a cult of female poisoners in the court of Louis XIV; *God and the Wedding Dress* demonstrates the failure of Pagan and Christian practices alike to allay suffering during the Plague Years of Restoration England; and *"Five Winds"* unleashes a Pagan Fury on the soul of a young man claiming the family estate.

The Carnival of Florence
"The Power is in the Ink"

This is a tale of a Pagan resurgence from an unlikely source—the enduring Ink of the manuscripts of the Roman philosopher Lucretius.

In the last years of the fifteenth century, the priest Savonarola expelled the ruling Medici and declared that Florence would be a New Jerusalem, the world center of Christianity. But it was a harshly puritanical regime. He usurped, in effect, the Epicurean ferment—as espoused by Lucretius—that had dominated the city, a Pagan philosophy radically at odds with fundamental Christian tenets. He proclaims, in one of his sermons:

> "O Florence! O Rome! O Italy! The time for singing and dancing is over! A mighty wind has arisen which shall wither all your flowers! Instead of carnival songs shall come the rattle of the death cart, and the dead shall lie unburied on all your pleasant places! Corruption shall stink where there was once sweet perfume, tears of blood shall be shed where once was the playing of viols! Ye who boasted

to be free shall be as slaves, your own wanton sins shall become whips for your backs, fathers shall rend their sons and sons slay their fathers, the land shall be laid waste and sown with salt, the towers of Italy shall crumble before the breath of the Lord. And Rome shall perish in her wickedness, and in her own abomination shall she stifle!" [160].

In reaction, the dying scholar-poet Mirandola, who is reading the Lucretian texts, weeps at the memories of what has been lost:

> At times the memory of the old sweet days would return, the warm friendship with Lorenzo, the joy of the new learning, the new art, the gaiety and the splendor of the hours spent in the Badia at Fiesole when Ficino expounded the Neoplatonic doctrine of love and loveliness; the days at Camaldoli, at Cafaggiuolo, at Careggi, all the varied beauty of that fair sinful time; and then he would wince at Fra Girolamo's fierce triumph and stern picture of Charles coming to punish the city Lorenzo had loved as Cyrus had come to punish Babylon [185].

The novel traces Savonarola's ascendance, his presiding over the notorious Bonfire of the Vanities, and his subsequent decline and fall in 1498. After his death by hanging and burning at the stake, the Medicis reasserted control during the next two decades.

Savonarola's rejection of the Medicis, was, in effect, his rejection of the Epicurean ideas known and endorsed in Florence, as espoused in the notorious Latin text known as *De Rerum Natura* ("On the Nature of Things"), by Titus Lucretius Carus (99–55 BCE), written around 50 BCE. Marjorie Bowen refers to Lucretius's materialistic attacks on the delusions of superstition and divine agency frequently in her work.[45] Indeed, it may be regarded as one of the wellsprings of her own existentialist philosophy. In brief, as Stephen Goldblatt argues in his book, *The Swerve*, "These subversive, Lucretian thoughts percolated and surfaced wherever the Renaissance imagination was at its most alive and intense." Lucretius holds that the pursuit of pleasure is the highest goal of existence. It appeals to interests in the pagan deities and the rich meanings attached to them: "What human beings can and should do," Greenblatt explains, "is to conquer their fears, accept the fact that they themselves and all the things they encounter are transitory, and embrace the beauty and the pleasure of the world.... [It was] a vision of a world in motion, a world not rendered insignificant but made more beautiful by its transcience, its erotic energy, and its ceaseless change."[46]

Miraculously, however—and this is very much to the point—Lucretius's manuscript, which, like so many Greek and Roman texts, had virtually disappeared had it not been miraculously located and restored at the time of the Medicis. Over the centuries, the ink of many Greek and Roman texts had been scraped away by monks to make way for Christian writings. Yet, as Greenblatt explains, "the remarkable durability of the parchment used in these codices kept the ideas of the ancients alive and well...." The original ink proved to be so tenacious, *it could still be possible to make out the traces of the texts that had been written over*. "These strange, layered manuscripts—called *palimpsest*; from the Greek for 'scraped again'—have served as the source of several major works from the ancient past that would not otherwise be known."[47]

The power of Pagan usurpation was in the ink!

Black Magic

"I sought God and have been delivered to the Devil!"

Black Magic is a gender-bending story about the relationship between two practitioners of Satanic Arts, Dirk Renswoude and Thierry of Dendermonde. Their machinations will topple the Papal Seat and bring the world to the brink of Apocalypse. Epic in scope, written in heavily perfumed prose, fraught with Bowen's penchant for architectural and scenic details, the novel features the most extravagant characters and situations this side of Matthew Lewis's *The Monk* (1797). In her Preface, Bowen declares: "In the following narrative the author has endeavoured to catch the spirit of such an atmosphere, and of times when these things were, and when belief in the supernatural and visions swayed the lives and destinies of many" (10).

No kidding. She warms to the chase.

Black Magic is based on the ninth-century legends of Pope Joan, a woman who reigned as Pope John VIII between the papacies of Leo IV and Benedict III. The secret of her disguise was carefully kept for two years and only revealed when she died giving birth to a still-born baby. After her death, whether by accident or murder, the Vatican mandated that future popes would be examined and certified as male. Most modern scholars dismiss Pope Joan as a Medieval legend.[48]

The story opens in Flanders in the ninth century, during a time when the coming of Antichrist and the end of the world seems at hand. Dirk and Thierry enter into a solemn pact to pursue their studies of Satanism. They travel to Frankfort, then the seat of Melchior, the Brabant Emperor of the West. During their days at Basle College, they cast their first successful spell as a punishment to their enemy, Joris of Thuringia:

> [Dirk] stepped up to the fire and addressed an invocation in Persian to the soaring flame, then retreated to Thierry's side. The whole room was glowing in the clear red light cast by the unholy fire; the cobweb-hung rafters, the gaunt walls, the books and jars on the bare floor were all distinctly visible, and the two could see each other, red, from head to foot.... The image lying in the magic circle and almost touching the flames (though not burnt or even scorched), was beginning to writhe and twist on its back like a creature in pain.... The figure, horribly like Joris with its flat hat and student's robe, was struggling to its feet and emitting little moans of agony.... The figure was making useless endeavours to escape from the fiery glare; it groaned and fell on its face, twisted on its back and made frantic attempts to cross the line that imprisoned it [59–60].

As he becomes more adept, Dirk begins talking of Antichrist: "The Devil has put me here and I will serve him.... He shall make me his archetype on earth" (100). Ten years later, now separated both men converge in Rome, Dirk assuming the name of "Cardinal Caprarola," and Thierry as a monk seeking absolution for his practices in the dark arts. Thierry at first doesn't recognize his old friend, now sworn enemy. "Betrayed," he moans, "I sought God and have been delivered to the Devil.... I have been seeking for what does not exist—God!—aye, now I know that there is no God and no Heaven, therefore what matter for my soul ... what matter for any of it since the Devil owns us all!" (224–226). But the strange bond between the two persists and Dirk proposes Thierry join him as the Emperor of the Western Dominion. Still under his thrall, but mixed in his emotions, Thierry agrees. "Though the world I rule rot about me," he declares, "though ghouls and fiends make my Imperial train—I will join hands with Antichrist and see if there be a God or no!'" (273). He leaves for the West to join his armies as their new Emperor.

Returning to Rome, victorious, on the eve of the Papal Coronation, he finds a city convulsing under a lowering storm and the advent of the Plague. Ghosts and devils are thronging the streets. "They say Pan has left his ruined temple to enter Christian churches and laugh in the face of the marble Christ" (273). It seems the Apocalypse is at hand:

> The storm that had hung so unnaturally long over the city had affected the people; bravoes and assassins crept from their hiding-places in the Catacombs, or the Palatine, and flaunted in the streets;

> the wine shops were filled with mongrel soldiers of all nations, attracted by the declaration of war from the surrounding towns; blasphemers mocked openly at the processions of monks and pilgrims that traversed the streets chanting the penitential psalms, or scourging themselves in an attempt to avert the wrath of Heaven.... The people lived with reckless laughter and died with hopeless curses; magicians, warlocks and vile things flourished exceedingly, and all manner of strange and hideous creatures left their caves to prowl the streets at nightfall [272–273].

Finally, on the eve of Dirk's Coronation as Pope, Thierry reunites with him only to announce that he is going to expose him as a fraud. Indeed, it is Thierry's inconstancy, not his sins, that will bring about his downfall and Dirk's ruin. Dirk reproaches his old friend for his vacillating nature, his shifting loyalties:

> Always have you thought too much, and not enough, of that; you served too many masters but not one faithfully? ... Do you suppose it matters to me that you are weak, foolish, or that you betrayed me? You are the one thing in all the world I care for.... Neither God nor Devil will do anything for you, for you are not single-hearted, neither constant to good nor evil [226].

Meanwhile, Thierry has long begun to have his suspicions about Dirk. Were his protestations of love actually those of a woman? As an inquiring mind, he wants to *know*. Approaching the Papal chambers, he finds Dirk already dead, an empty bottle of poison at his side. A note has been left for him:

> If I be a devil, I go whence I came; if a man, I lived as one and die as one; if woman, I have known Love, conquered it and by it have been vanquished. Whatsoever I am, I perish on the heights, but I do not descend from them. I have known things in their fulness and will not stay to taste the dregs [313].

When he leans down to gaze into his eyes, the head separates from the trunk. as he disarranges the clothing, the corpse disintegrates into dust.

The question is left moot. This is, indeed, the most interesting aspect of *Black Magic* and, to be sure, the sexual ambivalence of Dirk is what fascinates Bowen the most. Sounding against the fire and fury of the apocalyptic climax, her tempering note of compassion toward Dirk's love for Thierry is, ultimately, quite moving. She tempers his villainy with his emotional vulnerability. From our modern perspective, we might regard Dirk simply as a woman, or a trans man, or, at the least, bisexual. But such a revelation, even one hinted at, for a novel published in 1909, was pretty scandalous stuff. Certainly, for a woman in that era (or in more modern times, to be sure) to gain entre in politics and the Church, a male guise was necessary. And we recall details early in the novel Dirk's references to a woman named Ursula of Rooselaare, who had once been a nun and whom he had buried. It is important to note that Dirk's obvious connection with so much of Ursula's history borders on identity. And it is significant that his own features are typically described as displaying "feminine" qualities and features, with "smooth pale skin and cloudy dark eyes," small feet, and a throat that is "full and beautiful" (14). One might consider him not so much as a villain but as a person prepared to sacrifice everything for the course of love. All of which, for the record, has led least one commentator, Edward Wagenknecht, to declare, "female sex seems clearly indicated at the end."[49]

Circle in the Water

"The powers of the dark are loose here!"

Circle in the Water examines the practices of witchcraft in the historical context of the mid–seventeenth century religious and political turmoils, within and without Scotland.

Witchcraft is, variously, both a superstition, a stern belief, and a national expression for a country for whom Christianity is inadequate to reflect the spiritual hungers and needs of the people, Presbyters, Episcopals, and pagans alike. No sooner has young Thomas Maitland arrived at Castle Drum, in Galloway, as a tutor, than he confronts legends of witches and devils on all hands. No less a person than Richard Cameron, the leader of the Covenanters, warns him: "[The] powers of the dark are loose here. Do you know, young man, how mighty they are? Have you ever heard of the wilds and traps of Satan? Have you ever met the women who have yielded to his spell? ... You will need but one book in Castle Drum, and that is the Holy Bible" (53). And the mother of Thomas' young charges, warns: "There is much witchcraft in Scotland much secret worship of the Devil.... There's not a corner of Scotland where witches may be found if they are sought for" (84). Maitland, who has already heard much about Thomas the Rhymer and the Queen of Elfland, is intrigued enough to accept an invitation to witness a Witches' Sabbat. Atop an old belfry outside Castle Drum, he looks down into the center of a ruined church:

> Then, as I stared, I was conscious of something moving below. It seemed a grey shape, as if it were of the same substance as the weed-covered ground or the stained stone pillars. But it was moving and detached from these and seemed to be a human being and yet to be crawling. It moved towards the large stone that had once been hung with rich cloths and set with jeweled candlesticks in the days when the Pope was lord in Scotland.... As I stared again I saw that the whole space enclosed by those ruined walls was moving with these grey figures. It seemed as if the ground heaved as I had noticed a piece of rotten meat to heave with the maggots that were devouring it. I could not count them, they were there so thick, these grey palpitating shapes [88–89].

"How lightly we talk of the Devil and his evils," muses Thomas to himself, "how carelessly we jest about the monsters of darkness!" (88) Meanwhile—

> The first figures had reached the altar; they overflowed it in slow-grey waves, then mounted through the broken windows and began to disperse like torpid rings of smoke in the dim upper air. Then I heard a little wailing music like someone playing on the pipes that they had in this country, of someone singing. I looked up at the moon to steady myself, for I thought that the base of the ruined church was filled by globes of light that changed and intermingled one into the other ... and I held the little Cross that [Evan] had given me tightly in my palm, and managed to move my stiff fingers to my lips, then to open them and to kiss the Cross [89].

Finally, near the confines of the Castle grounds, he sees "a hunched figure playing upon the bagpipes, that I took to be no mortal thing. And I knew then that Castle Drum and all the ground about was truly infested with the powers of evil" (91).

This encounter haunts Thomas for the rest of the narrative. He feels ill, diseased, and frantic to get away from the place. Shaken in spirit, it matters little to him whether it was hallucination or reality, but "it was proof, intangible maybe, but proof that evil was about me, that evil was possible, and might take on these tormenting and disastrous forms to torture mankind" (101).

Months later, when he returns to the Sabbat, what he sees from close range is only a pathetic and tawdry travesty of what he had previously seen. It is led by a "wretch wearing a kind of tawdry robe stuck with stars" leading a clumsy dance around him. Yet, mystical dream or tawdry reality, Thomas knows these Satanic rites answer a great need among the people: "I began to understand," he says, "as uncouth words left their quivering throats chanting in some language older than even the rude Scots tongue, that this was the wretched remnant of some ancient religion far older than Christianity, and that these were the priests of some god whom they would not allow to drop into decay, though in the eyes of most of mankind he was already dead" (246).

Nightcap and Plume

"An infernal puppet show"

When King Gustaf III dabbles in occult rituals, his motives are both personal and political. As with *Circle in the Water*, the experiences are fraught with magic and hokum. Secret societies of sorcery and the occult are abroad in late-eighteenth century Sweden, including an Illuminati sect of astrologers, alchemists, and magicians, purportedly privy to the magic of the Comte de St. Germain. As a man who is both a rationalist and a dreamer, Gustav is vulnerable to, yet skeptical of, these meetings. But because he himself has employed artifice in the service of his agendas, he knows it is best to keep a close watch on these meetings, which may disguise a cabal against him led by his brothers Karl and Frederik. Moreover, because of a secret, keening grief he feels at the death of his beloved, Jeanne d'Egmont, he nurses a faint hope that a séance might contact her. "They knew all the means whereby the invisible world might be entered," he reluctantly muses, "and all the magic of all the ages" (133).

The séances are described in detail—the days of fasting, arranged seating, the somber décor, the pointed caps and dark gowns, the chalk-inscribed circles, the cauldrons filled with hot stones set at the four corners of the room, the placement of a crucifix flat on the floor, and "the crouching, swaying shapes of the magicians as they uttered incantations, composed of doggerel and bad Swedish and worse Latin, [while one of the magicians] lies prostrate over the crucifix, muttering and groaning" (154). The perfume of incense clogs the nostrils. Morphing into vague shapes in the clouds of burning gunpowder, are sea creatures from Norse mythology—the Stromkarl, the Nikr, the Nixie—who lure hapless mortals to underwater depths. Other apparitions appear, "faltering shapes, tattered shrouds, faces with staring eyeballs and gross, yellow cheeks, with the circlet of kingship on his brows." Gustaf recognizes his own father. Drums are heard that once sounded the ceremonies of his forebears. Suddenly, sharp, evenly spaced raps are heard, "green globular lights" appear... Gustaf, meanwhile, is recovering his amused incredulity. He rises abruptly, raises the alarm, and everything vanishes. The spooks are a disappointment. Worse, his late beloved fails to appear. He himself has created on the stage many such effects and passed them off as "wizard's spells": "Nothing would have been easier to arrange—a knocker in the next room, apertures in the wall into which lamps with coloured shades were inserted and withdrawn." Surely, he realizes, no one here could possibly think he is deluded by "any of this. He could himself have played with brilliant address, the part of a St. Germain, or a Cagliostro, but he would soon have tired of it." Now he wishes only, as he says, "to laugh away the spectre and the bats, the charnal house stench, the dusty foul shadows, all the mumming." Shall he disband these quacks? But, as he becomes aware that behind these meetings exists a cabal intent on bringing him down, he changes his mind: "No—their affected bold assumption of my credulity makes me desire to keep them observed. I think their pretensions a disguise for some political design" (151–166). He is right. He will be assassinated at a masquerade ball only a few years later.

The Haunted Vintage

"Nature is beating at the very doors of man's church."

Pagan assaults threaten to usurp a Christian monastery and vineyard in Bavaria in *The Haunted Vintage*.[50] Legend has it that long ago evil spirits had taken possession of the monastery at Eberbach monastery and debauched all the monks.

This is Marjorie Bowen at the peak of her powers. It ranks among her finest fantasies.

Lally Duchene, on the commission of the local Duke of Nassau, has left behind him his old life and the woman he loves to take on the position of Commandant of the Eberbach prison and lunatic asylum, where he oversees 250 prisoners and a hundred lunatics. His first view of the ancient monastery disturbs him: "How much more fitted for the worship of heathen gods was this building, placed in this rich garden of Nature's fairest fruits, than for the rites of a spiritual religion!" (85). Indeed, legend holds the place long ago had been chosen by a pagan spirit, a wild boar, which had appeared to Saint Bernard and had bid him to build a monastery on the spot, where the monks not only operated distilleries producing "essences, soap, and liquers" but practiced alchemy (43). Saint Bernard had been deceived: "The beast was supposed to have been a kind of devil or spirit that deceived the holy man, making him build what was really a temple for the pagan deities, where they reveled every harvest and held their orgies in the wine cellars and chapels" (227).

Now, centuries later,

> it is supposed that the valley is haunted by evil spirits, of which the Boar was one, and that when the monastery was built, they rushed in and took possession and debauched all the monks, and no blessing or consecration would get rid of them ... and that the place belonged to the devil (52). The influence of the wood is very powerful, Lally is told: "Anyone must feel that Nature is beating at the very doors of man's church." [152]

There are many portents of what is to come. His servant, Luy, is a peculiar fellow, whose grotesque features remind Lally of the hideous medieval carvings on the old cathedral walls. A painting is found in an old, disused chapel depicting "the bare limbs of women, uncouth forms of animals, wreaths of fruits and flowers, and inhuman looking creatures, horned, bearded, not pleasant to look upon" (56). One night Lally perceives outside his window a strange shape "draped, formless, dark against the pale sky, yet seemed to be observing him" (65). And there is a strange female in one of the asylum cells, identified as "Gertruda Gerhart, Dissolute," who is reputed to be a witch. It is said she had been turned out of the village, having lured several citizens into the forest, where they disappeared. Lally's first sight of her through the bars elicits his exclamation: "The moonlight plays tricks. She looks more like a nixie than what she is" (54). Her compelling gaze is both sensuous and repulsive: "She was of a type quite unknown to him—inhuman, with the god-like look of some noble wild animal. The face was peculiar.... The features were small, yet blunt and broad; the brow low, the eyes far apart, the nostrils wide, the lips very full, yet firm, the chin slightly cleft" (98). Moreover, during a scene when she entices him into the forest, she pours out a rich, intoxicating wine for him and asks, softly: "Who do you think I am?" Is he dreaming?

> Lully stared at her. Her eyes seemed like the holes in a mask—windows through which he peered on curious lands and seas. She seemed to tower above him ... she put her hand on his shoulder, and it

was as if something hot had touched his flesh through his clothes ... instantly his senses swooned away from him. He thought that he was falling backwards through water or the endless leaves of the forest trees ... that somewhere in a beam of cold light the face of a wild boar was peering at him [180–181].

Increasingly, the world around him dissolves into inhuman faces and dancing forms twisting from altar to garret, climbing over the tombs in the deserted cathedral. The scraping sounds of cloven hooves echo in the air.

Events pile up in quickening succession. Lally's employer, the Duke, arrives and is instantly smitten with Gertruda. A hidden, ancient temple is excavated on the grounds near the monastery. It is a temple to the god Mithias, an Eastern deity, a god who ruled over the sun and was attended by fire-worshipers. Inside are altars once used for human sacrifices. The Harvest approaches. Grains, ripening vines, flowers are burgeoning in riotous profusion. Stains of the grapes are everywhere. Intoxicating scents thicken the air. The statues everywhere seem to swell in size. A gigantic monk is seen. The local pastor fears aloud that "immortals lingering from an older time and an older faith, robbed of nearly all their power now, yet not quite all" are "remnants of the forces that overpowered St. Bernard" (263).

From the surrounding woods the vintagers arrive for the Harvest. They are of an "oddly foreign aspect" and speak in strange tongues. Working with expert, preternatural skills, they produce ancient Greek wines while speaking of the great Harvests of the world, when there were no cathedrals in Germany, when the gods were worshipped in grove and thicket, "and ghosts and nymphs and penates, kobolds and fairies, water spirits and wood spirits, devils and wild hunters had never been exorcised from the banks of the Rhine" (296).

The Harvest concludes with a fine pagan frenzy, replete with

> [A]ll the crude wildness, the black melancholy, the morbid glooms, the religious terrors, of Gothic fancy. All the fierce passions, the untamed imagination, of the North were in these uncouth fairy tales, which, darkened by superstition, saddened by fanaticism, sullied by ignorance and cruelty, yet showed here and there glimpses of a yet older world, joyous, human, lovely, the age of the Pagan gods before monk and nun, ghost and demon, robber knight and goblin, came to dwell on the banks of the Rhine [59–60].

All is unbound.

And then, suddenly, the Harvest is finished. The grapes pressed, the wine finished, the perfumes distilled, the unholy vintagers return to the surrounding woods. Left behind are two mortal men, Lally and the Duke of Nassau. They meet very different fates. The Duke follows the seductive Gertruda into the forest, where his body is found, "but not alive, and scarcely in human shape." Shaken free of his "poor bones and flesh," he now wanders "in some region of which it was best not to think" (320). Meanwhile, Lally Duchene, the Duke's friend and former commandant of the fallen Eberbach Monastery, fears a similar fate. "I am lost now," he confesses to his beloved, the fair Paulina. "I must go with them; there is no hope. I think they make a sacrifice in the woods." But Pauline puts her arms around him and "the touch of her warm humanity gave him a certain strength; and he breathed more freely; the air seemed less oppressive" (318). They return to the world, "loving each other at last in a kind and human fashion" (320).

Damnation and salvation, evil and grace, death and life—they all prevail, neither triumphant, neither defeated, but ongoing, together, everlasting...

The Haunted Vintage ranks high in Bowen's oeuvre. It is rich in sensuous prose and extravagant in architectural and floral detail. Edward Wagenknecht has declared it "a masterpiece of atmospheric invocation and concentration; the description of the harvest is a brilliant tour-de-force on both the natural and the supernatural level."[51]

The Abode of Love

"To give up witchcraft is to give up the Bible"

The Abode of Love ranks among Bowen's most probing and compassionate investigations into the thin partitions that separate faith from fraud, Christian orthodoxy from pagan mythologies. How do they both give testimony to our lives? Their kinship is suggested by a quotation from John Wesley: "To give up witchcraft is to give up the Bible" (61). Moreover, it is suggested that in the fellowship of the lapsed reverend, Stephen Finett's Agape there are echoes of pagan practice. Indeed, as one character avows: "White Magic lies very close to Black Magic" (72). Finett's Church is fraught with references to the "Triple Hecate" of Greek mythology. It will be recalled that Hecate is a mythological goddess from Greek polytheism, frequently depicted in triple incarnations, associated with magic and witchcraft and poisonous herbs. As Finett tells a member of his "flock," "[Hecate] was all the natural feelings we are ashamed of, and that have to come out somehow; and *if people—women, didn't worship her in secret they would go mad and upset society*, [which] had been made by the men—who didn't know anything about women" (35). Moreover, carved into the Church walls are the four creatures who appear in the apocalyptic vision in the Book of Ezekiel: Four cherubim—in some versions, four animals—born of a stormy wind and each with four faces and four wings that sparkle like burnished bronze.[52]

The lapsed Rev. Stephen Finett is one of Bowen's most finely drawn charismatics, who to his followers proves to be an unstable combination of revelation and fraud. The novel eschews some of the more melodramatic excesses of other false prophets and faiths found in *The Haunted Vintage, The Circle in the Water, Black Magic*; and ultimately it regards Finett as a pathetic figure lost in his delusions.

The action begins in the Valley of the Wye in Clapham Town district of Paulchurch. The time is the mid–nineteenth century. We meet the prospective members of Finett's newly established Church of the Agape.[53] We are not surprised to learn that in the area is the old Rectory, which lies forsaken and abandoned to ruins. There are hints that it once was the site of heathen practices. Two young ladies, Agnes and Rosa, will play an important role. Already, Agnes is predisposed to the "Rapture" promised by Finett:

> She felt an illusion of being on the frontiers of the invisible world, that only dedicated saints were allowed to enter; she was too feeble to be permitted visions of the eternal radiance beyond human darkness; but was it possible that, led by a strong hand, she might some day glimpse the eternal brilliancy of that region that she had not been able even to imagine, because her faculties were not equal to the effort of piercing the darkness that crowds in on all the human senses? [54–55].

Her aunt is Pamela Glascot, whose skepticism of the whole thing is the ongoing, necessary counterbalance to these effusions.

Finett has chosen to follow the "revelations" that are frequently granted him, without deference to his spiritual superiors. He preaches the second coming of Christ, the approaching Day of Judgment, and his status as a Divine mouthpiece. He has written pamphlets like "The Sinner's Slide to Hell." He has come to Paulchurch, in the words of his wife, Martha, "like a whirlwind, he will purge the floor and gather the wheat, but the chaff he will burn with a fire unquenchable" (15). The established Church, Finett adds, "is moribund, desperately in need of salvation, but the awful moment of awakening approaches" (26). Further, his disciples need not wait in discomfort for the end of the world, he says—"not if one was chosen" (27). Meanwhile, he preaches "sinless perfection" and hints at a "Love Feast" to come.

Agnes and Rosa are warned by Rosa's father at the outset that, despite appearances, Finett is neither Evangelical nor High Church:

> I wish I could make it clear to you that the conventions, orthodoxy, are essential to society. Rebels and heretics there are in numbers, but they only bring disaster on themselves and others. There must be rules. Those who break them, pay. Mr. Finett breaks rules—those drawn up by the Church. No one can understand the Divine will or purpose, all we can do is to be guided by the Church—a compromise, no doubt, but it suits our English nature; it casts out the wild visionary, the raving charlatan, it orders everything smoothly... [30].

But Rosas's nurse suggests that the real spiritual truth lies outside the Church:

> There is something besides Heaven and Hell, and that is the Earth. What is there in the forest, my dear, besides the good spirits and the bad? Little live, busy things eating, drinking, sleeping, not knowing anything of these mighty affairs. There are the ruins of pagan camps and pagan altars in the fields, and houses where the grand folk lived in the merry times. There are caves where warriors hid from their enemies and roads built long ago ... and there is magic abroad and queer things happen; the moon is kind to women [34].

And Agnes's brother, Adam, who serves as Finnett's acolyte, hints at the same thing: "The time may come when we shall not be so trammeled by human rules of conduct" (51). Finnett's message of the Wrath and Fury to come, so disrupts the congregation that they sink into convulsions and think they behold the church elders as birds with great beaks; and lest they repent they will sink into a black pit.

Henceforth, Finnett's name is Beloved.

Five years pass and a new church is built for Finnett, named The Ark of the Covenant. The walls are now emblazoned with the Four Beasts of Ezekial. Finett's Love Feast derives from ancient pagan festivals dedicated to their patron gods, where Bacchus is worshipped by the wine dealers, Diana by the hunters, Sylvanus by the wood workers. It transpires in the so-called Abode of Love, a walled-off enclosure into which only a select few women are allowed entry. What transpires there will not be made public. Finnett will soon select a Bride of the Beloved. Suspicions are aroused and voiced by the local press; and a bold headline proclaims: "Christ or Antichrist on Clapham Common?" (93).

Agnes and Rosa are soon accepted into this sanctified Abode. There is a strong sense of eroticism as they and the other women are clearly being groomed, their garments discarded, their group bathings in perfumed waters, their abandonment of the sense of Sin encouraged. Has not Finett proclaimed himself Christ come again; and as the Second Messiah, discarded what the Devil had created in man, the sense of self, and through that, sin? Has he not destroyed "the consciousness of self and sin, body and soul, so that the brethren become one with him, spouses of Christ, celebrating the mystical reunion?" (114).

But when Agnes notices the Sisters gazing lovingly at themselves in the mirrors, she realizes that the Serpent has invaded the Garden.

Comes the long-awaited Marriage Ceremony. Sister Rosa is chosen. Amidst the fumes of the burning incense Finett anoints her and proclaims: "After this feast and these espousals, Sister Rosa will not exist any longer, free from all sin, or possibility of sin, she will be spirit only. Whatever she does she cannot sin.... Her name is Eirene, for she is Peace and brings peace. By this name the risen Lord greets and espouses her'" (126). Disturbed, Agnes senses that "a door had closed on the visionary world" and that in that realization she is "allowing evil to enter the Abode of Love."

Dissension is rife. Some of the women become pregnant and attempt to escape the compound. Their disappearance is unexplained. The once-clean quarters are dirtied, garments soiled. Agnes, once the paragon of Finett's flock is dirty and slovenly. A new Love Feast is held, but the "ceremony of love and reverence" has become a debauch. Rosa, now "the Goddess of Love" is pregnant. Her union with Finett was anything but chaste. "Who do we worship here?" asks one member. "What holy virgin is this? None, but Hecate, who is Diana of the mystic wood by the lake named her mirror when the moon falls on these accursed waters" (150). Stephen Finett's wife has had enough. She and Mrs. Glascot warn Agnes that the good reverend is mixing up the Heathen with the Church: "We are all weary of myths, fables, and shams. They are dangerous to play with, for too long; we must keep our feet on the earth or be put behind bars" (143).

Mrs. Finett confirms the source of her husband's teachings: He had modeled his Love Feasts after paintings and old writings he had translated from the Latin, modeling the Agape after Pagan rites, baptizing his "spiritual bride" Rosa as Eirene. But, after all, she protests, Stephen must have *believed* in all this: "'He isn't the first to be deceived, is he? He *thought* he heard voices, didn't he? And saw visions—?'" (151). Mrs. Finett is a pathetic figure here, insisting that she had loved him, knowing his weaknesses and his struggles, because she was old and alone and he was all she had. But then, he had turned to the young and pretty girls..

This moment elicits one of Bowen's strongest denunciations of the Agape. The redoubtable Mrs. Glascot lashes out, extending her vituperation into Christian practices, in general, and Agnes in particular:

> Sinless perfection indeed! None of you seem in that state.... Sinless perfection is imbecility. People want to run away from trouble and difficulty—to make someone else responsible, so they throw the whole mess on to a scapegoat and pretend he is a god—that is all there is to sinless perfection, Agnes.... Only the feeble-minded could believe without understanding—it is the feebleminded who make all religions possible—the fools following the rogues.' ... It is such an old story. Mankind hasn't much power of invention, always the same rubbish—sacrifices, giving God his share of your meal, or cutting God up to eat so that his power passes into you, or turning your natural feelings from another human being towards some image or statue and writing love poems to that instead of to your mate, and going crazy and ill with the strain, always lamb and stars, and prophets and wise men and sacred virgins, and love feasts, and always human nature breaking through.... The Devil? I'd say he is always there when people go mad—when the priest begins to believe what he's preaching, and the people begin to believe the priest, then you've got the devil abroad.... If all women had always married young and had large families there would never have been any religions—the men might have invented gods to help them in their fightings and cheatings, but they'd never have bothered to keep them going. The women did that because they were crossed in love, or fancied the priest, or not being able to get a real sweetheart, they liked to think they were married to a god—or they wanted power and to feel superior to better-looking women, you ought to know all this. It's all so old. Moonshine, reflected in a bit of glass, or a piece of water [153–155].

The Church is in shambles, the reverend is in hiding, and his disgruntled flock plots a punishment that is the height of irony: They will crucify him. After all, Agnes's brother offers, wryly, in sentiments that reveal the commonality between Christian and Pagan practice: "Gods were always killed, sacrificed, and rose again, the flesh, the blood, the corn, the wine, the earth must be replenished before there is a harvest and a vintage to feed us all and to give us dreams, bread to make the body live, wine to indulge the soul" (160).

And Rosa, once the Beloved, takes her leave with her child. With a measure of compassion, she comes to Finett, by now addled and confused, and gently tells him: "Goodbye, poor soul—you had a little wonder and excitement, did you not? And so did I—and what else is worthwhile striving for? ... It is time I was away—with all the other sensible people. It seems you cannot be wholly spiritual and wholly sane" (171).

Literally under cover of darkness, Mrs. Finett leads her befuddled husband away from the area, while the noises of carpenter's hammers are heard in the distance.

I Dwelt in High Places

"This modern age is an epoch of wonders."

I Dwelt in High Places is a fictionalized account of historical events in the life of John Dee, astrologer and mathematician to the court of Queen Elizabeth, and his relationship with the alchemist, Edward Kelley. It is one of Bowen's most impressive blends of fiction with fact. She even provides an extended commentary on her historical sources.

These are turbulent "modern times," muses Dee, when, as it seemed, "most unexpectedly, and surely through the wish and guidance of Divine Providence, all the world was opened up to eager adventurers, and every day brought some marvelous discovery, either in the realms of Nature, or in those of science, or in the finding of strange countries and peoples" (28). This extends to Dee's New Testament itself, which in those times, as the pious astrologer discovers, includes experiences that are supranormal and ecstatic, including dreams, visions, trances, epiphanies, theophanies, "speaking in tongues" (the language of angels), and raptures to heaven.[54]

The story begins in the year 1582, when the 55-year-old Dee first meets Kelley. The ensuing six years cover their association as they travel through Central Europe to seek patronage with Emperor Rudolf II in Prague Castle, King Stefan Bathory in Poland, and Lord Rosenberg in Bohemia. After the two men part company around 1588, Kelley goes on to serve under Rudolph II in Prague. Having failed in the promise to produce gold by alchemical experiments, however, Kelley is eventually imprisoned and dies in 1597. Back in Mortlake, Dee dies alone in 1608.

Controversy surrounds the precise nature of the collaboration between Dee and Kelley and to what degree Dee might have fallen under the influence of Kelley's greed for power and position. Bowen closely follows the historical record as it is known and draws her own conclusions.

Standing between the idealistic Dee and the opportunistic trickster Kelley is Dee's wife, practical, compassionate, vulnerable. Revered by the former and seduced by the latter, Jane emerges as the "voice" of author Marjorie Bowen herself. Thus, *I Dwelt in High Places* not only deserved a "high" place in Bowen's oeuvre, but must be counted among her more autobiographical books.

Dominating the narrative is Bowen's fascination with the tensions between Dr. Dee's spiritual questing and Edward Kelley's alchemical pursuits. The two men constitute a kind of Elizabethan version of Don Quixote and Sancho Panza, i.e., Dee is portrayed as a rather naïve man whose preoccupation with spiritual matters blinds him to the more pragmatic realities and concerns of the pragmatic, manipulative Kelley. Having said that, Bowen is careful to reveal how easily Dee, a man of science and mathematics can be befuddled by the lure of magical practices; and how Kelley, a rank opportunist and charlatan, falls victim of his own delusions.

Although Dee is a sturdy paragon of established reputation as the wisest man in England—he had been a student at the University of Louvain, graduated as a doctor before he was twenty years old, lectured in mathematics at the College of Rheims, in Paris, was a personal friend of many of the great men of England, and was now Astrologer to the Queen—he thirsts for "the illimitable knowledge to set free the spiritual elements in all chemical substances and metals, and to attain the god-like powers of wisdom of healing, and to learn secrets hitherto unguessed at by man" (24). He senses that he has been visited by "angelic beings," but he is denied concourse with them. He has not yet tampered with hermetic experiment. For that, "he must be dependent on another person; and though he had been several times deceived and cheated, his faith in the possibility of find this person was by no means shaken" (31).

Just arrived at his door is a stranger named Edward Talbot, a rather mysterious fellow who has brought with him some mysterious red and white powders and a book he claims he has found in the ruins of Glastonbury, which he is unable to translate. "My name is Edward Talbot," he says; "I can skry very well. I have a number of spirits at my command. I feel sure that Dr. Dee would wish to try my powers'" (13). Over the objections of Dee's wife, to whom "the stars were but so many lights, far away and mysterious" (30), and against the warnings of his assistant, Roger Cook, Dee brings him to his laboratory; and after several visits, is convinced he is the man with gifts of vision he has been looking for. Talbot, whose real name is Edward Kelley, claims he has seen Uriel, the spirit light, in Dee's shrewstones, "who had told him that these experiments were to be blessed, and that if implicit obedience were given to the spirits, great benefits and glories might result" (43).

Kelley declares mathematics is insufficient for his purposes: "'I hear very little of such matters from the angels,' he tells Dee. 'I believe when I get into divine company mathematics is of little account'" (39). He seems to exert great influence over Dee and has persuaded him to purchase at great expense various items to showcase the crystal globes. He claims that although spirits remained in the globes, sometimes they stepped down and moved about the room, not seen by Dee, but their voices could be heard.

The observant Jane Dee has already taken his measures and observes a preternatural changeability in his aspect:

> He was a shadow among shadows. Often, she would stand at her window and see him ride out across the drawbridge, down the one crooked, winding street of the little town. And then, again, by chance, she would be looking out across the dusk, and see him riding in with his cloak flying and the long hat with a heron's feather on his flast cap. He was very richly dressed now and wore gold rings and a bright clasp of gold ast his throat [183].

Against her wishes, Dee invites Kelley to live in his house at Mortlake. And soon, Kelley's wife, Joan also arrives. Roger Cook immediately warns Dee and his wife of Kelley. His deceits are dangerous to Dee's own spiritual interests: "We have trouble with the spirits, because of the disbelief of Edward Kelley.... Juggling and conjuring and a blasphemous and dangerous use of the names of things holy and spiritual" (52). But Dee believes Kelley's claims he has summoned the spirits of Uriel, the Spirit of Light, and the Archangel Michael. "[Dee] believes what he wishes to believe and sees what he wishes to see," observes Roger Cook. "And I will not deny this wretch has a strange power about him. I myself have felt it, even when I have passed him in the passage of an evening" (45). Jane herself has seen that beneath Kelley's black skull cap are ears mangled through tortures inflicted upon him by those punishing him for coining bogus money. And soon she is aware that a warrant has been issued against him for coining money. But such is Kelley's growing influence that he forces Cook out of the house.

Meanwhile, Kelley begins to suffer fits of an apparent demonic possession, alternating with periods of confession. Against her incredulity, Jane herself witnesses these demonic episodes: "For it seemed to her as if she really saw an evil spirit let loose in the gold paneled parlour, for Edward Kelley's body seemed to lash about as if it were in the control of something stronger than himself, and it was with a movement as if he were swept away by an invisible power that he flung himself across the room..." (58). He sits before the shrewstones, seeing and hearing things denied Dee. And the messages are strange and ambiguous, voiced by the angel Madimi, "a pretty girl angel of seven or nine years," says Kelley:

> We open the eyes through the sun at morning and the sun at night. Distance is nothing with us, unless it be the distance which separates the wicked from His mercy. Secrets there are none but what are buried in the shadows of man's soul. Iniquity shall not range where the fire of His piercing judgment lights [66].

Sometimes the spirits leave the crystal and move about the room. And always they warn of the evil spirit Belmagel, while ordering Dee and Kelley to go abroad in search of riches. Such scenes are amusing as Kelley works his imagination upon everyone around him, voicing the spirits and graphically describing their aspect and activities. He even conducts imaginary disputes among the various spirits.

One day the Queen comes for a brief visit, although she fails to give Dee the funds he so desperately needs for household and experiments.

A new character enters the scene, a Polonian Count, Adelbert Laski. He also wants to study magic at Mortlake. But again, doubts: Is he nothing more than an adventuress? And does he really enjoy the favor of King Bathory of Poland? Kelley predicts great good fortune will come to them if they follow him. But it becomes apparent that his true interests are those of Kelley, the pursuit of gold and how to transmute it from base materials.

What follows is a methodical attempt by Kelley to usurp his patron's work and his mind. Along the way, it might be added, Kelley want to appropriate Dee's wife. From the very first, Jane can't help but be fascinated, while also repelled, by him. And he quickly sees this: "Do I disturb you, Jane Dee?" he asks, "in the way a man disturbs a woman? You are married to one much too old for you" (73). Her excited fancy depicts him as a fallen angel, "thrown before a celestial sphere" (77). Kelley's coming also excites a restlessness in her and dreams of travel and adventure:

> She felt, too, what she had not known since her marriage, a great unrest and desire to be away from Mortlake, even from England, and to join in those adventures which were taking place all over the world—the discovery of new worlds, the pursuit of new thoughts. She longed to be on a quest, even if it were but a quest of clouds [92].

"I do not know if I believe in his angels," she muses, "but at least he has made me discontented with the commonplace of every day" (92). Her pleas to Dee that Kelley is a rogue fall on deaf ears. She is reluctant to expose him, in a way: "Yet I shall never betray him," she says to herself, "for that would be to betray myself and to lose all the sparkle there is in life" (97). She is bitterly ashamed of herself for this. "If he is a devil or inspired by devils," she thinks, "then I am damned, yet I do not regret it, though life is short and one is in Hell for so long" (150).

Kelley knows she could denounce him, but won't: "It is true, is it not, that you have a deep faith in me beyond all that? You have never denounced me, but always in your heart you have taken my part. Is it that you cannot help loving me, Jane Dee?" (161).

Kelley and the Dee family and Count Laski plan to leave Mortlake. They undergo a long and tedious trip, full of privations, across Bremen, to Hamburg, to Cracow, to the Court of the King of Poland. to the Emperor Rudolph at Prague, and the Graf Rosenburg of Bohemia. There are even invitations from Muscovy [Moscow]. There are patronage and riches awaiting them. Of course, the interests of these titled men lie solely in their greed for gold, for providing Kelley with laboratories and means to make gold.

At this point, Kelley announces he will have nothing more to do with Dee and his spiritual questings:

> Do you not see they do not care for heavenly wisdom or angelic visions? They wish for nothing but gold. These visits of the spirits bring us no profit, and I, for one, will skry no more. Do you not see that that is all that any of them care about? ... What does anyone to whom we may go want but gold? ... Leave off then, these vain communications with the spirits, these delvings into these symbols and mysteries that have no explanation and let us indeed see if we cannot make that which is every man's desire [156].

Bowen catalogues abundant details about Kelley's alchemical procedures and apparatus. How much of this is substantiated by Bowen's research and how much is wholly fanciful is in question (166–167). Kelley does indeed produce small examples of what are judged to be pure gold. He assumes more and more power, leaving Dee and Jane in the shadows. He grows rich and increasingly power-mad. He has nothing but scorn for Dee's spiritual quest: "What have these spirits done for me? How many of their promises have they redeemed? Did I not say from the first that I was not seeking heavenly wisdom, but rather earthly good" (194).

Now old, broken, and forsaken, Dee cries to Jane that *he had wanted to believe*:

> I could not endure to believe that the angels were all false. For five years I have lived with them and believed in them and heard them speak, ay, and seen their movements across the room. No, Jane, it cannot be but the tricks of a rogue. Never tell me that, for it would be enough to shake one's faith in God Almighty [196].

At this point Bowen herself intervenes with her own voice: "[Kelley] had no refuge, save in his prayers, and of late it had seemed to him that the heavens were closed against him" (195). And her citing of the King of Poland's view of Kelley's experiments perhaps echoes her own judgment:

> I am neither convinced that angels are present, nor sanguine that they will ever appear. I believe that God has reserved to himself three things—the creation of something out of nothing, the knowledge of futurity and the government of the conscience [178].

Ultimately, the titled heads are credulous enough that they offer riches and support to Kelley and Dee. Only an Englishman, Edward Garland, expresses an open mind:

> I have travelled too far and seen too many strange things to doubt anything. This modern age is an epoch of wonders. Who knows what may be discovered or performed from one day to the next? Things are now possible which our fathers would have rejected as frantic impossibilities. The powers of man seem daily to stretch farther in every direction. I have, for myself, seen many strange things. I have voyaged in lands which our fathers did not know existed [186].

Just as Dee and Jane determine to return to England and Mortlake, Kelley comes to Jane entreating him to come to him; and he declares to Dee that the angels have told him of a shocking proposition—"that we are to share everything, even our wives" (203). At this moment, our narrator observes that Kelley "seemed then angel and devil both.... One damned and yet one who had tasted heaven, like an angel who had been immediately, on his first sin, cast down from Paradise" (204).

Although Dee almost begins to believe that angels have ordered this, Jane knows that now is the time to leave Kelley. It is a difficult decision that dominates the last pages of the book. She tells her husband he must let Kelley go. He protests if they do, the angels might never come to them. "We do not want such angels that this man can summon," she retorts (215). But Dee had been persuaded that he "felt himself at one with God" and had been on the verge of attaining the perfect wisdom which "was the end and be-al of Hermetic philosophy" (218). But now all the "airy shapes which rose from the crucible in which chemicals melted over the clear fire of the furnace" were gone; and "before him nothing but the increasing darkness of a weary old age, with all his long and painfully accumulated knowledge which he had been piling up since he was a boy…" (219).

Jane's final confrontation with Kelley is a magnificent scene, sad and painful: "She knew no tremors," we are told, "doubts nor fears; her faith was single, simple and infinitely strong. Nothing to her could obscure right and wrong. She knew neither subtleties nor hesitation, and duty to her could never have either two names or two faces" (225). Yet she sees within herself the difficulty of her rejection of him:

> She knew him, she thought, through and through, and in truth she knew him as well as anyone would ever know him, and yet she was in a wonder as to what was false in him and what was true—a strange, unstable, wild creature! She pitied him as much as she loved him and she wondered a little why they had not been allowed to meet when she was free.... This was the end, and she wondered what she would do in the future if duty should be insufficient to fill the long, grey days [227].

And yet, as she and her husband depart Prague, she briefly entertains the image of what her life could have been with Kelley and the riches that surround him: Would Dee have remained in his delusion? Would the spirits of Uriel, Madimi, and Michael remain with them? Had she denied her own vague, restless, intense desires for nothing? Would it have been wise and kinder to have assisted in Kelley's imposture, to have ignored the evil aspect of the bargain, to have dissimulated and led her husband, cheated but happy, to his grave? (235).

Dee and Jane return to a Mortlake that has fallen to vandals, Dee's papers destroyed, his books ruined. They are now penniless. Soon, she will die. Kelly will be exposed and incarcerated in a lunatic asylum.

At the end, we find an 80-year-old John Dee, who has outlived wife and family and now, in his old age, is spending his last days under a cloud of suspicion. Suspected of witchcraft, he is petitioning Parliament "that he not be confounded with devil-worshippers, and raisers of hellish imps" (239). His mind is clouded. He doesn't know that his onetime associate-turned-nemesis, Edward Kelley, is long dead, and that his former patron, the Emperor of Bohemia has been deposed and incarcerated as a lunatic. After years of futile gazing into his shrewstone, he now imagines a spirit named Raphael is bidding him to settle his worldly affairs and prepare for a long journey. And so it is that Raphael vanishes "into the azure glory of eternity" and takes John Dee with him, "far beyond the quest of clouds" (244).

Throughout this carefully researched story, Bowen maintains a careful balance between Christian faith and Pagan agency, theology and science, and the possibility of a genuine necromancy measured against the reality of fraud. If Dee ultimately rejects Kelley, it is more through the influence of his wife than any doubts on his own part. In her Notes to the book, Bowen claims to remain open-handed about such questions, simply cleaving to the historical record and utilizing such letters and "conversations with the angels" that are available. She feels free to observe, however, that after Elizabeth's death, the accession to the throne of James I led to the subsequent inauguration of a century-long persecution of witchcraft. What she calls "this outburst of ignorant malice, spiteful bigotry, interested loyalty, superstitious fear and genuine religious zeal ... swept away John Dee ... into a dishonourable obscurity, from which his reputation has hardly yet, perhaps never will, recover" (247).

As a "man of science," Dee became the mystic "without being conscious" that he had changed the direction of his studies into "Angelical conversation" and alchemy. Not just a search for gold, alchemy at the time—quite apart from Kelley's alleged chicanery— was also "revered as perhaps the first of the sciences bound up with transcendentalism" and held a "spiritual purpose" and "a quest for divine wisdom" (249). Thus, Bowen regards it as much like the Spiritualism of her own time: "John Dee's reverent and careful account of the conversation of the angels through the medium, might have been written to-day at any *séance*, save that the language is more beautiful and the thought more noble than that usually employed or expressed by modern seekers after psychic knowledge"(251). Bowen adds that Dr. Dee and Kelley "never endeavoured to raise the spirits of the dead," which he would have regarded as "the horrible blasphemy of meddling with departed souls" (251). Rather, he "stretched out to God himself" and his angels "spoke, often tediously, often incoherently, but never in a babble of childish patter, their language was always beautiful and they often expressed themselves in passages of great power and splendor" (252).

Bowen is even willing to cut Kelley some slack. "He must have been more than a common rogue, just as John Dee was more than a common dupe.... He must have been somewhere, well-educated to have been able, as he was able to cope at the age of twenty-six with the most erudite man in England" (252). Moreover,

> If one assumes that the angelic conversations were his sole deliberate inventions, they show him to have been a person of considerable literary ability, some poetic vision, a profound insight into character, and one possessed of at least the knowledge of much grandeur of thought, high moral precepts and desirable virtues.... He may have been often self-hypnotised, self-deluded, entirely confused, and the rages that passed as diabolic possessions may have been the conflict of a divided personality.... By what trick he persuaded so many people that he had actually persuaded so many people that he had actually made gold can never now be known [253].

In sum, Bowen's novel "makes no attempt to solve that mystery or to impose the deliberate inventions of fiction on to known truths. Because no imaginary characters are used, I have felt obliged to keep to what facts we possess about these people and to interpret them by what insight and understanding I may command" (254).

The Poisoners
"A Fantastic Farrago of Incredible People and Incredible Incidents"

> Now that I, tying thy glass mask tightly
> May gaze thro' these faint smokes curling whitely,

> As thou pliest thy trade in this devil's-smithy—
> Which is the poison to poison her, prithee?
> Robert Browning, "The Laboratory"

Nothing less than the reign of Louis XIV of France is threatened with the Furies of witchcraft. The notorious "Affair of the Poisons" chronicled here, as it was known in the late seventeenth century, might well be labeled, for our purposes, "The Affair of the Furies." Based on historical records, the majority of the female poisoners and blackmailers that populate *The Poisoners* may or may not have been inspired by supernatural agencies they presume to invoke. Bowen, as usual, cleverly balances both fact and fancy and allows us to draw our own conclusions. What is striking is that the malefactors are women, as de la Reynie, the Paris Chief of Police, declares:

> The women—always the women! ... They are kept so close, they lead unnatural lives, almost like prisoners—they have lively passions and no means of expressing them. And very often their husbands or their fathers are cruel. Well, they take the only weapon to their hand. It seems that we may find it is a weapon that has been used very freely [49].

And as the Minister of War in the Versailles of King Louis XIV declares, those weapons are readily at hand: "When has there been a moment that idle, great ladies have not amused themselves with charms, philtres and incantations?" (249).

As in *I Dwelt in High Places,* Bowen's novel is scrupulously researched and, aside from a measure of dramatic license, cleaves closely to the historical record.[55] Beginning in 1678, at the height of the French Monarchy, at a time when the King's diplomacy and his armies overshadow Europe, and continuing over the next four years, a series of poisonings alarm the public, whose authorship seems to extend from the low-born to Versailles itself. Poisoning and witchcraft are held to be connected, writes historian Anne Somerset:

> Through the ages witchcraft and poisoning had been held to be naturally affiliated, with many authorities maintaining that the devil enhanced witches' power to do harm by supplying them with deadly powers.... The reality of the devil was very evident and the devil dominated people's consciousness in a way that today we can hardly grasp. The counterpart to living in an age of faith, when religion afforded comfort to so many, was that the devil was not conceived of some remote entity, but rather as a malign being who could be visualized with horrible clarity.[56]

Indeed, continues Somerset, there were suspicions that one of the poisoners was the King's own mistress, "The Queen of the Left Hand," Mme. de Montespan. She "would herself be touched by the same scandal after she too was accused not just of poisoning but also of sacrilege, Satanism and infanticide."[57] She purportedly had exercised black magic to maintain a hold over the King against his presumptive mistresses.

There were many trials and many executions. But, reports Bowen, the scandals were deliberately hushed up by the Chief of Police, M. de la Renie and the King himself: "For a long time complete obscurity veiled the subject, until, in 1789, the taking of the Bastille by the Parisian mob brought to light the secret archives of this fortress prison." A large number of documents revealing facts in the case was sorted through by M. Francois Ravaisson and revealed to the public. He reconstructed events into "a wild, sinister tale of love and magic that would do credit to the imagination of any novelist and provide ample material for what is now called a 'detective story' or 'thriller.'"[58]

One can readily imagine author Bowen warming to the story, alert to the Hunt, and straining at the leash... What she has produced is, in her own words, "a farrago of incredible people and incredible incidents" (13).

To the roster of the actual people involved—Louis XIV; M. de la Reynie; the Marquise de Brinvilliers; the King's mistresses, Madame de Montespan and Mlle. De Fontanges; Catherine Montvoisin and her daughter, Marie; Mlle. Des Œillets—she has added the fictive characters of a young policeman named Charles Desgrez, his wife, Solange, and a mysterious character known for most of the story's length as The Grand Master.

The action is swift, the characters sharply delineated, and the tone decidedly melodramatic, recalling those wonderful French movie serials from the 'teens by Louis Feuillade, *Les Vampires* and *Fantômas*, with their masked Master Criminals, episodic structures, and nightmarish repetitions of pursuit-and-capture. Chief of Police de la Reynie, along with his assistant, a new police lieutenant, Charles Desgrez, pits his wits against this mysterious "Grand Master" who has organized and implemented a cabal of poisoners in an attempt to undermine the French aristocracy. He is a megalomaniac who is always just one step away from capture, who leaves behind mocking notes to de la Reynie that surely warms the hearts of Bowen's other megalomaniacs:

> You do not realize the joy it is to be God and Satan in one—to destroy for the love of destruction, for lust or greed or ambition, as one wishes! You cannot understand the superb sense of power it gives me to walk modestly, unnoticed, perhaps despised, and to know that I have power even over Kings! I could have removed you before—though it is true that you took great precautions—but I spared you because it amused me to pit my wits against yours. But I shall no longer hold my hand. Unless you get me—soon—I shall get you [395].

The "Affair" begins in 1678 with the sensational trial and execution of the convicted poisoner and murderess, Marquise de Brinvilliers. Two years later, it is discovered that she has left a legacy. A Parisian shop of perfumes and soaps, "The Lily Pot," is actually a cover for a dispensary supplying poisons to clients, including none other than two women close to the King, Madame de Montespan and Mademoiselle de Fontanges. There are also references to Saint-Croix and Exili, who had supplied de Brinvilliers with poison from Italy.

Under the authority of the King himself, de la Reynie proceeds with the investigation. He has become something of an authority on poisons and how they are administered—through arsenic-impregnated bouquets of flowers, for example, which, upon delivery, do their deadly work. This is an Italian invention, he reveals, and the victim need only inhale the aroma. Moreover, articles of clothing can be saturated with poisons, which prove to be fatal when touched to the skin: "The custom is to wash shirts or even bed-linen or cravats in arsenic soap—this produces on the victim an eruption and a slight fever. He is then put to bed and the doctor called in. The poisoner then gets to work; he doses the medicine, and the fever and the skin eruption pass as the disease that has proved fatal'" (232). Further, although a skeptic, he admits witchcraft may be involved:

> The witchcraft of two hundred years ago was a very potent evil—it was a network of secret societies dealing in every kind of abomination, directly opposed to Christianity and encouraging paganism and atheism.... A remnant exists here and there, perhaps, far more powerful than we know. These people may be mere ignorant imitators, and they may know nothing of the secrets of the true black magic cult—they may be mere dabblers in wizardry, but that they practice it there seems little doubt [168–169].

He speculates that perhaps the King may be one of the principle targets, since he is under the influence of the wicked Madame de Montespan: "I think he has never loved her. She is so imperious, so violent, such an adept at seduction and scenes of temper and fury, he has never been able to free himself from her" (172).

Rumors are rampant that a cabal of women is responsible. De la Reynie recruits his young protégé, Charles Desgrez, to disguise himself with a mask and infiltrate a meeting of a group of suspects. Desgrez' duly attends what seems at first just a gathering of ordinary, inoffensive people. However, it's not long before he realizes that something is very wrong. They talk of a vague conspiracy. Their faces blur before his eyes; they appear to be intoxicated; somehow he has become intoxicated; abominably dark shadows crawl around the room; and acrid perfumes choke the air. He grows dizzy and disoriented from the noxious perfumes in the air. He thinks he recognizes two characters who will be important in subsequent events, Catherine la Voisin and her daughter. He is astonished when everyone turns to him and addresses him as their "Grand Master." Apparently, he realizes, the identity of this man who is purported to be their leader is as yet unknown to them.

Subsequently, he is invited to attend a Black Mass at the *Impasse des Fleurs.* Accompanied now by de le Reynie and another masked companion, Desgrez finds himself in a cellar beneath an old mansion, a chamber that once had been a burial vault. Attending are two priests robed in black. The air is thickened from the fumes of a narcotic, black candles give off a sickly light, and the Host is produced (black, 3-cornered wafers) and trodden underfoot by the company. A general confession is voiced, cries and shrieks are emitted from the obviously drugged congregants, and a procession of black-veiled, black-cloaked women appear. "Some of the women are overcome by emotion when they reach the altar and fall down in a kind of fit or trance; one foams at the mouth and screams hysterically ... the air becomes thick and foul and is mingled with the reek of the perfume used by the women" (213).

At length, a woman enters, strips naked, and lays herself along the altar. Her "pale glimmering body looked like a length of stain laid on the three white linen cloths on the table" (217). A basket is produced. It contains a small, naked baby. There are shouts and incantations. The baby is carried to the altar. What transpires after that is unclear to Des Grez, whose senses are befuddled. He tries to deny what is happening, "to reassure himself he had not seen properly, the whole thing had been an hallucination, a nightmare; even if there had been a child, it would have been dead—or perhaps it was a child at all, merely a wax image" (218).

However, during an interview later with the King's Controller-General, M. de Colbert, the ghastly reality is revealed: Colbert had been de le Reynie's masked companion at the ceremony, and he explains what he had witnessed: "A child, newborn, and living as I think, though of that I cannot be sure, was sacrificed on the naked body of some woman, which was used as an altar ... a portion of the child was burnt afterwards to make a philtre" (221). Colbert goes on to enumerate the many women present by name and intends to place them under arrest. "I am tainted by the abominations I have seen to-night," he declares (223).

De le Reynie confirms to Desgrez that in his police work he has become aware that many women were trafficking newborn and aborted babies for ceremonies like this:

> The children, of course, have always been alive—when they could procure them. But this is a difficult matter to prove. Who has any care of, or kept any records of the base-born of great ladies who have gone astray? The bringing into the world of these children, dead or alive, and the selling of their bodies, dead or alive, have been the most profitable part of the whole business [234].

When apprised of all this, the King is alarmed. "These subtle poisoners abroad," he cries, "—so many insidious fiends administering poisons—who feels safe? In a shirt, in a bouquet, or rubbed on one's fork or spoon, on the rim of one's goblet, in one's handkerchief or medicine" (248). He has fears he may be the target of his former mistresses Madame de Montespan and Mlle. Des Oeiulets. He had already dismissed de Montespan and replaced her with Mlle. De Fontanges as his confidant and lover. She, in turn, fears she is now likewise a target. She's right to fear Montespan, who had already voiced her hatred of Fontanges and had conspired with Catherine la Voisin to poison both her and the King. If she, Montespan, cannot retain his passion—and she has tried with blood-rituals to effect that—Fontanges *and* the King must die. "But let *her* die first," she says; "let him see that! Let him stand by and see her suffer and die and be unable to help her! Then, perhaps, he will feel something of what I have felt, the agony, the despair, the humiliation, the shame of being powerless..." (294).

As for Mlle des Oeiùlets, she too has been active among the poisoners. "I'm in and I can't get out," she confesses. "There are no doors in hell, you know. It grows about one, little by little—it walls one in, and then there is no way out.... I have been in this business for years now. There is a good trade in these misbegotten brats—I've known as many as eighty to be sacrificed in one place alone'" (319–321).

With Oeillets in custody, de la Reynie wrings his hands in frustration at the obscurity of this investigation. Madame Montespan he had already suspected as one of the leaders, but the identity of the Grand Master is unknown:

> This case is too obscure, too mysterious, too far-reaching. We might sit here examining prisoners for years and still ne'er get to the bottom of it. All these people lie, contradict one another, create a confusion by sheer malice, or sheer stupidity. Even the sight of the torture chamber, the fear of the wheel or the stake only frightens them into fresh lies.

By now, de la Reynie has ordered seventy-five executions—"and where are we?" (338).

Indeed, a reported 150 people have already been executed for the crimes of poisoning, sorcery, infanticide and blasphemy, and many more suspects have fled Paris. Attempts to keep much of this secret from the public have only aroused the public's exaggerated gossip.

A breakthrough comes with the confession of Catherine la Voisin about her complicity in the poisonings. Defiant at first, but after witnessing the torture and execution of her mother, she relents and reveals that she and her mother and Montespan had all been present at the Black Mass: "She had not hesitated to perform the most revolting and detestable rites. She had permitted infanticide—the sacrifice of a new-born infant whose blood, as an offering to the Infernal Powers, had been poured upon her nude body, which had served as the altar" (382). She admits that Madame de Montespan had come to her mother for a love philtre some twelve years ago before the King had even looked at her, that it was by the means of these potions that she had drawn His Majesty's affection from Louise de Valliere to herself. She declared that during these years when Madame de Montespan had ruled as Queen of the Left Hand, she had been in constant touch with Catherine la Voisin, who had supplied her with drugs to keep the King faithful to her every time that there had been a weakening in his infatuation (381).

Further, she confirms that Montespan had been a celebrant of the Black Mass, where, la Voisin confesses,

> she had not hesitated to perform the most revolting and detestable rites. She had permitted, on her behalf, infanticide—the sacrifice of a new-born infant whose blood, as an offering to the Infernal Powers, bad been poured upon her nude body, which had served as altar [382].

In desperation, she had even considered saturating a document with poison to be handed to the King. La Voison's mother had not confessed any of this before, because she didn't think Montespan would allow her to die. Montespan thought herself safe from blame if she successfully poisoned Fontanges, because the King would not dare touch her for fear of scandal.

Alerted to this confession, the King comes in disguise to her cell. He asks her about the extent of the poisonings. Her response is remarkable: "No doubt you would be surprised, Monsieur, at the names of some of the great ones who made pacts with Satan—why, hardly a Captain went to the wars who did not come to us for a charm to render him bullet proof" (386). She is evasive about direct contact with Satan: "How do I know? The Masses were ugly enough—one was ways intoxicated. I've seen things" (387).

The scene shifts to Versailles. Fontanges is dead (probably from poisoning), and two scheming women are left to contend for the favors of the King. Louis now realizes that it was Montespan who had been subtly poisoning him all these years, authoring the illnesses that had so puzzled his physicians. Distressed at these revelations, he turns to Madame de Maintenon, a quiet widow of middle age, for advice. She has been patiently waiting for his attentions and gently rebukes him for having had so many mistresses. What is he to do about Montespan?

Maintenon suggests, perhaps he should keep up the pretense of keeping Montespan at Versaille—but should never see her *alone*: "Let Your Majesty's every look and glance, save those few formal ones you exchange in public; express your implacable hate, your undying revenge.... I should always be present. I do not think she will long endure that life. She will of herself retire from the Court and enter a convent" (408). He agrees, grateful at this way out. She muses to herself: "Is it possible? I have won at last, after all these years of patient waiting.... He grows afraid of God. He has found [Montespan] out at last. La Fontanges was his last love. I shall have him when he is old, burnt out, dull and pious, but I shall never be his mistress—only, if the Queen dies, I might be his wife" (406).

But Montespan is still clinging to her allegiance to the Devil. That she has failed so far is only because she has made mistakes in her spells. If she could eventually marry the King after the death of his Queen, she could then turn away from Satanism and embrace God. Have the cake and eat it too. Her thoughts are a fine example of her twisted reasoning—and perhaps Bowen's own sly critique of the practice of Catholic absolution:

> She believed in God as ardently as she believed in the Devil, and still trusted that a time might come when she would be in a worldly sense so safe that she could forsake the worship of Satan and return with an acceptable penitence to God. For this end she intended to force the priests to give her absolution [410].

Yet, when she confronts the King, it is Maintenon who blocks her. "Quite useless, Madame," Maintenon says, "I am here by the King's order—and by the King's orders I shall remain" (413).

Thus, not only is Montespan punished, but also the King. In a sally typical of Bowen's acid wit, de le Reynie observes, "No more light loves for him—he's turned to piety, and to Madame de Maintenon, who is a most virtuous women" (417).

Although many mysteries remain unsolved, de la Reynie decides to dismiss the investigating commission. He orders all records to be destroyed. The public is to be reassured that all the sorcerers and poisoners have been rooted out. Yet, he is dissatisfied. As he recounts to himself the almost two hundred people who have been arrested and gone to the rope, the wheel, the stake during the last four years, he has yet to unveil the mysterious Grand Master behind it all, that shadowy figure who has flitted in and out of the narrative, ever elusive, always concealed behind a variety of disguises. He has just sent another of those mocking notes: "Farewell, M. *le Lieutenant de* Police! I believe that our accounts are now squared, and that you will, after all, die without guessing my identity" (428).

But no. In a wonderfully vivid midnight scene, De le Reynie and Desgrez discover in a rag and bone shop, amongst rows of masks and the chemical apparatus of a brazier, an alembic, some tubes, retorts, phials, molds, a dwarf in a glass mask concocting arsenical potions. Standing near him is a young man wearing a doll-like wax mask. With a disdainful grimace, he escapes. A chase ensues, across streets and over the rooftops of Paris. Trapped finally, on the bridge over the Seine, the man who has gone by many names but who now is revealed at last to be none other than the Grand Master, plunges off the bridge to the waters below. Desgrez dives after him. The two bodies are borne away down the rapid current. Desgrez is found later, clutching the mask. The moment is vivid, like a scene from a Commedia dell'arte:

> With the staring wax mask with its painted, wistful smile in his hand, the long strings dripping water, Desgrez gazed about him; above was the moon, remote, high, cold, around was the gloomy outline of Paris roofs, towers, *tourelles*, black against the silver-filled atmosphere; below the boat in which he sat ... the powerful river swirled in muddy currents toward the sea [441].

A week later there is a notice in the weekly *Gazette* about a body washed ashore at Saint-Cloud. His face had "been entirely eaten by water-rats." He is identified only by the ruby ring he wears. He is Innocenzo Pignata. He is the envoy from the Pope in Rome.

Author's Note: Another mystery presents itself. In my opinion, of more than passing interest is the fact that a year after the publication of *The Poisoners,* mystery writer John Dickson Carr published a novel bearing a remarkable similarity to it—*The Burning Court* (a translation of de le Reynie's *chamber ardante*). Both writers were living in London at the time. Both novels are about the *affair of the poissons* during the reign of Louis XIV—the main narrative in Bowen and the backstory in Carr. Both cite the same historical characters of the Marquise de Brinvilliers, Madame de Montespan, and the police chief M. de la Reynie. And both foreground a cult of witches. We know about Bowen's abiding interest in witchcraft and the occult. Carr's biographer, Douglas Greene points out a similar preoccupation in Carr: "Witchcraft most perfectly combined Carr's interests in the occult, the past, and mysterious death. He was fascinated by witch beliefs" (164).

It is also interesting to note that the *invented* characters—Bowen's "Desgrez" and Carr's "Despard"—share remarkably similar names. And both are policemen investigating the same case.

By now, our heads are spinning at a high velocity. What do we make of this? May we conclude that Bowen and Carr knew each other? Influenced each other? (It's difficult to believe that did not at least know *of* each other). How do we account for the strong similarities of both writers and both books? I haven't a clue, as it were. I have written Carr's biographer, Doug Greene, about this, and he can offer nothing one way or the other.

As if that isn't intriguing enough, there's yet another element that binds both Bowen and Carr together: *The Burning Court* has a fictional character who is a specialist in writing true-crime novels of famous court cases. This is the reclusive Gaudan Cross. He takes one or two celebrated cases for each of his books… He devotes his research to unearthing picturesque crimes of which few people seemed to have heard at all: wonders in their own time, unquestionably, but appearing with a shock of novelty to modern readers. Despite photographs and documentary evidence, some of the accounts were so remarkable that one critic accused the whole thing of being an elaborate hoax. After another stir—again no bad advertisement—Cross was proved to have invented nothing (203).

Who does this sound like? Is this not an apt description of Marjorie Bowen's penchant for and methods of writing true-crime novels! (See a later chapter on "Joseph Shearing.") Moreover, Cross has an ancestor who was a poisoner. May we regard this as a sly reference to Bowen's own "ancestry" of the Furies?

Clearly—and this is the only thing that is clear—work remains to be done regarding these two writers whose works of gothic melodrama and historical romance invite comparisons.[59]

God and the Wedding Dress

"He was forced to admit that Christianity had here been merely superimposed upon Paganism, a palimpsest"

Neither the rituals of the Church of England, nor the revelations of Calvinism, nor the practices of Paganism—all of which are represented here—offer protection and redemption to the Plague-stricken inhabitants of a rural English village. The devastation of the little village of Eyam, material and psychic, and its inhabitants is utter and complete.

Based upon an historical incident, *God and the Wedding Dress* traces the relentless progression of Plague through a small English rural village in the span of just one year, during 1665 and 1666 during the reign of Charles II.[60] Contending against the devastation are an Anglican priest, William Mompesson and an outcast Puritan dissenter, Thomas Stanley. The village itself is under the sway of Pagan rituals, led by the local witch, Mother Sydall.

Mompesson is a man above his station, a modern fellow, taught "to despise the tricks and superstitions of mankind and to disdain the grossness of the self-seekers, the panderers, jobbers, and wittols who cluttered up all approaches to authority" (14). His counterpart, Stanley, holds illegal meetings with his flock in the hills. He exercises a hold over them that puzzles Mompesson: "Was it possible that Thomas Stanley did possess a spiritual power totally denied him?" (47). In his turn, Stanley mocks Mompesson: "What are you or your patrons, or your boundaries, to me? I perform the will of God"; and he accuses him of his worldly elegance, the refinements of his household, the Papist ornaments in his house, the frivolity of his wife and sister-in-law: "God will speak to thee in this place, which is to thee so wild and savage. And then thou wilt leave thy easy living, thy music, ribbons, idols, dancings, perfumes and curlings…. Take heed to these people in thy charge. Their souls will not be saved from the Pit by shows of images or lute playings or honey-sweet talk" (21–22).

In sum, Mompesson and Stanley each "claimed to be in communion with God, yet they regarded one another as lost, disobedient, if not damned" (152).

Meanwhile, since coming to the village, William Mompesson had been astonished at the survival of pagan customs handed down from parent to child since the Roman occupation. On the site is a strange temple of 16 oblong monoliths placed in an upright position and surrounded by a deep ridge of earth: "The use and antiquity of these stones could only be guessed, but Mr. Mompesson had a scholarly interest in such antiquities and knew that they were very old indeed and probably represented the remains of some heathen temple, in which hideous sacrifices had taken place with mysterious and accurst rites of shameful slaughter" (56).

He asked himself if the villagers—including the local witch, Mother Sydall, and the astrologer in nearby Bakewell—"were not the true descendants of those people who had watched their bloody priests slit the throats of their victims on the sacrificial stone. Even now, if they were allowed to, they would have their blood feasts, of animals if not of human beings" (56). For example, at the rituals of the harvest festivals of St. Helen's Wake, "Some of the games in which the villagers liked to indulge were so barbarous that Mr. Mompesson had forbidden them" (55). Mompesson is tempted to believe that somehow the rituals in St. Helen's Wake have played a role in the onset of the Plague. Indeed, "he was forced to admit to himself that Christianity had here been merely superimposed upon paganism, a palimpsest" (51). Under these circumstances, he doubts he can exercise any Christian influence in such a community.

In reality, the onset of the Plague seems to have originated with the arrival from London of a wedding dress. Unbeknownst to the villagers, a warning had been issued to avoid any goods shipped out of the Plague-infested capitol. Mompesson is alarmed at the news and immediately orders the dress to be taken out of the box and burned in the fields. Too late. The tailor and his assistant expired soon after opening the box. Soon after, a Pest House is erected and villagers begin to show symptoms of the Plague.

During the autumn season the body count increases. During the coming summer, it's worse.

> The disease varied little in its manifestations; it began with shivering, hot and cold fits, headaches, sickness, then delirium; then the appearance of the fatal tokens, the plague spots on the breast and thighs that meant immediate death. At best the illness never took more than three days; sometimes it was sudden.... A man or woman would fall down at his or her work, a child at his play, and be dead before they could be carried to the Pest-House [130].

Was it the Devil, it is wondered, who brought the dress to Eyam? The local gentry and the children are allowed to depart, leaving behind about 500 citizens.

Primitive remedies are resorted to, including such practices as scrubbing the skin vigorously with vinegar; or, taking an onion, hollowing it out, putting in a fig, adding a dram of Venice treacle, wrapping it in wet paper and roasting it in the embers, and then applying it hot to the tumor; or, roasting a dead toad over a vessel of yellow wax and smearing the fat on the sores. The infected Wedding Dress itself is "sacrificed" and burned on an ancient burial mound. Mompesson is uneasy at this:

> The dry, crisp muslins and buckrams of the trimmings and stiffenings soon caught fire and, fanned by the uneasy wind that seemed to come from the clenched fist of God.... It was curious to see ashes and charred fragments on this stone: so perhaps it had looked a thousand years ago after a bloody sacrifice had been offered to a pagan god [76–77].

But the Plague ravages on.

Mompesson and Stanley put aside their differences and join forces. "You know, sir," says Stanley, "that you can trust me with these poor people in their affliction.... Many Church of England clergy went into the sweet air and left the Nonconformists to do their work'" (125). He argues he is needed to administer to them and to bury them. And although it is against Mompesson's principles to deal with any who do not belong to the Church of England, he agrees to work with him.

Their plan is to seal off the community from the outside world.

With Calvinist relish, Stanley seems almost cheerful about the prospects of the village sacrificing itself for the good of the larger community of Derbyshire: "The dissenter's eyes flashed encouragement. Such a scheme, heroically bold, appealed to his stern nature. He had the temperament of a martyr, self-sacrifice delighted him ... and he says: 'We might put a cordon round the village and the outlying farms, beyond which they must not go. Though we were all to die here, it would be a triumph'"(134).

Mompesson offers his own bleak consolation:

> He spoke to his people of how brief and, as it were, worthless, was the longest and most splendid life. He declared that it was but a little play before eternity and given to us as time to prepare for Heaven, and that those who had the most crosses and afflictions in this life were likely to get the highest rewards, when His bright face should beam upon the righteous [142].

And one of the practitioners at the St. Helen's Wake bluntly declares: "I do not perceive the hand of God in this. Rather does it encourage the blasphemers. If there be a God, I think he has given his faith and given his fire into the Devil's hands" (181). The Plague ravages on. The village is sealed off from the rest of the area.

What a contrast we have between the broad-brush description of the idyllic rural pleasures of Eyam at the outset—

> The July day was warm, the hill air sweet with the pure scent of the wild thyme and mint, which showed their blue and purple flowers by the banks of the stream ; a soft wind stirred the upper boughs of the crest of trees that overhung the dale ... [12].

—compared with the dry-brush image of vastation that Stanley observes a year later from a high hill:

> Mr. Stanley could not doubt ... that the air in the village was infected.... He could look down and even count the graves that marked the neglected fields about it, he thought that he saw a kind of visible miasma hovering over the village like a noisome vapour. He shaded his eyes, trying to be certain if this were a fact or his excited fancy, and his mind was divided, his thoughts partly being that this was the contagion itself borne on the winds and hovering in this one spot, and partly that this was the visible wrath of God, the angry breath from His nostrils congealing in the air [178].[61]

The Lord Mayor at Chatsworth provides relief supplies and food to the village perimeter, where they can be picked up and dispersed. A pit is dug in the churchyard for mass burials, although others are buried where they fall. The supply of coffins is soon expended and the bodies are bound in sheets.

Eventually, inevitably, the plague is ended. Ironically, a few outbreaks in nearby Buxton and Derby have been quelled and the neighborhood is healthy. Only Eyam remains infected. It's a grim scene: The odor of putrefaction is everywhere. Houses are dilapidated, doors hung askew, window-frames empty, roofs broken, chimneys fallen. Grass chokes the streets. From a great space of burnt ground and ashes a column of smoke rises steadily into the air from a small bonfire. The few survivors wander like ghosts: "They were like strangers, stern angels clothed in the coarse habiliments of men, or supernatural creatures like those supposed to haunt the lonely moors" (214–219).

Mompesson, who has miraculously survived, looks about him, at a town, by now, "a veritable Golgotha, the place of the skull." He muses to himself: "My ears have never heard such doleful lamentations, my nose never smelled such horrid smells, and my eyes never beheld such ghastly spectacles" (210). Yet, he still can fall back on spiritual platitudes:

> What does all this suffering mean but a little waiting in the ante-chamber that leads us to eternal life? We must believe that God loves us. We must believe that He will respect our courage and our dignity. We must believe that in his infinite goodness, he sent the plague into Eyam in a wedding gown [209].

And his colleague, Stanley, as usual, surpasses Mompesson in his brand of gruesome piety: "Do not all things teach us to die, point out the way we must go? Do not birds, beasts, trees, flowers, herbs in the fields, take their leave and die? Have they not one large language—Death?" (207).

Bowen's intervening authorial voice adds: "Even an attempt to reason with God's dealings was a presumption, even to make an inner cry of anguish against the fate that had robbed him of his wife, that had put this task upon him—even that was a sin" (203).

Mompesson, Stanley, Mother Sydall are all, in Bowen's words, "monstrous in their virtue" (217). In what amounts to a Pagan ritual, they have sacrificed their town to whatever gods seem to be available. In that remote Derbyshire village nearly three hundred years ago, these people tried to serve their Gods to the best of their beliefs—but at a terrible cost.

"Five Winds"
"She became the countenance of the universe"

I conclude this brief survey with one last blast of Pagan Fury. Inasmuch as *"Five Winds"* is as much a ghost story as a Pagan parable, I examine it in a later chapter about Bowen's ghost stories. (Indeed, it has one of the great Old Dark Houses in the Gothic literary tradition.)

Although the Burgoyne estate may be haunted by a ghost that has survived several generations of the Burgoyne family, the estate's very name, "Five Winds," also hints at its Pagan ancestry. Indeed, the remains of a ruined abbey and a pagan monolith are to be found on the grounds. Unrelated to the conventional four winds of Greek and Roman mythology—Boreas, god of the north wind; Eurus, god of the east wind; Notus, god of the south wind, Zephyrus, god of the west wind—a "fifth wind" blows straight from Hell. Thus, when Denis Burgoyne, the last in the family line, claims the estate, he inherits far more troubles than he has bargained for. "I never heard of anyone living in 'Five Winds' who didn't go crazy or come to a violent end," he is told by a neighbor. "I heard the land was stolen from some heathen temple by Christians, and that began the trouble."

"Five Winds" begs our attention for one of the most remarkable and erotic scenes of a Pagan manifestation in all of Bowen. It begins with Denis's encounter with a strange local servant girl he knows only as "Nelly Natas." She has a deformed foot and bears a curious resemblance to an ancestress, Eleanor Engayne, whose painting hangs in the house and whose remains have been entombed in the nearby burial grounds. As time passes, and as Burgoyne learns more about the tainted past of "Five Winds," he succumbs to a strong attachment to the place. He has left behind him a career in architecture and a woman who loves him. To her urgings that he leave "Four Winds" and come back to her, he replies, "Kitty, it would be pure misery. I don't belong to your world—to any world that I know of. I'm alien to everything but a place like this" (237). Moreover, his increasing attraction to the servant girl is fueled by a strong erotic power.

One night, while he is trying to sleep in his rooms, he slips a ring on his finger that once belonged to Eleanor Engayne. Dreamily, he wonders, did it also belong to Nelly Natas? A feeling steals over him, detaching him from the room... What follows is an erotic passage, a cinematic montage of images fraught with erotic tensions, tactile sensations of earth and flesh, and the liminal presence of a female form seductive and monstrous. A ghost? A Pagan Fury? The sense of reality fades. A succession of images passes before his eyes:

> Now he's standing and opens the latch of a door.... Now he's in a long room with a noble and stately bed and filled with jewels. A seated woman is there, with graceful limbs and richly braided locks, whose head is crowned by a monstrous tower-like diadem with horns. In the dim light the crowned, immobile figure seems to grow in grandeur "till she towered above him on a vast throne, and he cowered below, catching at a corner of her robe ... now her horned diadem was among the stars" (230). He is drawn into infinity and the face before him is of the earth and sky: "[She] became the countenance of the universe, the diadem was the hills, the horns the moon, the slim, silver limbs were rivers, the dark garment was woven of flowers, the silver eyes were the planets; he was being swept through space into nothingness" (230). Now he's on the bed and the woman, normal sized, is beside him. When he kisses her, "it was as if he had laid his mouth to empty air. He put his head on her lap, and it was as if he had rested it on the warm earth. Her hands passed to and from his forehead, and it was as if a wind blew over him with gentle yet chill persistence" (231). But now what he is holding is a "beast form now, with hoofs beneath the purple robe and horns from above a furry mask with sharp fangs. And then a tattered skeleton, more rags of flesh, still horned and hooved. And then a woman, uncrowned, unadorned, who drew him down, away, into a pit, a long corridor—space" [231-231].

Denis cries aloud, "This is a dream! I must awake" (232). But when he throws open the curtains, he sees the woman again, now asleep, pressing the golden pillow, a web of pearls around her neck. But she's not asleep, her eyes are opening, and her hands are reaching out to him... He cries out again and tries to run across the room. But the effort is impeded by phantom-shapes and by "pale men with his own face." (233) ... And he looks down upon his own form in the bed and watches it as it rises with a cry— ... but now he feels himself flowing back into his own body...

Upon awaking, Denis immediately feels a terrible desolation, that "he's chained to this little fraction of time called to-day, that he had returned to the petty monotony of material existence, but aware that he had felt 'a voluptuous zest in thinking of that feminine shape, half-horned beast, half-crowned goddess, the vileness fascinated as much as the beauty'" (234).

There are more dreams and more nightly encounters with this woman, who may be a ghost or a goddess—or, somehow, both. Despite the anxious entreaties from Kitty to leave, Denis determines to stay on with Nelly. "There are some things seen better in the dark," says the creature who now calls herself "Eleanor Engayne" (252). "You'll never be without me now." At which "a second's pang of ghastly apprehension touched Burgoyne; as in a delirium he saw this creature as a fiend hounding him through the corridors of hell through all eternity" (304).

Indeed, there is one last, final, ghastly encounter. The truth of this creature is unveiled, once and for all. The creature that Denis perceives one night, crawling from the depths of the tarn, is no longer Nelly, or Eleanor, *but something else*. The awful reality is the monstrous equal of anything in the fevered prose of H. P. Lovecraft:

> [In the] lurid greenish illumination ... a form [was] rising stark behind the vile waters of the tarn. It was monstrous, of immeasurable size ... the dark, gigantic leaves that curled about the shapeless body fell back to reveal the hideous bust. There seemed to be bent arms, held to the side, with uplifted

hands yet flung out with clutching fingers, and a face that smiled, with slanting eyes, huge cheekbones, and full lips; this was crowned by a towering diadem, or casque, horned and festooned, that mingled with the clouds. The expression was at once gloating and gorged; the smiling visage, which writhed from hunched shoulder and raised hand to the other hunched shoulder and raised hand, was utterly evil and obscene; and the narrow eyes seemed to be hollows with a dead light [314].

As Burgoyne collapses, a destructive Fury shatters the pagan monolith.

THE SONG IS ENDLESS...

What ears can withstand the Music on the Hill? What conventional religious orthodoxies can survive the Pagan assaults? Putting it another way, what dark and uneasy symbiosis might prevail, leaving us in a profound confusion, where damnation and salvation, evil and grace, death and life all prevail, neither triumphant, neither defeated, but ongoing, together, everlasting... Thus, the precise nature of Marjorie Bowen's spiritual self—Apollonian and Dionysian by turns—may never be precisely understood, least of all by her. Earlier in this chapter, we cited her own ambivalence toward the historical figure of the controversial magician, Comte de St. Germain. In *The Courtly Charlatan,* Bowen writes that the Christian Church, "with all her panoply of impressive ceremonial, with all her inherited superstitions, with all her hold over the terrors and horrors of the human mind, had failed mankind," while the alleged sorceries of St. Germain had not: "In the half-light of the mind, between superstition and philosophy, one subject had a universal attraction. And that was magic" (46). St. Germain himself scornfully addresses the French Court: "What is it you desire?... You can pursue all the caprices that enter your mind. Philosophy, art, science, are all at your service, yet you come here to-night, looking at me with eager expectancy, hoping that I will tell you of some miracle" (139). Perhaps Bowen's great friend and champion, Edward Wagenknecht, best described Bowen's own position in his balanced assessment: "Mrs. Long [sic] has, indeed, the mind of a skeptic, but she has the heart of a poet and the soul of a saint. Mysticism holds her, even though she cannot quite believe in it."[62]

Just as Marjorie Bowen was always alert to that "enchantment that was around the corner," which she confesses in *The Debate Continues* (244), so too do we readers keep coming to her stories, alert and expectant for any such revelations that she might vouchsafe us about the Music on the Hill.

TWO

"Painting History": The Historical Romances

I thought that their spirits were about me like pictures depicted in primary colours, and the thought that they had once lived was enough to fill me with subdued satisfaction.—Marjorie Bowen[1]

During the crowning of William the Conqueror in Westminster on Christmas Day, 1066, the Archbishop of York demanded of the assembled nobles if they would have William the Norman for their King. The reply was so loud that it startled the Norman soldiers outside the church. "Supposing that an attack was being made on their Duke," relates Marjorie Bowen, "the troops set about the Saxon populace, killing a great number and burning the surrounding houses."

Bowen adds, with characteristic deadpan: "A bad start for the fierce and wily William, but which left him quite unperturbed."

But it's an entirely appropriate way to introduce Marjorie Bowen's lifelong penchant, if idiosyncratic passion, for history and historical writings. To be clear, virtually all of her writings, be they novels, short stories, essays, biographies have historical events and personages as their subjects.

This anecdote, among many others, was included in her beautifully illustrated book, *Royal Pageantry*, which was published on the occasion of the crowning of another English monarch, George VI, on 12 May 1937. I found this little book among the Marjorie Bowen Papers at Yale University, Box 180. Among so many other books of hers, it deserves a new publication for today's readers. "This imposing prospect," she wrote in the book's Foreword,

> is sufficient in itself to make everyone interested in the traditions and happenings connected with the ancient ceremony—an event which still has power to be an inspi-

ration to many millions of free people. Far back in mists of antiquity—through every age and among many peoples—the crowning of a King has been regarded as a sacred ceremony.... The rites of the sacring of Kings have been handed down from Biblical days, as we read in the Old Testament, and today the mystic and religious aspect of a Coronation still remains in the hearts and minds of the people.

With its gorgeous full-color cover of the Coronation Procession of Henry V (artist unknown) to the many detailed pen-and-ink interior drawings, it briefly outlines the symbology and the history of coronations of Kings and Queens over hundreds of years and showcases her love for the color and pageantry of history.

Coronation Procession of HENRY V.

Royal Pageantry

With a typical gesture to the "low-born" as well as the noble, she even adds two lines of her own to the first two lines of Alexander Pope's *First Epistle of the Second Book of Horace*:

> Pageants on pageants in long order drawn,
> Peers, heralds, bishops, ermine, gold and lawn.
> Tom, Dick and Harry, in a different way,
> Much more at ease and twice as gay.[2]

From first to last, from the appearance in 1906 of her "breakout novel" published when she was in her teens, *The Viper of Milan*, to *In the Steps of Mary Queen of Scots* in 1952, the year of her death, Bowen's preoccupation with the color and pageantry of historical characters and scenes was lifelong. *Viper of Milan* was a "historical romance," interchanging characters factual and fictive against the backdrop of northern Italy in the fourteenth century. *Mary Queen of Scots* was a biography told with the sober approach of the academic. In both we see Bowen's flair for narrative drive and vivid characterizations. The point is that whether fictional or historic, history was, for Bowen, a broad, colorful fresco, shot through, by turns, with flame and fury, nuanced deftly with incident and anecdote, tempered with satire and insight.

History Fact and Fiction

At the time Bowen began publishing, the genre of the historical novel, as well as that of "History Paintings" had fallen into disfavor. This is difficult to believe these days, when the bookshelves, cinema, television, and the proliferation of streaming platforms are flooding the market with historical films, romances and biographies, from the "Flashman" novels of George MacDonald Fraser, to *Wolf Hall, Versailles, Victoria, Bill and Ted's Excellent Adventure!* and countless others. Yet, according to Professor Harold Orel's study of the subject, *The Historical Novel from Scott to Sabatini*, the abundance of historical novels that had begun with Sir Walter Scott and continued unabated throughout the Victorian century with the works of Robert Louis Stevenson, Stanley J. Weyman, Anthony Hope, Rafael Sabatini, H. Rider Haggard, Arthur Conan Doyle, among many others—when "new perspectives on all kinds of historical situations had created a favorable climate for the writing of fictitious narratives dealing with the past"—peaked sharply at the turn of the new century and fell into disfavor for decades thereafter. Not a single one of the important novelists born after 1880, Orel declares, thought it worth their while to write historical romances. It did not matter whether they were traditionalists, such as E.M. Delafield, David Garnett, James Hilton, Constance Holmes, J.B. Priestley, Hugh Walpole, or were other writers willing to experiment with "Modernist" techniques, like Stella Benson and Ronald Firbank, Aldous Huxley, Virginia Woolf—"their interests lay elsewhere." The market would not flourish again until World War II, when escapist fare was in great demand. Which proves, Orel concludes, that readers will always thirst for a blend of history and fiction: "The interest of readers in how intensely-imagined men and women behave when forced to work their way out of extraordinary dilemmas is as old as the art of story-telling itself, and its future is both healthy and assured."[3]

Surprisingly, except for a passing mention of the historical novel, *The Third Estate*, the name of "Marjorie Bowen" is notably absent from Orel's discussion.[4]

This is an egregious and puzzling sin of omission. The woman who was most known and applauded in her lifetime for her dozens of historical romances and "straight" biographies—who was an invited member of the respected Royal Society of Literature, the Royal Historical Society, and a Diplômée and Honorary Fellow of kindred Societies in Utrecht, Leiden, and the Netherlands—has today fallen into an entirely undeserved obscurity. A resurgence of popular and critical interest is long overdue. Only her "true-crime" historical dramatizations, written under the name of "Joseph Shearing," notes Bowen authority, Edward Wagenknecht, have maintained any degree of notice. He reminds us that Hugh Walpole praised Bowen "as the greatest historical novelist England has produced in a generation"; that William Roughead particularly "admired her scholarship." Moreover, continues Wagenknecht, "I have never ceased to marvel at how little appreciated she has been. How can anyone who has written so much managed to escape the notice of so many people?"[5]

Bowen's "true-crime" novels are examined in the chapter on "Joseph Shearing."

History Fact

Before we venture into Marjorie Bowen's colorful and vivid historical romances, some attention should be paid to her so-called "straight" biographies, many of which appeared in the 1930s. These include *This Shining Woman* (1937, Mary Wollstonecraft), *Wrestling Jacob* (1937, John Wesley), *William Hogarth* (1936), *Patriotic Lady* (1935, Lady Hamilton), *The Angel and the Assassination* (1935, Charlotte de Corday), *The Lady and the Arsenic* (1937, Marie Cappelle, Madame La Farge), and the Comte de St. Germain (*The Courtly Charlatan*, 1942). Her *William Hogarth* will be discussed presently. Several others are discussed in other chapters and need not be repeated here: Her comments on the Comte de St. Germain and John Wesley are found in the "Music on the Hill" chapter; and comments on Lady Hamilton, Sophie Dawes, Charlotte de Corday, and Marie Cappelle in the chapters on "Joseph Shearing." Particularly pertinent here, at this point, are the two biographies of women, *Mary Queen of Scots* and *This Shining Woman*.

In both, Bowen works on a small canvas with a fine brush, a limited palette, and "close-up" scrutiny. Reading between her comments is her evident desire to remain a *novelist* in the face of a scientifically materialist approach. Rather than losing Mary Queen of Scots against the backdrop of history—no matter how closely researched—she separates the figure from the ground, achieving, in effect, the "shallow focus" of the telephoto lens: "The individual," Bowen says, "is so apt to be dwarfed and even hidden by the events that surrounded his personality."[6] Thus, in addition to the annotated list of previous biographies, she examines the extant portraits of Mary. As a painter herself and a haunter of museums and picture galleries, she explains they aid her in "forming a mental picture of the subject." It is not likely, after all, "that the most diligent of historians will ever discover further vital information relating to the history of Mary Queen of Scots." *Therefore, no historian can do more than offer his opinion of this subject* [italics added]. But that is precisely the passion with which Bowen approaches history and biography. Surely, she would have echoed the words of one of today's most respected biographers, Richard Holmes: "The past is not simply 'out there,' an objective history to be researched or forgotten, at will; but that it lives most vividly in all of us, deep inside, and needs constantly to be given expression and interpretation."[7]

Moreover, as Bowen knew full well, there comes a time when the historian, "must cease to be a historian and *begin to invade the realms of poetry and fiction*" [italics added]. None of us knows the truth about ourselves, so how can we presume to know the truth about figures long dead? Yet, we persevere: "The answer can only lie largely in the perversity of human nature—we desire to attempt the impossible. Without twisting of known fact, we long to rearrange these familiar materials *according to our own sense of design or of decoration* [italics added] to make our own deduction from bare facts, to re-tell, by the light of our own experiences.... We long to write our own love stories." Simply put, *Mary Queen of Scots* pursues *dramatic* agendas. "It is not intended for the student or the specialist, it sets out to be a portrait, broad in outline, but detailed in background and appointments, of a woman whose life and death *are as exciting and uncommon as any in history*" [italics added]. Modest as ever, Bowen concludes hoping "that there may be some interest in the attempt."[8]

The biography of Mary Wollstonecraft also foregrounds the face and form of the subject. It may also be read as a portrait of Bowen herself, so completely do the similarities of the one with the other border on identity. As much as Bowen projected her own qualities and circumstances, as we shall see, into her romantic portraits of William of Orange, she likewise locates them in Mary Wollstonecraft. For example, we are only a few pages in before we find a passage like this: "She was self-educated, not well-read.... She was sensitive to a fault, proud, delicate-minded, and like so many women who have endured a wretched childhood, enamoured of an ideal domesticity.... Her miserable circumstances had given all her thoughts a melancholy cast and a bitter opinion of humanity" (13). To a degree, this is Bowen growing up, neglected, marginalized, and forced into her own mode of self-education and self-actualization. And her description of Wollstonecraft at age sixteen almost exactly resembles that of Bowen at that age, struggling to write her first novel, *The Viper of Milan*: "She was sixteen years of age and knew a good deal of the miseries of existence; her intelligence, acute and precociously developed, wondered at her misfortunes, which seemed grotesque and unnatural, but she was forced to accept them with resignation, since she knew nothing else" (27). In her maturity, Wollstonecraft was, like Bowen, tough-minded yet of a passionate nature, the woman who impetuously, but unwisely, married her first husband: "Intellectual interests might fill her head, but her heart was empty, and, though not romantic, she was, as she began uneasily to suspect, passionate, and she felt the need of an heroic affection, an overwhelming interest to absorb her emotions, her dreams, to give point and lustre to her barren days" (143). Perhaps prescient of the obscurity that would befall her after her death, Bowen deplored "the complete neglect, that fell over the memory of a woman who had made such a stir in her time" (314).

History Fiction

Historical fiction first caught her eye in a book that became a prime influence on her work. Scattered among the Marjorie Bowen Yale Papers is a note citing her special approval of Charles Reade's *The Cloister and the Hearth* (1861). Declaring it "superior to the novels of Sir Walter Scott," she praises its style as "at once delicate and pungent like the odour of old parchment."[9] The story is set in the middle of the fifteenth century at the dawn of the Renaissance in Europe. As Samuel C. Chew points out, "its every level of life from palace and monastery to tavern and highroad; its every type of character from bishop and burgomaster to beggar and freebooter—is at once spacious and dignified and beautiful and wonderfully informed with life." When Gerard Eliassoen believes his wife to be deceased, he takes vows as a Dominican friar. However, he later discovers his wife and son are alive; but his vows prohibit him from resuming his marital concourse with her. The son grows up and becomes the great Catholic scholar and Humanist, Erasmus of Rotterdam. The central conflict of the book is between duty to the Church and the fulfillment of human love. Arthur Conan Doyle, who also loved the book, concluded that it is a critique of celibate priesthood.[10]

Spiritual conflict, intense emotion, historical color and detail... Prime elements that illumine Bowen's historical works.

Also among the Yale Papers are numerous unpublished and undated testaments to her early fascination with the subject. In a fragment of typescript, "The Value of Romance in Fiction," she writes: "There are so many tempting realms of history that have not been exploited, so many themes ready to the hand of the imaginative and romantic writer that lie in the endless records of the past." In another typescript, "Advice to Would-Be Writers," she advises, *"Your knowledge of your art will not come from books alone, but from scenery, architecture, pictures, the decorative crafts..."* [italics added]. In yet more typescripts, we see the germs of the novels and stories to come: She envisages a "Great Lovers Series," short accounts of famous lovers—"Casanova and Manon Balleti," "Emma Hamilton and Charles Greville," "Mary Wollstonecraft and Gilbert Imlay," etc.,—and a "Remarkable Women" series, brief accounts of "Madame de Montespan" ("The Woman who secretly practiced black magic"), Mary Elisa Gilbert (Lola Montez), "Catherine de' Medici," "Francis d'Aubigne, Marquise de Maintenon," and "Sophie Dawes" ("One of the most remarkable women who ever rose from the gutter"). Not to leave out the men, there is a "Little Poor Men Who Became Great Men" ("Antonio Canova," "Claude Gelee" [Lorraine], "Michael Faraday," "Heinrich Heine)." And she is already critiquing the research of other writers. In a handwritten note responding to Sisley Huddleston's *Louis XIV*, she rejects the author's allegation that "Louis had an inferiority complex, which helps nothing to understand the subject." And consider her fascinating comment that "humor and gusto," "gossip and anecdote" must flavor the necessities of historical research, since "there must be few writers who are able to clothe the characters for themselves." And of course, there are voluminous notes on "Mary Stewart and William III."[11]

THE COLOR OF HISTORY

Marjorie Bowen happily possesses what painters and photographers call a "great eye." "Write, write the colour," she declares in one of her short stories," the glitter, the glory and the power of it—

> [of] days burning into the nights with the lights of a thousand jeweled lamps glowing behind screens of silk, the marble halls strewn with flowers, the slaves with bands of scarlet on their foreheads ... the churches shining with burnished bronze and gold. Sometimes, I dread that Heaven cannot be so delicious.[12]

This quality in her work has been frequently remarked on. In their appreciation of her early novel of the supernatural, *Black Magic*, James Cawthorn and Michael Moorcock observe that the characters are not only "strongly drawn," but the scenic pleasures are abundant—as is true to one degree or another, of all her work:

In Marjorie Bowen's prose, the fields and towns of medieval Europe shimmer in a burning haze of sunlight or cower under the stifling purple pall of unnatural storms. Lightning forks and flickers about the characters as they act out their complex loves and hatreds. The interiors of cathedrals and villas swim in the sumptuous, many-coloured radiance of stained glass, reflected from gold, silver and crystal. Flowers mass on glistening marble, scattering petals on rug-strewn floors, drugging the air with languorous perfume. Gowns and doublets, armor and hose, blaze with orange and purple, crimson and green; great gems glitter from settings of precious metals. It is a hectic, high-key world, into which black diabolism fits without incongruity.[13]

On the other hand, Bowen can paint with an impressionist's brush, lightly touching here and there moments from Fairyland—as in this ceremonial procession from *Nightcap and Plume*:

[Gustav's] royal cavalcade moved slowly through the darkness flecked with snow flakes that showed, softly floating, in the lights cast by the torches.... [It seemed] a pageantry of spectres, some vision evoked by a wizard, so strange, so remarkable this procession appeared, half-seen shadows, dark unexplained forms, blazing torches, swinging lanterns, the huge chargers with rough-shod hoofs moving slowly ... the coach horses helped by running grooms and guided by ropes, sparks from the resin-fed flames and the flaring pine knots flying into the clear air, quivering with moonshine [300–301].

Obviously, a skilled painter is at work. Indeed, she always wanted to be a professional painter and designer. But that was not to be. Of immediate interest here, her palette and canvas became her ink and foolscap.

Despite the drabness of her surroundings, she was quick to respond to vagrant vestiges of color. "My earliest memories are jumbled," Bowen recalls, "like the pictures on a pack of cards flung down on a table." She writes about a "red flower in a pot," a room "with white cups with gold flowers," "black and white birds in a glass case," a museum with a "coloured relief in plaster of a fish," and the pictures she finds in books. A drawing in one of those books filled her with terror: "A book was shown me ... in which was a picture of an old man coming down a ladder through a hole in the ceiling."[14]

She draws pictures of her own on any odd scraps of brown paper that came to hand, with a stump of pencil and, "on great occasions, a penny box of chalks." She drew continuously, "fantastic objects, with never any attempt to copy what was about me." Against the "dingy and gloomy" world around her, she illustrated stories she made up "of beautiful scenes and beautiful people." She refers to her first readings as depicting "historical characters in crude simple colours."[15] These characters included "heroes" like William of Orange, whom, she thought "magnanimous, lonely and courageous," which she "secretly worshiped," admiring "all that was cool, lofty, generous and, above all, self-controlled."[16] She spends entire days in visits to galleries, where she sees the works of great painters, like William Hogarth, Jean-Antoine Watteau, and Gambattista Tiepolo, many of which will surface in her later stories and biographies. Hogarth holds a special appeal to her. Her *William Hogarth: The Cockney's Mirror*, in addition to its biographical details, is a careful examination of dozens of his images: "He wished to compose pictures upon canvas, similar to representations on the stage," and "to entertain and improve the mind."[17]

But again, her attention inevitably strays to the portraits of those historical personages "whose spirits were about me like pictures depicted in primary colours, and the thought that they had once lived was enough to fill me with subdued satisfaction." Thus, from the galleries and from picture books, it seems "as if I lived in those times that they depicted or related." As a result, the past "began to seem to me more real than the present," and she moved with the greatest ease in the seventeenth and eighteenth centuries that I saw, darkly but clearly, like a landscape under an approaching thundercloud. I had a deep and passionate nostalgia for the people and places I had imagined they had been. I was absolutely part of them.

To which, she adds, from the perspective of maturity. "It still does."[18]

She's drawing with whatever comes to hand. She remembers boxes of chalk and scraps of brown paper: "On these I was delighted to draw representations of the scenes that were beginning to fill my mind—heroes and heroines, from the history of England and from fairy-tales."[19] She admits, however, that she "was hampered by lack of material and lack of skill. I was capable of industry and of concentration, but I often doubted where I should be able to wait to express 'myself until I had mastered the technique of painting.'"[20] At age twelve, she is sent to a "famous art school" [the Slade School]—not to mention her habit of drawing and sketching all her life. Her great contemporary, G. K. Chesterton, also studied at the Slade at this time, and whose essay, "A Piece of Chalk," forever immortalized the application of colored chalks on brown paper. Chesterton's amiable lines might well be applied to Bowen's own "painted histories":

> Stand up and keep your childishness,
> Read all the pedants' screeds and strictures;
> But don't believe in anything
> That can't be told in coloured pictures.[21]

With her chalks and brown paper, with her pen, ink, and vellum, Marjorie Bowen is prepared to "restore" color to history.

For too long, our sense of ancient history has been through the excavations of cold, white marble statues and busts. Recent researches are revealing that the Greeks and Romans applied tints and colors to their statues that have long been thought to be of pure white marble.[22] And in several of his studies about the pursuit of color, Simon Schama notes that many historical figures, from Marco Polo to Van Gogh, brought color from the ancient world to their contemporaries.[23] Schama cites one particular example that must have been close to Bowen's wicked heart, i.e., that the Victorians loved Paris Green, derived from a highly toxic copper arsenite compound coating used for wallpaper and children's toys. This is the color of her Furies, the hue that Bowen "applies" to the gowns of many of her murderous heroines! We must grant her honorary membership in a long line of colorists in galleries who are restoring "black-and-white" history to its original colors and to filmmakers like Peter Jackson, who recently "colorized" old grainy, black-and-white footage of World War I in his memorable *They Shall Not Grow Old* (2018).

Bowen can deploy color schemes to dominate an entire novel. *No Way Home*, for example, depicts a post–Revolutionary world in a narrative whose three-part structure has its own color key. The Bavarian scenes suggest a child's paint box:

> [Florio's] taste was gratified by these South German churches with the windows painted in yellow and blue, the stone pulpits with lime-wood canopies, the shrines with the black figure in the tinseled robes, sparkling with sequins and tinsel, with gems and gold, the offerings of rich pilgrims, glittering in starry crowns, and the votive tablets depicting frightful disasters by land and sea. Such churches had, to the polished Italian, a childlike candour, even a crudity, that was agreeable after the elegance of his native edifices, cunning designs in light and space [46].

The Palermo scenes have a Whistler-esque feel for nocturnal hues: "The night was superb, the rich scene of rock, tree, shrub, aqueduct and valley lay in differing tints of blue and green silver under the moon that filled the upper air with a brilliant refulgence, broken by a few still clouds, white as lilies under clear water."

Finally, the London scenes are shrouded in a heavy chiaroscuro:

> [There is] heavy marsh air, the sluggish grey river, the narrow streets, the houses like grey rocks in the early twilight, the vaporous sky, the sun and moon shrouded in mists and without radiance or colour, the pressure of the alien crowd, all about business or pleasures of which he knew nothing and from which he felt excluded, as if he were a ghost returned to earth, mingling among men and unseen, unheard and unthought of [304].

The entirety of the aforementioned *Nightcap and Plume*, a chronicle of the last four years in the reign of Gustaf III of Sweden, is saturated with vivid imagery, contrasts of colorful costume and pageantry against the drear grey of the northern wintry landscapes. "Keying" most of the action are the colors of the House of Vasa—lilac, green, and silver. "You ask me what are my colours," Gustaf tells his lover, Jeanne d'Egmont; "they are those of the new order" (281). In the climactic moments, before the attempted assassination on his life, we see Gustav, proudly wearing these colors in resplendent garb amid the Opera House masquerade: "Gustaf stood up.... Across the ruffles of his cravat he wore the ensignia of the three orders, these crossed swords, seraphim heads and knots made his breast blaze in the candlelight" (303).

Moreover, the color red, which has been an important thematic element throughout—it has been prophesied that Gustaf will be assassinated by a figure clad in red—now plays its deadly role. Gustaf never sees the approaching assassin. He is shot from behind. And the only crimson color he perceives is, ironically, the slash of blood across his black domino.

In stories like these, Marjorie Bowen proudly displays her own version of "Vulcan's Shield." We recall, in Virgil's *Aeneid*, that Aeneas leaves Troy and goes into battle during his campaign to establish imperial dominance in Italy. The god Vulcan forges him a shield emblazoned with images conveying the whole story of power, corruption, and empire. Bowen's own vision of history is like that colorful shield, displaying, in words and pictures, on the one hand, the nobility of power and order; and, on the other hand, the corruption and collateral damage left in the wake of empire. This "torturous conflict between private fulfillment and public responsibility," writes cultural commentator, Daniel Mendelsohn, in his essay on Vulcan's Shield, "[would become] a staple of European literature and drama, showing up in everything from Corneille to *The Crown*."[24]

A Painter Has Her Critics

As we come to the gallery of historical fictions and romances, we should note at the outset that Marjorie Bowen is not without her critics, past and present.

On the one hand, writing in 1943, Edward Wagenknecht declared, "Where will you find better historical fiction than in *Dickon* [1929], with its daring rehabilitation of Richard III, or the trilogy on the spiritual life of England in the seventeenth century—*God and the Wedding Dress* (1938), *Mr. Tyler's Saints* (1939), and *The Circle in the Water* (1939)?"[25] By contrast, despite historian and novelist Pamela Cleaver's more recent admission that Bowen's "historical judgments are usually sound," she goes on to charge that Bowen's characterizations "lack depth" and "the thoughts and motives attributed to her characters (especially in the romances), are a little superfluous." Cleaver suspects an undue "bias" toward many of her characters, objecting to Wagenknecht's praise for *Dickon*, for example, declaring instead that Bowen's depiction of a physically attractive figure—with no mention of a withered arm or a physical deformity—could not be the villain capable of the murder of his brother Clarence or the Princes in the Tower. Bowen's Richard is "a perfect medieval knight, *sans peur, sans reproche.*" Likewise, Cleaver also objects to Bowen's portrayal of Oliver Cromwell in *The Governor of England* (1913) as "a compassionate private man who nevertheless believes that he has a divine mission and so reluctantly concludes that [King Charles I's] death is necessary." Indeed, Cleaver adds, "Bowen seems to have held low opinions of all the Stuarts, bar none." Cleaver objects to Bowen's harsh portrait of a "slobbering and fawning" James I in *The King's Favourite* (1908) and of Charles II as a man who but for his birth would "have spent his life as a tavern idler buying his indulgences with his quips." As for James II, Cleaver castigates him as "a pompous doll bigot—vain, sensuous and arrogant and to a curious degree cruel." And she takes great exception to Bowen's "worshipful attitude" toward her great hero, King William of England. Contrary to Bowen's portrait of a steadfast soldier and politician—a ruler who delivered England from the thrall of Louis XIV—Cleaver dismisses him as "one of our dullest kings, little loved by his English subjects and who had little liking for England"; and who "only accepted the English crown as a means of vanquishing Louis XIV."[26]

Indeed, as we shall see, Bowen's preoccupation with William of Orange is of particular interest here, and not a little controversial. Among all the historical figures to whom she dealt so much time and energy, William remained her lifelong priority.

As for the above critiques, let's see how they hold up as we venture into several of Bowen's representative historical novels.

A Young Professional Novelist

The Viper of Milan

"A Fantasia on History"

Marjorie Bowen bursts out of the blocks with *The Viper of Milan* in 1906. She dipped her brush in a palette of hot blues, burning umbers, and blazing scarlets. Begun in her mid-teens, the book was published when she was twenty-one, although the publisher persisted in passing off the final product as from a girl of sixteen. Here she is, in her first high flight, tackling a long form demanding a balance between historical research and dramatic speculation. There is a distinction, she is discovering, between the "scientific historian," who scarcely can draw deductions from his "carefully sifted collections of facts," and her own agenda:

> Once the historian begins to sort and to arrange his facts, to endeavor to correlate them by the light of his own intuition and experience, too often by the light of his own emotions and prejudices, he must cease to be a historian and begin to invade the realms of poetry and fiction.

Her contemporary, G.K. Chesterton, knew a thing or two about this dance of fact and fancy: "At the very outset," he observes, "the writer … has to decide whether he will confine himself to what he knows to be true, or speculate at length on many things which he can see to be possible, or even probable, but which may, after all (especially in the light of later research), be entirely misleading."[27]

Why take on such a tricky challenge? "The answer," she says, "can only lie largely in the perversity of human nature—we desire to attempt the impossible. We hear from our earliest childhood of a certain subject or a certain character until we become fascinated, perhaps obsessed." Although we may reason that all is already known and everything has been said on this matter—

> yet we long to rearrange these familiar materials *according to our own sense of design or of decoration* [italics added] to make our own deductions from bare facts, to re-tell, by the light of our own experience, these experiences with which everyone is familiar. Perhaps there is something which has not yet been said and that we can say it. In brief, we wish to paint our own pictures of the familiar scene, to give these legendary creatures faces of our own fashioning, to draw our own design on their robes.[28]

Undaunted by such challenges—audacity is her middle name—she is ready.

Marjorie Bowen, age 16

In this following overview of *The Viper of Milan*, we should bear in mind it is still the product of a girl without formal education, with scant worldly experience, and responsibilities as the sole provider for her family. It is also the first product of an eager and avid imagination and a quick study of fourteenth-century Italy.

The setting is Lombardy, northern Italy, 1360. An ongoing war for territory and power sets the villainous Gian Galeazzo Visconti, Duke of Milan, the last of the Visconti line, against the swashbuckling noble, Mastino Orazio della Scala, Duke of Verona.[29] And over it all waves the Visconti banner, a green figure against a silver field. As the story begins, Mastino's city of Verona has been sacked and burned. His wife has been captured by the conquering Visconti and imprisoned in a tower in Milan. Now, Mastino is on the road, in rags, disguised as the wanderer "Francisco," seeking revenge and the recovery of his wife and lands. He gathers his armies to launch a powerful assault against Visconti. But in the end, he is thwarted by treachery on the part of his allies and a vulnerability and weakness in his own nature. So desperate is he to recover his wife Isotta that he enters into an unholy bargain with Visconti: She will be spared and Mastino can live out his life back in his beloved Verona if he will cede his armies, his lands and towns—Verona, Ferrara, Novara, Mantua—to Visconti. But at the last minute, during the exchange, Visconti poisons her. Mastino, who in the meantime has admitted his treachery to his captains and his armies, is left dishonored and his

Title page of *Viper of Milan*

wife dead. Subsequently, his desperate attempt to murder Visconti fails. He dies, a hero irrevocably stained and humiliated, his armies and allies betrayed and fallen. Visconti, too, will die, betrayed by his own secretary, Giannotto. Neither the nobility of love nor the machinations of evil can prevail. Only a desolate sense of loss and futility remains.

Looming over the story are the two principal characters, Visconti and Mastino, both figures of power and doomed for their overreaching ambition. Headquartered in Milan, Visconti controls a dozen cities in Lombardy, is in league with France, and is favored by the Empire. He is a master manipulator. He concocts poisons in his secret chamber. He is a master of disguises and under the name of "Ambrosio," carries on in monkish robes a secret seduction of Grazioso, the lovely young daughter of a master painter. "He loved to be feared, to hold lives in the hollow of his hand, and play with them and death" (31). He exults in his triumphs: "A god can do more than say, 'I have succeeded—in all I have undertaken, I have succeeded!' And I can say as much. I have succeeded. I looked on life and took from it what I wanted, the fairest and the finest things that offered; and the price—others have paid it" (86). He tells his soldiers:

> I do not pay with ducats, Paduans, or measure my rewards with coin; follow me, and I will give you cities for your plunder, and nobles to hold for ransom. Like to the thunder will I circle Lombardy, and city after city shall surrender me its keys, and the meanest soldier in my train shall gain him fame and riches from my spreading greatness such as kings might envy! [182].

Yet, disaster always portends. As one of his allies warns, "Thou art not human, Visconti. Yet remember, even devils meet their punishment, and there will be the bitterest of all for such as thou art—failure" (154).

As for our noble hero, Mastino, we first meet him under the name "Francisco," a fugitive in rags, recently escaped from his sacked city of Verona. He sets out to enlist the armies of Lombardy against Visconti.

> He was a powerful man of gigantic size, clothed in coarse leather, undressed, patched, slashed, and travel-worn. His legs were bound with straw and thongs of skin, the feet encased in rough wooden shoes stuffed with grass.... The man's face and bearing belied his dress. He was not handsome, and a peculiar effect was given to his expression by the half-shut brown eyes, but he had a grave and stately bearing... [20].

Immediately, those around him sense he is no peasant but one "gently born" (67). As Francisco, he declares early on: "I am the Visconti's foe. For the sake of della Scala, whom I knew, for the sake of Verona, where I lived, for the sake of something dearer to as man than life, I am sworn to hunt him down" (22). At the end, however, we find him a broken man, his honor stained, his wife dead, his attempt against Visconti failed. "He was changed, so changed the boy would scarce have known him; his soft brown hair was streaked with grey, his fine face drawn and white, his eyes, once soft and kind, unnaturally bright, and, like his mouth, strained and hard" (262). He is quite mad, refusing to admit his wife is dead of the poison Visconti put on her wedding ring. He carries her body on horseback in the rain, bent on reaching Visconti: "Mastino's thoughts were centred on one thing—Visconti. There was no reflection in them; neither the past nor present had meaning. He was riding in a nightmare: He knew he carried Isotta and that she was dead; he knew too he was riding to find Visconti—nothing more" (267). In the grappling with Visconti, he is overwhelmed and his battered body tossed into the weeds.

Among the secondary characters are Valentina, Visconti's sister, his equal in scheming and determination.

Valentine's lover is Conrad von Schulembourg. Once a trusted friend of Visconti, he has been betrayed by him and left to die. Now, rescued by Mastino, he enlists in his cause.

Grazioso Vistarnini is the daughter of a painter and the recipient of the secret passion of the disguised Visconti. Her passion for him will result in her betrayal of Mastino's campaign to lead his armies against Milan.

Giannotto is Visconti's secretary. He is loyal only when it suits him; otherwise, he hates his master. "Long habit and constant contact had not lessened the secretary's fear of Visconti, nor mitigated the hate, nonetheless intensified for being forever concealed under the mask of cringing servility" (27).

Tisio Visconti is the elder brother. "Like all the Visconti, there was poetry mingled with his madness, and the sight of beauty touched even his crazy brain" (52–53). His father and his brothers have all been driven to their deaths. His key role in the story is the bringing Graziosa's jewels to Visconti early in the story.

The quickening last quarter of the novel is bloody melodrama at its most compelling. Betrayed by Valentine, Mastino's army is reduced by half and his prospects to take Milan ruined. When he is confronted by Visconti for terms of surrender, he considers accepting. It is an awful decision: The only way to save his imprisoned wife is to turn over his towns to Visconti and relinquish Verona to his rule. Mastino's captain, Ligozzi, is aghast, and he warns his chief of the consequences:

> You *shall* know what it means, before you lend yourself to such a thing for love of a woman! It will give all Lombardy to Visconti, it and hundreds to the sword; it will mean the burning of cities to the ground; it will mean the misery of half Italy! ... What triumph will it not give Visconti to see you fall? [235].

Mastino's reply reflects all of his despairs of the futility of his endeavors and the inevitability of the betrayals that have dogged his purpose:

> Have I not pitted courage and high purpose, and honourable dealing and a righteous cause, against craft and cruelty and force? And to what end? Visconti triumphs. Half my men are dead against the walls of Milan! And now, am I to choose again what thou callest honour, am I to leave [my wife] to die by his dishounouring hands.... Does not Visconti fling all laws, all humanity, all honour to the winds.... I cannot think of the welfare of unknown thousands; what are they to me? [236].

Ligozzi leaves him, returning his sword: "I had that sword from an honourable prince— I go to weep that I should have to return it to a traitor!" (239).

When he finally admits his treachery, his armies turn against him. He dies miserably at the hands of Visconti's men. Visconti, in turn, lies stabbed to death by the treachery of one of his loyal followers.

We can see that *Viper* is already pregnant with all the themes, density of scene and color that marks all of Bowen's subsequent historical novels. Here is a story that is liberally peppered with strong characters, an insistence on details of architecture and flora, and a sensitive eye for color and scene. Indeed, she takes great care to present each scene as if it is a painting or a stage setting, always careful to establish its light source and composition. Here, for example, is what amounts to a theatrical portrait of the villain Visconti at ease in his quarters as he plots his strategies:

> The background was mosaic, black and silver, gold and white, saints with glittering haloes, warriors in shining armour, placid and dignified—a splendid decoration; and against these the moving figures, brilliant in colour, scarlet mantles, doublets, purple and orange, glittering with jewels, and laughter

and talk—a riot of life and colour. Slashed sleeves and gorgeous tassels were laid on or swept across the many-tinted marble table, on which there stood gold and silver goblets of curious shape, and glasses, milk-white, azure, or painted, some delicate as flower-bells, others with twisted stems clasped by a snake with emerald eyes. And the centre of it all was Visconti, leaning eagerly over the map, with brocaded mantle thrown back [280].

And there is, undeniably, a certain bloodthirsty appetite for violence. In scenes rendered in affectless, blunt prose, Mastino's terrible humiliation is heartlessly described, as his soldiers, one by one, approach the silent, stoic figure and fling their spears and swords against his battered shield. Humiliated and cast aside, he lives now only to slay Visconti and recover the dead body of his wife.

His final confrontation with Visconti is a bloody one. Ravaged and defeated, he seems scarcely human: "[Visconti] was not sure if [Mastino's] face or that figure, struggling ever toward him, could be killed; that they were earthly, or that that was the voice of a man which, with no sound of the human left in it, called his name" (269). It takes fifteen men to subdue him. His inert body is casually tossed outside the room into the weeds. But the sounds without of him scrabbling at the door indicate he's trying to re-enter the room. A soldier cries, "It's blind, struggling—it—does not look like a man!" (270). The door is shut again, but not before "a livid face appeared, with dim eyes and a bare throat streaked with blood. For one moment the ghastly apparition showed there, then fell into the dark again." Despite the pleas of Visconti's men to accord some vestige of respect for Mastino's noble lineage, the last of the Scaligari, Visconti is unrepentant. Mastino, by now, seems scarcely human: "[Visconti] was not sure if [Mastino's] face or that figure, struggling ever toward him, could be killed; that they were earthly, or that that was the voice of a man which, with no sound of the human left in it, called his name" (269).

In his brief remarks about the novel, written from the standpoint of 1991, Edward Wagenknecht, one of her staunchest supporters, attempts an even-handed critique. "[Visconti] must be very nearly the blackest villain in literature," he begins, and it employs "every trick that the old-fashioned historical novelist ever dreamed of." It may be so "bad," Wagenknecht avers, "that it is good." He insists she would do "vastly finer work" later in her career but adds, "it was still an achievement for so young a writer, revealing not only a daring imagination but a strong mind and much organizing power."[30]

At its publication in 1906, the book was greeted mostly as a remarkable achievement for a teenaged writer. In "A Precocious Author," *The New York Times* reviewer wrote:

> It would seem to such a reviewer simply incredible that a mere child could succeed, where the best equipped and most experienced had so often tried and failed, in transferring to the pages of a novel the spirit, the scenes, and the people of a long-past ago, and infusing them with the breath of life and reality. But seeing is believing and it would not require the reading of more than the whole of Miss Bowen's first chapter to put that reviewer in a very repentant and receptive mood. It might still seem a fairy story that any girl at the age of sixteen could have read, studied, and understood enough Italian history, even if she had devoted every moment of her time to that one thing ... to have conceived such a picture of Italy in the Middle ages as is to be found in *The Viper of Milan*...[31]

Likewise praising the novel's precocity, *The Literary Digest* reviewer added, "It is evident that the young author has saturated her mind with the history of this period ... and upon the whole it may be described as a creditable performance for one so young."[32] Perhaps the greatest praise came from Frederic Taber Cooper in *The Bookman* for whom was left the Impression "of the flavor of old Italian chronicles."[33] The lone disparaging note I have found came from the unnamed critic in *The Nation*, which dismisses it as "silly and superfluous" and objects to its marketing as a precocious product of a young girl.[34]

No less than Mark Twain counted himself among its admirers. And he told her so.[35] In turn, she dedicated to him her third novel, *The Glen O' Weeping* [American title: *The Master of Stair*]. Graham Greene was likewise impressed. In his essay, "The Lost Childhood," he recalls that among the most influential books of his youth, few could match the excitement he had upon encountering *The Viper of Milan*. Not even *King Solomon's Mines*, he admits, could equal the impression *The Viper of Milan* made on him. It was that first reading that predicted his own future as a writer:

> I think it was Miss Bowen's apparent zest that made me want to write. One could not read her without believing that to write was to live and to enjoy, and before one had discovered one's mistake it was too late…. She had given me my pattern … perfect evil walking the world where perfect good can never walk again, and only the pendulum ensures that after all in the end justice is done.[36]

Small wonder her contemporaries, including her publisher, were incredulous at her precocity. She remembers that the publisher came to see her, asking if they had been defrauded, dubious that she could not have begun it in her mid-teens. She did her best to disguise her awkward youth:

> I was tall, serious and had put up my hair. I was also morbidly shy and awkward. I did not know then, and do not know now, why the book had been noticed. It was an

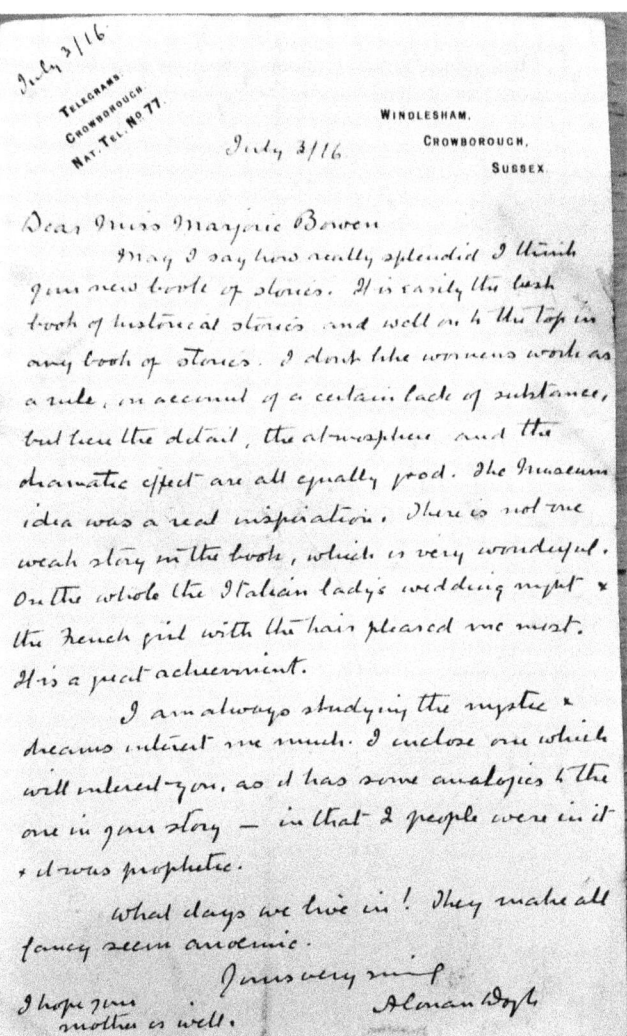

Left: **Graham Greene.** *Right:* **Letter to Marjorie Bowen from Conan Doyle.**

artless performance, and no one knew that better than myself. It had been written with sincerity and a certain amount of enthusiasm and care, and I was very young—these seemed the only points in my favour. But, somehow or other, this tale had attracted attention, perhaps because there was a dearth of any other books at that time.... I suppose, too, it was then something of a novelty for a young girl to have written a book. It has happened so often since that it could no longer excite the slightest interest. But then, it was considered odd, amusing, and surprising.

She also admits that many considered it "just a schoolgirl's dream," and the historical background of the book:

was wildly inaccurate and did not even pretend to have any verisimilitude. It was a kind of fantasia on history, but those who knew nothing whatever about the period thought that this book showed a wonderful knowledge and an accurate scholarship. I got credit for a good deal that I had not done, and for many gifts which I did not possess. The Italian atmosphere was supposed to be marvelous [*sic*]; it was really a little colouring got up from guide-books and pictures, and any one could have done it.

Although warned never to expect to repeat her success, the die was cast. Thoughts of being a painter were discarded. Her canvas now is foolscap:

I had already given up my first hopes [as a painter], but I knew my little gifts to be genuine. I was a born story-teller. I knew perfectly well that as long as I lived I could go on writing stories as good as, and I hoped to Heaven, far better, in time, than that I had already produced.... I had an inexhaustible fund of invention, a fluent and easy style, a certain gift for colour and drama, and such a passionate interest in certain periods of history that I was bound, in reproducing them, to give them a certain life.[37]

A life's work lay ahead. "I found myself then harnessed to a career of

Left: Letter to Marjorie Bowen from Mark Twain; *right:* Mark Twain.

hard work, and I had to earn all I possibly could, to chase every odd five-pound note in order to keep up with expenses." If not a "considerable" writer, she at least determined to be "always a conscientious one"; indeed, the more preparatory work involved, "the better I liked it." She had no "whims or caprices" about her work: "a table, a bottle of ink and a pad of foolscap were sufficient." She could work with "noise and interruptions going on about her." It was not difficult, she observes, "to be self-sufficient and independent, and envy and jealousy did not trouble me, because I would rather be myself than almost anyone whom I met."[38]

And there was this resolve: "I did not, indeed, desire to depict the life about me; it was too stale and wearisome. I tried to escape from it as best I could." Her ambition was nothing less than to enact "on a splendid stage" moving historical dramas "not of our times."[39]

As astonishing as was the precocity of *The Viper of Milan*, the sheer productivity of the next six years is more amazing,—even confounding. Consider: *Viper* is quickly followed by more historical novels, including *The King's Favorite*, a Middle Ages chronicle of Queen Giovanna of Naples; *The Leopard and the Lily* (1925), mid–fifteenth century courtly intrigue in Brittany; four novels about William of Orange (*The Glen O'Weeping, I Will Maintain, Defender of the Faith, God and the King* (all 1907–1910) and a collection of historical short stories, *God's Playthings*. (The latter is considered in detail in the chapter on short stories.)

All of this before she was twenty-eight!

SEVEN MAJOR HISTORICAL NOVELS

Under consideration here is a selection of seven of her major historical novels. First, there are four novels about William of Orange: A standalone debut: *The Glen O'Weeping*, followed by a trilogy: *I Will Maintain, Defender of the Faith*, and *God and the King*. (Two other novels about William's grandfather, "William the Silent" are beyond the scope of my study.) After that are *The Governor of England* (Oliver Cromwell), *The English Paragon* (1930, Edward the Black Prince), and *Nightcap and Plume* (1945, King Gustaf III of Sweden). As it happens, all but *The English Paragon*, which derives from the Hundred Years War of the fourteenth century, demonstrate Bowen's longstanding fascination with the seventeenth and eighteenth centuries, their politics, people, and places.

These were times answering to her many appetites for swashbuckling action and cultural and political turmoil, and which saw the emergence of powerful, if conflicted, ruling figures. Christopher Hill declares the seventeenth century, in particular, "the decisive century in English history, the epoch in which the Middle Ages ended." Indeed, the whole of Europe faced a crisis at the time, which expressed itself in a series of breakdowns, revolts, and civil wars. Whereas the republic of the United Provinces "enjoyed its greatest prosperity in the seventeenth century," Germany and Italy "failed to establish national states based on a single national market." England, meanwhile, moved toward national independence after defeat of the Spanish Armada and became "the first industrialized imperialist great power," ensuring "it should be ruled by a representative assembly." However, while Parliament was arrogating more power to itself, asserting its independent status in the constitution, rulers like James I and Charles I were retaliating by reasserting the Divine Right of Kings, "stressing the royal prerogative, the independent power of the executive without Parliamentary consent." Meanwhile, the rise of the absolute monarchy in France with Louis XIV meant continuing conflicts with England.[40]

Bowen is drawn to the powerful figures of William of Orange, Edward of Wales, and Oliver Cromwell because of those attributes which always fascinated, and sometimes bewildered her, notably, their ruthless ambition, valor in the field, and religious fervor bordering on fanaticism—countered betimes by a more feckless confusion and self-doubt. Regarding King Gustaf III of Sweden, by contrast, she responds to a figure at once more subtle and enigmatic, a figure who is a compound of political savvy and dreamy fantasy, a Harlequin-like player lost in his own masquerade. These are no cardboard heroes and villains, as the historian Pamela Cleaver has alleged, but men swept up in their time, tested, and sometimes defeated by their own actions. Ultimately, their destiny lies within them and are not solely conditioned by their circumstances. As King Gustaf realizes, "He himself knew that his success lay in his own character, his immense labours, his concentration on his purpose" (287). With her brush, Marjorie Bowen edges their portraits in high relief so they stand out, but are not apart from, the fury and flames of their backgrounds.

Why William of Orange

We begin of necessity with a brief consideration of William of his allure as a subject for Bowen. His titles were various—Prince of Orange, Stadtholder of Holland, and, from 1689 to his death in 1792, King William III of England, Ireland, and Scotland.[41]

Far from "dull," Bowen sees in William a complex character and occasionally a man of action, rooted in a time of turmoil in the last third of the seventeenth century in the relations among England, the Netherlands, and France. "Extravagantly maligned and hated by some," she writes in her lengthy, fair-minded, and solidly researched essay, which appears in *World's Wonder*, "extravagantly lauded by others, misunderstood by many, by others merely tolerated, amid a turmoil of stress of business, politics and war, with neither rest nor pleasure, did William III, constant to his own deals, pass the thirteen years of his reign." Here were the very qualities she was disposed to admire, and to which she remained loyal all her life: "[William] was deeply attached to his hereditary Faith and cherished a keen sense of personal honour.... Added to this were a tenacity of purpose, an indomitable fortitude, and a stern resolution that have seldom been equaled ... and a courage that nothing could shake."[42] And she may have responded to him in a more personal way. Having always regarded herself as an "outsider" in her family and in life in general, perhaps she felt an affinity, bordering on identity, with the view held by Williams's contemporaries that he was a "foreigner," an outsider sitting on the throne of England. She notes this in her full-length scholarly study, *William, Prince of Orange*, about his early years, from 1650 to 1673: "He was not English," she writes tartly, "he did not attempt to disguise disappointment and an aloof disdain for much that was English." This attitude was, "from first to last, unpardoned; his great services could not take the place of good fellowship; his wide policies could not excuse his scorn for insular absorption in local disputes; he never wholly succeeded, till on his death, in uniting the English in one common front against a common foe."[43] Moreover, she was in sympathy with William's great love for gardening and his sensitivity and support of the arts, particularly his love of paintings.[44]

In *The Church and Social Progress*, she acknowledges those who take exception to her positive view:

> Before the century closed, there was another effort for the liberation of humanity from folly. It came from the Netherlands and England, both of which were then represented by a man whose remarkable character and astonishing abilities have, at least in this country, been persistently obscured by the malice of party politics, national prejudice, and the repetitions of slanders by careless historians. Again, the credit of the liberal move belongs to the Protestants; William III was bred a Calvinist, and he was the first "good European," the man of whom a modern historian has written: "His views would be considered extremely advanced even to-day."[45]

Bowen claims him as the greatest statesman of his age and one of the makers of modern England:

> This Prince, who had read Locke and employed Newton, was in favour of, and gave universal toleration, and endeavoured to call a conference of the European nations in order that the affairs of the West might be settled on a rational basis and 'the million miseries of war' avoided.[46]

To accusations that William opportunistically and ambitiously grasped at power, she replies, with the objectivity and compassion of the scholar and the dramatist:

> Personal ambition, as his enemies aver, may have mingled with this design. William was of autocratic sentiments, a professional ruler, a professional soldier, accustomed to rule in close as in camp, and irking at restraint or opposition as much as any Stewart King. But it is impossible to read his huge correspondence, kept up with tireless energy through sickness, defeat, failure, and sorrow, without realizing the intense sincerity and simplicity of the resolve that lay behind the weary shifts, intrigues, submissions, and schemes to which the overworked, harassed, handicapped man was forced to set his hand.[47]

She objects to characterizations that emphasize the coldness and severity of his "lips of ice, the heart of fire, the unmoved Caesarean calm, the iron fortitude" and declares them "overstressed for the sake of dramatic effect, even by his admirers." She is quick to bring this legend down to size, citing his love of hunting, card-playing, billiards, love of jokes, showy skill at horsemanship, the "long, dark, melancholy features" so beloved of cruel caricaturists. In short, "he was passionately of his own time, deeply concerned in the events taking place about him, painfully serious in his approach to religion, politics, and those abstractions, liberty, patriotism, honour, and justice, that easy men of the world are ashamed to take seriously."[48] Inasmuch as her writings about him assume such a strong position in her work, we can only obey his injunction to his men during the Battle of Namur, as chronicled in *God and the King*, and follow into battle the sight of his uplifted baton.

A brief review is in order. Born in 1650 in the Dutch Republic, William had strong ties to England through his mother, the oldest daughter of King Charles I of England. He became Stadtholder, or head of state, in 1672. This was at a time when the strongly Protestant Dutch republic was at war with Louis XIV of France. William rose to eminence at age twenty-one as Captain-General of a small army that was falling back from the French. In 1677 he married his first cousin, Mary, the oldest daughter of the Duke of York, who soon would become in 1685 the pro–Catholic King James II of England. After the death of Charles II and the accession of pro–Catholic King James, intrigues among the Protestant majority in England conceived plans to remove James from power. Thus, in 1688, a faction of English bishops asked William to invade England to overthrow James by force. William agreed. With his invading Dutch Army, he proclaimed, "The liberties of England and the Protestant religion I will maintain." James II was forced to flee for his life; and with little loss of life, William was crowned King William III in April 1689 with Mary II as joint sovereigns of England and Scotland. In 1689 the Bill of Rights was passed, which established restrictions on the royal prerogative, providing, among other things, that the Sovereign, without Parliamentary consent, could not suspend laws, levy taxes, or raise a standing army during peacetime. She died in 1694 and he reigned as sole monarch until his death in 1702. His sister-in-law, Anne, became Queen Regnant. During the next five decades, *Jacobites* pressed unsuccessfully for the restoration of James and his heirs. William's reign marked the transition from the personal rule of the Stuarts to the more Parliament-centered House of Hanover.

This brings us to Bowen's remarkable series of stories, novels, and scholarly studies about the irrepressible William. As has been noted, he first appears in Bowen's third novel, *The Glen O' Weeping*, hard on the heels of *The Viper of Milan*, and thereafter in linked trilogy, *I Will Maintain*, *Defender of the Faith*, and *God and the King*, depicts him at various stages in his life and career. (Thereafter, he appears in a "cameo" at the end of *Circle in the Water*.)

The Glen O' Weeping
"What sins have we done to be so cursed?"

We first turn to Bowen's initial sketch of William of Orange. *The Glen O' Weeping*, her third novel, detailed his controversial involvement in the infamous Glencoe Massacre.[49] The Massacre transpired in the Scottish Highlands on 13 February 1692. An estimated forty members of the MacDonald clan were slaughtered by forces mandated allegedly by William himself and carried out by William's Secretary of Scotland, Sir John Dalrymple, the Master of Stair. Aware of armed resistance against him in Scotland by loyalists to the deposed King James II, William had mandated that those Scottish chiefs who refused to sign an Edict pledging their support to him would be punished. When the Highlanders, the MacDonalds, failed to sign the Declaration of Achallader in time—or, as is alleged, their signatures were disallowed—William signs a warrant authorizing John Dalrymple, The Master of Stair and Secretary of State for Scotland, to carry out the massacre. Military forces under the Earl of Argyll and the Earl of Breadalbane and Holland prepare to attack the MacDonalds.

Who should be held to account for this tragedy? Bowen has it that Dalrymple is primarily responsible, that he chooses to ignore the news that the MacDonalds have sworn the Oath. He has reasons to hate the MacDonalds and seizes this opportunity to rid the Highlands of them. He tells the Earl of Argyll and Breadalbane that he orders the attack on the MacDonalds: "I am the first minister in Scotland. I take the responsibility" (110). But Argyll insists he wants additional confirmation—from King William himself. This could be tricky, says Breadalbane, since "the King knew little of Scotland and seemed glad that so many of the clans had come in, and opposed to violence in dealing with the Highlands" (111). But Dalrymple lays out his plan to Breadalbane for the massacre:

> Let it be done swiftly and suddenly. I will send a regiment from Fort William to sweep Glencore clear of these bandits, another to stop the passes. You and my Lord Argyll shall hem them in (though I hope there will be no fugitives)—and so the thing is done. The name of Macdonald will be cleared from Argyllshire and Inverness-shire.... There must be no prisoners.... I will not have one left alive ... and you shall have the King's warrant [112].

In a subsequent conversation between Dalrymple and his father, the Viscount Dalrymple, he admits he has devised plans outlining the details of the coming massacre at Glencoe to be kept from King William: "I will make an example of [the Macdonalds], whether they took the oaths or not. But this must be kept from the King" (141).

But it is too late. The Viscount has already sent the papers to King William.

The scene now shifts to King William's chambers. William has been apprised of a Jacobite plot against him and now receives one of the accused, a young man named Jerome Caryl, who is carrying incriminating papers. While William peruses the papers, Bowen takes a moment to paint his portrait: He cuts a calm, moderate, and elegant figure, appareled in "a black velvet riding suit, heavily galloned with gold; a diamond fastened the long feather in his hat. There was a quantity of fine lace on his cravat and at his wrists; the gold handle of his sword was of most beautiful workmanship." His eyes, "of that hazel that is almost green, were large and very brilliant, his features clear cut, composed, and shaded by heavy auburn curls" (166). Caryl denies to William's face his legitimacy as King. William, unfazed, hands the incriminating evidence back to Caryl and says he tires of the many plots swirling around him: "I will not hunt down these bourgeois—what are they? I will not know their name ... wherefore did you think I would wish to be revenge'? I do not stoop, Mr. Caryl, to revenge" (169). Bewildered at this mercy and calm judgment, Caryl departs. The papers, meanwhile, are retrieved by William and burned.

Minutes later, Dalrymple enters. He is surprised that William has released Caryl, that the Jacobites and their plot will go unscathed. William mildly says that the discovery of the plots is enough to prevent France from being a threat. No retribution is ordered.

The conversation turns to Scotland. Dalrymple insists that it is dangerous for William to take such plots so lightly. William rebukes him: "Whatever game I play," he says, "it is not that of being your puppet, Sir John. I 'ave my own motives—if you cannot understan' them—very well, it make' no difference.... I will not be question'—you understan'? ... I will take no more, Sir John. You 'ave forgotten you are not in your parliament 'ouse'" (173). Sir John is taken aback: "He was face to face with a character that he could not understand, and a spirit every whit as masterful as his own" (173).

But Stair has the last laugh, as it were, since he claims the papers that have been sent to William for his approval are merely letters "relative to the preserving of peace in Scotland" (174). Assured they are "nothing of importance," William signs them.

Dalrymple bows himself out as William absently turns to his tulips. With "the interest of the born gardener," he remarks to no one in particular: "They are very well. If I 'ad keep them in water, they would not smell so. Is it not charming?" (175).

Moments later Dalrymple shows the signed papers to Argyll, declaring, "As for Makian of Glencoe and that tribe, if they can well be distinguished from the other Highlanders, it will be proper for the vindication of public justice to extirpate that set of thieves "(175). Shortly afterwards Jerome Caryl meets with the Duke of Berwick and his gang of conspirators. He unsuccessfully argues in favor of their abandoning their plan and respecting William's tolerance and clemency. A conspiracy to enlist the French is one thing, but the assassination of William is quite another. "This is not the way to win England for the Stuarts," he says (186). Caryl leaves the meeting. For his efforts, he is pursued and brutally murdered by the gang members.

And so to the Massacre. A tableau: Midday, February 13th. The red coats appear in the glen and their leader declares: "I come to root out your cursed den of thieves, by the command of Scotland and the King." The slaughter begins:

> The volley of musketry echoed down the glen; a savage cry of triumph broke from the Campbells as, flinging the guns aside and drawing their swords, they dashed on the MacDonalds.... The report of the guns echoed from the mountains, rang in her ears; she saw smoke curling from the huts, and one burst suddenly into a bright flame that rose into the sky.... Horsemen flew past her; one fell, and his companion leapt over man and animal and was gone into the smoke. Screams and cries of triumph and hate sounded all round; figures formed out of the smoke and were lost again; for a second time came the roll of musketry from the hills, nearer now.... From the burning hut a woman came running, alight from head to foot; without a sound she flung up her hands above her blazing hair and fell forward on her face.... To right and left lay the dead, frozen in their blood. Stained and torn plaids were scattered over the heather; here and there a musket was flung down, or a dirk, or a household implement hastily snatched up and cast aside [202–204].

Epilogue: It is May 1695 at Dalrymple's home in Edinburgh. The town is festering with anger at him, since he is suspected of complicity in the massacre three years before. William has ordered an inquiry into the affair. Stair is unafraid: "He was not afraid that all his enemies together could accomplish his ruin: He had England behind him, and during the last three years his worldly success had put him above the law" (213). The Earl of Breadalbane hints that Dalrymple is in danger:

> They say that the MacDonalds were murdered by your orders. They say that the soldiers entered the glen by treachery, feigning friendship, that they lived there for a fortnight, feasting and drinking; that they rose one night and murdered the clan in their beds—butchered them, men, women and children, with every cruelty [218].

Dalrymple retorts: "Every soldier under Glenlyon knows that this was a military execution—every man among them can disprove this ridiculous story" (218). "He refused to be moved by insults raked from the gutter," reports an onlooker, "he was impervious to tales in Jacobite pamphlets. No remorse troubled him with regard to Glencoe; he was too sure of himself, his position, the King's friendship, to tremble before the Scottish parliament" (218). But when he recalls his duplicity in making William sign the Warrant, he feels a vague uneasiness.

Meanwhile, the Estates of Scotland consider the verdict that blame for the Massacre rests with the Dalrymple. William of Orange is abroad in the Netherlands, but it is certain he will not come to his aid with clemency, since that would imply his own complicity.

Is Bowen fair in excusing William's alleged complicity in the affair? The whole incident remains to this day controversial, and details are muddled about the writing and distribution of the Oath of Allegiance, the responsibility of William of Orange and John Dalrymple, the details of just what transpired at Glencoe, and to William's behavior during subsequent proceedings of inquiry. In her treatment of the story, Bowen is clever—maybe too clever—in sidestepping William's complicity.[50]

By contrast to the blazing colors and harsh contrasts of Bowen's palette in *Viper*, *The Glen O' Weeping* paints its scenes of the chilly, snowy North in muted colors, employing a *sfumato* effect of veils of snow and mists partially obscuring the scene. Typical is this moment when a disguised Stair arrives at Romney Marsh on a dark and snowy night, bent on a mission of intrigue:

> It was snowing over Romney Marsh, the wide, desolate fenland sweeping down to the sea lay grey under the storm. It was almost dark and a light could be seen burning brightly through the snowflakes. To judge by its steadiness, it came from a window; by its size it was far off. There was the steady sound of the thud of the distant waves, now and then broken by the thin cry of a curlew or the hungry shriek of a seagull. In the broke marsh-ground grew a group of withered trees, the foremost bent and blasted by lightning, and against it leaned a man wrapped in a long cloak.... As it grew darker, the snow began

to cease, and over the sea the heavy sky broke into a patch of gloomy red and crimson; it was possible now to discern the line of shore and sand, and the glimmer of the waves [76].

Critical praise was generally positive. Fredric Taber Cooper, writing in *The Bookman*, singled out Bowen's gifts for "making men and women, long since a handful of dust, seem to us for the time being living, breathing realities." The female characters, in particular, are singled out, like the wife of the Master of Stair, Ulrica—"neglected, maligned, misunderstood; silently suffering under the shadow of his sinister presence..."[51] The critic for the *Sydney Mail* praised the book, declaring, "The promise contained in [*The Viper of Milan*] is more than fulfilled in the present novel," and "presents a vivid picture of the days when might was right in Scotland." Singled out for particular praise was "the delineation of the Master of Stair, which is in itself sufficient to give 'Marjorie Bowen' a place among the prominent novelists of the day."[52] However, another critic, writing for *Philadelphia Record*, complained that Bowen was too "soft" on the villainous Stair; moreover, that her handling of the Campbells's participation in the Massacre of Glencoe neglected to mention that the Campbells had been accepted by the MacDonalds into the clan for days of feasting *before* they turned their swords on their hosts. This last point, I might add, remains controversial to this day.[53]

THE WILLIAM OF ORANGE TRILOGY

The first book in the William of Orange trilogy, *I Will Maintain*, flashes back, in effect, to events in *The Glen O'Weeping* to William's early years leading up to the Dutch resistance to the French in 1672, when he became Stadtholder. The second, *Defender of the Faith* is concerned with how he reluctantly married his cousin, the English princess Mary, fought Louis XIV, and drew Holland together in a series of heroic actions, including his victory in the Battle of St. Denis. The third in the trilogy, *God and the King*, depicts William's invasion of England, his assumption, with his wife Mary, to the Crown, the Battle of Namur, his ultimate victory over the forces of Louis XIV, and his death in 1702. Bowen paints aerial views of vivid battle scenes throughout, frequently deploying the *sfumato* technique of viewing the combatants through veils of smoke and mists. By contrast, she wields a finer brush for the "closeup" intimacy of scenes between William and his wife, Mary Stewart.

I Will Maintain

"[He] carries himself with an air of unnatural,
almost dangerous, quiet and control..."

We first meet William as the seventeen-year-old young Prince of Orange. He has been brought up a Calvinist and educated by the State at the University of Leiden. Our first view of him carefully places him in time with a nod toward his future—and a hint of something rather sinister. He is "elegant, rather delicately made" and is

> pale and clear complexioned, with a high-arched nose and curved lips set firmly, wonderful eyes, hazel green, large and brilliant under dark reddish brows.... There was a look about his brow and mouth as if he controlled incessant pain, but neither that nor the expression of gravity that made him appear old for his years could destroy the charm of youth.

But there is that hint of something else: "*[He]carries himself with an air of unnatural, almost dangerous, quiet and control...*" [italics added].[54]

Our first glimpse of William in battle comes during Franco-Dutch War (1672–1678), in which the United Netherlands fought against the French in the attempt to preserve Holland's hard-won independence. In attempting to gain the town of Utrecht, William, who has been head of the army only a few weeks, has to lead his army against the enemy. To the amazement of his men, he is displaying for the first time "a gift of command that was worth everything to an army pitted against tremendous odds" (317). At dawn, entreating his men to stand firm against their privations, while facing superior numbers among the French, he orders the guns to open fire and the cavalry to charge. The French, under M. Spoubise, advance, irresistible, but reckless: "This was the French mode, reckless, showy, expensive, but irresistible, at once the glory and the ruin of their arms.... Again and again the French were to buy dashing and profitless victories at the price of their best blood" (322). For his part, William is transformed: "All restraint had gone from his voice, and there was a new eagerness in his expression," as he led his men straight against the French dragoons. Time after time, his band is driven back, and time after time he leads again the charge, amazing the French with his undaunted persistence. "I shall not be slain today," he tells his men, refusing to retreat. By now, the right wing of the Holland regiments is being cut to pieces; yet, still the center and the left fight on. "Get back to your places, you cowards," he tells his flagging men, "and never care whether the day be lost or no as long as you stay" (327). Yet, defeat is at hand. Utrecht is in the hands of the French: "No human endeavor could do any more. The Prince had kept up a fight of eight hours against overwhelming odds, holding at bay, with his raw, tired troops, the splendid forces of France" (328).

This is but the first of Bowen's descriptions of Williams's valor in battle. Lest we think this an exaggeration, biographer Bryan Bevan confirms that "of his conspicuous bravery in countless battles, there can be no question, and he never had any thought for his own safety.... He had carefully studied the art of war and his phlegmatic temperament found genuine pleasure in the excitement of the battlefield." Yet, Bevan qualifies, "He cannot ever be described as a great general. He met with many reverses. He could devise good plans and up to a certain point execute them, but his physical health debarred him from steady and sustained effort."[55]

A singularly touching moment comes late in the book when William testifies to his commitment to release Holland from French tyranny. In a "tight closeup"—a "two-shot," as it were—his mentor, the Rev. Cornelius Trigland, bestows on William a benediction and a charge.

> In this dark hour [he says] a time of misery, of bitterness, of despair, the tyrant triumphs.... But God, who planted in your breast this fervor, will not patiently endure the blasphemer.... Your way will not be easy; there will be dangers, disappointments, sneers, oppositions, failures.... When you long for peace, you will be driven into combat ... but in your heart you will know you are the elect of God, and that you fight His battles.

Clearly, Bowen sees this moment as William's baptism. Trigland warns: "Maybe you will die before this reward comes, maybe you will never see the result of your labours. Men may never give you the honour; but yours will be the glory if now you dare what no other man does dare—or will!" Humbled, his face "distorted" with emotion, William manages to respond: "I will not falter—I will not despair—even though I go forth alone and never reach the goal" (451–452).

The novel's concluding pages see him narrowly escaping assassination attempts and sorrowing over the deaths of two of his closest friends, even though they had been among his assailants.

In a long and detailed commentary on the novel in *The Saturday Review*, John M. S. Allison praised Bowen's handling of the character of the Prince:

> He was Dutch to the core and continental in his interests.... Before he became King of England, as Prince of Orange, he had had to risk his life, his future, and even at one time, his own popularity to save his land. His entire youth had been spent in the struggle. His had been a life of hardship with little time, if any, for the gentler amenities of princely existence.... This had been the education of the man who became William III of England, and this, in brief, is the theme of *I Will Maintain*.... This book is doubly welcome. It is a work of real merit and presents an almost unique interpretation of its subjects. Too often, the studies of William have neglected the formative years to the period just preceding the Peace of Nimwegen. In this first volume, Miss Bowen has purposed to portray the Prince against his Dutch background, and she has succeeded admirably with clear judgment and no taint of hero worship.[56]

Defender of the Faith

*"Monsieur de Luxembourg was the better general
as the Prince was the finer man"*

As a soldier, William cuts a gallant, swashbuckling figure in *Defender of the Faith*.[57] By contrast, he also comes across as a hesitant young swain, a suitor to his cousin, 15-year-old Mary Stuart, the oldest daughter of the Duke of York and niece of King Charles II. The alliance had been opposed, at first, by Charles, who had preferred she marry an heir to the French throne. Bowen is at her best in describing the tart dialogue between the stern William and the animated Mary. They warily address each other, each in turn taking the other's measure. Although he rebukes her showy dresses and gems—"Do not wish me to think that I have a thing of folly to my wife"—she cleverly sees that "he was not cold at heart but passionate and disguising himself from her." For his part, observes Bowen, "He admitted to himself that youth, gentleness, beauty, and meekness, though among the things he despised, yet had a value of their own. She had dignity through her very simplicity. He could not disregard her as a fool, though hitherto he had thought of her as little better" (207). The union quickly settles into amicable feelings and eventual love. She will continue to hold a certain allegiance to her English background and heritage, but never will fail to support her husband in the stormy times to come.

Meanwhile, back at the battlefield... William is in his element. And so is Marjorie Bowen. The scene is the immediate aftermath of the Battle of Nymuegen. The year is 1678. Bowen pulls back her "camera eye" for an aerial perspective to reveal the positions and the strategies of the contending forces under Prince William and the celebrated French general, Marshall Luxembourg. The first phases of the struggle between Louis XIV and William of Orange had come to a conclusion with the Peace of Nymuegen. To William, however, this was but a momentary truce. His protest came in the form of an attack with his 45,000 troops against Marshall Luxembourg's French forces near the village of St. Denis.

What follows is one of Bowen's many great battle scenes. M. Luxembourg rejoices at what he considers the defeat of the one man Louis really fears, the Prince of Orange. Suddenly, interrupting the nocturnal quiet, cannon fire announces William's unexpected attack. Luxembourg buckles into his cuirass, shouting, "This is a trick! He would fall on us while we rest under faith of a treaty—which is a move I was not prepared for!"

> It was said afterwards that no man but the Prince of Orange would have dared the attack and no man but the Duc de Luxembourg would have rallied so soon to meet it. The French battalions had to form in the face of the Dutch cannon-balls and bombs that dropped into their midst from the shelter of the slightly rising woods where the Prince had his artillery. Many a man dropped as he rode up to take his place.... Before the moon had paled before the hot august dawn, Luxembourg had recovered from the surprise and disposed his infantry in order of battle about the hastily constructed earthwork round the encampment. The cavalry rode up the incline, and succeeded, in spite of many losses, in spiking several of the Dutch guns; upon which the Prince sent out a regiment of Spanish horsemen which, skirting St. Denis, fell on the right flank of the French [269].

Seeing the disorder of the Dutch regiments, William orders them to dismount and advance with pike and musket to break the French line. He and Luxembourg confront each other, both on horseback: "The Prince saw him and instantly lifted his hat, smiling. Monsieur de Luxembourg uncovered and bowed with an answering laugh." The two bodies of troops rally and fall upon each other in a fierce, disordered combat. The Furies are unleashed:

> Time after time the cuirassiers and musketeers of France charged the ranks of the allies; time after time, the shock was met without flinching and a steady fire of shot emptied saddles and thinned ranks. The Prince led now this regiment and now that, dismounted to encourage the infantry and exposed himself with a reckless ardour that called forth the protests of his officers. He gave his usual answer that he did not risk his life needlessly out of mere foolhardiness, but on due consideration to encourage his comparatively unpracticed troops against the veteran arms of France. By midday, he had had two horses killed under him, and, mounted on a third steed, led a detachment of the Spanish cavalry right against the now slightly wavering centre of the enemy.... He rose in his stirrups to shout to those behind, when a French officer clapped a pistol to the forehead of his horse, and at the same instant, another knocked him out of the saddle.... A hand-to-hand fight followed round the Prince, who was actually under the hoofs of the maddened horses and in danger of being bruised to death. Two of his men dismounted and dragged him with difficulty out of the press. He was borne backwards, hatless, with a broken sword, the fire of the French so hot upon him that the balls struck down those about him and carried away the end of the pistol at his waist, even passing through the skirts of his coat ... [270–271].[58]

With death at hand, "he stopped the first riderless horse that passed him, flung himself into the saddle, grasped one of the swords offered him, waved it aloft, his arm streaming with blood, and again led his men against the French" (271). Throughout the stifling August day engagement followed engagement. "Monsieur de Luxembourg was the better general as the Prince was the finer man, and he put the whole force of his genius into resisting the attack, as the Prince put the whole strength of his courage and resolve into leading it" (271).

The purple evening drew on as the French and the Dutch, were in turn, pursued and pursuers ... "Toil, difficulty, discouragement, opposition, defeat, failure, sickness, and utter weariness of mind and body, that was the sum of it." And the Prince has only more intrigues and turmoil ahead ... (278).

Reviewing *Defender of the Faith* in *The Bookman*, Wilkinson Sherren wrote: "We step into the atmosphere of quick and robust action—the austerely told story of William of Orange, who is presented as a fine figure of a man. Nobly does he shine beside the intriguing purposes of Charles II and the French King's spies ... the incidents are tightly knit into a narrative of unflagging interest."[59] The critic in *The Nation* demurs, adding, "the great Prince is presented throughout as a human and fallible being, a leader more loved than feared, an indifferent soldier, though a great statesman, a cunning intriguer with an honest purpose."[60]

God and the King

"[William] was facing France, equal to equal"

The title refers to the oft-repeated anecdote that a soldier declared his allegiance is to "God and the King"; to which the response was "So do we all—it is merely a question of which god and which king."

God and the King spans the years 1688, as William is preparing his invasion of England, to his death in 1702.[61] While William stands center-stage, Bowen also devotes a sympathetic voice to Queen Mary, divided in her loyalties to her father, King James, and her husband.

There is agitation in England. King James has come to power after the death of Charles II. His favor of the Pope is causing the populace to break out in resentment, and there are burnings of effigies of the Pope in the streets. James is also concerned with rumors of plots against him. He fears that the Protestant Prince of Orange may be planning an invasion. Where the Duke of Monmouth had failed, the Prince may succeed.

We meet William as he is receiving letters from England that invite him, in effect, to effect his invasion. He is thirty-seven, a man has who has spent close on twenty years trying to induce England to shake off the yoke of France and who has wrested three conquered provinces from the French. He is,

> [T]he most respected statesman, one of the most feared generals and powerful rulers in Europe, the head of the nation which was supreme in trade and maritime dominion, the foremost champion of the reformed religion, first Prince of the blood in England ... and husband to the heiress of that country, the rallying point for the discontents and indignations of all those whom the King of France had injured or the King of England put out of humour [50].

Added to this was the

> glamour of past heroism, the history of his splendid house, the great deeds of his ancestors, his own breaking from unhappy childhood and desolate youth to power in one day of chaos and ruin, blood and despair; his almost miraculous deliverance of his country, constant devotion to it, and his firm adherence to the persecuted religion were unique in the history of princes, and lived in the minds of men [51].

Yet, despite this reputation, he appears as no climbing despot or figure of arrogance. Rather, he is possessed of a "rather severe and austere expression" and appears "as a gentleman of no particular appearance of energy, rather below than above the middle height, and of a frail physique and slenderness of proportion rare in a man of action" (51).

In a touching scene, he talks with Mary about his plans. "There is no other way to preserve Christendom," he says, "if I do not take this step, there is a life's work wasted, and we are no better than we were in '71." He realizes there is no way he can persuade King James to break with France: "I am forced to this decision. No consideration of justice, of ambition, nay, even of diplomacy or good sense, can move His Majesty to break off with France; his insults to the liberty of England are incredible" (62). She still has a sense of duty to her father, King James, but also knows her first duty lies with her husband.

She also knows how reluctantly William would deploy force against a near kinsman "that only a tremendous need could force him to this tremendous resolution, which was at once more daring and more necessary than any could realize save himself" (61).

Clearly, Bowen is sympathetic to her. This is a marriage bound in mutual trust and support. She is compassionate for Mary's failure to conceive a child after the first stillborn infant. Mary confesses to William: "I am a poor creature, to think of my wretched self at such a juncture; what are my own melancholies compared to what you must undergo? Yet, humanly speaking, I have no courage to face this crisis…" (63). Moreover, as she gazes out to the woodlands outside her window, she has a presentiment of an early death: "She thought that this pageant had ended for her, that though the wood might bloom and change she would never see it again after these leaves fell; she had been haunted, though not troubled, all her life by the presentiment of an early death, and now this feeling, which she had never imparted to any, became one with the feeling that the wood was passing, ending for her" (64). Much later in the narrative, there is a touching scene at Christmas as Mary prepares to submit to the smallpox that is fast overwhelming her:

> Her thoughts ran past her own death, and saw [William], lonely amidst his difficulties, without her aid to smooth over little frictions, without her company in his infrequent leisure, without her sympathy in his disappointments; in a thousand little ways he scarcely knew of she had been able to help him, and now there would be no one.

At this point Bowen pauses to paint a cinematic montage of the images past and present and future that stream before Mary's eyes (236–237). The candles gutter and die. The image in her mirror is of "a face and throat indistinguishable from her crumpled lace collar…" (238).

For his part, William has great compassion for her:

> He remembered how he had disliked and despised her, treated her with neglect, then indifference, made no effort to please or win her; and yet she, during the ten years of their marriage had never from the first failed in obedience, sweetness, self-abnegation, nor once faltered from a passionate devotion to his interests … and now, for him, she was doing violence to her own heart and setting herself in active opposition against her father, a tremendous thing for such a nature to bring itself to As he gazed at her fair youth, pale with anxiety for him, he felt she was the greatest triumph of his life, and her love an undeserved miracle [125].

Contrasting with these intimate closeups, Bowen paints a spectacular scene as William's invasion armada confronts heavy storms, while attempting to set sail to England. The forces comprise no less than sixty-five great ships of wars, seventy vessels of burden, five hundred transports, all of them carrying five thousand cavalry and ten thousand infantry of the magnificent Dutch army, the six British regiments in the employ of the States, the French Protestants, and the whole artillery of every town in the Republic. Watching the passing of the fleet from horseback is Mary. In her heart "all terror, remorse, sadness had been absorbed by strong pride, the doubts, shames, fears that had tortured her were gone; she did not think of her father, of her danger, of her loneliness, only that she, of all the women there, was the beloved wife of the man who led this—a nation's strength—into war for … the new liberty against the ancient tyranny … all that she symbolized by the word Protestantism" (129).

Thwarted by the storm, the fleet is forced back, only to sail again the following week, after the dispersed ships were retrieved. Finally, they all made the Channel, "along which it stretched for twenty miles in full view of England and France, the shores of both these countries being covered with spectators who viewed a sight such as had not been seen in these waters since the great Armada crossed the seas, a hundred years before" (138). What follows are the many details of the Prince's landing, the assistance of English supporting forces, the King departing London, William's assumption of power, the return of Mary to London, and the negotiations resulting in William and Mary to reign together as King and Queen.

His popularity abroad, however, is not matched at home:

> The industrious simplicity of the King, his dislike of blasphemy, evil-speaking, and frivolous amusements, his private tolerance, justice, and modesty were as so many causes of offence to a people regretting former princes so much more suited to their temper. They missed the pageant that had continually entertained them at Whitehall, the money that had been squandered by the Court in a manner so pleasing to the national extravagance, the continual spectacle of the King in the obvious exercise of gracious royalty, even the gay ladies whose histories had diverted a generation [226].

As for William himself, "he never flattered, and he took no trouble to please women; natural modesty and the languor of ill-health made him refuse to concede to the national love of display" (226)

August 1695. It is a different William that looks on at the siege of the Castle of Namur. St. Denis had been won twenty-three years ago; Charles II had died ten years ago; James II had been forced into exile three years after that; the "Glorious Revolution" of 1688 had seen William and Mary's accession to the Crown; and William's wife, Queen Mary, had died just the year before. Prostrate with grief, it is feared that he would be unwilling to continue his reign. Meanwhile, France's predominance in Europe is waning. The Battle of Namur would be a key factor leading to the Peace of Ryswick two years later.

> [William] was facing France, equal to equal; he was feared and respected throughout the world. The Protestant faith, once threatened with extinction by Louis, had been placed on a basis from which, as long as any faith lasted, it could never be displaced. His country was free, and prosperous, and foremost among nations again!

However, "after these years of toil, treachery, deceit, and constant strain, fatigue had done their work. The fine spirit did not shrink from its task, but never again could it recapture the early glow of hope, the early ecstasy of labour, the early pride of achievement" (279).

So now, here is William, rising at dawn on the nineteenth, riding from post to post surveying his troops, in the saddle from four in the morning till nightfall, with a mighty coalition of Allies, including all the principal countries of Europe behind him, preparing to attack the French at Namur. Across the plain of the Sambre and Meuse, "the starlight showed the huge French encampment stretching out of sight under the clear sky" (280). Rendered virtually impregnable, it once had been occupied by Julius Caesar. Early the next day, the Marshall of France, M. de Boufflers, refuses to surrender. The assault by William, the Dutch, the Elector of Bavaria, the Landgrave of Hesse, and other German potentates, will begin early this afternoon. The Allies have encircled the huge fortress. They will drive forward from four places at once. William is astride his huge grey Flemish horse, lightly trapped with red leather linked with silver gilt. "He had always been renowned for his consummate horsemanship, and this great beast, that had taken two footmen to hold in before he mounted, he held delicately with one hand on the reins, with such perfect control that the creature was utterly motionless on the narrow ledge of slippery rock" (289).

As the clocks of the Namur churches strike one, the steady beat of drums and kettledrums march the Grenadiers forward from behind their defenses. The French commence fire from behind their first palisade, which sweeps the ranks of the advancing

English with deadly effect. Slaughter, roiling smoke, bombs bursting at every hand, charge and counter-charge—

> The air was of a continuous redness; the half-naked French gunners could be seen, running in and out of their vaulted galleries and crouching behind the black shape of the guns; flying fragments of shell, masonry, and rock fell among the leaderless English, who hesitated, gave way, and retreated down the bloody slope they had gained, each rank falling back on the other in confusion, while a shout of triumph rose from the fiery ramparts of Namur [291–292].

William sweeps around the ramparts, his men following the wave of his baton; the Bavarians and Englishmen surge back into the fray, capturing batteries, climbing over corpses of men and horses. "The air was so full of powder smoke that the walls and turrets of the castle appeared to hang as in a great fog, with no visible foundations … and when the combined batteries of the allies opened on Namur … it was a bombardment as had never been known in war" (294). There is no change in William's composure, save "that he was more than ordinarily cheerful…" (294).

The French, lurking in the cuvette, recognize him by his great star and level their muskets. Displaying no concern whatever, saying, "We must get nearer than this," he sets spurs to his horse and, wheeling around "charged straight at the lines of France, the Brandenburghers after him with an irresistible rush." The ground ahead is so uneven, he dismounts and, "without leaving go of the reins, runs along by the horse's head, guiding him through the debris, and mounts again without touching the saddle—a well-known feat of the riding-school." An officer of Dragoons strikes up with his sword at the figure on the huge grey charger. "The King leant out of the saddle, parried the thrust with his weapon. The Frenchman, hit by a bullet in the lungs, rolled over with his face towards the citadel; the last thing he saw on earth was the King of England high on the distant heights of Namur, with the column of Brandenburghers behind him" (295).

Much later … the scene shifts to Holland.

While William languishes near death at Hampton Court, fatally injured from a fall from his horse, his delegated Grand Pensionary works alone in Holland at his desk. Sunlight and an absolute stillness fill the rooms. Suddenly, he is aware of a young man standing at a distance in the next chamber.

> He was very young—little more than a boy—but of a very grave, still carriage; he wore a violet coat, a black sash, a plain sword, and a cravat of Frisian needlework; his clothes were of the fashion of thirty years ago.… He was very slender and slight; his hair, which was long, thick, and heavily curling, of a deep chestnut colour, fell either side a thin hawk face. . Presently, the youth turned and came towards the Grand Pensionary's cabinet, walking stiffly, and holding his hat under his arm. M. Heinsius noticed the old-fashioned rosettes on his square-toed shoes…

The youth lifts a pair of eyes of singular power and of a marvelous brilliancy and flashes a smile at M. Hensius. "It is over," the youth says. "But you know what to do" (373).

Then, "as if one leaving something he loves," the youth moves away, "reluctantly it seemed" and passed out of sight, "with the sunshine all about him" (373–374).

It's a beautiful moment, captured in full daylight, the quietest of ghostly farewells to an enigmatic figure in history.

Bowen's sensitivity to such intimate scenes is contrasted by her evident mastery of battlefield campaigns. Her knowledge of military tactics and applied research, coupled with an astonishing pictorial imagination impressed even respected military historians. Lieut.-General F. de Bas compared her to "a skillful general" in her insights into battle tactics. "The characters and scenes she so vividly depicts undoubtedly show some remarkable insight into the past, which seems almost inexplicable.... Being an artist of no mean talent, as well as a born writer, together with the faculties of a soldier and tactician, she combines pen, brush and sword." Moreover, "her battles prove her to be a skillful general.... [Her volumes on William of Orange] have raised an enthusiastic admiration for the author throughout the whole of the Netherlands and its colonies. These works are of great educational value and are used in the various Dutch institutions and public schools."[62]

Critics rightly singled out *God and the King* for its sensitive and sympathetic portrait of Queen Mary II. The commentator for the *Boston Evening Transcript* observes *God and the King* is the final installment of the "William of Orange" trilogy.

> It is a skilled blending of fact and fiction, and famous historic figures make attractive and striking characters in the parts assigned to them. Princess, later Queen, Mary is a charming heroine, who endures many trials, the most serious of which is when she supports her husband in the war against her father, a war that made her Queen ... [Williams's] joys and sorrows are shown with a wealth of detail that indicates a rare imagination and a close study of history.[63]

And in *The New York Times*,

> Mary Stuart lives more vividly than, for most of us, she has lived in history, a sweet, sad woman, loyal and high-spirited always. It was his marriage to Mary Stuart that gave William of Orange his excuse for conquering England to wrest the control of Europe from France. It was Mary's devotion to her husband to the face of 'duty' to her father that made the bloodless revolution of 1688 possible and drove James II in exile from the country he had so misruled.[64]

AND OTHERS

The English Paragon

"Chivalry is not what it was, nor knighthood, nor feats of arms"

The English Paragon is a collection of interconnected short stories that collectively relate incidents in the career and decline of Edward Plantagent (1330–1376), K.G., Prince of Wales, putatively, the English hero of the Hundred Years War.[65] Bowen assembles her characters in discrete story fragments, like montage pieces, cross-cutting them into parallel narratives, much in the manner of the Soviet masters, Sergei Eisenstein and Vsevelod Pudovkin. In sum, it's a magnificent achievement, quite one of her finest historical novels.

"The following narrative deals," explains Bowen in her Preface, "in a broad, impressionistic manner, deals with the last few years of the life of Edward Plantagenet, K.G., Prince of Wales" (9). It includes Edward's doomed Spanish campaign of 1366 and the subsequent revolt of Aquitaine in 1370. Incidents include the revolt of Don Enriquez of Transtamara against Don Pedro, King of Castile, and the intervention of France, Aragon, Navarre, England, and the Pope, which led to the ruin of English fortunes in France and a renewal of the war between Charles V and Edward's father, King Edward III. "This very popular English Prince ... the victor of Crecy, Poictiers and Najera, has been the central figure of (I believe) a vast number of romances" (9). The novel concludes with the massacre of Limoges and Edward's death. Bowen notes that among her sources, "often admittedly unreliable or doubtful," include Jean de Froissart, the *Chandos Herald, Baker's Chronicle,* the *Calendars of the Patent and Close Rolls,* and biographies by G.P.R. James, Monsieur Moisant, R.P. Dunn-Pattison, and Armitage Smith's *John of Gaunt*.[66]

The players in this most cinematic of novels greet us like the opening credits of a movie: **Nunreddin**.

An occasional participant and commentator on the action is *Nunreddin*, a fictitious Arab philosopher and physician, who, in the guise of a Benedictine monk poses as the spiritual advisor to Edward Plantagenet. "I am a wanderer," he tells Edward; "I pass from place to place and find my amusement watching the follies of mankind" (225). He pretends to be an alchemist, but when questioned about it by Edward, he craftily evades the question: "Sire, the most curious and investigating of men must keep their lips sealed on some of these incredible secrets, until the time comes when it is the will of God to reveal all—the power of the elements, of the metals, of the principles of nature, and of the intellect of humanity" (120). Through his eyes transpires much of the action.

Edward of Wales

Looming large in events is the figure of Edward. We get all his titles: Edward of Woodstock, Knight of the Blue Garter, Earl of Chester, Prince of Wales, Duke of Aquitaine. Bowen portrays him, for the most part, as history has regarded him, as a figure of prowess, honour, and loyalty—of which prowess is valued most highly.[67] He is, however, a highly flawed figure, whose mistaken loyalties and military overreach condemned him to eventual ignominy and defeat. Our first picture of him comes from an observer:

> There was something in the contour of that famous face which reminded Nunreddin of a lion he had seen in the menagerie of the King of Granada—here were the same rounded, blunt contours, the flat cheeks, the short nose, the prominent chin and the upright carriage of the neck ... the tawny colouring of the Prince's short sleek hair and complexion, the same dark, bold look helped the likeness to the noble animal.... The eyes possessed a disfiguring feature—a drooping lid and a cast (that blemish which no Plantagenet wholly escaped), and which was supposed to be a heritage from some bargain Fulk of Anjou had made with the Devil, "Satan's squint" as the enemies of this great House named this hereditary defect [110].

He boasts to his new friend, the monk, Nunreddin:

> I am the strongest man in the world—do you hear, monk? I have never met my equal at feats of arms, at the six-foot lance or the broadsword. Since I was a boy, I have been accustomed to wear heavy armour. Nobody can ride in complete mail longer than I. I can endure fatigue or privation as well as any I have ever met. So much health and strength has God given me [126].

Contrast this with the final image of Edward, a dying man returning to England, suffering the ignominy of the slaughter of Limoges: "Nothing remained of his magnificence, save his great height. His hands were folded on his breast in an attitude of fatigue, defeat and resignation. Fur and silk coverlets were piled over him to keep his shivering sick body from the sharp January air" (310).

Presently, in a doomed enterprise, Edward is attempting to regain provinces England has lost to France. He has pledged his armies to support Don Pedro, the "legitimate" Christian King of Castile against the contending Don Enriquez, Don Pedro's bastard brother. Edwards support of Don Pedro is questioned by many, including Pedro's rival, Don Enriquez. Why, he wonders, does the Prince of Wales persist in supporting Don Pedro? "Sire," replies Don Enriquez' lieutenant, "all Europe wonders as to his motives. Some say he does it for pure lust of adventure and weariness of his long inactivity in Aquitaine; and some, say he does it out of joy to have a trial of arms with me" (212). Moreover, Edwards's advisor, the monk Nunreddin warns him, "It takes no prophet to tell you that if you leave Aquitaine with all your armed force to help this scoundrel [Pedro], regain his throne, you will commit, not only an unworthy, but a foolish action. Aquitaine will surely revolt in your absence" (123).

Don Enriquez of Transtamara

He is, by the will of the people of Castile, the rightful claimant to be King. Arrayed against him is his brother, Don Pedro, and Edward's armies. By contrast to Don Pedro, Enriquez is described as "just, wise, valiant and honourable." Well does he know of the might and power of Edward, and he fears the revenge of Don Pedro should his forces fall to the "rich flower of Gascon and English knighthood that followed Edward" (213).

Bertrand du Quesclin

He is the leader of the Free Companies, powerful warriors, mercenaries prepared to fight for either England or France—or to whomever they are hired to serve. He aligns himself in the service of Don Enriquez. Bowen clearly relishes these legendary warriors, for hire to the highest bidder:

> [The Free Companies] consisted of every type of fighting man ... their infantry was the best in the world ... the famous English archers carried six-foot bows and iron arrows.... Hard-pressed for men, the King of England had made contracts whereby various gentry of means agreed to furnish him with a certain number of men-at-arms at fixed pay for a definite period; when the peace came, these same contractors were quite willing to sell the services of their highly efficient troops to anyone who cared to pay the price, even to the previous opponents, but when they found no bidders, they lived by pillage ... [76].

Pope Urban V.

The Pope has been driven from Rome and is living presently at Avignon. The Pope is an amusing character who prefers his beloved flowerbeds and the lyrics of Petrarch to this dreadful business of warfare. He despises Bertrand's Free Companies of soldiers but knows they are needed as allies to Don Enriquez to keep the throne of Castile.

Charles de Valois, King V of France

The young King V of France, Charles de Valois, whose armies stands opposite to Edwards, is introduced as a person more interested in the arts and philosophy than in war and bloodshed. This estimation proves to be misleading. "It is said that I do not seek glory," admits the King, "that I do not know how to lead a battle of men-at-arms on the field of honour. It is quite true. Yet, without bloodshed, I hope to free France. When you go abroad again, my son, and hear contempt of me, tell them that the King has told you that" (146). He goes on to deplore the brutality of war as represented by Edward. The arts, by contrast, are far more important:

> Some men are born to destroy, some men to organize and administer. All may ruin a country in a few weeks, my son, and it may take centuries to build it up again. Do you love beauty, music, and painting, and carvings in stone and marble? I believe that in the service of beauty, and not in feats of arms, one may buy oneself a little place in Paradise [146].

Count of Armagmac

Formerly a Lieutenant of the King of France, he is now sworn to the service of Edward. He resists Edward's taxing of Acquitaine to raise money for his armies—money that was to have come from Don Pedro. He fears lack of funds will ruin Edward. On the other hand, he points out to his councilors the King of France is himself burdened with debts. Weighing his options, he is prepared to switch his allegiance once again to Charles V. He admits Charles is not the warrior to compare with Edward. However: "He does not make the show of the Prince of Wales, but he is a more useful man to serve. Do not despise him. He is very powerful, for all his books, his pieces of parchment, his clerks and his hymns and prayers" (251).

Charles II of Navarre

At the present time, he has to make a tough decision. His kingdom lies directly between Acquitaine (where Prince Edward is arming for his venture into Castile), and Spain, where Don Enriquez of Transtamara and Bertrand du Guesclin are rallying to resist the English invasion. He is under treaty with Prince Edward to do him service. At the same time, he has taken an oath to Don Enriquez not to open the Pyrenees passes to the invading English army. How shall he please both potentates?

Queen Philippa, Mother of Prince Edward

She is portrayed as an elderly, meek and simple woman weary of the wars that claim her husband, Edward III, and her sons Prince Edward and John of Lancaster. In a tender vignette, she encounters two small boys at play and remembers happier days when she played with her own sons:

> Yes, those were her happiest days when she had sat in the nursery before the children were taken from her and given to the knights to train. How she had brushed their hair, how it had shone, cunningly circled into their necks! How she had tried them in their new doublets and coats, anxious as to the cut and fit, watched their faces when she gave them some little gift or indulgence [161].

All the while, she muses to herself the waste of the fighting, the useless ambition of her husband to have another crown, the senseless pillaging of towns. But now she recoils in horror when one of the little boys boasts he is going to become a soldier.

Like most of Bowen's historical romances—although to a greater degree—*The English Paragon* interrogates and subverts the romantic notion of The Age of Chivalry in the thirteenth and fourteenth centuries.[68]

While in Aquitaine, Prince Edward is already suspicious of the ideals that had once sustained him. He laments to Nunreddin:

> We live in such base, degenerate times. These modern days are full of sordid dullness. Everything is in decay. Chivalry is not what it was, nor knighthood, nor feats of arms. To know the pride of honour and adventure one must read the old books of past times. To gain any satisfaction, one must lose oneself in a world of fancy [123–124].

He goes on to admit few moments of glory and satisfaction—such as the campaign at Crécy when he was sixteen years old: "There I won my spurs and proved myself a worthy Plantagenet, it was a good moment. I recall that once I was hurled to the ground and my standard-bearer, Richard de Beaumont, covered me with the great banner of Wales. I have known no such pleasure since." Was not the battle senseless? He replies: "I cared not for that. My father was in the right. England was in the right" (124).

But he now realizes that Money and power have become the determining factors of his ambitious campaigns. Countering the boasts of Kings is the view of the Ambassador from France's King Charles V (Charles de Valois):

Men like himself, the Pope, and the young King of France were the real rulers of the world. They always got the better of men of violence, of passion and uncontrolled lusts, even the dreaded mercenaries were but their instruments [72].

Count Armagnac says:

> Ay, money is at the bottom of it all. Money, money—always that. What is the good of this talk of chivalry and brave deeds, of the flaunting prowess of war, honour and glory? We come always to money, and there I say, sirs, do not pay this tax. Your example will be followed by other towns, and 'twill be the signal for which Charles of Valois waits [251].

In short, the complexities of war and peace and shifting loyalties are too much for plain men. As one of the councilors says:

> All these deep intrigues and shiftings to and fro of policies and underhand dealings are not for plain men like us. With all the quarrels and treacheries of these great ones we have much ado to keep our roofs over our heads, meat in our bellies, and a few coins in our chests [253].

And Bowen adds: "In their hearts they cursed all princes, men of war and politicians. They were peaceful traders, men who liked to live cozily and make their gains by labour, not through peril—men who enjoyed the thought of piling up fortunes for sons and daughters, of going to Mass regularly and feeling the priest generously, of perhaps endowing some hospital or chapel" (254).

The Battle of Najera

There are two great battle set pieces here. The first, the Battle of Najera, is vividly described in a series of "closeups"; the other, that of Limoges, is reported "off stage," as it were, through reported action.

April 1367. The Battle of Najera draws nigh. We are in the camp of Don Enriquez, who, with the support of Pope Urban, has declared his legitimate claim as King of Castile. The hour approaches. In full battle array, the Castilian force crosses the little river of Najerilla and pitches camp two leagues from the small town of Najera. The Free Company Captain, du Quesclin, anticipates the peaceful prelude with a sardonic eye:

> Pleasant in his nostrils was the fragrance of the budding orchard, the perfume of the heath and the odour of fresh green growing weeds in the fields near by—gracious and pleasant all this, although he was eager to destroy, in the tumult of a bloody conflict, all these fair evidences of a peaceful countryside offering rest, refreshment and joy to man [218–219].

Arrayed opposite, lie the spearheads of the English banners and lances. The Prince is with his councilors as the armies of the English, the Gascons, the Welsh, and Scotch prepare for battle. Lately, the Prince has been in pain, which he has been trying to conceal from the others. Nunreddin bids him think only of what lies ahead.

> Question not the mysteries of God. For the while, Prince, you are cured and may lead your battle, and whatever your fate, are you not the English Paragon who must bear all without lamentation? It is easier, Prince, to win battles and to endure bitter marches in winter and all the toilsome hardships of a campaign than in times of peace to bear the long, withering of the body, the blasting of health in the prime of manhood [226].

The Prince admits his fear of a wasting death, away from the battlefield: "I would that to-morrow might be my last battle, rather than live to endure what I must endure if a long mortal disease grip me" (227). But for now, he values highly the image he must present to his troops:

> The Prince of Wales, like all the Plantagenets but to an excessive degree, valued pomp and magnificence, and well knew the effect of superb spectacle on the minds of men. He had never neglected anything in his person or his surroundings that would overawe or move to admiration those who beheld him. Much of his success and fame was due to the way in which he had enhanced his great qualities by imposing and extravagant display. He always affected black armour, polished till it reflected a cold light like the gleam of midnight stars in dark water. In contrast, a princely coronet of finest gold, studded with rubies, pearls and sapphires, surrounded his steel helm. He had his visor up now and the links of fine steel, so exquisitely wrought as to be supple as a veil of silk that formed his coif of mail, fell on to his shoulders, framed his face close to the corners of the eyes and lips. His close-fitting jupon bore the Leopards of England and the Lilies of France, silver and blue, gold and white, and was buckled low round the hips with a belt of massive plates of gold [230–231].

The Prince gives the order to advance.

The two armies hurl themselves like Furies upon each other. The day grows ill for the Castile King. The steady pressure of the English and the Gascons drove the Castilians to the Najerilla river, which was deep and unaffordable. "Borne down by the showers of English arrows, even the stoutest ranks of Castilian chivalry had scattered and fled" (237). At length, Du Quesclin declares to his men they are "outmatched and outwitted," that "it is no shame to surrender," and advices Don Enriquez to flee the field (237–238). Du Quesclin is captured. English losses are less than a hundred, while "thousands of the enemy lay choked, drowned and dying in the river, besides hundreds scattered upon the plain" (239). The Prince has every reason to expect that the victorious Don Pedro will pay the monies he had promised when first he came to the Prince. But in the midst of the celebrations, the Prince talks Don Pedro out of beheading and punishing the foe. Sir John of Chandos warns that Don Pedro may not be good for the promised monies.

The next day is Easter. Nunreddin views the carnage and smiles sardonically at the sight of the Christian celebration of the Easter Resurrection of the God of Love—

> Amid the corpses of the fallen and the writhing bodies of the dying, slain hideously by their fellow-creatures on a sweet day of Spring, for no reason whatever. Most of all, Nunreddin pitied the mangled horses who had had no choice in this quarrel. The air was full of chants and bells, and Edward Plantagent took his part in the holy service very piously [244].

Limoges

Despite the Prince of Wales' victory over the Castilians at Najera, disaffection is spreading among the contending armies. Although he is the sworn ally of the Prince— he was one of the Captains at Najera—Armagnac deplores the Prince's inability to raise the money owed his armies. They know already that Don Pedro is refusing to pay the promised monies he owes Edward. Edward now is considering a tax, the so-called "hearth tax" (*fouage*) to be laid upon Aquitaine upon his return from Castile. If the taxes aren't paid, citizens risk going to prison. Moreover, Armagnac urges that they be rid of the Free Companies, who are ravaging the countryside: "Let us be rid of them by force. Why should we pay these thieves and brigands to cease cutting our throats? Let us rather drive them out of the country" (252).

Meanwhile, while Edward pleads insolvency, he nonetheless continues to live extravagantly. And the nobles of Aquitaine and Gascony no longer care if they are governed by Charles of France or Edward of England. Indeed, the shrewd and crafty Charles is proving himself to be more than the milquetoast people have labeled him. And there are rumblings of wanting to be rid of Edward. If no money is levied, Edward will be ruined. And perhaps those rumors of his illness contracted in Spain are true and may decide the issue... "We are men of peace, not war," they protest. "Though we, as Frenchmen, have a natural inclination towards the King of France, that is not the pressing question of the moment, but how we are to make our revenues meet out expenses" (248).

What follows is the infamous sack of Limoges in 1370. The city had renounced its allegiance to England and Edward III. The ensuing sack of the city by the Prince of Wales "has become, in some circles, a byword for violence disproportionate even by the lax standards of the fourteenth century." Details about the ferocity and the losses of the incident vary, but Green reports, "Whatever really took place at Limoges, the increasing frequency of sieges, brought about by changes in military strategy and advances in gunpowder artillery, had terrible implications for non-combatants, both those in a besieged town and those who lived in its vicinity."[69]

Bowen cleverly presents the Battle of Limoges solely through reported action. We are at an abbey on the high road between Limoges and Cognac, where Brother Francis and his brethren quietly go about their daily routines. Their lives are a quiet counterpoint to the preparations for battle. The armies of the French and the English come and go as Francis quietly tends his garden. When he learns that Chandos, the first ally of Edward, has been slain, he is glad that seemingly France has been left to the French. He has also heard that the Prince of Wales lies ill at Angoulême and that Edward's brother, John of Lancaster, has joined him in a last effort to keep control of the provinces.

At length, news of the capture of Limoges by the Duke of Berri reaches Brother Francis. Edward is said to have sworn a vow to take revenge on Limoges. And so, on a beautiful autumn day Francis and his brothers tremble as the English forces pass by on their way to besiege Limoges with three thousand men-at-arms, a thousand archers, a thousand footmen of English, Gascon and Free Companies veterans: "The monks believed that Limoges would at once surrender when this terrible warrior in his wrath appeared before the gates" (295).

Days and weeks pass by and Brother Francis hears nothing. He and the monks begin to think that maybe the dreaded Prince was not so terrible and that the town might hold out until French forces could come to the rescue. So Brother Francis walks in the garden, sheltering the little boy, Hugh, who had been rescued a year ago from the burning building of his slaughtered parents. He hopes that Hugh will not grow up to follow the sword and war. They walk and savor the multitudes of bright flowers, and the sweet fragrance of the honeyed air.

Then, the great English army passes, and it seems that they march on with the steady tread of a victorious force. Troubled, Francis hopes for news. Then, a wounded soldier stumbles into the church and reports that Limoges has fallen and almost everyone has been slaughtered by the English:

> Men, women, and children, even those poor helpless ones who had done no harm and knew nothing of the treason. All these poor creatures imploring mercy and finding it not. Although they threw themselves before the Prince of Wales, with many tears and supplications, yet he ordered that they should be massacred. And so they were. And I, who have seen many sights, have seen none so terrible as this, which made me think of God and hell and vengeance—to see little children, old women, and mothers who had done no wrong thus foully slain and crying out in their torment ... [302].

And Francis murmurs to himself, "This, is your English Paragon! This is your pattern of chivalry!" (302).

Spared by Edward are those valiant French knights who had been so valiantly defending themselves.

The dying soldier wishes to make amends. The Abbot tells him, "Kindness, charity and pity find it difficult to take root in this world. Yet, like weeds in a hard stone wall, here and there they flower." And Brother Francis adds, "Shall we not pray for these poor souls who were murdered in Limoges?" And the Abbot adds: "It is the tyrant, not the oppressed, who stands most in need of pity. They whom he caused to be slain are at peace in Paradise, but he must live to take his punishment.... God have mercy on Edward, Prince of Wales, and Duke of Aquitaine! God forgive his sins!" (304).

The French Provinces are lost, but Charles of Valois has triumphed: "This so-called craven and coward, who never left his palace on the Seine, but spent his time with astrologers, monks, and bookish scholars, had now by cunning diplomacy outwitted the famous Plantagenet" (308–309). John of Lancaster now had authority over the remnants of English power in Aquitaine, Guienne and Gascony. He and wife are now King and Queen of Castile and Leon. Nothing stands between himself and the throne of England but Edward's sickly infant, Richard.

As for Edward, nothing remains of his magnificence. He beckons to Nunreddin and asks what favor out of gratitude he could grant him. The "monk" refuses. Cheated even of this chance to be the superior to the monk, Edward pulls a large ruby ring off his finger and gives it to him. But Nunreddin, in turn, gives it to a malformed beggar he meets in the street.

At the end, weary of watching over the dying Edward, sorrowing for the loss of Edward's child, Edward, and tired of the detestable dreariness and cold, Nunreddin longs for Egypt, Persia, and Mesopotamia, "where he could hold out his hands and feel heat, like waves flowing over them. He yearned for the harsh sand burnt to silver by the sun, for the crude green of dry palm trees, for the little white houses with the green blinds and shutters, so glaring without, so cool within. He had had enough of Europe" (307).

He picks up on the street a white cat. "You are not troubled with sins or penances, triumph or failure," he murmurs to the cat. "You are the best company in the world" (312). Down in the harbor he watches the mighty vessel which has come to carry Edward of Wales home to die. Nunreddin turns away, his face turned to the East. "He went on his way gladly, leaving all these things behind him. He caressed the white cat which lay snug in his bosom and seemed content" (313).

The Governor of England

"I am in Grace"

The Governor of England traces the rise to power of Oliver Cromwell (1599–1658) in mid-seventeenth England, spanning his beginnings as a farmer, his military leadership during the two English Civil Wars, the dissolution of Parliament, the execution of King Charles I, and Cromwell's assumption as the Lord Protector of the Commonwealth of England, Scotland, and Ireland.[70] Of special interest to Bowen's scene-painting are the great battles of Marston Moor, Naseby, the assault on Basing House, and the campaigns in Ireland and Scotland. Like other military and political leaders in Bowen's novels, Cromwell thinks himself a force unto himself—in this case, a Puritan appointed by God to follow no laws other than those Divinely recognized. At the same time, he nurses inner doubts about the consequences of his actions.

The Great Moment comes to Cromwell one day at his farm in the 1630s. While entering a barn on his property at St. Ives, confused about the course of his life, he paces to and fro on the rough floor, strewn with the dried husks of the last harvest. As he grasps the hilt of his sword, "a sudden exaltation shot into his heart, his spirit leapt suddenly to a greater height than any it had touched before." And then, it happened. "A dazzle of unbelievable light opened before his inner vision; he fell on his knees, and, from a sword of fire, received the accolade of God." He cries aloud: "I am in grace. And I am chosen to be Thy servant in this work which is to be done in England." And he ventures forth, divinely anointed, "outwardly an ordinary gentleman, inwardly a soul newly awake to salvation, bearing a burning light no more to be quenched until it returned to Heaven" (16).[71]

Pursuing a policy of tolerance toward all Protestant sects—but not to Anglicans, "who are a mockery to the Lord—Cromwell despises everything Charles and his Church stand for." Like many leaders discussed here, whose charisma borders on fanaticism, nothing blocks their rise to power. In this case, Cromwell repudiates the Star Chamber, the power of the bishops, taxation without law, and all the incense, fripperies, and indulgences of Anglican ceremony. An ascetic rather on the order of Savonarola, he targets the "vanities" around him and banishes all ornaments and extravagances from his life. Moreover, he sets out to destroy every vestige of ornament in England, from Bishops to lace handkerchiefs: "He was not a man of exquisite sense; perfume and flowers, green trees and sunshine were as little to him as they could be ... and as for delights of man's making, he abhorred them all as vanities, from pictures and music, fine dwellings and costly gardens, to ruffles and fringed breeches" (127).

Despite his limitations as a politician and soldier, he trusted to Biblical Scripture to show him the way: *"Through God we shall do great acts; and it is he that shall tread down our enemies"* (47). Moreover, he possesses a quality of presence whose sheer force influenced others. "[Here is] a man of homely simplicity in appearance, yet conveying by some magic of the spirit, a splendor and force such as is found once among tens of thousands" (70). But, as a man of manic-depressive tendencies, he has moments of confusion and doubt about his actions and a foreboding of the forces he is setting in motion: "I think," Cromwell confides to a friend, "this dark air is full of portents and heavy with forebodings. You know, that we stand in a little mean street, in the cold and darkness, in the midst of a distressed and oppressed city" (72).

King Charles, for all his power, is surrounded by fears of a restless Parliament and anxieties about sedition and treason on all hands. Fear for the safety of the Crown impels him to condemn to death his traitorous friend, Lord Strafford. And he is intriguing in Scotland and Ireland to bring Northern armies into London. He has reason to be suspicious of this rising Puritan Cromwell and his "Roundhead rabble." He may be "a half-crazed fanatic or a very cunning hypocrite," but, admittedly, he is "an able fighter" (113).

In 1642 a Civil War portends, as Royalist forces contend with forces aroused by Parliament, the Roundheads, including those of Cromwell, now a Colonel and Governor of Ely, who has raised a troop of his own for the Eastern Association. Accused of leading a soldiery more fanatic than professional, Cromwell retorts: "I prefer them who know what they fight for, and love that they know, to any lukewarm hireling who will mutiny when his pence are in arrear.... For we wrestle not against flesh and blood, but against principalities, against powers, against the rulers of the darkness of this world, against spiritual wickedness in high places" (107–108). He continues to rise in the ranks, from Colonel and Governor of Ely, to Lieutenant-General.

Bowen is in her element as she paints mighty battle scenes: Cromwell turns the tide at Marston Moor in 1644 with his light cavalry, wrests the north of England from the King, and is instrumental in the creation of the New Model Army. The great fight comes a year later at the hamlet of Naseby where with six hundred men he confronts the King's last hope, his "flower of the loyal gentlemen of England" (120). It is English against English, enacted on English land. Like a general in her own right, Bowen lines up the order of battle: Cromwell at the head of his cavalry on the right, the infantry in the center, General Ireton's men on the left, the King's army in view across Broadmoor with the King in armor in front. The Furies are unleashed.:

> Then began the bloody and awful fight. Up and down the undulating ground English struggled with English, the colours rocked and dipped above the swaying lines of men, the demi-culverins and demi-sakers roared and smoked, the horse charged and wheeled and wheeled and charged again. The mounting sun shone on a confusion of steel and scarlet, sword and musket, spurt of fire and splash of blood, on many a grim face distorted with battle fury, on many a fair, youthful face sinking on to the tramped earth to rise no more, on many fair locks of loyal gentlemen, combed and dressed last night and now fallen in the bloody mire never to be tended or caressed again, on many a stern peasant or yeoman going fiercely out into eternity with his word of "God with us!" on his stiffening lips.

A montage of carefully selected closeups tells the story: "Uplifted swords, maddened horses, slipping, falling, staggering up again, the shouting, flushed Cavaliers, the bitter silent Roundheads struggled together toward the hamlet and church" (122). The left wing is shattered, but Cromwell's cavalry rushes into the breech. Charles' foot soldiers are cut down. His men are now outnumbered one to two. But they form up again and again:

> One after another these English gentlemen, pikemen, and shotmen went down, slain by English hands, watering English earth with their blood, gasping out their lives on the rabbit holes and torn grass, swords, pikes, and muskets sinking from their hands, hideously wounded, defiled with blood and dirt, distorted with agony, dying without complaint for the truth as they saw truth and loyalty as they conceived loyalty ... as long as they had a shot, they fired; when their ammunition was finished, they waited the charge with clubbed muskets [123].

As King Charles rides from point to point, rallying his Cavaliers, Cromwell forms his cavalry a third time. The parliamentary dragoons advance. Charles is restrained from throwing himself forward by one of his men, who cries: "Will you go upon your death in an instant?" (124) Charles replies: "This was a fight for all in all, and it is lost!" (124).

Bowen ends it all with a sardonic grace note: Across the grasses where the blood of both sides mingles, a lark soars up into the cloudless sky, "pouring forth his immutable song for which the living were as deaf to as the dead" (126).

Charles's attempts to negotiate with Parliament are proven to be disingenuous. He will not abridge his Divine Right and forsake the Church of England. Likewise, Cromwell stands by his own unflinching sense of power. Witness the slaughter, plundering, and burning he authorizes at Basing House, perhaps the most controversial of his military decisions.

His attempts to negotiate a compromise with the King fail. Charles' surreptitious last-ditch attempts to enlist a supporting army in the North for a second Civil War in 1648 are exposed. His attempts to flee to safety are foiled. Inevitably, perhaps, after almost ten years of strife, evasion, pacts made and broken, bloodshed and lives ruined, Charles is brought to trial, where he is condemned to the executioner's axe in 1649. "I tell you," Cromwell says, "we will cut off his head with the crown upon it" (231).

Throughout these affairs, and during the subsequent years when Cromwell declares himself the King, Bowen continues to portray a figure not without remorse and regret. "Ah, soul, my soul, are you wandering again in blackness, not knowing which way to turn? ... Yet did not the Lord receive you into His grace, and make with you a Covenant and a promise?" And while he thus exhorted, "he chided some inner weakness of sadness that was liable to come over him, most often at night" (163). Viewing the fallen, he admits, "Mine has been a dismal fate, to ruin all those I would most advance, to bring down those whom I would most exalt" (219).

Bowen, as is her wont, expends many pages on Charles' trial in Westminster Hall. Lengthy quotations from the trial records are given. Repeatedly, the charge is that the law is above the king; that the King had defied the law and was therefore answerable. At length, the execution is ordered. "I submit to your power, but I defy your authority," says the King, contemptuously.

The axe falls. Cromwell conducts thereafter brutal reprisals in Ireland against Papists priests, Papist garrisons are massacred, Papist peasants transported, Papist gentry forbidden their religion. In Scotland, he routs the forces of the young Charles, who flees for his life.

Back in London, at the close of 1652, he is ready for his final coup: A few years later, with his army behind him, he dissolves Parliament and declares himself "Governor of England" and "Lord Protector"—in effect, a King, although he rejects the word. "It is a call from God and the people," he declares, "and no man could ask for more. Yes, I know the Lord has called me as He called me ten years ago from St. Ives—this is your work—get you up and do it!" (277).

Bowen's balanced attitude toward Cromwell, labored as it has been heretofore, now is torn away, and her scorn is revealed at last:

> [Cromwell] might be going to rule for the people's sake, purely, but he was not going to rule by their wish. He felt this a weakness in his case and strove to cover it, even to deceive himself in it; a general election, a genuine appeal to the country, might have resulted in bringing in the second Charles Steward, and for the sake of the cause he dare not risk it.... His call might be from God, it certainly was not from the people of England [280].

In effect, adds Bowen with savage irony, "He was doing what no King of England had been permitted to do; he had, in fact, the power at which Charles had aimed, and he had what Charles had never been able to attain—the armed force to maintain him in that power" (284). His voice growing more shrill, he insists that God wishes England to go forward "to fight heresies and Antichrist!" ... which includes "putting down cockfighting, play-acting, and horse-racing, gambling, and such lewd sports..." (285). No, "His Highness," as he was now called, is oblivious to the charge, leveled at him by a former friend, that he murdered Charles solely to "climb into his place, succeed to his power, sleep in his rich bed ... and have a high name" for himself (295).

In 1658 his health begins to suffer and his mental faculties are strained by the constant apprehension of assassination attempts. At his death, it seemed as if this England, "so violently shaped anew into something of the form which was the ideal of Puritanism, purged and glorified, was no more than the vivified dream of this one man, and that when he passed from the earth, it would be as when a sleeper wakes—the dream would be dispelled and all things become as they had been" (316).

At the end, the dying man moves to rise from his bed. "It is a fearful thing to fall into the hands of the Living God," he cries.

Bowen is of two minds about this man. While she holds his protestations about

Divine Appointment suspect, she sympathizes with his last years of age and disillusionment, of his stoic shouldering of the burden of the Protectorate, and his moments of doubt and confusion about his Divine appointment. Moreover, while indicting his bloodthirsty campaigns, she clearly admires his sturdy pragmatism and his soldiery professionalism in the field.

Nightcap and Plume

> "The skill I learn in handling puppets helps me
> in handling my politics—'tis one art" (169).

Concluding this brief survey of Marjorie Bowen's historical novels is *Nightcap and Plume*. Of all her historical novels, it is the most idiosyncratic. It defies easy categorization. Densely plotted, fraught with convoluted intrigues, it vividly paints all the color and pageantry of which Bowen excelled. She creates in the character of King Gustav III (1746–1792) of Sweden an unstable compound of reality and myth, of public patriotism and private nightmare. Small wonder that in her "Author's Note" she pleads the book to be "read as fiction" with "no pretense to be dramatized history or biography." That being said, the historical backdrop of eighteenth-century political intrigues against which Gustav moves is astonishing in its granular historical detail and texture. While we dream with Gustav, we plunge into the very fabric of history. In short, there is nothing else quite like this in the whole of Bowen's oeuvre.

Late eighteenth-century Europe stands on the precipice of revolution and anarchy. National and political identities shift and blur. Bringing to a focus the disparate strands of this most complex of Bowen's historical romances is Gustav himself. Seen in a kind of half-light, he strikes an elusive aspect, stepping in and out of the shadows of fantasy and reality, both a master politician grounded in reality and a fantastic Harlequin-like figure involved in his own masquerade. She finds in him some of the qualities she celebrates in her portrait of William of Orange. Like the Dutch-born King of the previous century, Gustaf is a paradoxical figure: He is a political animal who is deeply involved in art and culture; he preaches religious tolerance while maintaining conflicting interests in Catholicism and Protestantism; and his elegant posture in manner and dress conceals his skill in battle tactics. Moreover, his investigations into the occult are counterpointed by a hard-nosed pragmatism. Pursuing an enlightened monarchy, he entertains a sympathy for the peasantry. Bowen's obvious sympathy for both Gustav and William might be construed as empathy.

Gustaf is Sweden incarnated. He embodies all the triumphs and tragedies of the House of Vasa.[72] He frequently loses himself in the Swedish landscape:

> He forces his thoughts to travel out over Sweden, over the untrodden snow ruffled by the wind that now lay deep, deep and deeper over the wild swan's way, to the magic land of the Laplander and his drum, the reindeer, the midnight sun ... the ruddy peasants cutting the barley with a scythe, the women working at their quilts of wool, the houses of the wealthy Scots merchants of Goteborg, with the rich painted furniture, the bridges with masks of knights and horses. All this he saw flowing before his aching eyes [271].

While considering a new Constitution in 1771, he is regarded as a mere "puppet" and dilettante on the throne of the Vasas, a weak inheritor of the glories of a free Sweden from the mighty Gustaf Vasa, whose reign, from 1523 to 1560, had marked the Swedish war of liberation against King Christian II of Denmark, Norway, and Sweden. But now, since the disastrous reign of King Karl XII, during which Sweden fell into decline, Sweden is caught in the crosshairs of violence and intrigue from the incursions of Russia, Prussia, and Denmark. The loyalty of Sweden's one ally, Louis XV, is wavering. The country is bankrupt, "blighted, bought and sold, appendage to Russia, pawn to England, victim to Denmark," while currying favor for the financial support of France (85). Meanwhile, at home, there is political conflict between the political factions of the "Caps," who represent the peasantry, and the "Hats," who represent the aristocracy—*nightcap and plume.*

Gustav strives to effect a reconciliation between the two, while maintaining a royal autocracy. "I do intend to overturn the state," he declares to his close associate, the soldier Johan Toll, "to make myself master in Sweden, to save her from Russia" (12). Indeed, the restoration of the glories of the House of Vasa and an independent Sweden is his obsession. His new Constitution curtails the Swedish Parliament, breaks most of the privileges of the nobility, and, at the same time, establishes him as an enlightened monarch, a sort of benign despot. His ambitions have been nothing if not idealistic: "He intended to abolish all differences between the classes, and to give to the *ofralse*, or unprivileged orders, the same rights as the *fralse*, or privileged, 'those rights which every Swede should enjoy,' adding an invitation to them to elect representatives to concur with him on the details of this matter" (262). He arrests his enemies and abolishes all the main privileges of the nobility, while conserving those of the other estates. At the same time, he encourages the royalists in France and hopes to achieve a secure peace with Catherine of Russia. All comes to naught, however. Growing unrest from his disgruntled and disenfranchised nobles results in his assassination from a gunshot to the back. Like a Swedish Julius Caesar, his presumption to absolute power results in his betrayal by a conspiratorial cabal.

Of primary importance to Bowen is Gustav himself. At times he seems to have stepped out of the commedia dell'arte: Indeed, masks and artifice are his stock in trade. They are his insight into the human condition: "None of us is ever without some disguise" (150), he confesses at one point. "I have dealt so much in disguises, it amuses me. My part has been something that of harlequin" (281). "We play in a masquerade all the time," he admits. "The only ease from pretense is when we are in mask and domino" (13). His friend and military advisor, Johan Toll see through this artifice: "Your balls and *fetes*, your concerts and card parties do not deceive me. Your elegant idleness is a disguise for your severe intentions" (10–11).

Gustav's devotion to the arts is part and parcel of his public statesmanship and his private identity. Amusements and politics serve each other: "The skill I learn in handling puppets helps me in handling my politics—'tis one art" (169). In particular, he finds in Gluck's opera of Euripedes' *Iphigenia en Tauride* and the Greek myth of *Thetis and Peleus*, which he adapts as Sweden's first national opera, important metaphors for defining Swedish identity. In Gluck's music he "hears" Sweden's own "summons of fate and the refusal to accept defeat" despite the onslaught of the Furies and "the stern refusals of the gods" (7). In *Thetis and Peleus* he combines Greek myth with Swedish folklore in a tour-de-force of staging. The story, he contends, contains a warning of the political attacks that await him and his striving for Swedish independence: "Was it not at the marriage of Peleus and Thetis that Discord threw the apple so disastrously disputed. Such fruit is tossed at most feasts" (71).

A theatricality of a different sort—what Gustaf calls "an infernal puppet show"— also preoccupies him (165). Secret societies of sorcery and the occult are abroad in the land, including an Illuminati sect of astrologers, alchemists, and magicians, purportedly privy to the magic of the Comte de St. Germain. As a man who is both a rationalist and a dreamer, Gustav is vulnerable to, yet skeptical of, these meetings. But because he himself has employed artifice in the service of his agendas, he knows it is best to keep a close watch on these meetings, which may disguise a cabal against him led by his brothers Karl and Frederik. His attendance at a series of séances are among the key scenes of the novel (they are examined in the "Music on the Hill" chapter). At one of them the medium— none other than his brother, Karl—has a vision predicting Gustaf's demise, "Let the ruler look to his measures. Now he swells with his power and overturns the state; in time he shall be over-turned and all be as it was before.... His reign will be transient, leaving no impression on history (155)."

Not just his life, but his death will be a masquerade: "Maybe we shall vanish with our masks on" (150). Near the end, before the assassination attempt, he dons his costume of purple silk domino and mask, with the orders of Vasa on his heart, and in his lapel a knot of ribbon with the colors of his new order, lilac, green, silver. "How many costumes have I worn!" he declares. "Every harlequinade ends at last, lights out, at last, one costume is the last disguise" (242). Having been alerted earlier that his assassin will be wearing red, he is watchful during the fateful Opera House Masquerade.[73] Ironically, he never sees the assassin. He is approached from behind and the gunshot to his back will lead to his death thirteen days later. The only red color he sees is the crimson blood splashed across his black domino.

A Final Royal Pageant

Ceremonial history has always been an expensive proposition. Consumers have always expended the big bucks to attend royal pageants, coronations, and the like the way moviegoers crowd the theaters for first-run historical epics, like Abel Gance's *Napoleon,* David Lean's *Lawrence of Arabia,* and William Wyler's *Ben-Hur.* Never did these entertainments come cheap. Millions upon millions of Coins of the Realm have been expended on Hollywood's historical epics.

According to Marjorie Bowen, the Royal Processions of times past didn't come cheap, either. "From the earliest times," she observes, "it was customary to charge for 'good places' from which to see Royalty in action—":

> Until the reign of Edward III a sum equal to one farthing was charged, this was then raised to one halfpenny, for the next two Kings the charge was one penny and the price was gradually raised until the sightseer had to pay sixpence to behold the glories of Elizabeth in comfort, half-a-crown for Charles II, five shillings for William and Mary, and as much as five guineas for George IV, though seats to view Queen Victoria's procession could be purchased for thirty shillings.[74]

Happily, we have the "best seats" for the Pageantry of History.

Courtesy of the painted pages of Marjorie Bowen.

THREE

"We Human Beings Cannot Endure Too Much Reality": The Ghost Stories

"I believe that I have seen and heard many ghosts, though some of them were dreams. And I believe that ghosts move in and out of dreams as they move in and out of waking hours, and the obscure memory of them dims the outline of reality in all our days."— Marjorie Bowen[1]

It all began when young Marjorie Bowen heard footsteps in the empty rooms. The lights suddenly clicked on and off. Groans broke the stillness. A wheel of light whirled down the stairs. "A small brown animal" appeared on her bed, "rather the shape of a turnspit, but with cropped ears standing on its hind legs." Then came the night when "a gigantic figure, hooded and cloaked, with very square shoulders" shambled down the stairs...

"There seemed an oppression of something intensely evil," she recalled, "an abstraction and yet something in concrete form." She was fourteen years old at the time, living in one of the many lodging houses her family occupied over the years in Bayswater, Hampstead, Maidstone, etc.

Finally, the Society for Psychical Research was called in. It determined that the house once had been "a private lunatic asylum, and that some unchronicled tragedy had taken place there...."

"It was strange now to me, looking back," Bowen writes, "how I could have continued to live in such an atmosphere."[2] Already she was learning to regard these terrors with the same mixture of incredulity and respectful acceptance that the mature writer we know

Five Winds

as "Marjorie Bowen" came to question and dissect in her many novels and stories the horrors of the world around her. As painfully chronicled in her long essay, "Margaret Campbell" (1938), and the book-length *The Debate Continues* (1939), the hauntings in that former lunatic asylum were neither the first nor the last of her ghosts.

As a child living in a dysfunctional home, the screams of her arguing parents were "like a battle of the gods overhead"; and all she could do "was to try and get out of the way for fear some of these Jovian shafts might fall upon me."[3] Convinced she was neither wanted nor pretty—she "regretted the miserable fact" that she was a girl—and wishing to "efface" herself—she became rather like a ghost, haunting her own house: "I grasped that I should not have been born, that I was a burden, a responsibility, that I had probably inherited a number of bad qualities from members of my family, whose fate was so tragic they could not be spoken of, and presently I grasped only too clearly that I was an outcast from the class to which I belonged."[4]

First encounters with books and pictures held their own terrors. A book illustration of a man climbing down a ladder through a hole in the ceiling haunted her: "I expected the old man nightly." Her first encounter with Wordsworth's poem, "Lucy Gray," threw her into "a state of terror approaching ecstasy."[5] What was it about those concluding lines about the dead girl—

> O'er rough and smooth she trips along,
> And never looks behind;
> And sings a solitary song
> That whistles in the wind.

—that gave her such a shock?

Religion offered no "relief," as she put it. Thanks to her mother, the daughter of a fundamentalist clergyman, "God joined my already manifold terrors.... This so-called religion as presented to me then was altogether repulsive to me. I suppose something may have been said to me about Heaven, but this could have made no impression. I could not visualize such a place. But torment, loneliness, unhappiness and pain—in other words, Hell—I could imagine very well." Churches seemed like places of "penitence and punishment," although the Catholic Church at least offered the "rituals of incense, subdued lights, the flowers, and the monks in their brown robes."[6]

Since her youthful encounter with the spectral figure sloping down the stairs, Marjorie Bowen admits that "we are no further in the knowledge of the supernatural than we were when Dr. Johnson marvelled [sic] over the death of Lord Lyttelton, or when the Wesley family were tormented by goblins at Epsworth Parsonage."[7] She acknowledges her "interest in the invisible world" and admits that "the intellect rejects what cannot be proved, and the emotions accept what cannot be explained."[8] The "most satisfactory kind of ghost story" resides in the "emphasis on evil, the malice

Marjorie Bowen, 1925

of the dead, the unholy power of fiend and phantom, the miasma, shuddering into palpable shakes of secret crime."[9] She firmly rejects ghosts of the Ann Radcliffe school, i.e., those manifestations which prove to be "shams and waxworks." Too much is explained away. (She does an admirable job satirizing this in her novel, *The Shadow on Mockways*.) A measure of ambiguity should be maintained. The issue comes up in her story, "The Accursed Portrait": "It has been agreed," declares one of the characters, facing the question of a family ghost, "that no one shall demand or offer any explanation of any of the marvels that we may hear; for, indeed, there is not much pleasure in a ghost story, if it is explained away."[10]

She declares that ghosts display no preference regarding past or present contexts. They haunt the contemporary scene as much as they do the Gothic cellars and attics of the past:

> A phantom motor-lorry (and we are assured that there are several haunting our busy main roads) is as dreadful as a phantom coach; a headless motor-cyclist (and they have been seen) is as grisly a spectre as a headless horseman. A telephone has been used with great effect in a modern ghost story … and there are obvious dreadful possibilities in the airplane that crashes and burns out in a lonely spot.… We have had ghosts in shops, theatres, modern flats, even in bathrooms. And we may assume that, the more unexpected the place in which these visitants appear, the more prosaic and unlikely the ambient, the more detestable will be their apparitions.[11]

With rare exceptions, comic ghosts, are "intolerable." And so are clanking chains. But she does have a grudging affection for that most "debased" of ghosts, the Victorian "gliding lady, who floats, always with tapping of high heels and rustling of silk, through so many well-worn old legends of so many well-worn old houses."[12]

She reveals herself as something of a scholar and archaeologist of the ghostly tale in the prefaces to her two edited anthologies, *Great Tales of Horror* (1933) and *More Great Tales of Horror* (1935). Although she enjoys the "historic value" of stories written before the age of electricity and the motor car—"There are no shades, no hints, no half-tones to these old ghosts; they jump out suddenly like a jack-in-the-box, and you either believe in them and run away, or you don't believe in them and say that you have been dreaming"—she searches for stories that "have not become staled through constant inclusion in anthologies and frequent re-publication in magazines and newspapers."[13] Thus, she has looked long and hard for forgotten tales and legends. Many of her selections were culled from nineteenth-century sources, like scrapbooks, chapbooks, and newspapers, whose authors were "anon." These derive from Scottish and German legends and are rooted in a core of fact: "Many of them were told long before they were written down and were the possession of the unlearned for generations before some professional writer gathered them for his scrapbook and cast them into the literary form of his day." She praises "these Scotch stories" for qualities we find in her own stories—

> Their solid dignity, shrewd humour, and an air of integrity that makes their queerest flights acceptable; there are no tricks, no padding, no flippancies to disguise poverty of material no cheap devices to lure or thrill the reader.

Contrast these, she adds tartly, with too many of those "tales of dread and of the supernatural" written today, which are all too often written to a formula. They become "a kind of puzzle, a combat of wits between the author and the reader, with no sentiment of compassion or terror on either side. The reader of these stories, in fact, only pretends to believe an invention which never expected credence."[14]

Among her contemporaries, she singles out for particular praise the work of M.R. James, Walter de la Mare, J. Sheridan Le Fanu, Algernon Blackwood, and Arthur Machen. She applauds Blackwood's and Machen's "spiritual quality," that their stories "are released from confines of time and space, and move, whether their authors intended it or not, in a world as indefinite and elastic as that of a dream; they are dateless." She praises Le Fanu's ability to provoke "the insatiable nostalgia for the past that gnaws at so many of us with its intolerable melancholy, and the infinite horror endured by disembodied and damned spirits chained to earth."[15]

Marjorie Bowen's own ghostly tales have, in general, either "some foundation of truth, are based on some ancient tradition that the author chanced to hear or to read"; or are, frankly, "inventions, expressions of the desire to relate the terrible, the monstrous, or the incredible."[16] They have elicited the admiration of many contemporaries in the field. Graham Greene, wrote, "[Her stories evoke] perfect evil walking the world where perfect good can never walk again."[17] Her most fervent admirer, Edward Wagenknecht pronounced her "one of our best writers of stories of the supernatural."[18] Aside from her ability to scare the wits out of the reader, however, Michael Sadleir and Jessica Amanda Salmonson single out a special quality that is as difficult to describe as it is cherished in its effect. It is a quality that transcends the genre: "[Her stories] possess a further element," writes Sadleir, "to which the old-time Terror writer did not aspire. Under the bitter fascinated realization of love turned to loathing, under the relentless evocation of gloom, decay, and tarnished grandeur, Marjorie Bowen has a capacity for anguished pity. Even in her most venomous conflicts … she seldom fails to sound a note of compassion."[19] Salmonson agrees, declaring that these "supernatural romances" transcend the mere excitation of dread; rather, they give "evidence that even at our lowest and meanest, there is something of merit and beauty in the transience and suffering of human existence…."[20]

We find her ghostly short stories and novels scattered among the thickets and bram-

M.R. James

bles of the vast output of her otherwise historical, social, and biographical works. Surprisingly, only a handful of novels and little more than two dozen short stories—among the more than one hundred and fifty books and two hundred short stories collected in the twenty volumes published under her name—qualify as overtly supernatural. Others are of a marginal nature, more concerned with disturbing emotional and psychological states than spooks and phantoms. If it weren't for two relatively recent story anthologies, *Kecksies* (1976) and *Twilight* (1997), many of her most famous ghosts would be lost in obscurity, threatening to slip away from our notice, wraiths themselves, their frights diminished, their horrors blunted, their screams reduced to lonely sighs. Many more, however, are obscurely tucked away in other collections published during and after her lifetime. Inveterate collectors seeking these volumes are like those hapless "ghost-hunters" that stumble through the dim corridors of cable television programming ... watching and waiting, for a sign, a glimmer; in this case, scanning the notices in the collectors' catalogues.

For the record, by my count, the following short stories qualify as ghostly tales. This may seem an arbitrary selection, inasmuch as other stories linger at the outer fringes of the genre. Stories of witches and black magic are omitted here (see the chapter "Music on the Hill"). Those marked with an asterisk are described by Bowen as "anonymous" but are probably her own work.

I begin with that most agreeable and traditional of the ghostly tale, the "Christmas Ghosts."; "The Murder of Squire Langton" (*The Gorgeous Lovers*); "Breakdown" (*Kecksies*); "The Crown Derby Plate" (*The Last Bouquet*); "The Prescription" (*The Last Bouquet*); "Raw Material" (*The Last Bouquet)*; "Heliotrope" (*Grace Latouche*); "Marwood's Ghost Story" (*Grace Latouche*); "A Stranger Knocked" (*The Fireside Book of Yuletide Tales*)

Other titles (in no particular order) include: Vigil" (*Twilight*); "The Sign-Painter and the Crystal Fishes" (*Curious Happenings*);"The Bishop of Hell" (*The Gorgeous Lovers*);"Florence Flannery" (*The Gorgeous Lovers*); "Dark Ann" (*Dark Ann*); "Accident" (*Dark Ann*); "A Persistent Woman" (*Dark Ann*); "The Last Bouquet" (*The Last Bouquet*); "Kecksies" (*The Last Bouquet*); "Madame Spitfire" (*The Last Bouquet*);"The Avenging of Ann Leete" (*The Last Bouquet*); "Red Champagne" (*The Knot Garden*); "Miss Lucy's Two Visitors" (*Grace Latouche*); "Sheep's Head and Babylon" (*Sheep's Head and Babylon*);"The Housekeeper" (*Crimes of Old London*);"The Blue Glove" (*The Pleasant Husband*);"The House by the Poppy Field" (*Kecksies*);"One Remained Behind" (*Kecksies*); "Nightmare" (*The Night Side*); *"The Ghost of a Head" (*Great Tales of Horror*);"The Grey Chamber" (*Great Tales of Horror*); *"The Dead Bride" (*Great Tales of Horror*);*"The Skull" (*Great Tales of Horror*);*"The Fatal Hour" (*More Great Tales of Horror*)* "The Sutor of Selkirk" (*More Great Tales of Horror*)

Note: For details about these stories, see the chapter on Bowen's short stories, "Curious Happenings," which places them in the contexts of their original first appearances.

THE NOVELS

Marjorie Bowen's ghostly novels have received little critical attention. Those titles examined here are, on the one hand, those of a traditional cast and effect—*The Veil'd Delight, The Spectral Bride, The Devil Snar'd, The Crime of Laura Sarelle,* and *The Fourth Chamber*—and others are of that distinctly "transcendental" quality described earlier by

Michael Sadleir and Salmonson—"*Five Winds,*" *No Way Home, The Sacked City, The Man with the Scales*. This latter group presents challenges to readers impatient for shock tactics and antic spooks. All of them together, moreover, compared to the brevity and concentration of the short stories, have complex plots, extended casts of characters, and a wealth of landscape and architectural detail that demand close attention and concentration. Their pacing, typically, is generally moderate, beginning at a measured tread, accumulating interest and pacing along the way, until hurling the narrative across the finishing line. Rarely do they pander to superficial melodrama or careworn ghostly tropes; rather, Bowen is concerned primarily with issues of identity among the living and the dead—and the consequences of their transgressions. In sum, as Edward Wagenknecht as observed, writing in the *New York Times*, they are "hair-raising fables with a hard, cool dry, intelligent, unsentimental detachment that never seems 'old-fashioned' to present day readers."[21]

The Veil'd Delight

"Perhaps she had never existed at all
and was but the creation of his starved fantasy"

The Veil'd Delight carefully walks the balance beam between the real and the ghostly, material manifestations and psychological projections. In its hints of telepathy, astral projection, magic mirrors, and necrophilia, it is Bowen's most unabashedly romantic ghost story. It is proof positive, as we shall see, that the mere excitation of dread is not always Bowen's agenda. Henry Darrell has lately come as a soldier from the field of war and now lives an isolated life in a "broken world." He is emotionally vulnerable, isolated, lost to the world. He cherishes a little, tarnished mirror he keeps with him. Of late, he seems to perceive in the glass a "veil'd delight," a woman of "scarcely shape or countenance" who may not really be there "but merely a phantom, created by his under-nourished body and too-active brain" (17–18). Is she a memory, "some face seen, perhaps in his childhood," or someone he had seen in his delirium during the war? "Perhaps she had never existed at all and was but the creation of his starved fantasy" (17–19). When he comes to Criffel Hall to tutor the children of Sir Thomas Brodie, he encounters seventeen-year-old Harriet, who, he is told, "is dull and stupid, not quite right in the head." But he is instantly on his guard. He senses "'something half-remembered' about her" (57). Although she is betrothed to another, his fascination with her grows apace. In a scene, delicately suffused with love, frustration, and erotic lust, he yields to temptation to gaze into the mirror while Harriet sleeps in another room. "Is it you, Harriet? Why don't you come" Preternaturally sensitive to every sight, sound, and smell around him, he hears a tap at the door. It is Harriet Brodie. "The dull, overcast expression which disfigured her delicate features by day was gone; she held her head high and smiled, 'See, I have come.'" She lightly enters the room, feet scarcely touching the floor. "He thought for a moment that she really was a disembodied spirit, there was something so ethereal about her delicacy, the quickness of her movement, that uptilted face, the long hands, the pale smooth hair" (143). There is a touch of the charnel house in her aspect:

> He thought how slight a chance she remained on earth. The harsh wind, a sudden shock, too fierce a sun, some hazard of illness, and she would be gone forever from him to rest with her mother in the monstrous brick tomb in the little wood where the dead leaves of the oak trees must even now be beaten down by transient gusts of rain on to the wet walls of the mausoleum [144].

He resists a sudden urge to take her in his arms. She moves back to the door. Was it real, or was it a dream? "Is this love?" he asks himself. "Or is this something more?" Perhaps he can summon her anytime he wants. "How do I know that she has not seen me in her mirror, as I, before God, saw her in mine?" (145). Or he could smash the glass and remove the temptation. If not, "Would he still possess that power over her, even when she was another man's wife?" (161). After several complicating intrigues involving Harriet's jealous older sister, Darrell leaves the house, convinced Harriet is lost to him. Finally, after months pass, he yields to temptation and sinks to his knees before the mirror. "And there was [Harriet's] face, distinct *behind his own* [italics mine], only faintly blurred." He rose and turned to find her standing behind him. Again, the moment smacks of the charnel house: She is splashed in mud and rain and dead leaves, "but a radiance of delight shone in her eyes, her cheeks, and on the dewy lustre of her rounded lips" (245) She says, "Didn't we make an appointment long ago?" Is she real? "He saw that there was an undulating light half over her figure; she seemed at once to waver and shine" (245).

The Spectral Bride

"It has risen again from its ashes. That would be all I should want"[22]

Two scenes from *The Spectral Bride* reveal two of Bowen's prevailing interests in her ghostly tales—occult practices and alchemical experiments. Regarding the occult, she is both wry and incredulous; toward alchemy, she displays an impressive historical grasp of the subject.

James Daintry, the last in the family line, is afflicted by "hideous tales" of a vengeful "spectral bride," or "fetch." She is named Harriet Bond. She had been murdered by his ancestor a century ago. She is now reaching out to claim him. Alarmed, Daintry attends a séance in the attempt to communicate with her. He is warned by a friend that "to concern himself in what might be glibly termed spiritualism might be perilous and that some who had tried to evoke the spirits of the dead at formal séances had lost their reason..." (115).

What transpires is a horrific experience for Daintry. The scene is the major set piece of the novel. Limited space here, however, permits me only a few excerpts:

Visualize a room in Bayswater: The candle light is dimmed. Participants sit in a row and grasp hands. The medium lapses into a trance. After a few minutes, James begins to feel slightly giddy and his senses begin to swim...

> The forms of the room, the lines of the floor and the ceiling became less distinct, and there was a faint buzzing, like running water, in his ears.... Then he heard, like so many claps of thunder, loud raps that came from the table as if violent blows had been struck there by an invisible hand. He saw his companions in slightly distorted shapes; they appeared a long way off like figures viewed through the wrong end of a telescope. The medium seemed to rise in her chair to the height of several inches from the ground.... Meanwhile the room had become blurred as if a thick mist of an equal density was obscuring it.... Sparks of light rose from the table to the ceiling and falling on the table struck it with audible sounds.... One of these lights condensed into the form of a hand, and this time it was small, delicate, white and rested on his sleeve; beautifully formed and dimpled, with a caressing motion it parted his cuff then placed between his fingers a sprig that seemed to be composed of small, dark-green spiked leaves and bright star-like flowers.... Then from the middle of the smooth and glimmering surface of the table that now had an icy appearance, as if it was extremely cold and made of rock-like substance, there rose the figure of a woman from the waist, clearly seen, of a comely shape but heavily-built, with bright hair plaited back behind her ears, a green sash under her full bosom.

James calls out "Harriet Bond, will you tell me what your desire is with me?" And the figure replies: "You have been away too long" To which the narration adds: "The ordinary words were spoken in a dreadful tone of voice that was like the feeble shrilling of a sick child and yet had something of the harsh notes of an old woman." The wraith disappears. "The whole room whirled round into circles that, spinning one around the other, made centre-point of an exceeding brilliance that after a second absorbed the whole of the young man's vision and seemed to burst into a complete brightness that was followed by a complete dark" (121–124).

He revives to find none of the others at the table had neither heard nor seen anything. Nothing in the room is disordered. Someone at the table murmurs, "I do not think that we need fear this evil.... I believe that [this devil] has no existence except as a distorted, deformed, and monstrous interpretation of the evil in each individual. And when I say evil, I mean everything in opposition to wisdom, goodness, and love. I know there are those who think that spiritualism is a satanic agency, but I cannot agree" (119).

Unconvinced, Daintry resorts to a second attempt to contact the spirit of Harriet Bond, albeit a most unusual one. He consults a friend, Abraham Steel, who is conducting experiments in *palinganesia*. This peculiar practice was based on an idea first put forward in a book published in 1650. Drawn from Greek mythological concepts of rebirth and recreation, it had been practiced by the seventeenth-century alchemist, Sir Kenelm Digby. He and others "possessed vases which contained ashes of plants," which were subjected to a "gentle flame." The original forms of those plants were thus resurrected:

> A small obscure cloud was first observed which then took on a faint form and showed a rose, or whatever plant or flower the ashes consisted of.... All are agreed, sir, that when a body dies its form or figure still resides in its ashes. I then went deeper into the subject and found that many of my predecessors, including the famous Sir Kenelm Digby, had practiced this art of bringing back the forms of plants from their ashes, and he had said that we may suppose that the earthly husk remains in a retort while the volatile essence ascends like a spirit, perfect in form, but void of substance [242].[23]

Daintry is intrigued: "The perfect signature, that might be so with *human* bodies?" To which Steel replies: "The line of thought is confused and uncertain. We make *experiments*. You know that when gas was first discovered it was supposed to be a ghost. There is a great deal that lies beyond our comprehension."

Daintry persists:

> Suppose we tried the human body or what is left of a human body ... supposing we took some corpse from the church-yard.... I say, supposing we obtained what was left of a corpse, perhaps only a few frail bones, and you reduced them to ashes and then treated them as you will treat the heliotrope, we might see *her* as she really was. That might decide whether the apparition and this woman who so often crosses my path really is Harriet Bond.

But Steel rejects the idea: "[What if] the wraith did appear, what use would it be? No more than your Bayswater spectre. It wouldn't speak or explain itself. The recalled rose has no colour, no light, no radiance—it is at first but a dim cloud and afterwards but a vague shape." James shrugs. He thinks he knows where the bones of Harriet Bond are interred: "It has risen again from its ashes. That would be all I should want" (246–247).

Before James Daintry can carry out his plan, events overwhelm him. At Harriet's burial ground, where he intends to excavate her bones, he meets a woman, Caroline Fenton, who has been blackmailing him. He mistakes her for Harriet. Seized by an impulse—

He raised the pick and struck her. She fell down and then rose. He struck again—five times. And now Caroline Fenton, slipping into the long empty grave where once the body of Harriet Bond had lain, did not rise again [314].

The Devil Snar'd

"It's the devil in ourselves we've got to snare"

Not only is the novel thoroughly layered with incident and subplots, it also serves as Bowen's own meta-textual commentary on her own practices as a writer. It can be regarded as a "literary haunting," rather in the manner of Henry James, whose characters in "Sir Dominick Ferrand" and "The Real Right Thing" are haunted by manuscripts. As such, *The Devil Snar'd* is a compound of text and meta-text and, to quote her words cited earlier, an intersection of "hallucination and spectre," and "delusions of delirium and the projections of an over-excited imagination." I have pared down its complex plot to its essentials:

At the heart of the story is one of Bowen's favorite gothic tropes—the punishment awaiting the transgressor. Fueling the tale is a wood carving which depicts a grotesque fiend advancing on an innocent victim. But the victim has turned about and now "snares" its persecutor. Grace and Philip are those figures, confronting each other in a "dance of death," which, as we will see, ends tragically when the prey becomes the predator. It's a question of which is which—and when. As one of the characters in the story remarks, "It's the devil in ourselves we've got to snare" (154).

Grace Fielding and her husband Philip have just come to Medlar's Farm, in Northumberland. It's far off the high road, and the nearest village is well away from the closest motor-coach route. There is neither electricity nor telephone. The stress of Philip's affair with another woman, Angela Campion, has left him and Grace ill and exhausted. Now, determined to put all that behind them, they settle into their new home. Philip is a writer whose new book will be an attempt to break free of the commercial taint of the thrillers and murder mysteries that have made him a success. But there's something immediately disturbing about the place: A hundred years ago former occupants Hugh and Susanna Vavasour had lived and died here. There had been something troubling about their deaths, and their rooms are reputed to be haunted.

Grace, in the meantime, is unconvinced Philip's affair is over: "His surrender had not been so warm or so eager as to make her feel safe" (11). Over the ensuing weeks, she becomes aware of the house's bad reputation: Years ago a woman named Susanna Vavasour had been murdered by her adulterous husband. She may have been poisoned. Although her husband was acquitted of any crime, he also died soon thereafter under unexplained circumstances. Susanna is supposedly buried nearby in Crompton Old Church. Soon the site will be submerged by an ongoing waterworks excavation and the bones recovered. "[Susanna] said she'd never sleep till the Resurrection," reveals the maid; "and they are moving all the bodies before they drown the church" (42).

Details are murky. But—"[The house] has got a nasty name," Philip admits wryly, "No doubt, the worst haunted house in the North of England" (34). The housekeeper, Mrs. Mace, adds, "You see, ma'am, it's the *influence*, that's what is so bad. That's why Mrs. Holmes [former occupant] took the children away—the medium they had down here said it was dreadful, pure evil, and if anyone was a sensitive, as they call it, or ill, or in trouble, it would be very dangerous for them to come here—" (48). But Grace protests that is not her main concern:

> She was not frightened by ghosts; they belonged, in her opinion, to the dimmest realm of fairytale. She was not troubled by such remote terrors; she was completely absorbed in her own averted tragedy—was she quite sure that it was averted, or only held in abeyance? [16].

Grace is forty years old, with no talents, convinced no one could ever want her just for herself; that Philip had opportunistically married her for her money and for the tireless work she had put in promoting his career. His own success as a writer had come, finally, and now the greater share of money was his and she seemed now only an irrelevant impediment to him. Her thoughts clot and fester. She suspects that not only is Philip's affair continuing, but that she may now be an encumbrance to his plans.

Meanwhile, Philip, surrounded by the moods and objects in the house, is busily working on his new book. He seems increasingly under the sway of what is best described as a "literary ghost," a presence that seems to be *dictating* his manuscript, writing its own story, as it were, even *revealing* itself. He tells Grace:

> I feel certain—the stories, I mean, and the people as well—[are] all here, telling me everything. It is the most fascinating pursuit in the world. If I could only get materialization.... [Just yesterday] I was reading of *them* lost on the mountain, in the mist, and I did feel my feet wet, dripping from the long grass, and then, suddenly, there was a portion of a brocade sleeve near my chair. I could see the pattern, the threads of the material, the outline of the figure was being built up—then, nothing! [37].

When Grace finds an unfinished letter to Philip's former mistress, Angela, hinting at some nameless action Philip intends to take against her, Grace confronts him. It's a painful moment. Philip seems genuinely puzzled and confused. Shaken out of his daze, he is suddenly remorseful. He promises they will leave Medlar's Farm soon. She doesn't believe him, lapsing instead into a near hysterical soliloquy:

> Something is wrong—with me—with the house; everything is worse than it was in London. Is it possible that these dead people are really impressing me, influencing me, filling me with—despair? ... Why do I disbelieve everything he says? Take no comfort from his promises, his kindness? [43].

While searching for any more letters from Angela, she comes across Philip's unfinished manuscript. In a telling detail, she espies a spidery form crawling across the pages... The title page bears the title, in all caps: SUSANNA VAVASOUR. It is indeed about a murder a hundred years ago. She turns over the pages. She reads in horror about the as-yet-unnamed husband who is pursuing an affair and yearns to be away from his wife to freedom. There are references to "a simple, tasteless, odourless, colourless liquid—cyanide of potassium [that] he had procured..." (44–45).

Disturbed to the point of paranoia, she is convinced Philip's manuscript is, in effect, plotting her own murder. That must be why the coincidence of the Vavasour murder fascinates him: "Was [Philip] not violent, impulsive, abnormal, like all men with a touch of genius? Did not his work deal, however beautifully, with crimes, cruelties, and the darkest of border lands? Had she not herself often heard him excuse a murderer and declare that every human being was a potential criminal?" (47). Writing this story is not just all "play-acting": "No doubt he was trying to cloak himself in the personality of the dead murderer, to learn from him how to be rid of a jealous wife" (47).

The remoteness of the house and the bottle of "headache drops" she has found among his effects lend itself to his plan. Her mind reels crazily: She thinks to herself that her body would rot away in a cellar for years while Philip indulges his lust for Angela.

She is especially disturbed that Philip has applied his own name to the murderer in the manuscript. She doesn't believe Vavasour's name really was "Philip" that it was "Hugh." He explains: "As for the name, I don't know—yes, I did alter that. I like to call him Philip." She retorts: "Aren't you rather betraying yourself?" And he adds, in words that describe the strains and priorities of any writer's life (especially that of a writer like Marjorie Bowen): "In what way am I betraying myself, Grace? Everyone betrays himself in his work. You can't keep it out…" (90).

Grace retorts: "Don't you see? That is simply our own story that you are dwelling on? We ought not to let these dead people get hold of us like this. There's peril in it, isn't there? We should never have come to this house. It might make one do things" (72–78).

Now thoroughly alarmed, Grace visits the Crompton Old Church, where she sees a woman who resembles the portrait painting hanging in the house of Susanna Vavasour:

> [She wore] a tight-fitting bodice of a green that seemed of the very darkness of the yew trees; her face was colourless, neat featured, and a small quantity of pale hair was drawn away from a high, smooth brow.… The woman now appeared to be seated on the tombstone and looking fixedly at Mrs. Fielding, with the almost painful intensity of one who wishes to convey an important message and may not speak.

The vision wavers, "but, before it had entirely disappeared, Mrs. Fielding observed a large spider crossing the crumpled flesh of the bosom"—the same insect Grace had seen creeping across Philip's papers (58).

Grace has also taken to wearing a dark green dress she found in the house…

The rest of *The Devil Snar'd* is taken up with the escalation of Grace's hallucinations, Philip's increasingly suspicious behavior, and yes, the awful manuscript, which is growing, page by page…

Grace has an epiphany. What about that story that alleges Susanna was poisoned by her husband. Was Susanna really the victim? Maybe she died *after* her husband. "How odd [Grace muses to herself] that people should have thought that Susanna Vavasour was the victim. She must have been very clever—yet how did she contrive it, when she must have died first? Only I, who have known her since she was dead, really know her. To me she is not disguised" (103). Her death may have been suicide after poisoning her husband.

In a crucial scene, Philip and Grace fall into a discussion about the manuscript. This dialogue is not just about their relationship, but about a writer's empathy with his characters—and, indeed, perhaps Marjorie Bowen's own empathy with this novel called *The Devil Snar'd*. In other words, it's a *story conference* involving the characters and their author(s). Here is an excerpt:

> Philip insists: "Why shouldn't I write it? *It just came to me, there didn't seem to be any effort at all* [italics mine]. *Besides, I believe it to be true*. I think I've seen [Philip Lavasour]. Those descriptions of mine aren't faked. They're just like he looked to me.… It seemed to me he was about eight feet from the ground, but I couldn't get him from below the waist. He seemed to rise on a kind of vapour.… It seemed to me that it would be quite simple to just, as it were, project myself into his mind."
>
> Grace interjects: "I suppose, that's where you're stuck in your story. When it comes to getting into the murderer's mind and wondering how he could do it."
>
> He agrees: "I'm stuck there. You see, one mustn't be outside, one mustn't blame or condemn, or say how horrible, or how ghastly, or what an atrocious criminal—one has to be actually inside the man to see why he did it. There's a justification for everything, you know.… I felt that I could get his viewpoint, when he didn't feel that he was doing anything ill or horrible at all, only something necessary, like killing a noxious insect, a spider."

She tells him she has learned from an old engraving that Mr. Vavsour's name was not "Philip" but "Hugh."

Philip replies: "I don't quite know. It's an idea that came to me. It seemed to bring us closer together." (123) ... "You're getting overwrought, Grace.... The influence is too strong for both of us. Now we shan't be able to get away" [122–124]

At which point, Grace muses to herself that she can write the rest of the story for him. And she will stay on in the house until they "bring up the body of Susanna Vavasour.... I'd like to see what's left of her" (129).

And so it happens that Grace rises from her sleep later that night and goes directly to the library and takes up Philip's manuscript. She writes, "as if she is taking dictation":

> Susanna wasn't about to be murdered; she wasn't going to let the other woman have him. So she murdered him with the odourless white poison he had prepared for her and he died with that horrible swiftness that he had prepared for her. All unknowing, Vavasour's mistress came to the house determined to murder Susanna and sleep in the marital bed as the second wife. She ascends the stairs to Philip's room and finds him on the floor, writhing, his voice choked. He tells her he's been poisoned and that Susann has gone to the lake [139–140].

The next morning she meets Philip in his study, where he is sorting through his papers. But the pages upon which she had written are now only blank...

Events come swiftly to a close.

She slips a colorless liquid she has procured into his coffee cup. She leaves the house in her carriage. A woman in a dark-green dress sits beside her...

At this very moment, Angela is arriving at the house to tell Philip she has decided to give up the whole mess and leave him. He tells her in turn that he had never realized that bringing Grace to the house would create in her mind a parallel with the house's Vavasour backstory. She replies that she is afraid that Grace might have stolen from her a bottle of poison.

Angela and Philip hurry off to the lake where Grace is purported to have gone. Along the way, they pass a hearse, containing a collection of exhumed bones. Nearby on the grass is something in a dark-green dress. It is the lifeless form of Grace. She had been pulled out of the water.

As Philip gets out of the car, "he seemed to have lost the use of his limbs." He is paralyzed...." He loses consciousness.... "His last thoughts are of Medlar's Farm, "where a jealous woman in a dark green dress was restlessly walking up and down, in and out, searching for another companion" (157).

The Crime of Laura Sarelle

"Do you believe in dreams of the dead?"

Several of the standard Gothic tropes are alive and well in this novel, albeit illumined by an acute sensitivity to psychological states and a sensitive eye to atmosphere and detail. Is Laura Sarelle impelled to murder by her namesake of the century before, or, is she merely the victim of a delusion that robs her of her identity and impels her to repeat the crime. Not just Laura, but the world and the characters who surround her seem at times to transpire in a dream-like state, a world that is neither past nor present, real or imagined. As always, Bowen's masterful and evocative prose holds the reader in its own liminal thrall.

Like so many of Bowen's stories, *Laura Sarelle* is based on an actual eighteenth-century crime. Captain John Donellan had been executed for the fatal poisoning of his brother-in-law. The evidence was circumstantial, and he died without admitting his guilt.[24] Years before the publication of *Laura Sarelle*, Bowen had published a short story, "The Intruder," in *Fond Fancy* (1928), that likewise dealt with the past impinging upon and almost controlling the present.[25] "There is mounting horror in this book of the romance of Laura Sarelle and Lucius Delaunay, a young man of a noble house and no money," wrote critic and novelist Sally Benson, "There are many adjectives to describe this book … evil, sinister, ghostly, strange, baleful, terrible, relentless, sinister, and malevolent. But these words seem pallid."[26]

The time is 1840. Nineteen-year-old Laura Sarelle and her older brother, Sir Theodosius, inherit Leppard Hall, a gloomy old manor house, near which flows the river Avon. It's a drab, grey Palladian building, "which had a horrid air of looming larger and larger as you gazed at it till it filled the whole landscape" (137). The Sarelles have been there since the days of the Plantagenets. Her brother is a sickly tyrant who has absolute control of her destiny. He intercepts her letters and withholds her inheritance from her until she marries the man he chooses for her. Laura, who feels restricted within these walls, can only feebly protest her freedom, dimly aware of the realities of her limited agency as a woman:

> She had to play the game that women have learned during the ages to be so skillful at, to watch her opportunity, to cajole; if need be, to deceive. She was not yet very clever at any of these slavish arts … [5].

It should be noted at this point that in the dining room of Leppard Hall hang two portraits that greatly disturb Laura. One is of a woman in a gown of primrose silk, who holds in her hands a laurel spray. She is Laura's namesake, who died in 1784.[27] The other is her husband, Captain Avershaw. A grim history attends these paintings: Laura had murdered her brother, also named Theodosius, by poisoning him with the deadly essence of laurel leaves. She shifted the blame to her husband, an adventurer who had married her for her money. He was subsequently hanged. Now alone in the house, she died within the year and was interred in the church with the emblem of laurel leaves. Legend has it that her will had requested that Leppard Hall be razed and burnt to the ground. If her instructions were not carried out, she had warned, "I think that my successors may find themselves accursed" (123).

Meanwhile, back in the present Laura begins to act strangely. In dress and appearance, she presents a strange figure, described as if not Laura, but a *third* person:

> A tall, pale young woman stood in the doorway dressed in a gown of rubbed primrose silk with the palest of blue ribbons at the bosom, her hair powdered, her dark eyes shining with excitement and in her hand a spray of dark laurel. She was the exact likeness of the portrait in the dining room [56].

Indeed, her fascination with her namesake increases apace,

"Yes, I think I'm glad that, after all, I didn't have [the portrait] taken away," she says.

> There are other things of hers up there too, and I dare say that after a while I shall feel that I am in the past again and that I am the other Laura Sarelle.… I shall close my eyes and imagine what she was like and what she did. Perhaps her whole history will come back to me in a kind of trance, or dream [57–59].

Two men now enter her life. Harry Mostyn is a fortune hunter whom her brother seeks to impose upon her affections. The other is Lucius Delaney, the steward of the estate. He is struck by her beauty, but rather troubled:

Something was wrong, he did not know what, in that exquisite and frail femininity, holding the laurel bough; he seemed to see the symbol of something that was doomed and evil. He had an impression that this was really the other Laura Sarelle, that she returned to earth either to accomplish some desperate purpose or to avenge some desperate wrong [60].

Aware that love is growing between Laura and Lucius, Theodosius abruptly banishes Lucius from the estate.

Distraught and frustrated, Laura is spending time in the hidden closet where her namesake had experimented with distilling poison from laurel leaves that grow beneath her window. As if under running water, images of the world around her waver and blur. She seems to slip in and out her present identity and that of her namesake. Indeed, the whole house seems to waver between past and present. Laura's suitor, Harry Mostyn, while dining, is struck by what seems a hallucination:

[While] looking at the table with the filigree service and the rich appointments of silver, porcelain and glass, he had a sudden impression that he looked at a banquet that he been set for the dead, as if the table had been arranged thus for years, as if the wine and fruit had been kept intact, the china shining, the glass gleaming by some enchantment. He felt as if he peered through a window at another world [129].

The maid has this momentary impression of those around her:

Not in their faces so much as in their costumes, which seemed to slip and blur into the fashion of another day.... The candlelight was playing tricks, she was beginning to be infected with poor Laura's fancies. She moved abruptly and the scene seemed to shift into reality again ... [25].

And when Lucius looks at the painting of Laura Sarelle, he muses to himself: "One can imagine almost anything into a portrait. The eyes will seem to follow one, the lips change, the expression, too. It's a matter of light and shade" (29).

Now mad with love for the absent Lucius, Laura hatches a plan: She will marry Harry Mostyn solely in order to obtain her dowry and then run off with Lucius. She then contrives to poison Theodosius with a poisonous distillation of the laurel leaves and shifts the blame to her bewildered husband. Harry protests his innocence and is absolved of blame. He is convinced she is insane, and he says to himself: "I suppose she will have to be put away" (235).

When Lucius returns to the scene, he is startled by her behavior. She tells him to wait for her, that they can be together after Harry is hanged. Harry and Lucius, now allies, realize Laura must be taken away. Disoriented now, lost, she appears to them in the twilight, a pathetic figure in a clumsily-wrought yellow dress—a duplicate of the dress her namesake had worn—and tells them: "I have run away. I shall hide for a while. They are telling lies about me." She turns to Lucius: "You should not be here. I was going to write to you—but I forgot. You should not be here until Harry is hanged. Then I shall be rich and free" (254).

She runs off. They see her, "a pale figure that like a petal before the breeze hastened towards the grey river hidden behind the sedgy banks" (254).

The last lines of the book are chilling in their simple horror: Harry has hurried after her, but returns, sick and exhausted, a witness to a ghostly sight:

I feel ill. Have you any brandy? I don't know what I am saying. Let her go! I had to let *them* go—there were two of them [255].

The Fourth Chamber

*"What do you suppose happened in the
fourth chamber on the night of April 20?"*

A profound unease attends *The Fourth Chamber*, a greater disquiet than we have felt before. The dead reaching out to impact, or even control the living is a disturbing enough proposition, to be sure. But there are no such shivers here. Rather, a liminality in character and subject, in the living and the dead, elicits a confusion over identity. Any discussion of *The Fourth Chamber* necessarily involves a few other of Bowen's stories that so far have eluded discussion. I refer to four other novels, *"Five Winds," The Sacked City, No Way Home,* and *The Man with the Scales*. Neither, like *The Fourth Chamber*, could be considered a "ghost story" in any traditional sense. They are of a kin with certain of the works of Bowen's contemporaries, Henry James and Edith Wharton, that in their reach that eludes their grasp.

To begin, I'm not even sure if *The Fourth Chamber* is a ghost story at all. It has the trappings of one, to be sure: A mysterious murder in a secret tower room, a company of characters touched with the supernatural, a protagonist haunted by his ghostly double, and a ghost that periodically visits the scene. Indeed, Olivier Decorchemont may be either a living ghost or a dead man. He seems both, by turns—or simultaneously. He's not sure. And neither are we. By story's end, he is a homeless victim of treachery, dispossessed of family, shorn of his noble lineage, despised by the populace. Even though he has escaped a murder plot, everyone thinks he is dead. A witch with "second sight" thinks he is dead. He thinks he is dead. *We* are almost convinced he is dead.

What, indeed, happened that night in the fourth chamber? Is there a supernatural element here? Can there be *two* narratives here, running parallel—one in which Olivier was murdered, and one in which he is a living man? The implication may very well be that both propositions *are interchangeable*.

France, 1694. Olivier Decorchemont lives in his comfortable manor house du Plessis-Doray. He's a 25-year-old bachelor whose mother died two years before, and who's advised by his aunt and godmother, Madame de Bournon, to marry and extend the family line that went back to the 11th century. He occupies one of the two towers—one round, one square—that are a distinctive feature of the house. His square tower has a "fourth chamber" that is his special den, where he keeps a cache of gold under lock and key.

At the outset, Olivier and his world are seen in a kind of half light. The surrounding woodland of du Plessis-Doray is said to be haunted by spectres and goblins, "by serpents guarding hidden treasures, by whispers of old and terrible stories" (13). "Magic and superstition seem to infect everyone and everything. Wealthy, handsome, yet curiously detached from the reality around him, Oliver himself possesses a tendency to dream, to ponder on fantastic themes, to ride with loose bridle in the forest, or to wander there on foot" (9). The villagers are suspicious of him: "Olivier Decorchemont had, indeed, charms of person wasted in his rural manor, and that unnameable splendor that had some hint of darkness in it, for all his blond colouring and sunburnt glow, his good-natured air that at times appeared stupid" (13). The village witch, Mère Baffier, shares in these views: "He was marked from his birth, he is not like other—his eyes, his hair show it" (18). And there is a servant, Marguerite, who purportedly possesses second sight. She will play an important role in the story.

Madame Bournon warns him his feckless ways will bring him disaster: "You must marry, spend some money on the manor house, entertain, take a house in Chateauroux for the winter, and live according to your rank" (6).

At length, Olivier agrees to M. Bournon's advice and marries. Madame de Duclair is a widow who had borne two sons, both of which had died in infancy. He finds her, at first, humble, sprightly, and properly submissive. No sooner have they married and moved into du Plessis-Doray, however, than she shows her true colors. Literally. Her preference for yellow dresses alarms the citizenry. The village has a superstition about the color yellow. The peasantry believes it is "the colour of bile, of jealousy, of the Sulphur of Hell... [moreover] the yellow broom plant is believed used by witches to fly through the air.

The servant, Marguerite, who claims to have second sight, confides to Olivier's half-brother, Rene, her worries about the new bride—which from now on the novel refers to as "Macée": "She has the eyes of a wild beast," warns Marguerite; "—flaunting in her accursed yellow gown—do you not see ... that his evil demon comes to lodge with him?" (25).

It's only a matter of time before Macée drops her submissive manner, adopts a cold and imperious attitude toward her husband, discards Olivier's personal things, behaves rudely to the servants, especially Marguerite, and greedily regards Olivier's favorite "fourth chamber," where she believes he keeps his hidden wealth. Worse, she invites a stranger into this house, a priest named Brother Etienne. All we know about him at the present is the rumor that he had taken vows after disgracing himself in civil life.

In a hurry to quit this domestic nightmare, Olivier becomes a soldier and temporarily turns the household over to Macée and Brother Etienne. Only the faithful Marguerite laments his going. She gives him for protection a golden Roman coin engraved with the name of "Philippe Risse." By the time he returns, bearing the scars of several battles, he scarcely recognizes his own home. Brother Etienne advises Olivier to leave altogether and turn over his affairs to him and Macée. Oliver is so disgusted he's all to ready to comply. He leaves again, once and for all, with Macée's departing words in his ears: "I can have no objection. Our marriage is no more than a legal tie, and I for my part am prepared to resign myself to a life of retirement and piety" (75). He turns over the keys to the fourth chamber. Big mistake. Marguerite, mysterious as always, comes to him with fears for his future: "You are in constant danger, but who can speak to one so unsuspecting? I should not be credited" (77).

Indeed, he barely eludes several mysterious attempts on his life.

The scene changes. It is now 1701. A man in peasant farmer's attire arrives in the village. He confides to the disbelieving Rene he is his brother Olivier: Having narrowly escaped death at the hands of ruffians, he had been rescued by a widowed farm woman, Philomena, and been taken into her household. He fell in love with Philomena, married her, invented a backstory for her, and assumed the name on the Roman coin around his neck—"Philippe Risse." He has been happy with her and is now returned only to claim the cache of gold that is hidden in the tower room. He declares he will switch identities, resume his soldier's uniform and appear to Macee and Etienne as Oliver De Courchemont and demand his money. No one need know anything of the farmer named Philippe Risse.

Back at the estate, his appearance throws everyone into a panic. His money is gone. Macée and Etienne had thought to have contrived his death. "I am no longer your fool," he accuses them, "you squander my estates, you rob me, even of the gold in my peculiar chamber.... I was in your way, you planned to be rid of me" (113–114). But his threats to go to a local lawyer falter when he realizes that in doing so he leave himself open to charges of bigamy: "In a blunder of passion he stepped into a hideous tangle; he raged to think that two inexorable enemies were under his own roof, basely plotting against him, and cursed himself for having lost all circumspection in dealing with the situation" (117).

Olivier disappears again. His sword and clothes remain behind. Sounds of violence emanate from the fourth chamber. Blood stains cover the room, the walls, the bed sheets. Investigations lead to the arrest of Macée and Etienne. Marguerite steps forth and gives a chilling account of witnessing his murder at the hands of Macée and Etienne:

> The Dame held a dark lantern, the Prior stood over Messire, who lay across the bed, with the clothes stripped off, blood came from his side ... [the victim] struggled up, and she took a knife she had in her right hand and struck him twice in the side—saying: 'This is the only way to silence those who know too much.' ... Then, by the moonlight, they took up Messire's body and many of the bloody sheets and his shirt and carried him away ... while the Dame mopped up the blood with sheets and the coverlets and then went down after them [141–142].

Macée is subsequently seen in the courtyard below, washing the sheets. And an unidentified corpse is subsequently found in the nearby meadow.

Abruptly, another scene change—

The man called Philippe Risse is back at the farm of Philomena. A policeman is seeking the fugitive Olivier de Courchmont. He tells Philippe that Macée and Etienne have been arrested on suspicion of the murder of Olivier. A body was found but its identity has been unknown. Philippe goes to Philomena and confesses his bigamy. Rigid in her moral outrage, Philomena rejects him and orders him to leave the house. Dazed and confused, he returns to the village and gives himself up to the magistrate. He dons his military uniform, but no one believes he is Olivier. They are convinced that "Olivier" died at the hands of assassins, that this stranger must be Philippe Risse or, more strangely, the "ghost" of the dead Olivier!

By now, an already strange narrative has acquired a weirdly comic tone. Under torture, Macée and Etienne both confess they had indeed murdered Olivier. The body found in the field is now positively identified as de Courchmont. Two ruffians confessed they had been hired to murder him. When the ever-faithful Marguerite sees him, face to face, she protests: "You cannot be Messire, for I saw him murdered.... I can only repeat what I told M. Bonnet at the du Plessis-Doray.... You are an imposter. I loved Messire. Now he is dead I can say so.... God would not allow me to be so deceived. Have I not *proved* my tale?" (208–209). And the lawyers consider that the prisoner might be Philippe Risse, unsettled in his wits, accusing himself of bigamy through a craving for notoriety, an adventurer of dubious character who was neither Philippe Risse or M. Decorchemont, who had married Philomene for the sake of her farm, tired of her and taken this opportunity pose as a noble, hoping to be pardoned the bigamy for his heroic revelation of himself and, in the end, to "claim the du Plessis-Doray estates" (191).

So persuasive is all this that the reader—this reader, at least—wonders if indeed Olivier had been murdered, after all, and we have been following a ghost! Delicious. Even the man who is now calling himself Olivier begins to doubt his own senses. In his dream one night he encounters his double:

> The darkness was still thick about him and his senses were bewildered so that he believed he was on his bed in the fourth chamber at du Plessis-Doray; he sat up and listened, expecting to hear footsteps on the stairs; there were none, but the opening of the door was visible by the blurred light it allowed

to fall into the dark room.... M. Decorchemont was gazing at his own spectre, that looked at him with staring eyes full of appeal.... The apparition grew taller, so that the bleeding wounds were drawn out like the pale red ribbons that fastened Olivier's travelling cloak, and the dead face wavered like a mask.... "So. I should have looked if they had murdered me. This is a messenger from Hell, warning me to give myself up." M. Decorchemont sighed heavily, for this spectre had, he thought, come as a sign of the Devil's impatience to be at the soul of an impenitent sinner ... [182].

Confusions, dreams, identity transfers are running amuck: "Now, he wondered if he were not indeed the spectre he had seen last night and had not in truth been butchered by Macée and the Prior; his mind, ever given to fantasy, trembled before this ghastly supposition..." (188).

And so, off to prison, where he lingers for a year and a half while awaiting a court procedure to sort out who is who, and whether or not there was a murder, and what was the relationship between Macée and Etienne. He is registered as "M. l'Inconnu," [M. Unknown], a title "to which he soon became accustomed" (189).

The scene changes. The year is 1703. Nine years since this story began. A trial is considering the case for and against Olivier as Philippe, or Philippe as Olivier Bowen. Detailed testimonies conflict. If he is Philippe, Macée and Etienne are guilty of the murder of Oliver; if he is Oliver, he is guilty of bigamy and faces severe punishment. It is declared, at one point: "If he is an imposter he is an even more remarkable personage than M. Decorchemont" (231). As for Marguerite, she is in prison, too, still protesting her testimony. And Philomene? She refuses to recognize this man as Philippe and is content to righteously protest that she has been living in sin.

At length the verdict is in: Olivier is who he says he is. Charges of his bigamy will be lessened. Macée and Etienne are absolved of guilt. Marguerite is judged to be a perjurer and condemned to public flogging and humiliation. Philomene leaves with her children. In a heartbreaking aside, he bids them farewell: "He kissed his unheeding children, and went away, leaving a legend behind" (255).

All this man now pronounced to be Olivier can do is stand by Marguerite during her punishment in the village square. To the end, she insists Olivier's ghost attends her: "She believed that the spirit of her late master had been sent to support her in her agony as a reward for her persistent, if useless efforts to secure the punishment of his murderers" (232). Out of prison, dressed in shabby clothing, worn and out of date, Oliver scarcely seems to himself a living person: "Am I then to be for the rest of my life regarded as a ghost?" (236).

And one night, while he slept—"He saw his own phantom again, with the bright locks, the blood-stained shirt and the gold on the breast" (249).

Olivier's house is now boarded up and empty. The Fourth Chamber is locked. However—"At each full moon the shivering peasant who dared to pass that haunted way saw the Dame [Macée] washing bloody sheets at the trough in the courtyard" (255).

Epilogue. A curious sight greets the villagers one day. Macée and the priest Etienne quit the village in a hurry: "As if the Devil had snatched them away, leaving goblets full of wine untouched on the table in the manor house parlour; some peasants laboring in the fields declared they had looked up to see a coach swinging past, with a dwarfish coachman on the box, and the pace of the horses such that it seemed some infernal hand must be guiding them to Hell" (253).

Space limitations here prohibit a synopsis that more fully describes *The Fourth Chamber*'s wealth of detail, secondary characters and plot complications.

From Within: Bowen's Precursors to the Postmodern Novel

> *Our Phantasie ... intrudes a thousand fears, suspicions, chimeras on us ... so many things are offensive to us, not of themselves, but out of our corrupt judgment, jealousie, suspicion, and the like; we pull these mischiefs on our own heads* [157].
> —Robert Burton, *The Anatomy of Melancholy*, 1621[28]

The confusions of identity and the dislocations in time and space in *The Fourth Chamber* point to a number of Bowen's novels that contest even further the conventions of the ghost story. "*Five Winds,*" *No Way Home*, *The Sacked City*, and *The Man with the Scales* are populated by characters that seem to lose their moorings in maze-like worlds. Long before anybody decided there was something called the "postmodern" novel, Bowen is at work, playing with magic realism, elliptical narratives, temporal dislocations, displaced narrative arcs, dark irony, and unreliable narrators. Bowen herself wrote that some of her stories "are released from the confines of time and space and move ... in a world as indefinite and elastic as that of a dream; they are dateless...."[29] Moreover, ghosts emanate from within, not intrude from without. In that regard, writes Jessica Amanda Salmonson, Bowen surpasses the more conventional ghosting of a writer like M.R. James: "[James] was too healthy in outlook to grasp how Darkness reaches *outward* from within, rather than intruding from the outside [italics mine] ... never letting the reader forget that she and we are each of us as much the perpetrators as the victims of inexplicable urges and activities"[30] As we have seen, Olivier de Courchemont, in *The Fourth Chamber*, is haunted, in effect, by himself. Maybe the novels that follow here, are not ghost stories at all. Yet, do we not linger on the threshold, unsure...?

"*Five Winds,*" *No Way Home*, *The Sacked City*, and *The Man with the Scales* have all the charm and deadly irony of the entertainments they frequently evoke—machinations of the puppet show, the masks of the Harlequinade, and the illusions of the magic box. The living and the dead dance on a vaudeville stage. Reality and fantasy conjoin and are lost in each other. The character of Julius Sales, in *The Man with the Scales*, speaks for the existential dilemma of all the characters: "*I have inherited some curious story, and I do not know what part I am to play in it*" [italics added] (63).

"Five Winds"

We begin with one of Bowen's most Jamesian tales. "*Five Winds*" has already been discussed in the "Music on the Hill" chapter in terms of its Pagan elements. Here, we turn to its protagonist, Denis Burgoyne, and the part he plays in the hauntings of the titular mansion.

Young Burgoyne stumbles into an identity crisis when he inherits the titular family estate. As had happened with Laura Sarelle, who succumbs to the influence of her ghostly namesake, the burden of Burgoyne's ancestry weighs heavily on him. During the weeks he has come to the house, he seems scarcely himself anymore, "hardly conscious of the externals of present life," as if he "stood on the segment of a circle and might be as likely to go backwards as forwards, to meet the so-called dead as well as the so-called unborn or the so-called living" (25). He begins to hear footsteps in the rooms. He follows them. He pauses before doors, then opens them. Nothing. He mounts the stairs to the footfalls overhead.

He had left his own door ajar, and he watched the beam of fluttering candlelight and listened to the footsteps that came from behind it; a panic terror that was beyond fear held him rigid. He had not the strength to open the door. The footsteps continued—they sounded like those of a person walking up and down in deep distress or agitation, and were accompanied by deep breaths or sighs.... Nothing there but shadows" [259].

He is haunting his own house.

"*I might have known*," he mutters to himself, "*that sometime some one would find me in this house*" [italics added] (260).

What is it—*or who?*—he has found inside his own house?

The answer comes when the woman who has come to take him away from this place stands below the windows and looks up at his window—

> Burgoyne was looking down from one of the windows of the great bedroom.... He seemed one with the spirit of the building. There was a menace in his face, like the menace in the grim of the sightless masks, and an ironic smile on his lips like the irony of the empty house that had been so superb and pompous and was not settling to a long decay.... He looked less like himself and more like his ancestors.... It was the countenance, not of one man, but of a whole breed, an entire race. Not one Denis Burgoyne looked down at her with that sardonic, compassionate glance, but a whole family of Burgoyne ... [277–278].

Who is he, now? A man? A ghost? Both? Either way, in his confusion he seems to achieve a transcendent moment: "He might for the first time have found sanity; he might be in torment or might be in ecstasy" (284).

The following three novels from Bowen's post-war years, barely a few years before her death in 1952, carry this existential dilemma even further.

No Way Home

This novel depicts a Europe torn apart during the aftermath of the French Revolution. Bowen provides a cryptic introductory note: "All life," the old play has it, "is but a wandering to find home, and when we're gone, we're there."[31] Citizens, soldiers, statesmen alike are everywhere strangers; refugees claim no place in the world and struggle just to survive:

> [There were] people who had been driven from country to country during the long European wars, who now had no longer any thought of home, and who picked up their livings as best they might and with no great nicety.... Many of them were refugees.... Some were deserters from the one-time conquering army of the French and the one-time conquering navy of the British.... They preyed upon one another.... The death bell tolled incessantly [175–176].

Time seems at a standstill, "neither past nor future existed ... the present was dim" (70). The action sprawls across southern Germany, Sicily, and England. Few people use their own names, and many wear masks as if they are participants in a puppet theater. Amid this "comedy of travelers" are two principal protagonists: M. Florio is a Jamesian observer, a dreamer, who distances himself from the lives he contrives to influence; and M. Calamy is a hero straight out of Joseph Conrad, fleeing from the humiliation and guilt of mysterious past transgressions.

They all are in ghostly exile from a world that is no longer recognizable.

It all ends in a last masquerade of deception and murder during a game of chance in a London gaming table.

Significantly, Bowen wrote *No Way Home* during the years immediately after World

War II. She had survived under the shadow of the Blitz, uncertain of the fate of her three sons away at war in Japan, Germany, and North Africa. It was a time when "Home," for all of them, was nowhere to be found.

THE SACKED CITY AND THE MAN WITH THE SCALES

Here we encounter another arena beyond space and time. The main events have transpired before the story opens. We are left, like the characters, to sort things out and make sense of dimly perceived story fragments and images. Romilly Darrell, late of Stockholm, arrives by ship at a remote island in the Baltic, where he seeks sanctuary with his cousin, Klara Linderoth. Immediately we sense the very *strangeness* of the place: All around him an overabundance of exotic flora in a region so far north hints at some fertile power on the island. And overhead, "There was no sky, only a steady, limitless radiance" (5). In the island's past a violent invasion had sacked the city, leaving it at the mercy of the ghosts of its pre–Christian Norse and Scandinavian past. In Romilly's past is a murdered brother and guilts that have driven him away from home. He is like the walled city, remote, lost, enclosed within himself. Ahead of him lies suspicion, even hostility from the villagers who resent the disruption he brings with him. But there is also the promise of love and redemption, although he first has to discard the distortions of his obsessions and dreams—the wall of egotism, in effect—that have confined him like the walls that encircle the city. Only in the denial of self can he find a release from the oppressive reality around him. "We human beings cannot endure too much reality," Klara advises him. "Leave that to the trolls" (247).

Compared to *The Man with the Scales*, the foregoing novels are childish scrawls. Edward Wagenknecht's pronouncement that *The Man with the Scales* is a "difficult" novel is a thumping understatement. Here is a baffling tale of a death that may or not have been a murder, and a subsequent trial verdict that is neither guilty nor innocent. Martin Deverent is the son of the accused murderer and lives in exile. Julius Sales is the son of the dead man and lives comfortably in his vast estate. They live in a region simply referred to as Border Country, a land of "sad enchantment." Here, "there lived a kelpie in the stream ... who had accounted for the death of many travelers," who had been seen on land, "with great splay hooves and a thick mane of green colour, feeding with the herds." Nearby is a hillock "given over to the fairies," where "a girl in a white dress and a green bonnet waited to lure any youths who might carefully pass by. She would take them in a chariot, traveling at sixty-miles an hour to Ireland, and they would never be seen again, though the lady would return alone to the hillock, waiting for other victims" (157).

Julius and Martin are bound in a symbiosis of shared guilt and innocence. And both are trapped in a narrative, fugitives dodging fantastic dreams and prosaic realities. Intervening in their lives are two mysterious figures: The manipulative Baron Kiss is a Mephistophelian puppeteer plucking at their strings. He comes and goes, peeping in and out of the narrative, changing his names, by turns a Field Marshall in medals and plumes and a poor charlatan in tacky rags. Seeming to hover above it all is the magisterial Dr. Jerome Entrick, the titular "Man with the Scales." Julius is told he is "one of the signs of the Zoiak [the ninth astrological sign whose symbol is the Archer]—or the dreadful Sagittary" (78). He is assured Entrick will see "justice done" (78). Julius's servant, Maryon, explains, further: "Dr. Entrick spoke of the Three Fates, she who spins, she who guides, she who cuts the thread ... and how all three might be disguised in a single person [who] moves according to his own whim" (205).

Meanwhile, the narrative trots along in non-linear fashion as time and space are fractured and double back on themselves. It's a Commedia dell'arte funhouse, where characters pop in and out of the narrative, appearing and disappearing in a wink; where windows and doors open onto seascapes and vaudeville theaters; where Christians and Pagans dance in a vaudeville theater; and where present and past and future tenses are entirely conditional. At one point, pauses to check the time: "Chimes were striking; two different clocks clashed the quarter-hour together yet not exactly in unison" (17–18). Some of the characters are transparent—you can see through them. Literally.

"I have inherited some curious story," moans Julius, "and I do not know what part I am to play in it" (63).

Maybe the whole thing is an invention of the wicked Baron. In the end, do Julius and Martin find a resolution, or at least a separate peace? Only the Man with the Scales knows for sure ... and he's not telling.

Marjorie Bowen's last novel was published posthumously two years after her death. Which is entirely fitting, somehow. If the whole thing seems to be a ghost of a narrative, we might go further and proclaim it *the ghost of a ghost story*. It belongs in the company of the nightmares of G.K. Chesterton, the parables of her beloved George MacDonald, and the fairy tales of E.T.A. Hoffmann. "The line that divides dream from reality, fiction from fact," writes Hoffmann scholar, Ronald Taylor, in words that perfectly describe *The Man with the Scales*, "has been obliterated; the products of the imagination have the same validity as the facts of empirical experience, and the essential dualism in the shadow of which man lives out his existence—the conflict of body and spirit, of the finite and the eternal—is brought to an imaginary, and therefore false resolution."[32]

The real miracle is that *The Man with the Scales* never lapses into incoherence. It compels us in the way a dream sweeps us past the obstructions of reason and logic. Like the other books in this group, as Jessica Amanda Salmonson observes, the ghost is *within*. We are as much the perpetrators as the victims: "Darkness reaches outward from within, rather than intruding from the outside."[33] Bowen shares with us her pity and anguish about these existential dilemmas, notes Michael Sadleir: "Even in her most venomous conflicts between unforgiving jealousies or cheated ambitions, she seldom fails to sound a note of compassion."[34]

I leave here Romilly Darrell, Harriet Brodie, Grace Fielding, Susanna Vavasour, Laura Sarelle, James Daintry, Harriet Bond, Olivier de Courchemont, Julius Sales—and the other characters, living and dead, to their own devices. Only for the moment. Writing in 1938, Bowen confessed, "I am still absorbed in my own world of make-believe. I shall never tell all the tales, describe all the scenes and fantasies that possess me. I sometimes wonder how many will be untold when I am dead. And I regret the dear dreams that will die with me...."[35] When the end came, fourteen years later, she did indeed leave behind those ghosts she knew and the ghosts she had yet to meet.

FOUR

"Curious Happenings": The Short Stories[1]

Men taste the brittleness of success, the women the limits of beauty; all, men and women, pursue each other in vain, hoping to clasp the long-lost, the perfect lover, and always embrace delusion.... They believe in nothing save their own secret and endless disappointment.—Marjorie Bowen[2]

"The Accident" is one of Marjorie Bowen's briefest tales:

> Murchison was amazed at the speed with which he escaped from the flaming car, across the common, for he could now see the red blaze on the lonely road in the distance: they were fools to quarrel, he and Bargrave, and send the cursed vehicle over like that; he had not ceased running since he had felt the first shock of the released fire from the wreckage.
>
> He wondered why they had argued: the fright had seared his memory; but he certainly knew he loathed Bargrave; the landscape was oddly dim, like the dimness of an eclipse.
>
> Murchison, still fleeing, suddenly saw Bargrave in front of him, also hurrying—an attenuated, grey wisp of a Bargrave, blown thin by the forlorn breeze.
>
> Murchison yelled in triumph:
>
> "So you were killed, you silly fool!"
>
> "Do you think that you're alive?" jeered the ghost of Bargrave, then Murchison knew that he also had no body and that the red flames were not the blaze of the burning car but the light of their future destination.[3]

Brief, pungent, a sharp snap at the end, and not a word wasted ... a superb example of Bowen's mastery of the conte cruel.

Throughout her lifetime, Marjorie Bowen was a very busy writer, indeed. In addition to her many book-length novels, historical romances, and social commentaries, she published more than an estimated 250 short stories in a variety of British and American and Canadian magazines bearing familiar names like *Argosy, Harper's Monthly Magazine, The Strand, The Pall Mall Magazine, Hutchinson's Story Magazine, The Story-Teller. Ellery Queen's Mystery Magazine*; and less familiar names like *The Passing Show, Britannia and Eve, Maclean's, Colour, The Grand Magazine, The 20-Story Magazine*, and *The Regent Magazine*. In her lifetime, they were collected in twenty volumes, from *God's Playthings* in 1912 to *The Bishop of Hell* in 1949. Others appear in posthumous collections; and many others remain unprinted since their magazine appearances.

By contrast to the plot density, expansive scope, and measured pacing of her novels, these stories are relatively brief and to the point. To be sure, they share with them their pungency and variety of moods and subjects. They are preoccupied, as are all her works, with "the inexplicable course of human emotions and passions."[4] They are like pen-and-ink sketches as contrasted with the broader watercolors and oils of the novels. This is not to say that each doesn't reveal a careful craftsmanship that demands close attention. They do. They belong to the best traditions of the sharp and piquant "conte cruel." Virginia Woolf's definition is singularly apt, particularly when applied to Bowen's work:

> [They are] always showing us some affectation, pose, insincerity. Some woman has got into a false relation; some man has been perverted by the inhumanity of his circumstances. The soul is ill; the soul is cured; the soul is not cured. Those are the emphatic points.... Nothing is solved, we feel; nothing is rightly held together. On the other hand, the method which at first seemed so casual, inconclusive, and occupied with trifles, now appears the result of an exquisitely original and fastidious taste, choosing boldly, arranging infallibly, and controlled by an honesty for which we can find no match, save among the Russians...[5]

The rewards are many. Only in the comprehensive overview that follows, the stories chronologically and contextually arranged, can her achievement be fully assessed.

In addition to the subjects we have come to expect—pagan creatures, witches, ghosts, and alchemists—there are many more that explore the nooks and crannies of historical subjects and personages, from the Middle Ages, to the Hundred Years War, to the Kings and False Prophets of the Netherlands, France, and England in the seventeenth and eighteenth centuries. Others dissect the betrayals of contemporary love and marriage; provide autobiographical glimpses of her personal and professional life; evoke the philosophy of Lucretius; and amuse with lyric and gentle whimsies arts and artists—such as the music of Handel and Nicola Porpora, the Jacobin and Pantomime Theater of John Webster and Mezzetin, and the paintings of Tiepolo and Watteau. Taken together, it is not too presumptuous to suggest that this colossal achievement is nothing less than Bowen's own *La Comédie humaine*. I can think of none of Bowen's contemporaries who can boast such an extensive, learned, and varied output.[6]

Marjorie Bowen and the Conte Cruel

Mention of the tradition of the conte cruel, to which Bowen displays such mastery, demands a brief digression. Brief, tart, edgy, contes cruels are "warning shots" across the bow of our pretensions, self-delusions, and preoccupations:

> Grandmadam often told this story, as a relish of past follies and a warning of those to come, in the way the old have, enjoying the remembrance of what they would warn you against.[7]

Always has the mode of the "cruel tale" been with us. Bowen finds a particularly tasty example in the pages of a nineteenth-century issue of *Lady's Magazine,* of all places:

> Alexander, being now entirely at liberty (and coming into 700 pounds a year), determined to travel into foreign countries, and in a letter to Amasia, informed her of his design; the reading of this had such an effect on her that she was found hanging in her chamber.[8]

But we can look back further. As early as Chaucer's *Canterbury Tales* we find in "The Pardoner's Tale" a prototype: During the time of the Plague, three thieves are determined to seek out and slay "the faithless traitor, Death." They are directed by an old man to a nearby tree, where they find at its roots a goodly treasure of "golden florins, minted fine and round." They celebrate their good fortune. One of the men goes to town to fetch food and wine while the other two stand guard by the treasure. They plot to stab him to death upon his return. The first thief, in the meantime, "put in his head that he should buy poison wherewith to make his two companions die." He returns with the poisoned wine. The two thieves kill him before he can administer the wine. After that, they drink the poisoned wine and expire after horrible sufferings. Indeed, they have found Death— in the heap of gold. Quoth the Poet:

> Thus died these murderers of whom I tell,
> And he who falsely poisoned them as well.[9]

"That is a good story," says an admiring G.K. Chesterton, "and contains a grim crescendo of dramatic action." Moreover, he adds, "This element of mere pleasure in narrative must be allowed for...."[10]

This "element of mere pleasure" is at the heart of the dark irony of the conte cruel. It speaks to a great paradox, that in pain and cruelty reside a certain satisfaction, even pleasure; that the line separating a gleeful cruelty from an outright sadism is thin indeed.[11]

The degree to which wit, grue and gore are combined is variable. At one extreme is the *grand guignol,* which critic John Clute describes as "affect horror," referring to the experience of the visceral affect, or "the atrocity of the thing itself."[12] At the other extreme is the brittle social satire, the Balsacian "human comedy," where the pretensions of manners and morals are rudely punctured, and the veil of a romantic ideal is ruthlessly ripped away.

The roll call of practitioners, to which Bowen assumes her rightful place, is distinguished. Nineteenth-century American masters include the names of Washington Irving, Edgar Allan Poe, Ambrose Bierce, and Bret Harte. Inheriting their precedent, yet expanding their achievement at home and abroad are modern masters Villiers de l'Isle-Adam, Guy de Maupassant, Maurice Level, Saki, John Collier, Fredric Brown, Lewis Padgett, Richard Matheson, Roald Dahl. Beginning in the 1940s radio and television brought many of these stories to popular audiences via series such as *Lights Out!, Tales of Tomorrow, The Twilight Zone,* and *Alfred Hitchcock Presents.*

A few of the most celebrated modern practitioners are selected here for brief comment. They provide a measure against which to regard Bowen's own achievement. In writing about the conte cruel, H.P. Lovecraft in *Supernatural Horror in Literature* cited the work of Villiers de l'Isle-Adam as the inheritor and master of the form:

> "Villiers de l'Isle Adam followed the macabre school; his *Torture by Hope,* the tale of a stake-condemned prisoner permitted to escape in order to suffer the pangs of recapture, [is] held by some to constitute the most harrowing short story in literature. This type, however, is less a part of the weird tradition than a class peculiar to itself—the so-called *conte cruel,* in which the wrenching of the emotions is accomplished through dramatic tantalizations, frustrations, and gruesome physical horrors."[13]

Easily his equal in horrific stories was the French master of the form, Guy de Maupassant. Suffering in later years from a damaged mind and body, he turned from the satiric and frivolous sketches of his public life to his "desperate unhappiness and inner world of morbidity and terror," as revealed in late stories like "The Horla" and "Who Knows?" Appearing in the last years of life before his death in 1893, these are pages, that, according to scholar Arnold Kellett, "contain some of the finest descriptions ever penned of what it is like to be scared to death."[14]

The new century ushered in many notable writers who specialized in the conte cruel. "Saki" (1870–1916) was perhaps the most playfully nasty of these masters. Hector Hugh Munro derived the persona of "Saki, the Cup Bearer," from Omar Khayyam. Saki was both the messenger of "joyful errands" and the "Angel of the Darker Drink." In yet two more pseudonymous personae, "Reginald" and "Clovis Sangrail," Munro further distilled his spite and malice. No one, wrote critic Christopher Morley, has better described the unique achievement of the delicately satiric ("The Open Window") to the heartlessly cruel ("The Interlopers" and "Sredni Vashtar"): "Delicate, airy, lucid, precise, with the inconspicuous agility of perfect style, he can pass into the uncanny, the tragic, into mocking fairy-tales grimmer than Grimm."[15]

Max Beerbohm (1872–1956) was not as prolific in his sardonic short stories, yet two tales, "Enoch Soames" and "The Crime" reign supreme in their blending of the sardonic with a more savage cynicism. Of this ambivalence, he wrote: "Life—even such part of it as our limited human brains can conceive—is a very weird, august, complex, and elusive affair. Any single dogmatic point of view, any coherent 'message,' is an act of impertinence." Yet, no matter how fantastic the event, there must be a wise insight of human behavior: "All the greatest fantastic art postulates the power to see things, unerringly, as they are."[16]

Lord Dunsany (Edward John Moreton Drax Plunkett, 1878–1957) was the supreme fantasist of this group, and his creation of an entire cosmogony, complete with a pantheon of ethereal but balefully powerful gods displays, notes S.T. Joshi, the influence of Graeco-Roman mythology. But it is with the six volumes of stories chronicled by Dunsany's immortal spokesmen, that immortal wanderer and teller of tall tales, Joseph Jorkens, and the travelling salesman named Smethers, in which we find the true conte cruel. Sometimes only a few pages in length, they encompass social satire, science fiction, and detective fiction that, in the words of Joshi, "reveal a wry, owlish humour that constitutes a virtual parody of the 'gods and men' scenarios that had enraptured his early readers."[17] No conte cruel has ever more cruelly—or more startlingly—concluded with the closing words of "The Two Bottles of Relish," which explain the fate of a missing corpse.

John Collier (1901–1980) was the most cosmopolitan and urbane of these masters. His was a gentlemanly, world-weary cynicism. Even the most guignol of his stories, such as "Another American Tragedy," is expressed in an eighteenth-century style of elegance and wit. The felicity of his language is rivaled only by Saki and Beerbohm. Yet he faced the absurdity and the foulness of the world alike—be it atomic holocaust or domestic carnage. As he wrote in 1933, "There seems to me a definite bias in human nature towards ill, towards the immediate convenience, the ugly, the cheap…. I rub my hands and say, 'Hurry up, you foulers of a good world, and destroy yourselves faster.'"[18]

Relatively unknown to American readers, Maurice Level (1875–1926) was applauded by H.P. Lovecraft: "As a matter of fact, the French genius is more naturally suited to this dark realism than to the suggestion of the unseen; since the latter process requires, for its best and most sympathetic development on a large scale, the inherent mysticism of the Northern mind."[19] More recently, S.T. Joshi has observed, "Without a wasted word, Level's tales progress from the first scene to the last in a manner that fully exhibits the conflict of emotions that is at their heart ... and reveal such an economy of means that nothing could be added to or extracted from them without destroying their very fabric."[20] Level's brief tales lent themselves readily to theatrical adaptation in the "thrillers" of the Grand Guignol. A particularly gruesome example is Level's "The Last Kiss," in which a mutilated man exacts his revenge on a faithless woman by pouring vitriol acid on her face during their embrace.

The gleeful subversions of societal pretensions in the best stories of Roald Dahl (1916–1990)—collected in the early volumes, *Someone Like You* and *Kiss Kiss*—all too soon morphed into a crude misogyny and sadism. But as Joyce Carol Oates observed of his contes cruels (and she should know), his best work is that of a "writer of macabre, blackly jocose tales that read, at their strongest, like artful variants of Grimm's fairy tales; Dahl is of that select society of ... satiric moralists who wield the English language like a surgical instrument to flay, dissect, and expose human folly." He knew himself and he knew his readers to be one and the same, in the words he puts into a female character in "My Lady Love, My Dove": "I'm a *nasty* person. And so are you—in a secret sort of way. That's why we get along together."[21]

Roald Dahl

Note: A common misunderstanding is that the so-called "surprise ending" is a prime feature of the conte cruel. The turn-of-the-century American writer, William Sydney Porter, better known as "O. Henry" (1862–1910) is most commonly blamed for what all too often was merely a cheap and contrived effect. "Any list of plot summaries," observed critic Eugene Current-Garcia, "would immediately show that most if not all of these surprise endings that O. Henry contrived were based on sheer coincidence, the plausibility of which is unacceptable to those who seek in fiction a reasonable reflection of events in actual life."[22] (138). Rather, the wicked jaws that snap shut at the end of these stories must reveal something that has been properly prepared for, but whose unexpected effect is more like a shock of recognition.

THE STORY COLLECTIONS

Love, death, betrayal, and the whole damned thing. They all are here in Marjorie Bowen's contes cruels. The first three collections, *God's Playthings* (1912), *Shadows of Yesterday*, and *Curious Happenings* (both 1917), may be considered together, inasmuch as all three contain primarily historical sketches and anecdotes. They were written during the ten years spanning the appearance in 1906 of her breakout novel, *The Viper of Florence* and the death of her first husband in 1916. The precocious teenager was rapidly developing into an assured professional writer. These were stressful times, as we know, for despite the passionate desire of this newly married mother for a tranquil domestic life, she was forced to write as the sole family provider under the duress of wartime conditions in England and Italy; years, moreover, during which much of her energies were expended in child rearing and the care for an invalid spouse. "Few or none of the tales I had in my head were pleasant," she confessed, "[but] often full of dark and sinister shades."[23] As fast as the Mirthless Cosmic Jester poured misery into her," observes Jessica Amanda Salmonson, "she made ink of bile to fill pages with dark visions, calamitous adventure, and cynical romances—tales populated by innocents and villains alike ill-fated."[24]

God's Playthings (1912)

Mortality hangs heavily over all the historical characters and incidents depicted in Bowen's first collection, *God's Playthings*. Contes cruels all, fate is unkind to the humbly born and the aristocratic, by circumstance or pretension. They are victims of betrayal and death, by guillotine, by hanging, by burning, by stabbing, by poisoning, etc. For example, James Crofts, The Duke of Monmouth (son of Charles II), failed rebel, hangs from the scaffold in "The King's Son"; Lucrezia Borgia, Duchesss d'Este, embittered and deathly ill, far from the notoriety of the Borgias, expires of ghastly old age in "Twilight," leaving behind "a ghostly apparition"; Philip Duke of Wharton, Jacobite rebel, flees his enemies in "A Poor Spanish Lodging"; Madame Du Barry, mistress of Louis XV, dies on the guillotine, in "Woman of the People"; Henriette-Ann d'Angleterre, Duchesse d'Orléans, sister-in-law to Louis XIV, fears the exposure of her many infidelities in "The Cup of Chicory Water"; the Marquis de Condorcet, French philosopher and mathematician, fails to escape from Robespierre and the Terror, in "The Aristocrat"; and Michael III, Emperor of the East, is assassinated in the year 866, in "The Macedonian Groom."

Cruel twists and turns mark these lives. In "The Aristocrat," when the philosopher Marie Jean Nicolas Caritat, the Marquis de Condorcet, peer of France, after enduring days of torture, takes a fatal dose of poison, he murmurs to himself, "*Someone bungled when the world was made*" (248). On November 3, 1793, as the blade of the guillotine separates Madame Du Barry's head from her neck—"She saw and smelt blood and slime; she felt herself being swung forward. She shrieked once—twice—and the knife descended, sending her common blood gushing over the other blood that stained the oak and iron" (224). And in a cruel twist at the end of "The Burning of the Vanities," Fra Girolamo (Savonarola) dreams that the public burning reveals a prophetic truth: "The Friar gazed up through the smoke and flame, and in the horrid blaze saw another figure dangle at the rope's end, then drop; again, in the instant's downward fall, he saw the face—livid and despairing This time it was his own" (198).

Several of these tales were later amplified into novels—"The Burning of the Vanities" is expanded and included in Chapter XIV of the novel, *Carnival of Florence*, published three years later; "A Camp Outside of Namur," about the last days of Don Juan of Austria, is included two years later in *A Knight of Spain*; and two stories about the Hundred Years War—"The Betrothed of Pedro el Justicar," about Jehanne Plantagenet, sister of Prince Edward of Wales and daughter of King Edward III; and "Defeat," about "Edward Plantagenet of Wales, Duke of Cornwall"—both appear in *The English Paragon* in 1930.

Shadows of Yesterday (1916)

Bowen's second story collection, *Shadows of Yesterday*, contains twelve more historical stories from England, France, Italy, and Spain in the seventeenth and eighteenth centuries. The conceit that loosely binds the stories together is that a "very small museum," found in "a back street of a little Italian town," contains "the toys and the trifles of art and antiquity" once "handled by living figures," that reveals the "back stories" of characters and artifacts from the Past: "If one could look, writes the unnamed Narrator...,":

> —beyond the dust, beyond the years to the time when all these dead things were fresh—when the originals of those portraits moved and worked and laughed, when beer was really brewed in those jugs and tea drunk from those cups;, when those cards were dashed on to the playing table, when that sword graced some gallant's thigh ... might not one find curious stories, sad stories, and gay stories attached to these old worthless objects?—as staring at ashes one may recall the flames [5].

Among them are two stories about the Argyll's Rising against James II in 1685 ("The Soul of Jeannie Duncan" and "Sophia Fielding"); and a savage indictment of religious bigotry against Morisco Christians in Spain ("The Half Brothers"). Conte cruels include a satire on greed ("Pearls"), love betrayed ("Candlelight" and "Camille Rochfort"), religious piety ("The Scarlet Cup") and "The Fair Hair of Ambrosine"), and a strange testament to love beyond the grave ("Petronilla of the Laurel Trees").

Herein is the first appearance of the oft-anthologized horror story, "The Fair Hair of Ambrosine," wherein a man's dreams of a slain former lover prefigure his own death. Another story, "Giuditta's Wedding Night," famously attracted the enthusiastic attention of Mark Twain. In eighteenth-century Venice a trap is set for the faithless Giuditta Frimaldi, who deserts her new husband for a nocturnal tryst with her lover. But the face and form revealed to her at the last moment is her lover's corpse—"his livid, mottle face showing the manner of his death. The plague" (81). By contrast to these two grim tales is the amusing "Sir Basil and Rue," a trifle suggestive of Roald Dahl. Lovely young Ruth Fairfax finds herself the object of a gambling bet between her betrothed, Sir Basil, and his rival, the ruthless Lord Muskerry. Desperate at his losses, Sir Basil offers Ruth as part of a wager against Muskerry's wealth. When Sir Basil loses, Ruth blithely deserts her betrothed and agrees to marry Muskerry. "My hand is yours," she announces; "you may be a devil, as I make no doubt you are, but you are not a coward or a fool" (34). As Muskerry slips a ring on her finger, he leers, "You and I together, madame, will make our way in the world" (34).

Curious Happenings (1917)

Curious Happenings, published a year later, is Bowen's first volume to scatter a few contemporary fictions and dark fantasies among the historical sketches. Perhaps the single oddest of Bowen's short stories appears here for the first time, "The Sign Painter and the Crystal Fishes." In its lurid color, grotesque aspect, and assortment of shape-shifting characters it resembles the nightmares of G.K. Chesterton. The first lines effectively set the scene:

> The house was built beside a river. In the evening the sun would lie reflected in the dark water, a stain of dirty red in between the thick shadows cast by the buildings. It was twilight now, and there was the long ripple of dull crimson, shifting as the water rippled sullenly between high houses [231].

Characters die violently, then rise again. A painter's studio is filled with images of "horrible and fantastic things—mandrakes, dragons, curious shells and plants, monsters, and distorted flowers" (231). A boat carries its passengers to an unknown destination, while a one-eyed gypsy plays faro and sings to her companion: "There is no tomorrow for such as you. You had your neck broken an hour ago.... Presently we will go home ... your deal" (249). "The Sign Painter and the Crystal Fishes" eludes easy classification. It haunts us long afterward, as it teases and baffles. It may lay claim to be Bowen's finest Gothic tale, although at least one commentator confesses his confusion: "It is dreamlike and packed with symbolism. But though its appeal to the imagination is powerful, I must confess that for me at least it is the one tale of its author whose meaning, if there is any, remains opaque.... It is a unique tale in her oeuvre."[25]

Other stories, in their variety, include a denunciation of war ("The Quack"); a lyric elegy of death ("A Venetian Evening"); and a series of bitter contes cruels, satires on love, death, and betrayal—"Failure," "Honour," "Belle Hutchinson," and "Folding Doors" (the latter a story of the consequences of infidelity set against the outbreak of the French Revolution). And then, standing by itself, is one of Bowen's cruelest stories, "The Pond." Its calm, objective prose quietly describes a young woman's deliberate drowning of her half-brother. She strokes the dead body: "It was strange that anything could die so easily; she tried to prop him up in a sitting position, to lift him to his feet; she thought of all the dead things she had seen, birds and rabbits, and tried to remember what they looked like" (24). Moments later, back in the house, she quietly considers her fate: "The big gallows on the London road suddenly became of interest to her" (25). Then she turns to the jam jar. Had censorship permitted, it would have made a particularly effective episode on Alfred Hitchcock's television series. It's interesting to note this story arises from an early childhood memory of her theft of a jar of jam, after which, by contrast to the child in the story, she felt a consuming guilt: "I left some sticky finger-marks on the high-polished surface; the crime was discovered, punished by an application of the hair-brush and being sent to bed in daylight. There I lay for hours in the pale pink sunshine streaming into that hideous room, thinking of the ghosts and devils that were marching overhead and who, no doubt would soon descend upon me."[26]

By contrast to "The Pond." "A Venetian Evening" displays Bowen sensitive, lyric gifts. A man says farewell to the Venetian life he knew before his family came to financial ruin. A ghostly form appears before him, a former servant girl. They spend their last night together as their gondola slips away into the night and oblivion:

> Now the open sea was all about them, and the stars were flung nearer, nearer like a veil; the waves were larger now and presently began to overwhelm them; the splashing sounded to them like the music of flutes and guitars, and the starlight seemed like the lights of the great Piazza in carnival time [266].

We will find more lyric evocations of the Italian twilight in the story collection, *Bagatelle*.

Crimes of Old London (1919)

The fourteen stories in *Crimes of Old London* contain a subset of stories collectively titled "'The Seven Deadly' Sins." These darkly pungent contes cruels are like stark and sharply-etched medieval woodcuts. Here is Bowen at her rowdiest and most cheerfully guignol. Witches and devils and sorceries abound; and taken together they prove to be a wickedly congenial bunch. They originally appeared in *Pall Mall Magazine*, December

1913–June 1914 and were beautifully illustrated with sketches executed in a medieval manner by "Phyllys Vere Campbell" (the author's sister). The illustrations were not retained in the stories' later appearance in the stand-alone volume, *The Seven Deadly Sins* (1926).

An old monk, Father Aloysius, sits by the fire on long winter evenings and relates parables to a group of novices. "They liked to listen to the holy stories the old monk told them, for there was always a good comforting moral and some matter of interest too, for he had been in the world once, and remembered it well enough, though he was now so far on the path to heaven" (175). Here are grotesque contes cruels in the manner of the later John Collier—fables about witchcraft ("Pride," "Wrath," "Avarice"); ghosts ("Envy"); anti–Christ ("Luxury"); guignol ("Gluttony"), and alchemy ("Sloth"). The latter is an amusing counterpart to the deadly seriousness of Bowen's novel, *I Dwelt in High Places*. "Wrath" is especially amusing. Two rival old hags, Ottilia and Trina, contend with another in an old medieval town. Caught in the crossfire of their spells is the hapless Sheriff: "Whatever hag he decided for, the other would destroy him with her spells; and the Sheriff saw no escape for it but to die miserably" (234). Meanwhile, as the chaos reaches a peak, suddenly, with a thunder-clap, the Devil himself appears:

> He was as tall as the cathedral; he had a tail that lashed over the house-tops, and his long hair shook in the sky like banners. So he puts one hoof in the market-place and glances down with his red eyes; then he takes up the two witches as a man might take up to hens and tucks them one under each arm; and off he goes over the houses—stride, stride, stride—and disappears with another clap of thunder [287].

Among the remaining stories is the horrific "Scoured Silk." The setting is London, 1733. Beneath the placid, scholarly manner of Humphrey Orford is a man who has abused his first wife and now, twenty years later, is set on marrying again. But his fiancée is alarmed at rumors that the man converses with the ghost of the first wife behind the doors of his chamber. One day, on the eve of the planned marriage, Orford is found, stabbed to death within his locked chamber. A tiny scrap of dress, wedged into a crack in the wall behind his desk, leads to the discovery of a hidden room—the dwelling place of the first wife, who because of an affair, had been imprisoned there and kept alive all these years, subject to the nightly tortures of her husband:

> She wore the ragged silk skirt, the end of which had been shut in the panel.... Her hair was grey and scanty, her face past any likeness to humanity, her body thin and dry.... [He had] fed her on scraps, letting her out only when the household was abed, amusing himself with her torture ... [while she sat cramped] in the almost complete dark, a few feet from where he wrote his elegant poetry [32].

Her revenge was deadly. A scarf knotted tightly around her throat revealed how she had finally died. She had never been able to cry aloud. Her tongue had been cut out.

There are contes cruels, of course, including a ghost story, "The Housekeeper," about a woman whose determination beyond the grave to set her husband's house in order drives him insane; and several mordant views of love, marriage and betrayal (usually in that order)—"Brent's Folly," "The Gilt Sedan Chair," and "A Quiet Woman." Rounding out the collection is a melodrama of masks and identity switches in the manner of Chesterton, "The Extraordinary Adventure of Mr. John Proudie."

The Pleasant Husband and Other Stories (1921)

This collection contains fifteen stories. Many of them continue the series of contes cruels that Bowen had begun in the preceding volume, social satires about men and women, husbands and wives, behaving badly. The outstanding entry here is the tender ghost story, "The Blue Glove." A potentially maudlin situation involving a mother mourning the recent loss of her baby is redeemed—even illumined—by a quietly intense sincerity and compassion. At the end, poor Mrs. Trevennick is hardly alive herself, almost a ghost, certainly "unraveled" in body and mind. (And we are reminded that Bowen herself lost her first child at just six months.) Among the best *conte cruels* are the title story, "The Pleasant Husband," with its nocturnal duel between a husband and his wife's lover; "My Lady Played," a grim conclusion to a night of excessive gambling; "The Story of Lady Fanshawe and Lucilla," a battle of wits among lovers who thought they could defy marital conventions; and "The Wages of Sin," a classic confrontation in the manner of a "city mouse"–"country mouse" fable. Two stories reflect one of Bowen's favorite themes, the clash between Christian and Pagan gods—"The King's Orchard" and "A Princess of Kent." And there are three sketches, mere anecdotes, couched in pastiches of archaic diction, "Knight Ogier le Dois and the Christ Child," "The Adventures of King Ban of Benoie," and "The Viking."

Seeing Life! and Other Stories (1923)

A rich variety of stories appears in *Seeing Life! and Other Stories* (1923). Two of the highlights reveal extremely contrasting natures. On the one hand, there is the amusing John Collier-esque "The World's Gear," a delightful satire on writers and writing (doubtless owing much to Bowen's own experiences in the commercial literary world). It reminds us of the delicious—and sometimes savage—sense of humor in which she occasionally indulged. On the other hand is "Decay," what Bowen enthusiast Jessica Amanda Salmonson describes as "her most wholeheartedly cynical statement about society's standard mores."[27] It stands at the topmost rung—or is it the lowest?—of her acrid portraits of marriages gone bad. Poet Cedric Halton and wealthy Jennifer Harden have been married for three years. They present to a visiting journalist what seems a perfect marriage: "[Jennifer] had just snatched [her husband] away from all that was ugly or crude or mean or distressing and lapped him in love and Beauty and Service" (70). Her love and caring pervades the rooms. She keeps their house, called "Enchantment," trim, ordered, and perfect in every way. But, strangely, Cedric looks "strained, aged, and thin" (70). He no longer writes. Jennifer's perfection is marred by a display of bad teeth. And there is the matter of the *smell* ... "so creeping, foetid," observes the narrator, "I thought of drains or even dead birds in the chimney.... I woke up in the night drenched with it, sick and shuddering with the horror of it ... potent as a live thing" (73). After hastily leaving the place, the narrator reflects on the marriage he has just witnessed. Nowhere in all of Bowen, do we find a more savage dissection of a marriage gone bad.:

> It was all dead, love, ambition, kindness, the souls themselves, shut in, stagnant; he sold for money, his comforts; she sold for her satisfied lusts, each exacting the price ... each *hating* the other—no children, nothing let in, nothing going on—putrid, rotten ... each caged and caught by the other—stinking themselves to Hell [74].[28]

Two of her oft-reprinted classic ghost stories make their first appearance here: "The Avenging of Ann Leete" and "Ann Mellor's Lover." They remind us how frequently her ghost stories depended so little on stock, gothic effects but deployed a more subtle and sensitive effect, in the tradition of the enigmas in Henry James and Edith Wharton. "Ann

Leete" begins with a mysterious painting of a woman in a green dress and concludes with her green-clad ghost returning to the lover she had left many years before. The whole scene is suffused in a rich autumnal light:

> Through the gloom I saw a dark-green silk gown, a woman's form, a pale hand beckoning. My impulse was to fly from the spot, but a happy sigh from my companion reproved my cowardice. I looked at the ancient man whose whole figure appeared lapped in warm light, and as the apparition of the woman moved into this glow, which seemed too glorious for the fading sunshine, I heard his last breath flow from his body with a glad cry (128). [Note: pagination from the story's reappearance in *The Last Bouquet*]

"Ann Mellor's Lover" also begins with a drawing of a mysterious woman which triggers a young man's search through time to find her. Bowen's ongoing ambition in her work to connect with the past is eloquently confessed in the young man's words:

> My peculiar affinity with the past has always been rather overwhelming—a kind of haunting preoccupation, wholly pleasant but teasing, like something you can't place or explain or reason about. It's a great diversion to me, a great interest, and sometimes a queer sort of pain, too (91). [Note: pagination from the story's reappearance in *Twilight*]

The story dabbles in clairvoyance, time travel, and dark revelations about the close ties between love and hate. It's not unlike one of Jack Finney's gently time-twisting stories, although it goes dark at the end.

Another time-travel story is a personal favorite, "The Proud Pomfret," in which a mild-mannered postman, while waiting for his train, is thrust backward in time at the eighteenth-century estate of Lord Pomfret, listening to a pagan chorus from Handel's oratorio, *Theodora*. Then, abruptly, he's back in the present, with only a "faded glow in his memory" of what *might* have happened.

Other stories include Bowen's fascination with Pagan mythologies, in this case the Welsh *Mabinogian*, in "He Made a Woman—." Here, the magician Gwydion creates from "blossoms of broom, of oak, of meadowsweet" the beauteous Blodeuwedd. She entrances a young writer, but when he tries to clutch at her green robe—"She vanished; there was a heavy coil of perfume in the air, and Charnock's thin hand grasped a spray of oak flower, a twig of broom, a cluster of meadowsweet" (220). Two longer tales involving astral projection and psychic transfers were probably intended later for novels: "The Tarnished Mirror," is a trial run for *The Veil'd Delight*; and "The Cabriolet" is an anthology of brief, linked stories spanning generations in its history of a family-owned carriage. (No novel ever appeared, although a 1956 Hollywood film, *The Solid Gold Cadillac* bears distinct similarities.)

Some of these contes cruels are bitterly cruel, indeed: "Hush" involves an imbecile child; and "White Hyacinths"—one of Bowen's great flower pieces—concludes with a devastating revelation involving a deformed woman. "Miss Moss" is a pathetic portrait of an old woman overwhelmed in her grief over a lost lover who, we learn, is very much alive. That's her secret: "He don't mind," she says; "he don't know—no one here don't know he's alive, and he don't know he's dead. Where's the harm?" (59). And "Green Garters" is about a painter who translates his hatred of women to his canvases: He admits he endeavors to depict "the ugliness, the wickedness of women throughout the age'" in images of women "tusked and taloned, armed and foul [whose] wings were not those of butterflies, but monstrous bats" (239). Roald Dahl's story, "Nunc Dimittis" might reveal its influence; and Bowen herself amplifies this kind of imagery in her novel, *"Five Winds."*

The Seven Deadly Sins (1926)

The Seven Deadly Sins reprints the subset of seven stories that had originally been collected in *Crimes of Old London*.

Dark Ann and Other Stories (1927)

All of the nineteen stories in *Dark Ann and Other Stories* are contemporary portraits of women entangled in damaging relationships and marriages. It is a fact that such conte cruels appear in greater profusion in these later short-story collections. Moreover, some of them bear a distinctly autobiographical stamp. These include "Dark Ann," one of her best ghost stories, whose female narrator, a writer, bursts into a startling declaration of love's opportunities lost in the last lines. "Expiation," one of Bowen's most personally moving tales, is told much in the manner of a Thomas Hardy rural idyll; and it, too, concludes with the sudden hammer blows of a personal confession by the female narrator. The brittle contes cruels of corrosive marriages include "Nocturne," a gossipy tale about an extramarital affair that ends in brutal violence; "The Truth about the Hobart Marriage," a hard-nosed portrait a la Arthur Schnitzler of erotic intrigues, whose protagonist admits to the narrator (Bowen herself?): "I suppose that I am the type the modern novelist would love to write about ... thirty-seven, unmarried, dissatisfied—pages would go to my complexes, inhibitions, and repressions—but I'm not conscious of feeling any of these things" (305–306); "Praeludium," perhaps reflective of Bowen's second marriage; "Un peu d'amour," involving the cruel betrayal of a middle-aged woman's fantasies; and the briefest (and choicest) of the lot, the afore-mentioned "Accident." Others are "Suitably Rewarded," "Night Blooming," "A Flower of Carnival," "Bright Petals," "Is it Genuine?," and "Suitably Rewarded." There's a flower piece, of course, the wistful "Petunia," whose concluding lines compare the doomed protagonist to the eponymous flower: "To watch her fine and rapid fading is like watching one of her petunia blooms when it has been unnaturally plucked and cast away—too swift a withering" (188). Two psychological portraits of women are particularly nasty in the Roald Dahl manner, "Mrs. Smith and Rose—" and "The Scapegoat." The latter indulges in a savage portrait of a frustrated middle-aged woman hopelessly in love with a reprobate painter. When she sees in his studio a painting by William Holman Hunt, "The Scapegoat," she compares the plight of the abandoned, starving goat depicted therein to herself: "She saw herself as Mallot would paint her, and her heart withered suddenly as her face had withered slowly." And she tells him, "You needn't paint my portrait, you've got it there" (284).

Exits and Farewells (1928)

This story collection reprints the historical sketches that appeared under slightly different titles earlier in *God's Playthings* (1912) as noted in the parentheses. One story from *God's Playthings* is omitted here, "Burning of the Vanities."

Bowen's prefatory remarks explains, "Some of these studies are essays in style, the result of avid reading of old books, pamphlets, documents and letters; when they were written, expression in this manner came easier to the author than it did in the idiom of the present day. On re-reading these attempts one finds no anachronisms; youthful industry and keen absorption of past mannerisms have produced a tolerable imitation of the originals" (9).

Some are in seventeenth-century diction; some are in the manner of a news sheet and preserve "the old use of capitals" (9); and one "is a purely fanciful attempt to see Byzantine splendor and horror through the eyes of a contemporary" ("Michael III, Emperor of the East") (9). Notes appear before each to contextualize the subjects and names.

Old Patch's Medley; or, A London Miscellany, Being Some Adventures of the Old Gentleman in London City Some Two Hundred Years ago or So, Here Recorded (1926)

Among the sixteen stories of *Old Patch's Medley* are several that are retitlings of stories from earlier volumes. "Harry St. John Lord Bolingbroke, and Two Ladies: Lincoln's Inn Fields, 1705" appeared as "Dorinda Dares" in *The Pleasant Husband*; "The Orford Mystery: Covent Garden, 1734," as "Scoured Silk" in *Crimes of Old London*; "The House Near Hampstead Heath: Hampstead, 1770," as "The Gilt Sedan Chair" in *Crimes of Old London*); "The Mystery of Dr. Francis Valletort: Soho, 1690," as "The Extraordinary Adventures of Mr. John Proudie" in *Crimes of Old London*; "The Discretion of Lady Dorcas: St. James's, 1718," as "The Mystery of Hannah Power: Drury Lane, 1696," as "Heartsease in *Crimes of Old London*"; "The Confession of Beau Sekforde: Holborn, 1710," as "The Housekeeper" in *Crimes of Old London*; "The Story of Belle Hutchinson: Spring Gardens, 1690," as "Belle Hutchinson" in *Curious Happenings*; "The Countess of Ellesmere Plays: Lincoln's Inn Fields, 1740," as "My Lady Played" in *The Pleasant Husband*; "The Mystery of the Umbrella-Mender: Hampstead, 1770," as "The Umbrella Mender" in *Curious Happenings*; and "The Return of the Soldier: Islington, 1742," as "The Quack" in *Curious Happenings*.

Five more stories—"The French Mantua-Maker: Lincoln's Inn Fields, 1795," "The Bookseller of St. James's: St. James's, 1780," "The Mystery of Lady Arabella Ware: Vauxhall, 1785," "The Queer Story of Charlotte Charke: Red Lion Square, 1735," and "The Marriage Contract of Eliza Adair: Queen's Square, 1750"—are currently unavailable for review.

Fond Fancy (1928)

These nineteen stories embrace a wide range of topics and styles. Touches of the supernatural are mostly absent here, except for the masterpiece of the set, "Beltarbet's Darlin": Catholic Ireland is rent with strife and rebellion against Protestant English conquerors. County Clare is the site of recent "risings." Two men, one Catholic (the deposed Irish patriot, Lord Beltarbet, a Prince of Clare) and one Protestant (the conquering Lord Maskell), contend for the ownership of a magnificent horse. At stake is Irish pride. Enveloping the action are references to Celtic folklore and the "Shee," the fairy folk, and their High King, Finvarra. The name of the horse in question, Diarmuid, refers to another figure in Irish folklore, a hero who had slain the great enchanted Boar of Benbulten. A decisive moment in the action transpires on a legendary hill in County Clare, where Finvarra had his castle and phantom warriors walk. It's an extraordinary performance.

Ghostly touches also pervade "Two-pence Only," a strange tale of an organ grinder possessing "an infernal immortality" paired with an ambitious writer who fails to find success. The latter perhaps represents Bowen's own rueful doubts about her career: "In trying to commercialize his talent, he had killed it. He had pleased neither the vulgar nor the elect by his essays, his articles; his verse that had never been gathered from the pages of magazines and newspapers" (179). "The Intruder" may be seen as the forerunner to Daphne du Maurier's *Rebecca*. Upon entering her husband's estate for the first time, newly married Ann Vereker is rebuffed by the perceived presence of his late first wife, whose portrait still hangs in a locked room. "She is still here," says Ann, "in this room. In this house. In the church. How she must laugh at me!" (287). Feeling her inferior, an intruder, Ann departs, as "the painted figure seemed to step from the frame and dominate both of them" (288).

Among the contes cruels are several mordant portraits of damaged marriages and satires on conventional wifely roles, "Rust," "The Gate," "Powder Blue," "Reasons for Failure," and "Les Fantoches." There is a grotesque caricature in "Rust" of a predatory woman, a writer of little talent, who outlasts several husbands, thriving like a vampire while they waste away. Bowen skewers her with a deadly thrust, indicting her as "a Guy de Maupassant diluted with toilet vinegar" (30). There are references to motion pictures in two stories, "The Careful Youth," with its pungent depiction of a crowded movie theater, the site of a failed romance; and "Would You Believe It? A Film Close-up," a hilarious tale pitting crass moviemakers against the virtues of the local vicar's daughter, a country lass who outsmarts their attempts to make her into a glamorous movie star. Finally, in "Les Fantoches" ("puppets"), Bowen devises the striking metaphor of a weathercock circling in the capricious wind to convey the doubts and hesitations of two lovers who, "after years of weary arguments, protests, miseries, debates" attempt a reconciliation (264). As they listen to the titular song, "Les Fantoches," one of the lovers realizes it suggests their mutual indecisions: "You know the weathercock figures that go round and round with every wind and never get anywhere? ... We have gone round and round so often, and never come up to it before.... Even now, perhaps, something might blow us—round away—" (265). And, indeed, so it does.

Fond Fancy book cover

Sheep's-Head and Babylon and Other Stories of Yesterday and To-Day (1929)

Here is another wildly varied roster of stories. A personal highlight is the title story, a delightfully folksy conte cruel, in Scottish dialect, which pits a sanctimonious cleric with the Powers of Darkness. Guess who loses?! The Rev. Zachary Barlas of Drumknockie Manse battles evil with his new book, *The Snares of Satan Exposed*. But one day his door opens to the sight of the lavish, forbidden pleasures of Babylon and a fair lass with a cloven foot. Back to the real world, he is shaken: "Auld Mahoun nearly had me that time," he confesses, "I was half-way home to his cauldron, nae doot" (9). But the girl returns in all her infernal aspect, transformed into a sheep's-head that grows arms that pull him down into the Pit. His body is later found, frozen stiff in the snows, the sheep's head in his arms. The servant pronounces his Satanic book was his downfall: "It's nae wonder that the douce man should gang queer in the head wi' a' that book making an' learning, but preserve us a'! Why should he tak' wi' him the heid o' the willie goat" (15).

Several more stories are likewise touched with fire. "The Necromancers" is an amusing battle of wits (and magic) between two rivals. Whose magic? Which is the Witch? "The Prescription" is one of her best Christmas stories, about a ghostly murderer forever seeking a doctor to reverse the deadly poison with which he had killed his wife. "Appointment with Stiffkey" is one of Bowen's strangest stories, where time and space seem fractured, the narrative sequence of two murders is confusing, and the identity of the killer is unclear. Indeed, there are hints that *all three of the characters* are ghosts! It teases and confounds much in the manner of a riddle by Robert Aickman. "Pat-A-Too" is a swashbuckling intrigue, a game of disguise and plot-counter-plot, all conducted right under the nose of a French king.

Bowen is at her cynical best in several contes cruels: In "A Posie for Fanchon" the twist is that a man and wife actually love each other—a decidedly unfashionable thing, and one that can do them irreparable damage to their social standing; "False Pretenses" has an O. Henry–like snap at the end as two women exchange coats, with comically disastrous consequences for them both; in "All the Same Price" a vain bachelor's marriage scheme is undone by a clever woman.

On a more serious note, a cruel irony underpins two stories of women, whose self-proclaimed lofty virtues and hardy ideals have dangerous consequences: "Crowd—with Flags" portrays a young lady whose stern and misguided sense of morality blocks her mother's chances for a second marriage. She is something of a monster: "She was, of course, often considered hard; virtue always seems hard to the feeble and uneasy; and it was that she was more in love with ideals than with humanity; there was something cold in her detachment from the trivial and the foolish, the fond and the sentimental" (187). "Mrs. Hopeton at the Flower Show" is a psychological study of a mother whose grotesquely possessive love for her son cannot survive her disillusionment with his philandering ways. Flowers are everywhere, as is so often the case in Bowen, and their "grotesque" abundance reflects her own excessive passion: "Too many flowers—flowers over everything.... Mrs. Hopeton felt overwhelmed by these endless blossoms.... Why were there so many kinds of flowers?" (275). At story's end, the air is tainted by their "dying perfumes"; like her ideals, they have wilted—"A universal decay after so much pride" (289).

The Gorgeous Lovers and Other Tales (1929)

The fourteen stories in *The Gorgeous Lovers and Other Tales* are mainly cautionary contes cruels with an antique touch: "*Grandmadam often told this story, as a relish of past follies and a warning of those to come, in the way the old have, enjoying the remembrance of what they would warn you against"* (102). And Bowen herself steps forward to observe, in her "Advertisement to the Reader":

> Half of these short tales, and certainly the most dramatic, are true tales, and told (which may make them appear unlikely happenings nowadays) in the mood and language of the times in which they occurred; the source of the others may be found in the sub-titles or in the atmosphere of the period chosen; none of them pretend to anything but an offer of entertainment or a possible change from things and people as they may chance to be at the present moment [vi].

They are divided, on the one hand, between anecdotal contes cruels of lovers and losers (usually at the same time!) set against historical settings and characters; and, on the other hand, some of her most celebrated dark fantasies. The historical pieces range from late seventeenth-Century Versailles ("A Panel from Versailles"), Revolutionary France ("Madelon—and all the Graces"), Renaissance Rome ("The Jewels of the Contessa Testanegra"), late 18th-century Venice ("Four Farewells in Venice"), Colonial America ("The Complete Lover"), and mid-19th century Cornwall ("Sea Piece"). There are cameo appearances by John Calvin, poet Clement Marot, and Cardinal Armand Jean Duplessis. And in one story, "Jasper Hilton's Comedy," the music of her beloved Handel plays an important role.

Three masterpieces of horror appear here for the first time and have been subsequently anthologized: "Florence Flannery," "The Bishop of Hell," and a Christmas Eve chiller, "The Murder of Squire Langton." They all had appeared in different versions in an earlier novel, *"Five Winds,"* and appear here as self-standing stories.

"Florence Flannery" is a decidedly creepy and complex tale that defies easy summary, involving a centuries-old curse, a horrifying, fish-like creature, and a grisly revenge.

The second story, "The Bishop of Hell" is the first story I read by Bowen. Its horrific ending remains with me to this day. Indeed, at the start, how could *any* reader resist the narrator's opening lines: *"This is the most awful story that I know; I feel constrained to write down the facts as they ever abide with me, praying, as I do so, a merciful God to pardon my small share therein..."* (127)? An ordained clergyman, Hector Greatrix, has fallen so low in life that his intimates in the gambling dens have dubbed him "The Bishop of Hell." While his cousin, Colonel William Buckley, is abroad as a soldier, Hector promptly seduces the man's wife and inducts her into his dissipated life. Upon his return to London, Buckley vows to kill Hector, who tries to avoid him. Meanwhile, in desperation to preserve a shred of legitimacy, the mistress unsuccessfully implores Buckley for a divorce so she can marry Hector. At length the two men meet and Hector is severely wounded and his jaw shattered. "Hell!" Hector declares, "as if I believed in Hell.... One goes out like a snuffed candle; just blackness, blackness, nothingness, nothingness" (143). But that is not the fate in store for him. A short while after Hector's death and burial, a man is founded, seated in the narrator's rooms. It is Hector. When he turns around, we see something as awful as anything in all of Bowen:

> His face was alight; where the visage should have been was a ripple of flames quivering upwards; and through this crimson veil of fire gleamed his infernal eyes with an expression of unutterable woe. The flames rose above his head, shaped into a peak, a double peak; he wore a flaming mitre glittering with lambent fires of green and blue like hellish jewels [151].

For all that, the real horror, the masterful touch, resides in the reference to "the unutterable woe" in the creature's eyes.

The third story, "The Murder of Squire Langton" is a Christmas Eve tale of a consuming guilt that robs a man of his sanity. Lord Falkland watches silently while two men are hanged for the murder of Squire Falkland. The victim was a coarse, abusive man whose villainy certainly deserved his fate; but Falkland, the actual perpetrator of the crime, had contrived evidence to throw the burden of guilt upon those innocent men. Falkland had been in love with a young lady who was the ward of Langton; but when one wild Christmas Eve she tried to escape him and the advances of his companions, Falkland fled the ugly scene. "I am a coward," he tells the narrator. "I crept home that night and let them do their will with her.... It was I who betrayed her" (297). He subsequently tracked down the Squire and stabbed him in the back. Since then, each Christmas Eve he has relived the horrors. Hearing this, narrator is alarmed. He now finds himself complicit with his friend's crime: "We live in dread and horror of one another," he says, "and that one day I shall be driven to denounce him, and he will guess; in some way, he will guess my intention, for he has me watched, and then I shall be destroyed" (299).

The English Paragon (1930)

Unique among Bowen's story volumes, *The English Paragon* is a collection of fifteen interconnected short stories about Edward Plantagenet and his father, King Edward III of England in the years from 1366 to 1371 of the Hundred Years War. Is it a novel or a loose confederation of short stories? In her Foreword, Bowen declares: "The present novel is not a biography or study of this famous Prince of Wales, but an impressionistic relation of the fatal Spanish campaign of 1366 and the subsequent revolt of Aquitaine in 1370, considered from many points of view" (9). Each story introduces a character, historical or fictional, who plays a major and/or an incidental role in the course of events— the mysterious moor, Nunreddin ("The White Cat of Seville"); Pope Urban V ("Flowers at Avignon"); the Free Company Captain, Bertrand Du Quesclin ("The Free Companies"); the young King of France, Charles de Valois ("New Loaves"); Queen Philippa, the mother of Prince Edward ("Little Boys"); the ill-fated Charles II of Navarre ("The Leper"); the Count of Armagnac ("The Pot of Green Ginger"); and Joan [here called Jeanette], wife of Prince Edward ("Constancia"). Events include the revolt of Don Enriquez of Transtamara against Don Pedro of Spain; the intervention of France, Aragon, Navarre, and the Pope in the quarrel which became the cause of the ruin of the English fortunes in France; and the renewal of the war between Charles V and Edward III.

The mode of the *conte cruel* is best exemplified in the amusing "New Loaves," in which a humble young apprentice baker goes to work for a passing stranger, who is revealed to be none other than the young Charles de Valois; and in the altogether more grim "The Leper," in which Charles II of Navarre fails to elude his awful fate. And Bowen at her most personal seems to confess her own travails as the mother of sons destined to go to war in the portrait of the Queen Philippa in "Little Boys."

See the chapter on "Painting History" for more details about this remarkable volume.

Grace Latouche and the Warringtons (1931)

In the mix of sixteen contemporary and historical stories in *Grace Latouche and the Warringtons* (1931) are a number of repeats as well as some new stories. Here we find the first appearance of the frequently anthologized "Kecksies" and several Christmas ghost stories—"The Crown Derby Plate," "Heliotrope," "Raw Materials," and "Marwood's Ghost Story."

"The Crown Derby Plate" has a delightfully gruesome quality to its ghosting. Only in a conte cruel would we find such oppositions working together in such entertaining fashion. Martha Pym has never seen a ghost but hopes to encounter one in the old Hartley Place, allegedly haunted by an antiquary, Sir James Sewell, who once possessed a prized collection of fine bone china. Instead, she only finds an old lady, Miss Lefain, presiding over Sewell's priceless collection. Although Miss Pym is desirous of obtaining one of the plates for her own collection, she leaves the place in great haste. She discovers that the place is really a charnal house inhabited by the ghostly Sir James himself, whom she had mistaken for an old woman. Years before, Sir James had frightened away the real Miss Lefain and is now guarding his precious collection of Crown Derby against other collectors. The fun is how Bowen cleverly lays out the clues to the ghostly presence in broad daylight, as it were—that the furniture is covered with sheets, that the "old woman" wears "shapeless apparel stained with earth," that "she" has to "frighten away" strangers looking for her china, etc. The comments, "I was taken out of myself some time now" and "I haven't felt the cold for a long time" acquire a comically grim significance. And it is in one of the closets that Miss Pym smells "something damp rotting somewhere" (141–142). The delicious subtleties and pathos of this lonely ghost rank the story with Edith Wharton's classic, "Miss Mary Pask."

"Raw Materials" is a light-hearted Christmas romp, a conte cruel featuring a most amiable ghost. Robert Linley is a storyteller in search of the "raw material" of new and novel ghost stories. "Ghosts? Yes, of course, I've had any amount of experiences with ghosts, with people who've seen 'em, and people who think they've seen 'em, and with ghosts themselves." And so, he recounts a ghost story that is not quite so "threadbare" (329): Spinster Ursula Beane had been living with her nephew James and niece Louisa Catchpole when she died of arsenic poisoning. No guilt had been assigned to the logical parties, the Catchpoles. Many years later, however, James Catchpole, now a dying man, confesses to Linley that he had indeed poisoned Ursula for her money. Ursula's ghost had returned, threatening to harass him unless he and his sister use the money to "have a good" time. And invite her along. And so they do, with her ghost accompanying them the whole time. "Why," he says, "I tell you we've given the old girl the good time she ought to have had years ago" (347). No regrets; hadn't Catchpole felt The Furies behind him? Not at all. But now the money is gone, he says, and his death is imminent. That night, Christmas Eve, narrator Linley relates a strange sight, of—

> a dreadful old woman creeping up the stairs with a look of intense enjoyment on her face—Miss Ursula Beane—not a doubt of it.... I saw her so clearly that I could have counted the stitches in the darns at the elbows of her black sleeves.... When I came up to the bedside, James Catchpole was dead, with an extremely self-satisfied, smug smile on his face [348].[29]

Bowen is having a good time with this, and it is rather suggestive of the ribaldry of Thorne Smith.

"Heliotrope" boasts a "flower ghost." Or, at least, the scent of one. One can readily imagine a painting by Paul Klee with the title, "Flower Ghost." Bowen and Klee—surely an unlikely pairing—are alike in their love and employment of all manner of blooms and plants in their work. Phantom blooms are found, we recall, from an earlier chapter, in her novel, *The Spectral Bride*. At any rate, the effect of the heady scent of heliotrope blooms in the garden bed below Alicia Gates's window prefigures the action to come. Her grandfather had been obsessed with these flowers and had mandated that she plant them every year. Having "planted" that plot point, the tale begins... With his recent death, rumors are flying around about a lost will that allegedly involves great riches. Alicia takes up the search. Her destination is her grandfather's castle in Belgium, where his last wife, a Baroness, has presumptuously laid claim to the inheritance. The Baroness fears, however, that when the will is found, it might prove to disinherit her—unless she finds it first and destroys it. So, she has been searching the house, from room to room. Meanwhile, Alicia, on her way to the castle, is joined in the carriage by a stranger. Oddly, he bears a distinct resemblance to her grandfather. Odder still, he has about him the aroma of heliotrope... At the castle the Baroness announces she has just now found the papers and is determined to burn them. Alicia resists, and there is a scuffle. The old lady dies, clutching in her hands the lost papers. But they contain nothing. Except for one thing—of course—a recipe *for making heliotrope perfume.* A strange, hallucinatory quality hovers over all this. Alicia can't be sure if it has not all been just a dream. Who was that stranger, really, and why did he bear the scent of heliotrope?

By any standard, the most preposterous of Bowen's Christmas stories is "Marwood's Ghost Story." It is subtitled, "A Puzzle Piece"; and, indeed, it is. Marwood is a writer of solidly real stories, yet he wonders if he could bring off a ghostly tale. What better opportunity could there be than a Christmas trip to the country to attempt "a tale that would grip and chill and pester the imagination of the unfortunate reader?" (189). The problem is that *he doesn't believe in ghosts,* and surely that is a prerequisite? His wife, moreover, who does believe, can't understand why ghosts should come out on Christmas Eve. "It's all an absurd invention," he retorts (191). After weeks of fruitless attempts to encounter a ghost, Christmas Eve rolls around and he has a strange premonition: "Fancy sitting up in bed at night and feeling the Devil pulling the mattress from under you, or hearing an empty box opening and shutting, or something with eight feet shuffling around the house" (193). Indeed, after locking up their cabin up tight, he does hear a "shuffling, scraping, peculiar sort of noise ... broken by a hoarse, quickly suppressed laugh" (196). Across the room the window glows with a reddish light. Marwood is shaken, and shrieks, "It's true! It's true! ... Devils, ghosts—there, outside—legions of 'em." And then, "the howl took form and substance, and became: '*Hark the Herald Angels Sing!'* with trombone and triangle accompaniment. His wife shrugs; maybe it's the neighbors?" Neighbors? They're miles away from the nearest inhabitants. Not only is Marwood not convinced, but, in the final lines of the story, we are told: "Marwood never wrote his ghost story; he composed instead an essay on 'Fear,' but he would not care to have it published" (196–197). Do we accept the mundane explanation that the voices outside are merely those of Christmas Carolers; or do they come from ... *something* else ... as a hellish parody of the custom?

Among the others, "Kecksies" is a grisly tale set in desolate marsh country, where two travelers encounter the strange death and life of the villainous Richard Horne. When first encountered, he is quite dead; when last seen, he is a torn and ravaged creature murdering the woman, Anne Crediton, who has spurned him. What do we have here, a ghost? A shape-shifter? All the above? The word "kecksies" refers to the weeds that grow in the area. Elements of witchcraft are a normal part of the simple rural life of the area. And Horne's fate is nicely summed up: "The Devil's proved an ill master, then. He could not help Richard Horne into Anne's favor—nor prevent him lying in a cold bed in the flower of his age" (27).[30]

Of the non-supernatural contes cruels, the title story presents one of Bowen's most sturdily independent women. When Grace Latouche discovers that the man she has had an affair with is married, she confronts his wife and, aware that in her eyes she is only as a cheap adventuress, defends her actions with hard-headed practicality: "I suppose you think, Mrs. Warrington, that with women like me love does not enter into our—shall we say, without offence—our bargains? Marriages can be bargains, too, you know.... Love does not always last, but that does not say that while it endures, it is not genuine" (20). She leaves the scene, without a further word. The grimly guignol "A Traveller's True Tale" is a melodrama of confused identities, when in a bleak woodland, an idealistic young man encounters a horrible murder and an inconstant lover. This is his induction into "the horrible, the marvelous, the fantastic," and the world is forever changed for him "into a dreadful bleakness; the moon appeared to languish in a blank sky, the hill-side was covered with grass withered to the root" (226). Another melodrama, one with a pointed social commentary, is "The New Housemaid." A nocturnal confrontation in an old, deserted mansion between an innocent servant and a terrible thief and murderess becomes a savage indictment of the terrible and unjust working conditions of the working class in Victorian England. Finally, in the delicate and sensitive "Miss Lucy's Two Visitors," the frail and sickly Miss Lucy has a presentiment of her imminent death. Her world seems to exist under an enchantment. Her house is curiously empty. She herself seems to become a ghost to join the other ghosts that haunt the place:

> For the first time in her life, Lucy Middletone did not seem herself to belong definitely to her own time and generation, but to be part of the silent empty house, the silent empty garden, and one of the company of all those other people who had once crossed this terrace [35].

A handsome young man, surely a Prince in her eyes, comes to call. But she only tells him that she wishes that "I might not live to grow old" (46). That night, she senses another visitor. As she lapses into her last sleep, she murmurs to herself, "I'm going ... someone has come to take me.... I can't stay" (50). More a prose poem than a ghostly vision, "Miss Lucy's Two Visitors" is another of those stories that puts the lie to Bowen's reputation as primarily a writer of terrible dark fantasies.

Bagatelle (1931)

Bagatelle is, in my opinion, Bowen's finest volume of short stories. Published under the pseudonym of "George R. Preedy," the eleven stories and a one-act play all display exotic, historical, and imaginative settings. And, like so many stories under the Preedy name—most notably, the novel, *Nightcap and Plume*—motifs of masks, masquerade balls, and commedia dell'arte characters appear everywhere. The locations include an early eighteenth-century Italian villa ("Homage to the Unknown"), the roofless towers of seventeenth-century Karolsfeldt, in Nuremberg ("A Tune for a Trumpet"); an eighteenth-century Florentine palace ("Serenata"); and an eighteenth-century chateau close to the Russian frontier ("A Flourish for Drums").

In her remarkable Prologue, Bowen confesses the stories are "easily peopled by phantoms that soon take a definite shape and play out their own story without any help from the writer, who takes the part rather of transcriber than that of author." "They are all dead," she continues, and are "seen through the medium of a dream." Celebrated painters, composers, and actors flit in and out of the pages, such as the composer Porporo, painter Antoine Watteau, castrato singer Farinelli, and commedia actor Mezzetin. There is a wonderful tribute to Tiepolo in "Capriccio" and to the philosopher Lucretius in "A Visit to Verona." Their "tragedy," continues Bowen, shows through a "veil of resignation"; and their "comedy" is "hard, cynical and grotesque." Lest they seem "mere puppets adorned with tinsel," the reader should know "they have the essence of accomplished, successful humanity, disappointed (as always) in its final achievement.... [T]he men taste the brittleness of success, the women the limits of beauty; all, men and women, pursue each other in vain, hoping to clasp the long-lost, the perfect lover, and always embrace delusion." In sum, "They believe in nothing save their own secret and endless disappointment" (v–vii).

The set piece is the Burletta, "Homage to the Unknown." It ranks among Bowen's finest achievements. The time is "Midnight to Dawn, Summer, 1718," and the setting is "a lonely villa on the Brenta." A night coach has broken down and a stranger named Mezzetin, "a clown of the Comedia Italiana," appears to lead the occupants, Lord Charles and his tutor Theodosius Prose to the safety of a nearby inn, the "Villa Malconta." The Harlequinade begins, a fantastic dance of masks: The tutor is identified as Panteleone and Lord Charles is "Florio" or "Crispino" (162). A lady appears, and her name is "Incognita," the Unknown. Mezzetin appears, vanishes, and reappears several times, donning disguises, including that of the guitar-playing clown in a famous painting by Watteau, *L'Embarquement pour Cythère*. Who is he, really? He proclaims his essential mystery, in one of the great speeches in all of Bowen:

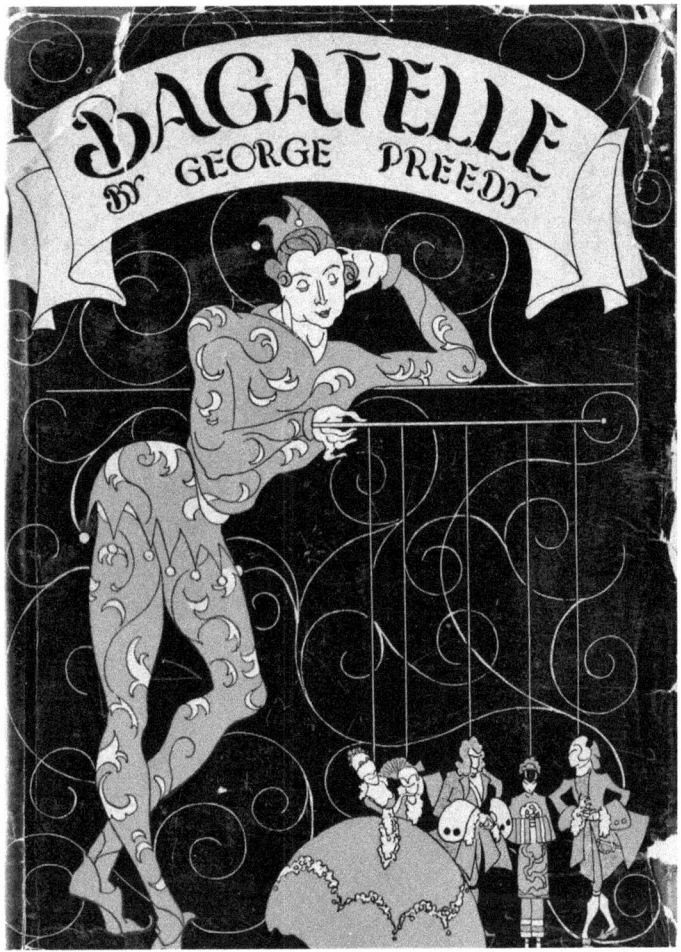

Bagatelle **book cover**

> I am Fantasy, day-dreaming and the unattainable. I beckon just round the corner where no one has been yet. I reside in those violet horizons which no man has reached. I am all you missed in the past and will evade you in the future. I am all that is incredible yet pursued, all that is never credited, yet longed for [174].

Erotic intrigues ensue. There is a duel. A masked figure falls to the floor, dead. But no, he rises again. His mask is removed. It is Mezzetin. Again. He turns to the audience and proclaims it is all a foolish charade:

> You see a variety of experiences—love, fear of death, killing a man, wooing a widow, and the knowledge that there is nothing in any of it! [189].

Comes the dawn and after the revelry, all is quiet. The two travelers depart. Mezzetin turns to the audience again for his valedictory speech:

> We remain and shall prepare our entertainment for the next wayfarers.... We have welcomed so many travelers, if we are good for nothing else we offer them, at least, a trifling diversion.... Perhaps you want to know who we are? We do not know ourselves. We have a thousand shapes, a thousand names. Yet I am always Mezzetin.... Good night and good morning both, for, if you are going home to bed, to us it is always the beginning of a new day [193–194].

What is it all about? Bowen's adopts the personae of Mezzetin to step back and confess that her stories are all a game of life and death, reality and fancy, faces and masks. That closing speech confirms Bowen's kinship to Shakespeare, particularly, to Prospero's closing speech in *The Tempest*, V, I, 2404, and Puck's closing speech in *A Midsummer Night's Dream*, V, 1.

Largely absent are the more overtly dark fantasies and graphic images of horror for which Bowen is most remembered today. Rather, *Bagatelle* stands in a class by itself and claims consideration as one of the most important collections of short stories by any writer of the last century.

Perhaps it is curious, even arbitrary, to append the self-standing short play, "Captain Banner," to this overview of *Bagatelle*. But inasmuch as it is also authored by "George R. Preedy," that it was performed and published at the same time as the release of *Bagatelle*, and because it reveals thematic affinities to "Homage to the Unknown," it seems useful to consider it here. Loosely based on an historical incident, events transpire in mid-eighteenth century in the isolated fortress prison of Wisberg. Herein gather three characters who all hide their identities under the masks of illusion and dream. Captain Banner is the Governor of Wisberg. His former lover is the servant girl, Katrine. And into their midst arrives a woman recently forced into exile by the mad King of Denmark and Norway. She is no less than the Queen of Denmark, sent to Wisberg to face death for her alleged adultery (her lover has already been beheaded). Stalwart Banner initially is cold to his captive, but her charms and protests of innocence turn his head. "I have done no wrong," she says, "The man they murdered was my friend, not my lover. For three years I have been faithful to an imbecile—I even loved him when he was kind" (47). For Banner, she is the dream of royalty he has always longed for: "I always dreamed to love a Queen" (65). For the Queen, he is the Hero she hopes will gain her release. In a moment of passion, both doff their presumptions and appear before each other as they really are—she as an adulterer and he merely a "hesitant, undecided, soul-divided, dream-tormented man and my own enemy" (65). Or, as it turns out, we wonder if these are merely more masks? At the end, the death of the King allows the Queen to return safely to the Court. She promptly resumes her haughty Queenly demeanor and invites Banner to be her adulterous lover back at Court. Banner realizes he had fallen in love with a fantasy and refuses, "flaunting in stars and ribbons as the Queen's lover" (100). He will remain in Wisberg. His former lover, Katrine, offers to put on the Queen's now-discarded attire: "I have learnt so many of her ways. Could you not think if I stood so, within the shadows, I was the Queen?" (104). But no. Banner sees her in the light of the open window and suffers an epiphany: "Take off that mummery," he tells her "—come to me as yourself. The light is good—it shows us as we are—what is left when all the dreams and illusions of the night have vanished—just man and woman loving one another" (104). It is one of the great moments in Bowen/Preedy. All the characters are unmasked, and reality has finally banished false dreams and illusions.

The Knot Garden (1934)

Published three years after *Bagatelle*, *The Knot Garden* is the second volume of short stories under the authorship of "George R. Preedy." The fourteen stories include historical fancies from Revolutionary France ("The Hyacinth Bloom"), late-eighteenth century Sweden ("Hurry! Hurray!"), late-seventeenth century Spain ("Mother o' Pearl"), mid-eighteenth century Russia ("Lally of Dillons"), and nineteenth-century Bavaria ("Heroic Landscape" and "Sonata for an Ugly Princess").

The outstanding contes cruels here are two brief sketches—a wonderful ghost story of bloody retribution in "Red Champagne" and the amusing symbiotic relationship between master and servant in "Hyacinth Bloom." Other effective contes cruels are a charming allegory of the redemptive power of music in "Sonata for an Ugly Princess"; a foolish young woman's eager embrace of carnal corruption during time of war in "Crab-Apple Harvest"; the fatal consequences of a woman's loss of honor in war-torn Poland in the grim "The Eye of War"; a whimsical tale of a missing celadon vase in "The Celadon Vase"; a carnal romp in "Minions of the Moon" (a reprint of "Four Farewells in Venice" from *Gorgeous Lovers*); a brittle satire of love and marriage in "A Group in Porcelain"; and "Mother o' Pearl," a cheeky servant's anecdotal account of the murderous career of the notorious Madame de Montespan. A fine guignol melodrama of murder and consuming guilt is "Graf Maarten and the Idiot." Less easily classifiable is "Heroic Landscape," a variant of Poe's "The Masque of the Red Death," a story of the spread of Plague with overtones of Pagan myth. Of the two tales of swashbuckling intrigue, "Lally of Dillon's" and "Hurry! Hurry!," the latter is especially interesting. As a pungent account of a failed assassination attempt against King Gustaf III of Sweden, "Hurry! Hurry!" is a preliminary sketch for the far more ambitious novel, *Nightcap and Plume*. This chronicle of the rise and fall of King Gustaf concludes with his death from an assassin's bullet in 1792 (see the chapter on "Painting History").

A personal favorite is one of Bowen's finest contes cruels, the aforementioned "Red Champagne," a brief ghostly tale of grim retribution. Marco Gherardi has pledged his eternal vow to Geva Gradenigo by sharing a glass of champagne containing a few drops of blood drawn from her arm with a silver bodkin. That night, a poisoned fly from the marshes stings Geva's open wound and within a day or two she dies. Months later, at Carnival Time, amidst the revels of figures from the Comedia, Marco forgets his vow and secures an engagement to Camilla Andreini. As the music of Tartini's "Devil's Trill" sonata is heard—"that inhuman music that Tartini heard in a dream"—a strange masked woman can be seen, quietly sitting nearby. Moments later, there are screams. Everyone is drinking from glasses of champagne stained with the color of blood. Marco's cries are heard behind the closed door of the bridal chamber. Bowen delivers the final blow in the last lines:

> The air blew very chill from the sea, and they all were silent as if something passed through the room and out by the grand entrance; then they rushed and broke open the bedchamber door. There was no bride, but on the bridal couch lay Marco Gherardi dead, and staining the white velvet coverlet was blood, for all his wrist vein had been opened by a silver bodkin, such as women use to pin their hair [208].

The Last Bouquet: Some Twilight Tales (1933)

The Last Bouquet: Some Twilight Tales contains mostly supernatural stories, many of which are gathered together from earlier volumes, such as the oft-anthologized "The Avenging of Ann Leete" (originally from *Seeing Life!*); several from *Grace Latouche* ("The Crown Derby Plate," "Raw Material," "Kecksies"); others from *The Gorgeous Lovers* ("Florence Flannery"); from *Shadows of Yesterday* ("The Fair Hair of Ambrosine"); and from *Curious Happenings* (the ever-inscrutable "The Sign-Painter and the Crystal Fishes"). New to the book are four outstanding dark fictions that demand special attention—"The Hidden Ape" with its murderous, shape-shifting psychopath; "The Last Bouquet," a delicate evocation of the psychic bonds between two sisters; "Madame Spitfire," with its no-holds-barred collection of Gothic terrors; and the extraordinarily sensitive and piquant "Elsie's Lonely Afternoon." They deserve special attention.

"The Hidden Ape" features an interesting debate between kindly Professor Awkright, an academic, and his young assistant, Mr. Joliffe, who is tutoring his ward, Edmund. Their joint study of Minoan languages elicits a discussion of the value of human life in Western culture. Against the professor's protests, Joliffe asserts: "I always think we attach too much importance to human life. No civilized people would consider murder a crime" (101). Alarmed, Awkright wonders if such "indifferences to right and wrong [are] manifestations of the hidden ape, still lurking within so many of us, alas" (99). And he shudders, "imagining a fantastic image of Joliffe, suddenly agile as a monkey, scaling down those rocks after Edmund" (105). When Awkright determines to dismiss Joliffe, the youth disappears. From his window Awkright views through the midnight landscape "a thin, darkly-clad figure proceeding across the lawn, half leaping, half crawling through the shadow; the arms looked very long; now and then the lanky, uncouth shape appeared to sink to hands and knees in a scrawling effort at haste" (110). Rushing to Edmund's room, Awkright finds his lifeless body. Meanwhile, the weird figure outside disappears "in the triumphant haste towards the wilderness, in the challenging thrown back head which seemed to howl at the moon that swung in an unfathomable, dreadful void" (110).[31]

Beyond its ghostly aspect, "The Last Bouquet" is one of Bowen's most important statements on the status of private and professional women in the mid-nineteenth century. Martha and Kezia are twin sisters who exemplify the contrasting lifestyles open to women at the time. Martha is the beautiful and successful actress working in the big city; and Kezia is a plain homebody living in the country. Their relationship is complicated. Martha is one of Bowen's strongest female characters, fiercely independent and proud of her status as a professional woman (who was at the time termed "The New Woman"). Surely, these words from Martha to her sister is Bowen writing in her own "voice":

> I daresay you think I am completely degraded, but pray don't waste any such pity on me. I am successful—I always have been successful. I am, in a way, triumphant over everything, over the usual conventions, the traditions that bind women, over the usual stupid emotions that cause them to waste their hearts and lives; over all the pettifogging duties and obligations that wear away a woman like you [11].

At the same time, Kezia, despite her feelings of inferiority before her sister's "opulence and splendor," feels pride in her own conventional virtues. In short, despite their differences, each feels a certain connection, albeit envy, of the other. One day, Kezia, who has never had the pleasure of receiving the sumptuous bouquets of flowers customarily lavished on her sister, is promised by Martha that she will have her "last bouquet." The years pass, and neither sees the other. Living alone, surrounded by her furnishings and charities, mortality beckons. Kezia begins to feel a vagueness in her senses: "The world around her grows strange ... the garden seemed too large and the sky too vast, and the bright light of the sunset too overwhelming..." (25). At that moment, Martha appears, holding out to Kezia a bouquet of roses. "Kezia took it, and as she did so, all the roses turned to blood and emptied themselves into her bosom" (28). She falls dead. At precisely that same hour, after an unfortunate encounter with a young rake, Martha is found, murdered, her room robbed of jewelry, with nothing left "but a large bouquet of crimson roses, which were found flung down carelessly on her bosom, profaned, drooping, and dappled with her blood" (29). Ghostly encounter? Or a kind of psychic connection, borne of violence and death? As usual, Bowen offers no conclusions.

"Madame Spitfire." Here is a romp. Bowen is full throttle, her dark Furies on display. Told in the manner of an "antique legend," it is boldly atmospheric, "dark with evil passions, fierce ruminations, the black clash of a high tide of bitterness" (38). There is a diseased house, Dower House, where the widowed Madame Spitfire lives with Agnes, the rumored illegitimate daughter and presumptive heir to the late Squire's fortune. Still in the prime of life, Madame is attracted to a newcomer, another contender for the fortune, the handsome and dashing Francis Rowe. Unfortunately, he is indifferent to her and more interested in Agnes. In a complex twist of erotic frustrations, intrigues, and bitter recriminations, events move quickly to murder and worse. What a grandly guignol melodrama this is, highlighted by Madam's dream vision of the visiting apparition of her late husband. The grotesque moment rivals anything in LeFanu or M.R. James:

> She did not move, in this dream, from the heavy bed with the dark baldaquin and stiff curtains.... She observed what she thought to be a fat dog, wheezing, uncomfortable; but a closer glance showed that this creature trailed drapery, knotted like a bunch of leaves above the head. It was her husband. He appeared to be nosing round the room on a tense quest.... He rose; his sagging body was stout and flabby as she remembered it, but his legs had dwindled to mere bones, his shroud tied on the top of his skull was rotted into tatters, his face was shapeless; she saw the dying fire through a hole in his cheek; his decayed eyes had the glitter of foul, stagnant water.... Abruptly, he came at her, gathering together his corrupted members for a leap on to her sumptuous bed [488–49].

At the end, the local parson claims the dead Squire still haunts the place, "an errant shape, like a globe of pale, wavering light, starting through the ground mist and floating towards the house" (58). As for Madame Spitfire, she lives on, alone, in the house; and when she ascends to her bed chamber, "she knew what awaited her there" (60). Whatever became of her no one knows, alive or dead; but when twilight falls, "the nettles give out a rank sickly odour; it is then that you may believe that Madam Spitfire is buried beneath them" (47).

The poignant "Elsie's Lonely Afternoon" stands in stark contrast to Spitfire's gothic hijinks. It is in a class by itself, although one may discern something of the delicate ambiguity of Walter de la Mare's "The Riddle." A conte cruel with a delicately whimsical touch, it allows us a glimpse into the mind of a lonely, emotionally abused seven-year-old girl living with her grandma in a lonely old house. "It seemed to Elsie not only a pity that she had ever been born, but that anyone else had" (180). There may be the ghost of her "Uncle Tom" in the house, but grandma says: "If you ever meet one who says he's your Uncle Tom or says he's any son of mind, you tell him that he's a scoundrel and a liar.... All my sons are dead—dead" (186). But, of course, when she does meet Uncle Tom, who has been prowling the attic looking for a treasure allegedly hidden there, she assumes he's a ghost—*isn't he?* ... How she sees the world around her is not unlike the limited perception of the little girl in Henry James's novel, *What Maisie Knew*. There's also a similarity to Patrick Hamilton's *Angel Street* [Gaslight], which debuted five years after this story, in that there is a plot element involving a man in secret exploring an attic in search of treasure.

There's much pathos here, and we have the sense that Bowen is talking about her own lonely and neglected childhood. In that respect, it belongs in the company of four more stories from a later collection, *Orange Blossoms*—"Vessels of Gold," "Wounded Bird," "White Hares," and "Jessie's Pink Balloons."

Orange Blossoms (1938)

Orange Blossoms is Marjorie Bowen's last volume of new stories, and it is the only collection that bears the byline of "Joseph Shearing." It is also the only one comprised entirely of contemporary stories, several of which bear an autobiographical stamp. None of the seventeen tales had appeared before. Highlights include a comic *guignol*, "Two Rose-Bud Wreaths"; two Hitchcockian stories about murderesses whose frustrated loves lead to murder and betrayal, "Love-in-a-mist" and "She Knew What to Do"; And "Blood and Thunder," is a splendidly atmospheric account of the grisly London dockland murders that had also inspired Thomas De Quincey's classic true-crime account, *On Murder Considered as One of the Fine Arts* (1827).

Of particular interest are five stories: "They Found My Grave," a wickedly amusing conte cruel about an arrogant ghost; four outstanding portraits of troubled children that bear the autobiographical stamp of Bowen's own abused childhood ("Vessels of Gold," "Wounded Bird," "White Hares," "Jessie's Pink Balloons"; and a masterpiece, "A Famous Woman," that evades easy classification.

"They Found My Grave" is an amusing conte cruel about séances and an arrogant ghost who delivers literally a deadly kick in the proverbial pants at the end. Ada Trimple, despite her skepticism regarding séances, reluctantly agrees to attend a sitting with a medium aptly named "Asra Destiny" at her "Bloomsbury Temple of Eastern Psycho-Physiological Studies." But when a disembodied voice intones a Latin inscription—"*Blessed is he who understands the poor and has pity on the unfortunate*"—and in a boastful and arrogant way identifies itself as "Gabriel Letourneau," who had died in 1837, Ada admits to herself she is *moved* by the experience. Although she finds the spirit's words and his manner insufferable, boastful, and arrogant, yet, she admits: "He spoke to me and, you know, I wish that I could have gone on talking to him" (277). The more she thinks about it, the more she is determined to obey the spirit's injunction to come and visit his grave. After many inquiries and searches, she finds a shabby stone with a Latin inscription identical to what she had heard in the séance. At a subsequent séance, the voice of Letourneau returns, taunting Ada with mocking remarks about her appearance and intelligence. The presiding medium is shocked, confessing that an "evil spirit" has been raised, but assures everyone not to be afraid: "There might be no danger. Any weakness on one's own part always gives the spirits a certain power over one" (288). Ada leaves. Suddenly, at the head of the stairs, a deep and harsh voice whispers in her ear—"*Canaille!* [fool!]." Startled, she trips, falls, and breaks her neck at the base of the stairs. Madame Destiny has the last word: "A pure accident. Everyone is witness that she was quite alone at the time. She has been very nervous lately—and those high heels..." (290).

In "Vessels of Gold," a young girl, Margaret (Bowen's own birth name) lives in poverty with a mostly absent mother, a shiftless, uncaring father, and the sense that she should never have been born. She spends her time drawing pictures with a box of chalk from the few pennies her father gives her. Yet, despite her privations—or because of them—Margaret has developed a curious sense of self-sufficiency. Her thoughts grant us an insight into Bowen's own mindset as a child:

> She began to think that it was a secret austere pleasure to be able to sacrifice everything, to have nothing but what she could get from herself. She felt, vaguely, that she possessed a great power in this self-sufficiency, and the joy of the lovely, sunny afternoon returned to her; she glanced up at her mother, completely detached from that unhappy creature [66].

"Wounded Bird" pits a manipulative 16-year-old boy against his mean and possessive aunt. While Bowen emerged from her lonely childhood a sturdy and independent person, prepared to exploit her psychological scars in the service of her writing, the boy in this story falls victim to his upbringing and learns to manipulate self-pity as his weapon against the world. The victim becomes a victimizer. A "wounded bird" he may be, but he enjoys—and exploits—his wounds. His only friend is Mary, two years younger than he, who contrives an escape plan. But a storm foils the plan and he abandons her and returns to his comfortable bed. His resolve for freedom dwindling, he realizes he loves his comforts too much: "Much as he loathed his aunt, he could manage her" and he decides to endure "with sickly patience" the meal prepared for him. Mary is left outside in the rain, a wounded bird nestled against her breast. Simon tells her to go away—and returns to his bed, "feeling with his toes for the warm place left by the heating pan" (167).

"White Hares" is a sad, sad story, whose cruel denouement is neither shocking nor wicked, but a painful revelation of a woman's delusionary state. Once upon a time there was a little girl named Margaret (Bowen using her birth name again):

> Her childhood was dateless, marked only by small, emotional events. Often, she had been happy for no reason at all, save the way the rain-drops fell from the rose bushes after a shower, or because someone said, "There are lardy buns for tea." Often, she had been bored and sad because of the blank faces of the adults, their mysterious humours, their vague tyranny [171].

One day, while watching three white hares at play, she had been so enchanted by the moment and its "augury of good fortune" that she had never forgotten it. Now, many years later, Margaret returns to the meadow, happy about an anticipated romance with a man whom she hopes to marry. Maybe he will share with her the "almost intolerable pangs of nostalgia for a lost past that had not been happy, yet which had been brilliantly lit by expectancy" (178). But now the moment is empty, the late afternoon grows dark, and she is "chilled by the phantom who had seen the white hares" (176). It was all a lie. "I never saw the white hares," she murmurs to herself as walks heavily back to the house where her tea awaits—"towards a life that always had been, always would be barren, save for her own falsehoods" (182).

Another sensitive and lyric glimpse into the world of childhood is "Jessie's Pink Balloons," which must be numbered among Bowen's most moving fantasies. Its honest sincerity saves it from cloying sentimentality. Is it a ghost story? Seen through the eyes of Jessie, we can't be sure. Little Jessie Pomeroy has just returned from the circus, with its "fantastic animals ... and untidy people moving about with pails and pans; and in the corner by the pond and the split thorn the balloon-man's stock-in-trade—dozens of shining balloons swaying together like gigantic bubbles" (185–186). The balloon man tells Jessie that when her own balloons are set aloft, they will come to rest at a place where she will find a treasure. She can't inflate them yet, however, because they are a frivolity—"that God, who came out on Sundays and went in on Mondays, like the cuckoo in the clock, disliked to see about" (187). Meanwhile, upstairs in her hooded chair, in the shadows, sits Great Grandmother, lost in the memory of an unhappy love affair with a man named Gilbert Hammond. She sends Jessie out to the meadow to release her balloons. One of them sails over the fence that divides her family's property from the Hammond estate. Following it, she meets a young man who seems to know her. An odd conversation transpires: He points out that his and her names are inscribed on a tree. She responds that her Great Grandmother wants her to bring him to her. "I thought you would be very old ... but I don't believe in time, do you?" (197). Escorting her back to her house, he tells her he is the great-grandson of the very Gilbert Hammond that once had quarreled with the Great Grandma. Back in Grannie's room, Jessie puts his hand into that of the old woman. She murmurs absently she had had a dream of her true love—"And I saw you, my dear" (199). Jessie falls asleep, fearing she might be punished for flying the pink balloons on Sunday—"but if God did not see the pink balloons, he certainly saw Mrs. Pomeroy; she died that night and no one remembered how naughty Jessie had been" (200).

Finally, we come to the poignant ambiguity of a Christmas tale, the richly atmospheric "A Famous Woman." A traveler interrupts his journey with a stop in a small town. "[Mr. Tellow] liked to do out-of-the-way things, to go to unlikely places and afterwards to make up little adventures with which to fill his loneliness" (139). All too often, however, "familiarity with every scene bred disillusion ... that the magic vanished after a short residence" (139–140). And so it happens that during a train stop he goes on a nocturnal stroll through the tinsel-strewn streets, visits the "monstrous church whose vast doors seemed too large for human use" (142), and, finally, pauses before a statue of a woman bearing only the inscription, "Gabrielle Buzot." Standing before it, "he feels a curious, pricking sense of chivalrous love ... as if he had known her intimately for years" (144). Inquiries yield no information about the woman, although there is a vague, muttered hint that it should be removed because of a "scandal." Back on the train, Mr. Tellow glimpses a peasant woman on the platform. The porter tells him she has just learned of the death of her only son. "She claims," continues the porter, "to be descended from a famous woman—Gabrielle Buzot" (148). Mr. Tellow impulsively calls out to her as the train begins to move. No response. In a guidebook, he finds only two lines about the town: "Worth visiting for the splendid fifteenth-century Gothic church. In the public gardens is a statue of the famous Gabrielle Buzot" (148). Only twenty years old before she died, muses Tellow, how could somebody become so famous in so short a time? Never mind, he has business to attend to. The town already belongs to the past. It had been foolish to run after this fancy. Still ... "Who was she, left behind in the out-of-the-way town in the deserted gardens, under the snow? He would never know, and by to-morrow he would cease to care" (148). But we, the readers, *do* care. This simple little tale is Bowen at her most masterful, leaving us to wonder about the many women who live and love and labor, but who finally must languish in obscurity. That is the fate that has befallen Bowen, herself.

The Bishop of Hell (1949)

This was the last volume of stories to appear in Marjorie Bowen's lifetime. According to Michael Sadleir, who contributed the Introduction, the twelve weird tales were "selected" by Bowen from her previous story collections. One exception is "The Grey

Chamber," a grisly guignol of two ghosts who contend nightly over an unresolved act of violence. It had appeared in print only once before, when Bowen included it in her edited anthology, *Great Tales of Horror* (1933). The classic contours of the ghostly tale are here: A solitary traveler takes refuge during a storm in a friend's ancient house. The only room available is purportedly haunted by the ghost of a woman named Gertrude. On the eve of her induction Graf Hugues "despoiled her by force of her honour"; but when she revealed this to her confessor, Gertrude was refused entry into the convent and subsequently committed suicide. Graf Hugues went unpunished. Since then, Gertrude appears every night in the Grey Chamber, a dagger in one hand to slay the false lover, and a crucifix in the other to reconcile her rapist with Heaven. Our traveler duly encounters not just Gertrude, wrapped in a shroud, but her rapist, "his ghastly face, on which still hung a remnant of skin and muscle, was distorted in a frightful grimace" (139). Finding himself between the two contending phantoms, he sinks to the floor, unconscious. He hastily leaves the scene without telling his host: "If he was able to persuade his host of the reality of his vision, who would dare to continue to inhabit the castle where Gertrude and the hideous skeleton of her lover had a rendezvous every evening?" (139).

Kecksies (1976) and *Twilight and Other Supernatural Romances* (1997)

Two more collections of Bowen's weird tales, *Kecksies* and *Twilight*, appeared after her death. *Kecksies* seems to have been planned before her death by Bowen enthusiast Edward Wagenknecht for August Derleth of Arkham House. In addition to a selection of her best-known weird tales, *Kecksies* added three previously uncollected tales, "The Breakdown," "One Remained Behind," and "The House by the Poppy Field." Their published origins are unknown; neither can be found in the listing of her magazine publications.

"The Breakdown" is a Christmas Eve ghost story along classic lines. On his way to meet a former college chum named Blanchard, John Murdoch loses his way and finds himself at the Wishing Inn, where he seeks shelter for the night. "There are stories about the place," says the landlord. "It is said that those who pass Christmas Eve here are allowed the fulfillment of one wish" (134). Idly, John remembers a painting of a lovely girl, "Marie Blanchard," he had seen before, and he wishes he might see her now. Sure enough, a figure appears in the doorway who resembles the painting. She confesses she is indeed Marie Blanchard. She entreats John to join her in her coach as she goes in search of her lover. During the journey, she suddenly disappears. Moments later, here she is again, walking toward a cemetery. She stands over a heavy stone bearing the inscription: *"Marie Blanchard and Tobias Grieve."* Confused, John is distracted by a glimmering light in the distance—the house that belongs to John's friend. He loses consciousness. The next morning, John learns from his host, Blanchard, that the Wishing Inn had been pulled down a century before; and that Blanchard's ancestress, Marie Blanchard, had run away there one Christmas Eve to meet her lover. But he had never arrived, and she died of a broken heart. At that moment in the story, the door opens and a young woman appears to John. She resembles the mysterious woman of the night before. She is the sister of his host, and her name is Marie Blanchard. "Murdoch thought of his last night's wish, and his heart thrilled as he looked into the fair girl's eye—to meet—to love—to win—Marie Blanchard!" (140).

"One Remained Behind" is subtitled "A Romance a la Mode Gothique." And indeed it is, a no-holds-barred Gothic conte cruel full of magic, three wishes, violence, and grim retribution, rather in the manner of Matthew Lewis and E.T.A. Hoffmann. Bowen is obviously having a great time. As a result of a poor university student's dabbling in the alchemical arts, he learns all manner of potions and spells and rituals. Everything quickens to his magical arts—his old coats on the peg wave their sleeves, his empty trousers kick a polka, and a host of strange faces leer at him from the mirrors. Finally, as a result of elaborate preparations and encounters with the Satanic spirits Astaroth, Beelzebud, Belial, and Beleth, he pronounces his desires for three wishes—fame as a poet, luck at cards, and vast wealth. Needless to say, everything ends in disaster, and a wicked female phantom refuses to leave his side. "Never!" she threatens. "One remains behind!" (165). At the end of his wits, the hapless student drowns himself in the river. And a good time was had by all.

"The House by the Poppy Field" is a personal favorite, one of those quietly elegiac mood pieces in which Bowen excels. Rich in atmosphere, the whole is gently saturated in intimations of Satanism, illicit romance, and death. Bothal House awaits the return of its rightful owner. Is John Maitfield, who has recently arrived, that rightful heir? The poppies are in full bloom, and "an unutterable nostalgia shakes him, the sense of something regretted, something sought: 'He had pursued his chimera in many parts of the world and never felt so near her hidden presence as now'" (168). Curiously, the house has been kept clean and tidy but is devoid of a human presence. He wanders through the rooms, marveling at how little light the candles give out. Outside, the silence is broken only by the gentle *swishing* sound of a figure with a scythe. John finds in the nearby churchyard a nameless gravestone on which is inscribed "the semblance of a strange instrument, something like a pair of compasses with an odd attachment, set in a pentacle." (174). A stranger nearby tells him a former owner of the house, also named "John Maitland," had long ago dabbled in the Black Arts and one night had been visited by a witch. He had died that night and no one has since slept in Bothal House and lived. John wonders, did he hear that story? Or did he invent it? "He felt that past and present were joined, and that escape by returning to his childhood and by death were resolved into one deliverance" (176). He is alone. The church is barred to him. Back in the house, returning to his room, one last vision remains to him: " On the threshold of his room stood a shadowy figure with wild flowers in her hair, a poppy coronal, surely, floating among her tresses. Maitland blew out his human light, entered his room, moving delicately among the shadows, and lay down on his clean bed and slept" (177).

The *Twilight* collection of stories was edited by the redoubtable Jessica Amanda Salmonson, one of the most perceptive of Bowen's critics and enthusiasts. To an assortment of Bowen's hitherto published stories are added three new ones, "The Recluse and Springtime," "Vigil," and "A Stranger Knocked." Salmonson reports that the first two had been hitherto unpublished and had been rescued from oblivion by Bowen's youngest son, Hilary Long (xxii). The only prior appearance of the third had been under the byline of "Joseph Shearing" in an anthology edited by Edward Wagenknecht, *The Fireside Book of Yule Tide Tales*.

"The Recluse and Springtime" features three of Bowen's favorite elements—flowers, alchemy, and, of course, ghosts. As for the ghosts that cluster around Prince Riccardi and are the awful consequences of his alchemical experiments with the dead. They do linger on... Riccardi has been living alone in his Lucca palace after losing his wife, son, and brother to the Plague. When a young flower seller comes to call, her visit awakens the old man's startling confession that the ghosts of his family *have never departed*. He tells her:

> They always follow me. I cannot kill the dead nor can I escape from them. As you see, I am a haunted man.... They never change. I grow old, but they are always the same. She has no grey hairs, no wrinkles. He is still a child. My brother never becomes a man. Always, always, the same! They are dead. Their bodies lie in the Cathedral and their souls hang between Heaven and Hell. They cannot be free of me, nor I of them [186].

And then, he adds his most awful confession: "And when I die, we shall still be together—hating each other—I and my thoughts of the dead" (186). Indeed, the spring will not stay; and the girl's flowers will all wither away. She flees from the blasted garden.

"Vigil" is a compact ghost story set in an Italian palazzo in the not too distant past. It has many autobiographical details reflecting Bowen's own sojourn in Italy during the early years of World War I while nursing her dying husband. Told in the first person, the narrator voices Bowen's own affinity with ghosts—"I believe that I have seen and heard many ghosts, though some of them were dreams; and I believe that ghosts move in and out of dreams as they move in and out of waking hours"—and strong sense of *place*—"The atmosphere of scenes, houses, streets is usually most poignant to me, far more so than human personalities" (188). There is even a detail about the narrator reading the book Bowen kept with her during those years, *Julius Caesar*. While maintaining a nocturnal watch over a dying invalid, the narrator catches a fleeting glimpse in the feeble lamplight of an "obscure," hooded figure wearing a garment with a green design. "I thought I was surrounded by an incredible concentration of evil, hate, cruelty, and revenge," muses the narrator; "—that I had in some fearful manner become part of this, almost understanding, almost rejoicing in it" (190). "*Almost rejoicing...?*" Comes the dawn and the old man is dead. He was a heretic, it seems. And the palazzo had once belonged to the Office of the Holy Inquisition. "I did afterwards discover that among the devices of the Holy Inquisition was one that resembled green leaves on a white ground" (190).

"A Stranger Knocked" is a richly atmospheric Christmas Eve fireside tale about a magic flower, an angelic visitation, and a miracle. A stranger arrives in the midst of a Christmas Eve celebration. He declares he's a botanist who has returned from China where he had found a mysterious flower with magical restorative properties. After years of travel, he had brought them back to his home, where he expected his betrothed, Isabelle, would be waiting for him. Instead, she has recently married to a man suffering from an illness of the lungs. In a fury, he intends to kill them and destroy the precious flower. But the mysterious appearance at his door of a ragged man begging a bed for the night changes all that. The flowers come to life and wriggle in his grasp "and flew upwards like rockets, into a shower of stars" (44). Later, from within the alcove sheltering the beggar, emerges an angelic creature with wings. "There, calmly watching me," recalls the botanist, "was the most beautiful, beautiful being.... Such wings!" (444). The following Christmas morning, repenting his hate, the botanist seeks out Isabelle and her ailing husband. The restorative plant cures him of his lung disease. Who was the man in the alcove? "I never saw him again," concludes the botanist. "He might visit you any time. Especially when I think you feel most forsaken" (445). Was it all a dream? The botanist produces a feather he had found on his pillow: "A feather that seemed to be of the finest gold, but delicate beyond all mortal workmanship" (445).[32]

STORIES FROM TWO ANTHOLOGIES OF WEIRD TALES

In 1933 and 1935 Marjorie Bowen edited two anthologies of weird tales, *Great Tales of Horror* (1933) and *More Great Tales of Horror* (1935). Each contained "strange stories of amazement, horror, and wonder selected, with a Foreword, by Marjorie Bowen." One of the stories in the 1933 volume is Bowen's own "The Murder of Squire of Langford," which had initially appeared as part of the longer narrative, *"Five Winds"* and later reappeared in *The Gorgeous Lovers* (1929). None of the other stories are attributed to Bowen, although a few are listed as "anonymous, translated from French or German sources by M. Bowen." To what degree these were either revised or wholly invented by Bowen is unclear at this writing. To add to the confusion, one of the stories, "The Grey Chamber," listed in the 1933 volume as "anonymous, translated from the French"—which she described, perhaps disingenuously as "the ancestor of 'the night in the haunted bedroom' that has been given with such an astonishing variety of treatment since"[33]—appears later under her own name in *The Bishop of Hell*. This would seem to hint that Bowen had a great deal more to do with these "anonymous" and "translated" stories than she has acknowledged. Certainly, her description of the collections, as a whole, could be readily applied to her own work. As she noted in the 1935 volume, "All the stories are released from confines of time and space, and move, whether their authors intended it or no [sic], in a world as indefinite and elastic as that of a dream; they are dateless; all we know of them is that they were written before the age of machinery or ignore it."[34] Their antique modes of storytelling are not unlike the cycle of "Seven Deadly Sins" in *The Crimes of Old London* (1919).

Stories from Great Tales of Horror (1933)

"The Two Sisters of Cologne" is a grisly tale of sisters who murder gentlemen travelers, dismember the bodies, and collect the hair and teeth. The sisters are arrested and executed: "The head is held down by two men, by a rope around the neck. The limbs are then broken, one after another, from above by a heavy wheel. At the end, the head is severed from the body by a sword. The elder sister's agony was prolonged to the very end" (94).

"A Ghost of a Head" is a grimly comic conte cruel about a severed head that won't stay in one place or keep quiet. An ambitious village prosecutor has so enthusiastically convicted an innocent man that the severed head comes to call. Later, a doctor examines the head "without discovering the slightest trace of anything resembling a soul" and dismisses the event as a mere "hallucination proceeded from an over-extension of the cerebral fibre" (125).

"The Dead Bride" is a long and complicated tale of ghosts who haunt faithless lovers. A story-within-a-story, about a "spectral bride," was probably the genesis for the 1942 novel of that name under the byline of "Joseph Shearing"

"The Skull" is about a troupe of acrobats whose leader, a charlatan, is found guilty of a crime during his performance. "The life we live," he tells his audience, "has on either hand that black abyss which we name death. To penetrate this darkness has been the aim of many.... What do you know of what is possible or impossible, true or false, light or darkness? How can you be sure that a whisper is not sometimes heard across this black gulf.... I claim the power to make the dead speak" (270). And a skull, which has been part of the performance, takes him up on it and promptly indicts him of murder.

"The Legend of Dunblane" is not so much about the terrors of a haunted room than the agony of a dysfunctional marriage. The childless union between Lord Dunblane and Miss Cameron disintegrates into mutual recriminations and hate. "Children are a horrid bore," declares Lady Dunblane; "thank heaven, I have no brat" (356). Indeed, admits the story's narrator, "The devil was in the woman" (356). And with their deaths, the Dunblane line is extinct.

More Great Tales of Horror (1935)

"The Fatal Hour" recounts the strange bond that binds together two sisters, even unto the grave. The character of Seraphine is one of Bowen's liminal women, half in and out of life, not quite of this world or the next. She is aware of a prophecy of her approaching death and of the end of the family line. After her demise, she appears to her sister, Florentine, "surrounded by rays of a pale, unearthly light." The words, "With you, for ever" are heard; but no one knows if they were uttered by Florentine, the phantom, of the two sisters together (108).

"The Accursed Portrait" is a story so complicated that it tests the reader's patience to sort it all out. But it does contain a conversation in which a crucial issue is debated: Should the mysterious be *explained* away? What is gained or lost in the process? A disputant declares: "If we knew the truth that lay behind the cause of these strange and terrible incidents, would they not lose for us all their mysterious fascination?" Which elicits this response: "Who knows what the explanation might *not* be? Might it not be as mysterious and terrible, as thrilling, as the tales themselves?" (326).

"Fairy Bride" quietly inflects an air of mystery into a young statesman's meeting with a bewitching young lady, their marriage, her death, and the bitterness of his subsequent days. We are in the mid-seventeenth century and the Scottish struggles of the Presbyterian Covenanters against the Episcopacy of the Stuart Kings. The woman is looked upon by the villagers with superstitious awe as a Nixy. After she dies during childbirth, the husband, once a mild and gallant soldier, is now said to be influenced by "unholy powers" as he seeks vengeance against the Covenanters. "Even yet, does his memory," go the final lines, "and that of his Fairy Bride, live in popular tradition like a thunderstorm, gloomy and desolating, yet not without the lambent flashes of more than earthly beauty" (267).

"The Murder Hole" is a ghastly guignol that transpires in a desolate stretch of country where there has been a series of unexplained disappearances. One stormy November night the crimes are traced to an isolated shack where an old woman and her sons have been murdering and dismembering passing travelers. The remains are then discarded into the "Murder Hole," a deep fissure in the earth nearby. "The Murder Hole is the thing for me," declares one of the sons—that "tells no tales; a single scuffle—a single plunge—and the fellow's dead and buried to your hand in a moment.... It sucks them in like a leech" (379).

A few brief comments on some of the "anonymous" tales are offered here, and I leave it to the reader to sense those hints therein that identify the stories as essentially Bowen. "Elie Anderson's Revenge" is attributed to "Anonymous. From the Odd Volume." It is a gruesome study of a pathological serial killer, a woman who has abducted, murdered, and mutilated a number of children in the village. The small bodies are laid out side by side in a crawlspace of her cottage and crosses have been carved into their chests.

Her motive? The killings began when, taunted by a child who had overheard nasty gossip about her, Elie had shaken it so violently that the child died. Immediately, a strange thought entered the old woman's head: "It cam [sic] into my head that it had been the means o' saving her frae sin, and frae haein' muckle to answer for; an' this thought made me unco happy. At last, I began to think that it would be right to save mair o' them, and that it would atone for a' my former sins..." (124–125). The citizenry seize and execute her in a grisly and prolonged manner. It takes a long time for them "to deprive her of sense and motion" (124–125).

"The Sutor of Selkirk" is told in a mock archaic Scottish dialect. It even delivers a moral instruction. Attributed to an "anonymous" source, it is surely the work of Bowen herself. Or is it? Again, I leave it to the reader with this brief summary:

Once upon a time there lived in Selkirk a shoemaker named Rabbie Heckspeckle. Early one morning he receives a commission from a mysterious customer to make a pair of shoes. The stranger not only smells "plough-tail," perceives Rabbie, but carries a purse spotted with earthly mold, from which drop a toad and a beetle. While measuring the man's feet, Rabbie is perplexed by the "splay" of the toes. The transaction complete, the curious shoemaker follows him to the local graveyard. "There's something no canny about this," he declares (203). When the grave is dug up, a corpse is found "with a pair of perfectly new shoes upon its long, bony feet" (203). The shoemaker, who is a greedy fellow, retrieves the shoes before the coffin is nailed back shut. But later, he rues his action, fearing that the corpse might be troubled by "cold feet," as it were, and might demand the return of the shoes. But then, he reasons, the customer is lawfully dead and cannot apply to the court for redress. So he's safe. But not for long. The next day, Rabbie has disappeared. Once again, the coffin is disinterred and the lid removed. The townspeople flee in consternation at the sight: The stranger's corpse is there, the new shoes are back on his feet, and Rabbie's red nightcap is clutched in its skeletal hands. Rabbie is never found.

"Nightmare" has appeared only once, in August Derleth's anthology, *The Night Side* (1947). It is unclear if Bowen wrote it expressly for that volume or produced it from hitherto unpublished work. In its description of an abandoned monastery erected on the site of a heathen temple, it bears a strong kinship to her novel, *The Haunted Vintage*. Under a strange compulsion, a woman travels through the twilight woods to a monastery where lies entombed her lover. Just as the stony figure quickens into flesh, she is recalled from her dream. She retreats to her rooms in a nearby inn. The stony figure follows and reappears on her balcony. "I knew then," she concludes, "that this was no waking hour, and the disappointment was profound, for I had resolved to put all to the test of reality" (372). The last lines suggest yet another reality: "I sighed as I turned on my hard, straight bed and felt the memorial stone above me...." Is this her dream? The man's voice answers: "Yes, but whose dream? Yours or mine?" (372).[35]

Note: The following are uncollected stories that have been retrieved from three sources, *The Girl's Own Annual*, *Harper's Monthly*, and *Maclean's*.

From *The Girls Own Annual*

"Reasons for Mercy." Vol. 61 (1940), 169–173, 192

Political intrigue ends in an unexpected act of charity. A prisoner named Martin Bampfield is taken to the Duke, who is aware the man was a Cromwellian, intriguing treachery against him, the Papists, and the King. But in a flash of charity, he agrees to release the prisoner to a waiting ship. The Duke is asked why he released the prisoner. "Because I hated him," said the Duke. "Even as my father must have hated his father in this room I hate him" (192).

"Purchas, His Princess." Vol. 60 (1939), 531–539

A flower piece. Rejected by Mistress Grant as unworthy of her, Peregrine Purchas retires before the scorn of the village. But when word reaches Mistress Grant that he has taken on the interests of another Princess, she is stung. Newly aware of her true love for him, she is jealous. She tries to obtain a potion from a local witch which will newly secure his favor. But upon secretly entering his chambers, she rejects that approach and hurls the bottle from her. But the magic bottle rebounds back upon her and knocks over Peregrine Purchas's flower pot. He appears and rebukes her. His new "Princess" was this favored bloom! He says it was near to blooming and would make him famous! It had not scorned her like Mistress Grant had done:

> You've killed her—she was to have been at her full bloom to-morrow—she would have made me famous; she was pink and yellow, the size of my hand. I have no other root. Get out of my house. You had done with me—laughed at me—you and the others; she was beautiful and did not scorn me— [539].

He orders her to leave. And as she departs, she hears him sob—*but not for her* ... (539).

"The English Free Lance." Vol. 61 (1940), 130–138

Sir Nicolas Oldcastle, an English mercenary soldier, has come from Naples to Tuscany, where he has sold his services to the Malaspina. But before he can launch his campaign, he is approached by a fair young maid named Palmira, who belongs to the enemy. Will he switch his allegiance to the forces of Malaspina's sister, the Duchesse Malaspina? He agrees on condition of a bargain that after he wins the field for her, she will marry him. She agrees, although warning him that another man has already sought her out. Subsequently, peace unexpectedly breaks out between the contending forces. Sir Nicolas demands his reward. "And that was how the English mercenary won his Italian wife" (138).

"A Sicilian Autumn." Vol. 60 (1939), 481–487

It is September. The Feast of the Madonna. In the golden light Agrippino, a young squire, rides forth to a castle. He intends to elope with the fair Constanza and carry her off to his own people in Taormina. In secret, he leaves the merrymaking in the castle and goes to the prearranged trysting spot. The clothed and veiled young lady meets him. On the road, she begs him to stop so she can eat. Annoyed at the delay, he agrees. But during their pause, they are approached by a young Lord. Constanza is revealed to be not Constanza at all, but the noblewoman Vittoria degl' Innocenti. Agrippino realized he has been hoaxed and that, in effect, he has abducted the Conte's daughter! As a reward, Agrippino is offered to come to Palermo and take up the position of Knight in the man's service.

From *Harper's Monthly*

"The Apple of Venus." February 1909, 370–377

A piquant little conte cruel about a young married woman's revenge on the man who spurned her love five years before. Although engaged to stodgy and middle-aged Sir Gilbert Fraser, Sophie had loved Paulyn, Lord Frere in secret. But because he was poor, the budding romance was blocked. He possesses a beautiful jewel that Sir Gilbert had desired to buy. Paulyn refused to give it up.

> It is an apple of pure gold, perfectly modeled, with two curling jade leaves, set against the stalk. Lord Frere took it out and touched a little spring; the apple flew open in four quarters against the leaves and disclosed a diamond as large as a lady's nail and beautifully cut [372].

Inside each of the four quarters is a likeness of beautiful women—Helen of Troy, Cleopatra, Queen Guinevere, and Lucretia Borgia. He swears to Sophie he will never part with it, unless—He implies, until it is hers. She refuses. He is scornful. She leaves and he mutters, "Until tomorrow."

But there is to be no tomorrow. Five years pass. Sophie has married Sir Gilbert. And now Paulyn, recently endowed with wealth, appears at Sir Gilbert's door. Sophie realizes at the sight of him now that her marriage

> had been filled with merely mechanical actions and aimless thoughts; now, like a tide damned and suddenly set free, her blood flowed passionately. She knew that her husband was old and dull, that her days had been as dust; she knew what she had missed, and she looked with narrowed brown eyes at the careless figure of the man who had cheated her of it [375].

Paulyn, now Lord Clare, had sold the jewel to Sir Gilbert a few years ago while still impoverished. He now appears at the door, declaring an interest in Sir Gilbert's treasures, but Sir Gilbert knows he really wants to retrieve the jewel—even if he has to steal it.

Paulyn arrives, there is dinner table chat. He feigns disinterest in Sophie. Sir Gilbert knows Paulyn has really come to buy back the jewel. He asks Sophie to wear it beneath her bodice lest Paulyn steal it. But surreptitiously he writes a message on Sophie's fan to meet him afterward in the garden. They meet and he asks Sophie to leave her husband and come away with him. He knows she is wearing the jewel. He wants her to steal it and come away with him. She rejects him: "Listen to me, Lord Clare. You went out of my life utterly. I only heard of you once—when my husband told me he had bought this toy from you. I never thought to see you again until to-night—now, what can you imagine are my feelings towards you—now, what do you mean me to say?" He says she belongs to him, that he is here to "claim" her. She asks, "Me-or the jewel?" "Both." He says. "[Your husband] thought to outwit me; he thought I should not guess where he had concealed the jewel; he thought it would be impossible for me to steal it from such a hiding place." (376).

"You woo me too late," she says. "Stand away from me." Disdainfully, she removes the jewel and chain and tosses it at his feet. The story's narrator adds, "He gathered the jewel into his pocket without looking at it and stepped into the street ... what he had come for—yes—perhaps." He thinks to himself, "After all, the jade cares, or why did she give me this?" (377).

Imagine his dismay, as the final lines of the story reveal that instead of the golden apple at the end of the chain, Lord Clare finds only "a little gilded skull." He laughs mockingly: "And do I care to have missed the apple—or to have missed—Venus?" (377).

Note: An enigma. It leaves both former lovers betrayed.

"An Initial Letter." April 1910, 663–666

A wholly delightful whimsy set in the 1380s as Geoffrey Chaucer and John of Gaunt join a procession that surely references Chaucer's *The Canterbury Tales*. This bespeaks Bowen's love of colorful processions and lyric tales and whimsies in invoking the historical characters of Chaucer (1343–1400), his patron John of Gaunt, and John's wife, the Duchess Blanche), and Katherine Swynford (mistress of John and later his second wife) and Otto Swynford. In microcosm, Bowen's little procession of characters is her pilgrimage to Canterbury, her own "New Canterbury Tales."

"Holy Mr. Herbert." May 1910, 839–845

Bemerton, England, 1630. A brief sketch involving clergyman George Herbert (1593–1633), his writing of *The Priest to the Temple*, and his meeting with a recently married young woman in distress. This woman has gotten separated from her new husband, Tom, when robbers beset them. Alone, she comes across Herbert in the woodland. He is writing on sheets of paper a work he titles *The Priest to the Temple*. He offers to escort her to a nearby house where she can rest. While she rests, he goes in search of Tom, leaving behind his packet of papers. She is horrified to see that two sheets are missing. She retraces her steps in search of him. She encounters Tom, who is looking for her. He discovers that the packet of papers is not missing any sheets at all. Herbert has apparently wrongly numbered them.

FROM *MACLEAN'S*

"You Ought to Be Thankful." 15 April 1924

The marriage between Madelaine and Randal Compton is jeopardized when the actress Lucy Bolton comes for a visit. While Madelaine has grown weary of what she has given up for husband and family, Lucy as a single woman fantasizes about running away with this new man in her life. When the Compton baby nearly drowns, the threatened marriage is restored and the actress leaves the Comptons alone.

"Fleur Ange." 1 May 1926

Fleur Ange agrees to give up her wealth for the sake of her new husband, whose pride prevents him from living off her money. But her resentment at sacrificing the luxuries they could have had creates frictions. She decides to leave her husband and enjoy the money that affords her the lifestyle she thinks she deserves. But in a fit of remorse, she quits her fortune and returns to her husband. He, in the meantime, has come into money on his own. They are happy once more.

"Different Drummers." 15 December 1922

Opera singer Marianne Considine and Harry Dobree, scion of an aristocratic family can't agree on marriage. He can't accept her pursuing an independent career. But during the course of their conversation on Christmas day, she relinquishes her position. She agrees to marry him.

"The Pink Shawl." 15 February 1925

Rose Smith and her mother run a shabby lodging house. When a new lodger arrives, Rose believes he is interested in her. When he admires a red shawl in a shop window, she believes it is a sign that he will buy it for her as an engagement present. Instead, no shawl and no promises of endearment are forthcoming. Desperate, Rose takes all her money and buys the shawl herself. But when the lodger sees Rose in the shawl, he declares her to be a flighty and foolish spender. He leaves. Soon after, his marriage to another woman is announced. In the list of the marriage presents is Rose's shawl.

"The Masterpiece." 1 June 1923

Wealthy Margaret Lennox pities "poor George," the man with whom she was once engaged. She has remained single and gone on to commercial success in her painting, while he has given up his own ambition to be a great painter and saddled himself with a wife and children. During a visit to George and his family, however, Margaret suffers a shock: George is living happily with a beautiful wife, baby boy, and a tiny study where he continues to paint. Moreover, one glance at a painting George is working on yields another shock: It's a masterpiece. Margaret can do nothing more but depart with mixed feelings of regret and surprise.

STORIES' END?

Marjorie Bowen once described herself as surrounded by her fancies, of people, "whose stories are perfectly clear to me.... There is not time to write it all down, one must select and be concise." Sometimes, "the figures move too fast, like a wheel of light.... It is hard to have gallery on gallery of pictures before one's inner eye, and only a few sheets of paper and pen and ink with which to interpret them!"[36] As readers, we try to catch up to these glimpses, these *contes cruels*, of characters, masked and unmasked, living and dead, all moving in their own *comedie humaine*: In doing so, do we not recognize ourselves? "[T]he men taste the brittleness of success, the women the limits of beauty; all, men and women, pursue each other in vain, hoping to clasp the long-lost, the perfect lover, and always embrace delusion." In sum, "They believe in nothing save their own secret and endless disappointment."[37]

FIVE

"Angels of the Darker Drink": The True-Crime Stories of Joseph Shearing

> *"Mr. Shearing" has given us a new quality of exquisite shivering, of sophisticated naivete, of dried rose-leaves soaked with blood, of a distinction which can entrance the scholar as well as the roughneck seeking to forget the state of his neck and his ill fortunes.*—Sinclair Lewis[1]

The Port of London. 1812. The scene is fraught with "continuous thunderstorms, the quick darkening of the tempestuous days, the obscurity of the highway and all its alleys and courts during the long evenings and nights." A murderer is loose. "No one knew but that his neighbor, the man he passed in the street, or whom he served at stall or counter might be the murderer. At length he is found and jailed, but before he can be brought to trial...."—

> ...he was found hanging by his braces from an iron hook where a lamp had formerly been placed. At the inquest it was ordered that the suicide should be drawn on an open truck through the capital and buried at the cross roads ... thrown into a hole in the ground, a stake driven through the heart and a cartload of lime thrown over it...[2]

This short story, "Blood and Thunder" is from Joseph Shearing's collection of short stories, *Orange Blossoms.* Shearing's dramatization of an actual British crime case from 1812 involved a series of eleven murders, committed during two separate incidents, twelve days apart in London's East End. The alleged killer, John Williams, hanged himself before he could come to trial.

The sensational case had alarmed the general public and fascinated the noted essayist, Thomas De Quincey. His classic essay, "Murder Considered as One of the Fine Arts," appeared a few years later.[3] De Quincey's biographer, Robert Morrison, observes that the essay "brought De Quincey great contemporary notoriety and inspired a long line of writers on crime, detection, aesthetics, and violence." They include writers as diverse as Edgar Allan Poe, G.K. Chesterton, William Roughead—and Joseph Shearing. "[Their writings] also hold a peculiar appeal to the modern reader," continues Morrison, "for they presage academic and popular assaults on conventional morality, the highly diverse commodification of violence, and the world-weariness that regards the spectacle of murder with both cynicism and fascination."[4] De Quincey himself summed up his attitude toward the subject: "People begin to see that something more goes to the composition of a fine murder than two blockheads to kill and be killed—a knife—a purse—and a dark lane.... *Design, gentlemen, grouping, light and shade, poetry, sentiment, are now deemed indispensable to attempts of this nature*" [italics added].[5]

Several sources in Britain and America fed the appetites of writers and public alike eager for true-crime fodder. *The Newgate Calendar* was established in 1773 and specialized in murder trials, with their dramatic denouements of acquittal or sentence of death. The gossipy *Police Gazette* was another source, first published in 1772 and continued into the 1970s. *Notable British Trials* appeared between 1921 and 1959 and featured transcripts of murder trials. The dramatic element was never far away, reports Theodore Dalrymple:

> Could there be a more definitive closure than the words uttered by an English judge, after he had the black silk square placed upon the top of his wig, in sentencing a murderer: "The sentence of the court is that you be taken from hence to the place from whence you came, and thence to a place of lawful execution, and that you there be hanged by the neck until you are dead; and that your body be afterwards buried within the precincts of the prison in which you shall have been confined after your conviction, and may the Lord have mercy on your soul?"

Dalrymple adds, "I love that unctuous after thought, so Anglo-Saxo in its hypocrisy: You order a man killed and then you wish him well in the afterlife."[6]

Among the distinguished writers who wrote introductions to these volumes was a retired Edinburg lawyer named William Roughead (1870–1952). His carefully researched accounts of true crimes, scrupulously researched and dramatically reported, intrigued readers in England and America throughout the 1920s and 1930s. "Connoisseurs in murder," said Dorothy Sayers, "will probably agree that William Roughead is far and away the best showman that ever stood before the door of a Chamber of Horrors."[7] For roughly six decades, Roughead attended almost every murder trial of any importance at the High Court of Justiciary. These experiences provided the material he would submit for publication in the *Juridical Review*, a monthly Scottish legal journal; in later years, he would collect his contributions to the *Juridical Review* as well as much new material into several anthologies of essays, including the two volumes at hand, *The Murderer's Companion* (1941) and Luc Sante, *Classic Crimes* (2000).

He wrote long and fascinating essays on the murder trials he had himself witnessed, as well as on a number of historical incidents and personalities. With a cheerful aplomb he speculated on motives and demeanor, although he was generally unsympathetic to the accused and applauded their comeuppance. Not for him, however, were neat resolutions: "He is not nearly as fascinated by the clue-hunting and deductive cogitation aspects of his cases as he is by their elaboration in the courtroom. A murder for him is of interest chiefly insofar as it provides the premise for a rich, complex trial at which personalities can clash, unfold, reveal their wrinkles."[8]

As the acknowledged master of this form, it's significant that Roughead considered Joseph Shearing a worthy colleague. In her 1942 *New Yorker* praise of Shearing's novels, critic and novelist Sally Benson confirms this: "Such experts in murder as Edmund Pearson and the former Scotch barrister William Roughead have declared openly that the Shearing novels are the best of their kind published today." She goes on to declare, "Mr. Shearing is a painstaking researcher, a superb writer, a careful technician, and a master of horror. There is no one else quite like him."[9] And as reported by an authoritative historian of the genre, James Sandoe, "The crime fictions of Mr. Joseph Shearing ... are in a class by themselves."[10]

Shearing's novels are not to be confused with the "whodunnit" form of mystery story, or the procedural tale where a detective or a policeman sifts through clues for the solution of a crime. Rather, critic William Charlton best describes their idiosyncratic pattern: "Murders, real, supposed, or projected, do occur in all of them, but the focus is upon the predicament of the women accused of murder, driven to it, or fascinated by its perpetrators."[11] Enhance it all with the principles of De Quincey—"design, poetry, and shade"—not to mention Shearing's abundant detail of atmosphere and scene and his insights into the psychopathology of the malefactors, and we have narratives that gently coax us into the story while gradually tightening the noose of our attention until we arrive, gasping, at the overwhelming force of their denouements.

"Joseph Shearing is drawn to crime and mystery as Conrad and the Brontës were drawn to them," writes Edward Wagenknecht, "not because they can be wrapped up in neat little artificial packages but because it is in the extreme situations that the real capacities of human nature are revealed, and because human life itself is a mystery; unless we are willing to explore the mysteries, you must leave large areas of human character unexamined."[12]

Shearing began his cycle of true-crime novels with the publication in 1932 of *Forget-Me-Not* and concluded it eighteen years later in 1950 with *To Bed at Noon*.

Note: It should be stated at the outset that many other novels, short-story collections, and scholarly histories authored by "Marjorie Bowen," "George R. Preedy," "Robert Paye," "John Winch" involve criminal behavior to one degree or another, fact-based or not. But it is only in Shearing that we find an exclusive emphasis on historical crimes.

Here is a list, in chronological order of publication, of Shearing's true-crime novels and scholarly biographies. The fictional female protagonists and brief notes on the crime's factual sources are included.

Forget-Me-Not (American title: *The Strange Case of Lucile Clery*). 1932. Lucile Clery. In 1847, the Duc de Choiseul-Praslin, a member of the court of Louis-Philippe, was accused of the murder of his wife. The motive allegedly was his anger at her charges of his infidelity with the governess, Henriette Deluzy-Desportes. The scandal so disgraced the King and his government that it contributed to the Revolution of 1848. Before the Duke came to trial, he committed suicide by arsenic poisoning. Meanwhile, suspicions of Henriette's infidelity with the Duke led to her temporary imprisonment, after which she was released. She fled to America where she married a minister.

Album Leaf (American title: *The Spider in the Cup*). 1933. Lavinia Pierrepont. Based on a case in a book of French criminology. Shearing claims the book and the specific case are lost.

Moss Rose. 1934. Belle Adair. Based on a murder mystery of 1872, "The Great Coram-Street Murder." A Lutheran minister, Dr. Hessel, was arrested for the murder of Harriet Boswell on Christmas morning. Hessel was dismissed and the case remained unsolved. Shearing leaves no doubt that he was guilty. Note: There was no woman directly involved in the outcome of the case; Shearing has inserted a fictional character, Belle Adair, who blackmails the murderer.

The Angel of the Assassination. 1935. A scholarly account of the life and death of Charlotte de Corday, who was found guilty by the *tribunal revolutionnaire* of the murder of Jean-Paul Marat and guillotined on 17 July 1793.

The Golden Violet (1936). Angelica Cowley. The female novelist in the story is based on Letitia Landon, a poet and novelist of the early 19th century who enjoyed a measure of notoriety. Luc Sante quotes Bowen: "This owes ... to an incident of about a hundred years ago," not more fully specified, "when a half-caste of education was hanged for inciting Negroes to a riot."[13]

Blanche Fury (1939). Blanche Fury. A quarrel over the rightful ownership of Stanfield Hall resulted in the murder in 1848 of Isaac Jermy and Jermy's son by the presumptive claimant, James Rush. During Rush's trial, the governess at Stanfield, Emily Sandford, delivered incriminating testimony that contributed to the conviction and hanging of Rush.

Aunt Beardie (1940). Lady Sherlock and her daughter Jenny. Based on a tale of the French Revolution in *Vielles Maisons, Vieux Papiers* (1908), by G. Lenôtre.

Laura Sarelle (American title: *The Crime of Laura Sarelle*). 1941. Laura Sarelle. Based on the murder in 1780 at Lawford Hall, Warwickshire, of Sir Theodosius Boughton by Captain John Donellan. Donellan was hanged, but irregularities of the case were subsequently revisited. William Roughead reported the case in *The Fatal Countess*. Shearing's version cites the 1780 murder and moves the narrative forward to 1840 in a repetition of a similar crime.

The Fetch (American title: *The Spectral Bride*). 1942. Caroline Fenton/Harriet Bond. Based on William Roughead's "The Ambiguities of Miss Smith" in *The Fatal Countess* and "To Meet Miss Madeleine Smith" as reprinted in *Classic Crimes*. Madeleine Smith is accused but acquitted of the arsenic poisoning of Pierre Emile L'Angelier.

Airing in a Closed Carriage (1943). May Tyler. Based on the Maybrick Case, a much-debated murder trial in England in 1889. Florence Maybrick was accused of the arsenic poisoning of her husband James. She was tried and sentenced to death by a judge, who was later found to be insane. Her sentence was commuted and after ten years she was released, after which she disappeared.

The Lady and the Arsenic (1944). A scholarly account of Marie Cappelle (Madame Lafarge), who murdered her husband by arsenic poisoning in 1840, was tried and convicted and sentenced to life imprisonment. However, irregularities in the trial procedure led to her release in 1852.

For Her to See (American title: *So Evil My Love*). 1947. Olivia Sacret. In 1876 Charles Bravo, a lawyer, died of antimony poisoning. After two inquests a charge of "willful murder" was issued, but no one was arrested. Implicated were Bravo's wife, her companion, and her lover. The case was never solved. The case was reported by William Roughead in "The Balham Mystery," reprinted in Luc Sante, *Classic Crimes*. Shearing implicates the companion.

To Bed at Noon. 1950. Challis Allen. Based on the so-called "Kentucky Tragedy" from 1826, involving the murder, trial, conviction, and execution of Jeroboam Beauchamp for the murder of Kentucky legislator Solomon P. Sharp. An accomplice was Beauchamp's wife, Anna, who subsequently committed suicide.

Several of these cases, involving "Madame Lafarge," "Madeleine Smith," "Florence Bravo," "Florence Maybrick," are examined in detail in Mary S. Hartman, *Victorian Murderesses* (1976). The reader is advised to turn to the solid research and commentary afforded by this invaluable book. "It is possible to conclude that it was wise to be female and respectable if one intended to dispose of somebody in the nineteenth century," wryly declares Hartman. "The victims were the women's husbands, lovers, rivals, pupils, siblings, offspring, and grandchildren.... It is tempting, of course, to regard the murderesses as extraordinarily gifted in deceit, but nineteenth-century middle-class conditions were so favorable for developing female skills in mendacity that the judgment would be hasty.... In the Victorian age, deceit, in matters large and small, was elevated as a socially prescribed form of female behavior."[14]

THE FURIES

Shearing's gallery of historical malefactors—most of whom are drawn from the nineteenth century—is primarily female.[15] Their presence, as Shearing pointedly observes in the prefatory chapter in *The Lady and the Arsenic*, "considerably heightens" the drama.[16] As "angels of the darker drink," they are virtuosos in the concoction and administration of their poisonous potions, face washes, flypaper distillations, etc.[17] Poisons of all descriptions are everywhere and fairly saturate Shearing's pages: "The gas that lights our boulevards kills our trees and flowers," Lavinia Pierrepont's lover teaches her, in *The Spider in the Cup*, "the people who are employed in our most important manufacturers die constantly of the poison they inhale.... It lurks in the most unexpected places, in gorgeous blooms in toads, snakes, spiders, in exquisite plants, in glittering minerals." To which Lavinia, eager to learn more, breathes, "It is a powerful weapon in a feeble hand..." (219). And Jenny Sherlock in *Aunt Beardie* is astonished to learn that as long as women use cosmetic makeup they are all potential killers: "One must be careful," she is told, "you silly girls sometimes have enough poison in your beauty recipes to kill a man" (195).

They are among the many Victorian women who face the consequences of the severe limitations on employment and the rigid requirements of social standing. For some, continues Shearing in *The Lady and the Arsenic*, marriage was an option, but potentially degrading in its servitude; spinsterhood was a life "barren of dignity, importance, and excitement"; and, save for the very few ...

> "a career" was not to be thought of; the market for feminine talents and activities was extremely small. A lady had no training for anything but a post as governess; the arts were out of the question unless one was very gifted; actresses were not recruited from the ranks of gentlewomen; nor was it easy to become a famous courtesan. Lack of gifts, opportunities and courage prevented most well-born women from taking up this career that was so seductively romantic.

Driven back to the conventions, continues Shearing, a woman "sullenly acquiesced in her destiny and tried to do the best with the material at her command—her dreams, her books, her scribblings, her albums, her chance secret opportunities for adventure, for rebellion, for realization of her own potentialities." She began to "invent the exciting life she was denied, to lie, to combine real details with an intricate pattern of falsehood, to intrigue to gain her ends; she became skillful in provoking the passions of those about her, in creating 'sensations,' in making mischief, in assuming poses, even often an adept in the most subtle duplicity." In short—"To achieve a double life with the ease of natural duplicity and that elegant feminine dexterity for which hypocrisy is too coarse a word." In the face of criminal behavior, "not even the shrewdest, best-trained legal brains of the day could cope with the fearful complications created by the perverse egotism of the hysteric female desperately anxious to be the center of some powerful drama" (25–27).

Indeed, Shearing sees something almost "Satanic" about this, inasmuch as "the inventions, poses and half-unconscious actions of some irresponsible, emotional woman bring misery, disgrace and ruin and perhaps death to innocent people, where the lurid incidents of melodrama blend with the grimmest realities of life and death" (32).

Grim, tawdry, pathetic, dangerous—yes. But assuredly they seduce Shearing as much as they seduced their victims and are now seducing the readers and certain critics of his books. As Sally Benson declares, reading one of these novels is a hypnotically compelling experience:

> At times the reader of his books is almost disconcerted by the pleasant chitchat of the dialogue, the bell shapes of lilac, silk, the dresses of dark-and-light-blue striped taffeta, the little velvet jackets of prune color with fringes of the same hue.... Yet underneath the surface of this pool of prettiness lie the weeds rooted deep in the soft mud, while myrtle creeps along the banks ...

Benson concludes that you may come away from these novels, incredulous of their events and their women, "but you are forced to admit that once they existed; you may refuse to credit these events, but you must acknowledge that they once took place..."[18]

Joseph Shearing's gallery of poisoners, blackmailers, and seducers—including Olivia Sacret, Belle Adair, May Tyler, Laura Sarelle, Blanche Fury, Angelica Cowley, Lucile Clery, Lavinia Pierrepont, and Challis Allen—all owe their duplicity, their fantasies, their self-delusions to the figure whom Shearing regards as the definitive example of the notorious and complicated female poisoner of the nineteenth century—Marie Cappelle Lafarge (1816–1852). Lafarge went on trial in 1840 for the arsenic poisoning of her husband. She was convicted and sentenced to life imprisonment. Her case was one of the first trials to reach the public through daily newspaper reports, and she was first person in modern jurisprudence to be convicted largely on direct forensic toxicological evidence. However, much about the case remains unresolved. Not just a *cause celebre* of its time, inflaming and dividing the public, the precise nature of Marie's guilt remains a baffling riddle to this day.

Shearing wrote a book about her. Of course. *The Lady and the Arsenic* is a long and detailed scholarly study with references to court documents and Lafarge's own *Memoires*.[19] For the first two thirds of his account, Shearing indulges in minimal authorial intervention. As such, we are invited to be members of the public, or onlookers at the trial, weighing the evidence. However, in the last chapter, "What Was the Truth?" Shearing steps back for the longer view to reassess the evidence and present his own verdict. "It is now impossible to hope that the mystery," he begins—dashing our hopes for a clear-cut solution—

> will ever be cleared up. The trial and investigation were conducted with such a careless, violent and partial spirit, so much irrelevant matter was allowed to obscure the main issues, so much hearsay, rumour and gossip was admitted as evidence, that it is, even after a most careful reading of all the available material, impossible to come to a conclusion as to the truth of the matter.... Lafarge may have been guilty, but the evidence against her was weak, vague and confused. It was not even absolutely proved that Charles Lafarge died of poison; it was certainly not proved that his wife administered to him the poison" [261].

More to the point, Shearing probes into her emotional and psychological character and permits a few speculations: "Was Marie Cappelle a pathological liar, a fantasy-dweller, one of those criminals who are able to convince others of their innocence because they believe in it themselves?" Or was she merely a woman "so highly-strung, nervous and excitable as to be almost a dual personality ... given her pathological state, Marie Cappelle might easily have persuaded herself of her entire innocence" (267–269).

We may go so far as to suggest they are inheritors of the Gothic archetype of the "Madwoman in the Attic," i.e., a malignant female agency that goes back to the Hebrew mythology of Lilith and reaches forward to the fictional characters in Euripedes' Medea, Shakespeare's Lady Macbeth, Racine's Phedra, Keat's "La Belle Dake Sans Merci," Arthur Machen's "Helen Vaughn," Peter Straub's "Eva Galli," etc. We met their real-life counterparts briefly in the "Music on the Hill" chapter; and now, here they are, wrapped in stiff black bombazine, erotic but cold, splendidly self-propelled agents of the Furies.

Their closest relative is May Tyler in *Airing in a Closed Carriage*. This complex book, although based on the infamous Maybrick trial—Shearing moves the location from Liverpool to Manchester—could also claim as its source Lafarge's story. Indeed, the resemblances between the stories of Marie Cappelle and May Tyler border on identity. Like Marie, May suffers an abusive marriage in a claustrophobic house, where her lack of education and skill in the arts allows few distractions; like Marie, her only escape seems to reside in the poisonous arts; and like Marie, the fantasizing May remains an enigmatic figure whose guilt or innocence is unclear to everyone—least of all to herself: "She was never at one with the people into whose midst she had married, never able to understand even her own fortitude, even her own attempt to escape, even why she had married John Tyler" (205). As her husband lies dying, the entire house, like that of Marie Lafarge's, seems awash in arsenic. Indeed, *Airing in a Closed Carriage* is the "Citizen Kane" of Shearing's books, where we find "packets of arsenic in a chocolate box, arsenic in solution in a scent bottle, traces of arsenic on aprons, handkerchiefs, and dressing gowns ... [May] saw Stone Pynes as soaked in arsenic from floor to ceiling" (289). Like Marie, she is convicted during a trial that is reported and analyzed from a variety of points of view. Released after ten years from the women's prison—whose crude conditions are reported in ruthless and clinical detail—she too wanders forth into a netherworld of fantasy and self-delusion, where she dies, anonymous and alone. In sum, the "closed carriage" of the book's title is May's whole life—"the narrow social circumstances of her childhood, the claustrophobic setting of the Stone Pynes mansion, the hatred toward her of its servants, the sooty pollution of Manchester, the broader context of English national decay, the corruption of the courtroom, and the prison to which she is condemned." Her elegy is voiced by a stranger: "I wonder if she did do it. I think I've read most of the arguments for and against—you remember at one time the press was full of it and books were written championing her, but I never could make up my mind" (349).

Edward Wagenknecht pronounces it "first-class Shearing" and handles facts "in the manner of a novelist" and deploys imagination "to explain what life left unexplained." The resolution—or lack of it—is arrived at, "not by study of actions only, but by the study of the characters and events that produces these actions." Everywhere apparent is "the author's deep, bitter indignation against cruelty and wrongdoing [which] is all the more impressive because of the apparent coldness of the style."[20]

In a fascinating footnote, a story appearing in a 1943 issue of *The Age* recounts the death in 1942 in a remote Connecticut town of a woman known as "Florence Chandler." "Her death would have passed unnoticed if an old scrapbook had not been found afterwards in the cottage. It contained faded newspaper clippings about a celebrated murder trial of the last century ... shy, retiring Mrs. Chandler was actually the famous Mrs. Florence Maybrick."[21]

Two more women, Angelica Cowley in *The Golden Violet* and the titular Laura Sarelle, employ poison as a way out of marriages that have failed their fantasies and expectations.

Cowley, a London novelist, finds in her new Jamaican home the time and leisure to indulge in adultery—"she was pleased at the thought of her own duplicity" (165)—and homicide. Laura finds the time to hide away in her secret closet where, with the expertise of a master chemist, she has all the apparatus and ingredients necessary to distill laurel leaves into a deadly poison: "She had to play the game that women have learned during the ages to be so skillful at, to watch her opportunity, to cajole; if need be, to deceive" (5). For her efforts, she goes mad and drowns herself. As for Cowley, she escapes punishment altogether and as a successful novelist gains social position in high society back in London. (Note: For more details of Sarelle case, see the Ghost Story Chapter in this book.)

By contrast, other women lack the means and opportunities for marriage and leisure and must resort to more desperate measures to survive. Lucille Clery, in *Forget-Me-Not*, defends her life of blackmail and extortion with this justification: "Good God! Have I not been trained to be an adventuress? If there is no place for me in society, must I not make one? … I have had nothing out of life, nothing at all, my duty to myself is to get all I can" (82). The delusional Mrs. Sacret, widow of a missionary, in *For Her to See,* sets her blackmailing sights on wealthy Susan Rue: "What have I done," she wails, "a poor defenseless woman, but try to look after myself?" (183). The titular Blanche Fury is the archetypal "poor country cousin" who, in order to secure the wealth and estate she thinks is her due, craftily adopts a superb mask to hide her wicked machinations: "She had no emotions that she wished others to know; she was well aware that most of the passions that she hid behind that smooth exterior would be considered blameworthy by those who surrounded her and whom hitherto she had invariably deceived with her self-control" (29). But the lover she enlists in her ambitions is no less duplicitous, and the fate they incur spells disaster for them both. Belle Adair, former prostitute and failed actress in *Moss Rose*, greedily seeks an income by blackmailing the Rev. Maarten Morl. But, like Blanche Fury, she meets her match. Literally. As a predator and serial killer in his own right (or wrong), he proves every bit her equal. Both end up locked in the symbiotic embrace of victimizer and victim. "We shall never escape from each other," declares Belle, with a certain exaltation; "we shall never understand one another—eternal enemies, eternal companions" (180).

Evil moves within and without these women. Make no mistake about it, all of Shearing's aforementioned sociological, psychological, and gender-based insights must ultimately fail in adequately understanding these women. And Shearing knows that, too. He declares in *The Lady and the Arsenic,* there is "a miasma of the most refined and fastidious evil" hanging over them (21). Challis Allen in *To Bed at Noon* "accepts without question the dark and nameless passions she so carefully concealed" (115). Jenny in *Aunt Beardie* sees the evil within her as beyond her control: "I will imagine that I am one of those marionettes, that someone is pulling the strings, that I do not know what I am doing" (209). Belle Adair is empowered by a nihilistic attitude: "She was sustained by the precise and arid philosophy that considers all action, virtuous or vile, as so much mere passing of the hours before the final annihilation" (109). And May Tyler observes that the woman around her in the prison, *"are so hardened that they will break into furies and tumultuous rebellions"* [italics added] (341).

This reference to the Furies is no accident. The vengeful poisoners of Greek and Roman mythology, as we know by now, always seem to be around in these stories. "Fury" is Shearing's favorite description of a state of malice, mind, and being. This is overtly acknowledged, as we learned in the earlier "Music on the Hill" Chapter, in Shearing's *For*

Her to See, which cites "The Messenger of Tisophone, the Third Fury, the avenger of blood" as the source of the poisonings (219). Their assault on Shearing's women is no less disastrous than the supernatural agencies that hurl themselves against the Christian citadels and monasteries in *The Haunted Vintage* and *"Five Winds."*

Who Is Joseph Shearing?

Before we examine in detail some of the novels cited above, let's pause first and ask that pesky question: *Who the hell is Joseph Shearing? And what is he doing in a book about Marjorie Bowen?* There's a mystery here that lies behind the cases he writes about. Heretofore cloaked in shadow, Shearing has been waiting patiently to be recognized in his own right. Shearing himself revealed the mystery in full view of the reading public in 1937 when, in *The Lady and the Arsenic,* he placed this "clue" in the introductory chapter:

> There was something in this case that no man could wholly understand, but that would be clear to all women without much trouble. [italics added]

Simply put. But complicated.

We can argue this remark is uncomfortably sexist. But what is inarguable is that they *were written by a woman.* Which may or may not grant them special privilege. Joseph Shearing *is* Marjorie Bowen. Putting it another way, Marjorie Bowen *is* Joseph Shearing. The secret was well kept for almost a decade. The truth was not generally known until 1942 in the publication of *Twentieth Century Authors,* edited by Stanley J. Kunitz and Howard Haycraft. This revelation created a bit of a splash, as reported in *The Wilson Literary Bulletin.*[22] Just as *Twentieth Century Authors* was going to press, the editors made the discovery, but since it was too late to make the change, there were allotted two biographical sketches—one under "Joseph Shearing" and the other under the two names, "Marjorie Bowen" and "George R. Preedy." And it's amusing to see Jane Steadman, writing in hindsight, conflating *both* personae in her assessment, moving back and forth from the pronouns "he" and "she" with breathless ease: "Shearing sometimes follows known historical details, but interprets them anew. But sometimes, as in her foreword to *Moss Rose,* she reports, 'Nothing but the bare outline and a few unimportant details have been used'; and sometimes, as in *Laura Sarelle,* 'the setting is authentically Victorian, but the crime and characters are largely imaginary.'"

Moreover, Steadman continues, "Shearing was obviously well-read in the cases she re-created, but retained the novelist's freedom of interpretation and invention," in the attempt "to try to arrive at the truth not by study of actions alone, but by the study of the characters and events that produce those actions."[23]

I will continue to refer to Shearing as a "he" as the author of these stories.

By the way, it is not precisely known when William Roughead first discovered Bowen's ruse. But by the 1940s we find in the Yale Archives letters addressed to her by the name of Gabrielle Long.[24]

Selected Novels

The Golden Violet

"Now I begin to know myself—to understand the woman that I am."

Joseph Shearing bases the character of the female novelist, Angelica Cowley, on a real-life a poet and novelist of the early nineteenth century, Letitia Landon, who enjoyed a measure of notoriety. She may or may not have been involved in an incident in Jamaica when her half-caste lover is hanged for inciting a riot. Before the tale is done, Angelica, who has heretofore been a model of English propriety, unleashes her Fury and shoots her adulterous husband. But her aim is bad. So, while nursing his wound, she finishes him off with a deadly poison. Words she had heard earlier—"White people rather go to pieces"—have proven viciously prophetic.

"[Joseph Shearing] has given us a new quality of exquisite shivering," observes Sinclair Lewis in his Foreword to the 1941 edition of *The Golden Violet*. Shearing presents to his public a character of "sophisticated naiveté" in a tale that is like "dried rose-leaves soaked in blood." Angelica Cowley is the epitome of the Victorian lady, frigid and delicately erect, who moves "against the fire and slaughter of a rebellion of slaves in tropic Jamaica." Lewis continues, "Underneath the grand story, underneath the creepiness of a tropic dusk ... you have one of the bloodiest, reekingest murders on record" (6).

The time is the early 1830s. When first we meet Angelica Cowley, she is a young, spoiled, middle-class woman who makes her living writing frivolous romantic novels. Her latest, *The Golden Violet*, is yet unfinished. Like her other novels, it is about the sort of woman Angel most wishes to be—"one of those lovely creatures whom she delighted to create on paper," and who was "such as she could write, so easily, with such zest" (11). She has recently met Thomas Thicknesse, a plantation owner in the British colony of Jamaica, and accepted his proposal of marriage. They leave London for a new and exotic life on his Jamaican plantation. Always the fabulist, Angel foolishly imagines that she would be "a ministering angel among grateful savages, as a fair white Queen among bowing slaves..." (22). Yet at every turn she is disgusted with the climate, the slaves, and her empty domestic life.

Compare that image with the woman we see eighteen months later. Now, "She belonged to the tropic night" (197). Disgusted with

Golden Violet **book cover**

the constant tension with her husband and his infidelities, she indulges in an affair of her own. And with cold deliberation murders her husband.

Indeed. Outwardly, she remains a successful and respected women, in and out of society. Not even the efforts of a few enlightened plantation owners had been able to erase the rot that eats away at the place. Prejudices die hard: "Some of 'em are very good to their slaves, but there is that feeling that you can't eradicate that they *are* slaves, that they're not ordinary human beings" (176). But the inner emotional and physical turmoil that she has endured on the Island, abetted by the corruption of the slave trade which supports her husband's lavish lifestyle, has released a new and dangerous sense of self.

Flashback to earlier events on the island. The marriage between Angel and Thomas is deteriorating. Thomas has been brutally candid that he has married her for her money. He has taken on a lover, the mysterious and beautiful slave girl, Luna. Angel, disgusted with him and disillusioned with her isolation, has also taken on a lover, John Gordon, himself a slave owner. Her adultery fulfilled herself as a woman: "She was pleased at the thought of her own duplicity, and the way in which she had fooled and hoodwinked, and, according to his own code, disgraced Thomas Thicknesse. 'Now I begin to know myself—to understand the woman that I am'" (165). She grew obsessed with her lover, in love and in lust for the first time in her life. "When she had known nothing of love she had been able to write endless love scenes that had completely satisfied her readers. Now that she thought of nothing but love herself in all her waking hours, and dreamed of it when she slept, she was incapable of putting a word of her experience on paper" (110).

The plantation owners face an impending slave uprising. Angel is no more enlightened than her husband in her disgust at the slaves, her conviction of their racial inferiority, and her support of their ill treatment. For her husband, it is a harsh necessity born out of maintaining the plantation's trade in sugar and cotton. For her is it borne out of the inbred prejudice of her privileged English upbringing. Therefore, it is with a shock that she learns her lover, the dashing and handsome John Gordon, is what was termed at the time a "mulatto," a man who in the eyes of the whites on the Island, is nothing more than a black man. But no sooner does she realize that her love for him transcends her bitter racism, than he is captured and lynched during the slave uprising sweeping the island. He had been trying to negotiate a truce between the slaves and their masters had resulted in his capture and lynching at the hands of the whites. Complicit in the act was her husband.

There is retribution to be meted out. With the assistance of a mulatto Luna, formerly the mistress of her husband, with whom Angel has formed an unholy alliance, Angel murders her husband with a rare and deadly poison.

A sense of dread touched with hints of the supernatural suffuses the novel. One of the first things Angel discovers on the island is the family mausoleum. She views with apprehension the ebony slab upon which lay the coffins of her husband's family and his sister, Betty, dead prematurely at age eighteen. "I suppose [my husband] thinks that I shall lie there some day," she says—and the thought "held for her an unutterable horror" (86). She pictures the mausoleum with deep fear; it seems "worse than death to have to lie there forever" (227). Moreover, Betty's ghost—an apparition dubbed by the natives as a "duppy"—can be seen about the Island. Angel tells Gordon she identifies with it: "I feel like that—disembodied—perhaps my spirit will come to tap at your shutter" (133). The slaves are afraid of the dead; and perhaps Betty's *duppy* is only one of the many ghosts raised by the charms of a "witch woman," an aged slave named Obeah. And there is the grim chant sung by the slaves she hears one day, about a slave owner who used to cast his sick slaves into a gully to die. The frock worn by the dead and the board upon which he had lain was always returned to the master. "People don't do things like that now, do they?" protests Angel. "I don't know," replies John Gordon, "sick slaves are a nuisance and an expense, and these people think it kinder to find means of allowing them to die" (105).

Shearing's prose richly captures the beauty and terror of the Island in granular detail. Its exotic aromas and vivid colors of plant and animal life, so graphically presented in luxuriant detail, becomes to Angel ultimately merely a sign of decay: "She hurried away from the plantation; the vegetation appeared to have grown since she had been there last; the leaves and flowers were monstrous in their size, overwhelming in their vivid colour, oppressive with their perfumes, which she now found rank" (183).

Important scenes are etched with extraordinary subtlety. Led by Luna, Angel finds the bridge where John Gordon has been hanged. What could be more gently moving than this moment:

> Angel turned her head to catch the wind on her face ... she turned to look at the bridge, now clearly visible in the rarefied air.... She could see patches of white and light brown—yes, that might be shirt, cravat, kerseymere trousers, that patch of dark might be a man's bent head, the hair falling over the face [204].

The sequence in which Angel prepares and murders her husband is deftly handled. Presaging it is this telling exchange between her and Luna. "You were wondering, were you not," says Luna, "what women can do to revenge themselves on men?" Her soft reply: "Yes, I was thinking that" (206). Her first move is the gunshot with which she wounds her husband. Accidental? The reader is not sure, until we have this tart passage with a snap at the end: "Revenge and convenience went together for her—with a little cleverness she might in this bloody day have satisfied both. But she had aimed badly and he would live" (222) Later, with cool dispatch, she nurses the wounded and bewildered husband. "I still don't understand your being so calm and cool," he says. "Have you really no heart, no feeling?" She replies: "I shouldn't enquire into that, if I were you." (237). She admits to him that when he recovers, she will be at his mercy and she will have lost her reputation and be ruined. She moves away and in the slightest of gestures receives the poison from Luna. "Sleep with pleasant thoughts," she says as she administers it. He's suddenly wary of her. "I've done what I had to do," she says. "You've had what you ought to have. Be quiet, lie still, sleep."

And she just waits ... "with an expectant smile." (239–241).

Back in London, the newly widowed Angelica marries the former Governor of Jamaica and enjoys a glittering social life. At last she completes *The Golden Violet*. Its genteel story is showered with critical praise as "an exquisite romance written in the sweet strain of moral humanity" (253).

"Forget-Me-Not"

"What a relief to think that I shall not go to his heaven" (239).

Mademoiselle Lucille Debelleyme is also known as Mary Showalter, Lucille Clery, and Lucy Meadows. There is a superb irony beneath these personae: Her fierce, crafty preservation of her virginity and public respectability spells nothing but disaster for the men she leaves in her wake. Like Angelica Cowley, her presumption of propriety is her weapon and, as it were, her saving grace in the face of notoriety: "It must have been my virtuous training that set me on the wrong path!" (155). This doesn't mean she is a passive character; rather,

> She watched contemptuously the helpless disorder of such other women as there were, how they clamoured for the protection of father, husband, brother, making a parade of foolishness and helplessness, how they lamented the distress of the voyage, and retired to the cabins immediately with smelling salts [28].

The story spans roughly 1840 to the mid–1850s, during the reign of the "Citizen King," Louis Philippe I, whose reign began in 1830 as the leader of the Orléanist party. He was deposed as the leader of the Orléanist party in 1848.

Clery comes to the household after several misadventures involving a feckless lover, Robert Morrison, a brief employment as a governess with Lady Anfield, and, finally, a position as governess in the home of M. and Madame du Boccage in an upper-class neighborhood. She has learned to efface herself, to hide her conniving spirits beneath rigid decorum:

> Her demeanor was perfect, respectful without being servile; her personality was completely effaced in her post; she was the governess in a rich gentleman's establishment and could never make the mistake of asserting that she was a human being [19].

No man yet had incurred her favor. "I should be better off in a brothel," she declares to herself (24). In the home of the Madame Boccage she immediately sees opportunity. The woman is a fool and her husband is dependent on her wealth. Clery curries favor with the Duke and soon gains a foothold in the house. "She felt like a general who takes the enemy's outposts in a slow, steady progress" (74). The harder Madame tries to oust her, the more determined is Lucille to stay, gaining steadily the support of the Duke. They are akin in their scorn of conventions: "Neither [of them] believed in God, neither of whom felt the lack of that belief, both hedonist, epicurean and passionate, [and] looked at each other with increasing excitement" (97).

As a sense of scandal grows up around their relationships, King Philippe warns the Duke that this sort of behavior jeopardizes the propriety of France and feeds those who would wish to topple his reign: "You have some idea how affairs are in France, the feeling of the people against us, the difficulty of maintaining this role of liberalism, the hatred there is for the aristocracy, for the Chamber of Peers, the avidity with which every scrap of scandal is leaped upon" (109).

Alarmed at what is happening all around her, Madame persuades the Duke to remove Clery from the home. No sooner does she find temporary employment in a humble little children's school than the news arrives that the Duke has been arrested for the bloody murder of his wife. Clery is also arrested as his accomplice. The public is aroused by the murder:

> There was an explosion of rage against the House of Peers, against the aristocracy, against the King himself, against the whole insolent, arrogant world of money and leisure which, in the eyes of the people, had fallen into disrepute with the murder [185].

The Duke is held under suspicion, protected momentarily from the guillotine by his aristocratic title. Before he comes to trial, he commits suicide by arsenic poisoning. Lucille is incarcerated for questioning, but the lack of evidence and her blameless demeanor and protests of innocence win her freedom. "It gave her some pleasure to reflect how few would guess that in this insignificant humbly-born young woman was one of the main causes of the revolution which meant the downfall of a dynasty" (231) "Good God!" she exclaims, "have I not been trained to be an adventuress? If there is no place for me in society, must I not make one?" (56). As a result, she feels, "I have had nothing out of life, nothing at all, my duty to myself is to get all I can" (82).

Alone and friendless, she considers suicide until she attracts the attention of a young American minister, Nathaniel Meadows. He is dazzled by her beauty and considers her "a worthy helpmate expressly sent him by God" (238). They remove to America. The novel ends with glimpses of her life in his pious household. Her "ceaseless work makes her the admired centre of a group of prosperous, comfortable, Puritan New Englanders" (233). She takes care, in the meantime, to destroy a packet of newspapers with headlines of the scandal with the Duke. To Nathaniel she is a seductive enigma: "He could not read the sincere contempt in her smile as she glanced up at him, he had never been able to understand her at all and never would be. He was perfectly satisfied with the artificial self she so contemptuously offered him…" (240). Of course, inwardly, she has nothing to do with his religion: "'What a relief to think that I shall not go to his heaven,' she thinks to herself" (239). He persuades her to publish a small collection of her charming vignettes about her life in Paris, entitled *Forget-Me-Not*.

Forget-Me-Not should be read as the cynical, shadow side to another novel about the same subject, Rachel Field's *All This and Heaven Too*, published six years later. Sally Benson notes that when the Rachel Field novel was published, "there was a threatening sound of offstage noises made by a select group of extras, numbering perhaps about two thousand. Their complaint was that the story of the Duc de Preslin who murdered his wife had been done before, and done superbly, by an English writer who signed himself Joseph Shearing."[25] In 1940 an Oscar-nominated film adaptation was directed by Anatole Litvak and starred Bette Davis as Clery. That film, like the Field novel, is determined to prove Bette Davis is an innocent, even saintly figure. This radical departure from Shearing's sharply cynical portrait of a ruthless female opportunist only proves the superiority of Shearing's version. It must be ranked as one of his finest achievements, about a woman whose cunning and wit brought about not just the unhappy demise of one of France's first aristocratic families, but contributed to the fall of the reign of Louis Philippe.

Moss Rose

"Who are these people that I should not take advantage
of their follies, their weaknesses—their faults?"

Belle Adair, by contrast to her sisters Angelica Cowley and Lucile Clery, makes few pretensions to respectability. She possesses neither great beauty, charm, nor aristocratic pretension, but her finely calibrated eye for the main chance will afford her a measure of success and failure, in equal proportions. And when she finds love, it is a most peculiar condition, borne out of darkness and degradation.

The facts in the historical case are these: On Christmas day, 1872, a woman of the "unfortunate" class was found murdered in her room in a house at Bloomsbury, London. The police arrested two men belonging to a German ship, recently arrived in port. One was the ship's surgeon and the other was the chaplain. The former was released, but the latter was brought up at Bow Street police court, where, however, he was released after establishing a satisfactory alibi. "Much public sympathy was expressed with the chaplain as a victim of blundering by the police, and a subscription was raised for him. Mr. Gladstone wrote him a letter expressing sympathy with him in the ordeal."[26]

Shearing moves the crime closer in time to the Jack the Ripper slayings. Here is a story of a young music hall dancer named Belle Adair (or is it "Rose Rastell," or "Laura Pryde," or "Rose Vere"?), who has recently left a tawdry life of prostitution for employment as a dancer at the seedy local Cambridge Theater. "She never made a success, there was something remote and alien about her, some quality of disdain and coldness that made people uneasy, even hostile" (13). "Even those men who had desired her, who had petted her, spent money on her, given her praises and caresses, had been very soon disenchanted. They had treated her as if she were, after all, nothing out of the common—merely a pretty complacent woman, with some breeding and no scruples" (233–234).

Shearing description of a London street scene on Christmas Eve superbly conveys a sense of the gritty atmosphere throughout:

> The gin palaces of Holborn were nearly as sumptuous as those of the Tottenham Court Road or Drury Lane. Belle had the choice of several brilliant establishments as she proceeded slowly over the greasy pavement through the murk. It was about eleven o'clock and the shopkeepers were putting up shutters and lowering their blinds; there was a glimpse through the fog of scarlet cheese and pallid butter as the cheesemonger shrouded his windows; there was the tinkle of the chemist's shop-door bell as it closed for the night, a glow of light from the baked-potato man's fire, where a few ragged children clustered to enjoy the warmth, and in the gutter a woman railed with her arms folded in a ragged shawl, muttering a song in a broken falsetto [19].

Later, at her lodgings in No. 12, Hogarth Street, she inadvertently stumbles upon the scene of a grisly crime. She catches a glimpse of the upturned face of a handsome, well-dressed stranger hastily leaving the rooms of Daisy Arrow. Entering Daisy's room, she finds her dead of a slashed throat. Instead of crying alarm, Belle methodically looks around the room and picks up items left behind by the killer—a plumed headdress bearing blood stains, a German bible, and the key to the door. She places the items in her carpet bag and conceals the key under a floorboard in her room. Surely, she thinks, the stranger she saw exiting the room is the killer. Excitedly seeing an escape from her drab existence, she plots a scheme to benefit from the tragedy. "Belle was upheld and even stimulated by the tragedy and by her part in it. Here was what she had longed for and needed—action, suspense, excitement" (39). With her knowledge, she felt a new sense of power, "a release from her present degradation" (48). Yet, Belle has moments of brutal self-assessment. "I suppose I never was so degraded as I am now. Perjury and blackmail. But those are mere words. It is no shame to fight with the only weapons I have. Who are these people that I should not take advantage of their follies, their weaknesses—their faults There was always someone to take advantage of me" (156).

She slyly learns what she can of the investigation by Scotland Yard of possible suspects. One such suspect is brought to the dock but, against testimonies incriminating him, Belle denies his guilt. The man, identified as Maarten Morl, a Lutheran minister on holiday from his native Germany, has had an alibi supported by his fiancée, Lily Schoppe, and his prospective father-in-law. He presents a public image as an upright, moral character, and he is acquitted. All of London comes to his defense and raises funds to compensate for his ordeal. Although the alibis put forth by his family and fiancée seem airtight, Belle knows he is indeed the killer. She had sketched his face at the moment after first seeing him on the stair.

After he is acquitted, Belle sizes up Maarten. They take each other's match: "She was quite certain that he was more nearly her equal and more to be respected and admired than she had supposed. Yes, that air of bewildered innocence, of manly simplicity that he had maintained so skillfully in the dock must have been a pose. This conviction of his strength made her more ruthless" (122). Another time, she muses: "He possessed the qualities that she much admired, cool elegance of mind and person, of speech and gesture, hard sophistication—he seemed a man who had fashioned his own personality to his own liking as she had fashioned her own personality to her own liking" (130).

Belle cares nothing about the tragedy and its victim. She regards them as merely a convenient passport to a better, more comfortable, more "respectable" life. Now known as "Rose Rastell," she approaches Maarten and his fiancée, Lily, and her father with offers to withhold incriminating information against gaining money and position as the "gentlewoman" she longs to become. As she ingratiates herself into the household, it becomes clear Maarten's family and fiancée are already becoming suspicious of him. During one of his visits to his mother's house, Maarten himself alludes to a criminal past, including the murder of a newborn baby. But Rose's blackmailing ambitions seem to sag as time goes on. Bored, she thinks it best after all to quit the family with whatever money she can get and pursue Maarten with romantic ambitions of her own. She had already noted that common bonds seem to unite them—a sordid past, a rejection of social and religious morals, their complicity in the crime itself. They play cat-and-mouse with the question of his guilt and her own blackmailing: He keeps protesting his innocence, and she deludes herself that her blackmailing is only an opportunity to gain the better life and opportunity that as a woman she has been hitherto deprived of. She even begins to wonder, against all the evidence she has, if Maarten is really innocent, after all!

Later in the story, as the details of blackmail seem to recede from her consciousness, she is aware that other more mysterious ties bind them together: She gazes upon his expressionless mask of a face and muses to herself: "We shall never escape from each other, we shall never understand one another—eternal enemies, eternal companions. Yes, that, for I do not mean to let him go" (180). He returns her passion and they leave together for Munich where they feel free to pursue their affair.

She recognizes his divided nature: "He is at odds with himself like I am, searching, lonely—we ought to suit each other very well" (211). At length, "She pitied the man whom she was tormenting, for his existence seemed like her own, out of control, distorted, dark and unescapable" (177). Yet, in the final pages she is experiencing what she thinks is love for him; "She considered what life would be without this exciting sense of power, this hold over another human being—what life would be without this odd intimacy with a man who began to stir her senses and hold her fancy in a way that had not, for long, happened to her…" (220) It's a most peculiar love, borne out of darkness and degradation. Belle muses to herself: "What would it concern them if they had come out of darkness to meet one another? Yet she could see no future for them—none. That did not matter, either; they were both vague, transient, incoherent creatures of base instinct and brutal passions; she judged herself as no better than he was, even if he had, cornered and desperate, struck down Daisy Arrow; she had been able, without pity, to turn that to her own advantage" (222).

Then, one night after heavy drinking, Maarten takes a drunken Belle to a cheap brothel in a dubious part of the city. Belle's confused mind sees it as a return to the brothel's rooms at No. 12 where the murder she had witnessed had been committed. Indeed, details of the moment are exact duplicates of the scene of that crime—down to the clasp-knife Maarten produces to slit her throat.

A movie was adapted from the novel and released by Twentieth Century–Fox in 1947. See the Appendix on media adaptations.

For Her to See

> "Life was only tolerable [to Mrs. Sacret] because of secrets hidden within her mind, guarded, seldom considered, never revealed."

Mrs. Olivia Sacret presents quite a dowdy contrast to the exotic and polished Angelica Cowley and the equally refined Lucile Clery. Like her sister from the streets, Belle Adair, Olivia's grasp of money and position will doom her just as quickly as they are realized. Her main chance proves to be not a chance at all. Like poor Belle, her penchant for a murderous lover finds her at the quick hands of man whose Fury matches—even surpasses—her own.

The novel is based on the so-called "Balham Mystery" from 1876. The death of Charles Bravo, a lawyer, was the result of antimony poisoning. After two inquests a charge of "willful murder" was issued, but no one was arrested. Implicated were Bravo's wife, her companion, and her lover. The case was never solved. The case was reported by William Roughead and reprinted in Luc Sante, *Classic Crimes*. Shearing's version implicates the companion, whom he names "Mrs. Olivia Sacret."

Olivia has just returned from Jamaica, where her late husband, a Dissenter, had been doing missionary work. Her past life has been, in her own estimation,

> incredibly dull, like a waterless, featureless plain.... How had she endured her barren childhood, the humiliations of her poverty-blighted schooldays, her marriage to a Dissenting, invalid missionary, those years in Jamaica where she had been cut off from everyone save a handful of fellow zealots and negroes, who were to her unsympathetic and aloof temperate, as degraded as slaves [48].

She lives now in humble quarters with no expectations of finding employment. After noticing in the newspaper the name of a former friend, Susan Rue, announcing her new residence in a fashionable part of London, Mrs. Sacret decides to visit her. She finds the pretty but foolish young lady she had known years ago living in luxury. She quickly realizes the woman is lonely and under the domination of her husband—a banker who had married her for her wealth—and a controlling mother-in-law. Susan is more startled than glad to see her old friend. She remembers that years before she had confided to her in a series of letters her affair with a married man, Sir John Curle. Alarmed, and needing to retrieve those letters, Susan invites Olivia to her home as a paid live-in companion. Olivia, for her part, realizes those letters could be her ticket to extortion and blackmail. Not that she is conscious she is doing anything wrong:

> She believed in God, she knew herself for a righteous, self-sacrificing woman who desired nothing from life save a decent position where she could maintain her genteel pretensions and expend her energies in good works.... The poverty of her childhood, her humble marriage, a dread of sinking to menial labour, unavowed fears of loneliness and the passive scorn or apathy of strangers who glanced at her once and never again, all made her cautious, unambitious, anxious for security [8].

It's no accident, she realizes, that she had always liked her name, "Sacret," so close to "Secret": "Life was only tolerable because of secrets hidden within her mind, guarded, seldom considered, never revealed" (9).

When Susan anxiously asks her if she has kept the letters and would agree to burn them, Olivia evades the question. She deludes herself into thinking it would be a pity to destroy such happy memories of their earlier friendship:

> It seemed harsh to destroy those letters without glancing at them again and recollecting the warmth and the pleasure of those few weeks when she had received Susan's wholehearted confidence.... She did not glance at the packed lines of Susan's crooked words, she read them carefully, intently, as she had never read them before, read them by the light of Susan's fear and distress and extravagant offer. Then she folded them up carefully and the blood showed in her face, making her appear younger, more comely. [22].

Sacret is positively blooming. Here is a way out of her sordid existence.

> She had always lacked enterprise, boldness; she had never made anything of herself.... She felt as if at last she was in her rightful place and that the social aspirations of the haberdasher's daughter and the squire's son, frustrated in themselves, had now been realized in her. This was what she really was, a lady, not a missionary's widow. [27].

Accepting Susan's offer to come live with her, Olivia rents out her little house to a rather mysterious character who suddenly appears—a painter, named Mark Bellis. She looks at him and is smitten. He looks at her and sees the main chance he's been looking for.

Bellis is very full of himself. He is a very dangerous man. He seems to know all about Olivia and her schemes. There is something elusive about him, something distinctly infernal: "A hundred years ago they would have said he had a familiar or was himself a limb of Satan" (251). Bellis is an artist of passable talents, at least to Olivia's eyes. He describes himself as an agent of the Greek goddess, Tisiphone—"I might term myself the Messenger of Tisiphone, the Third Fury, who was the avenger of blood" (219)—and again we recognize Shearing's own service to the vengeful goddess. He fairly relishes the portrait he is drawing of Bellis, whose artistic credo might well apply to Shearing: "As an artist, human material must interest me. I might have to draw a murderer or his victim. I must assimilate their characters" (91).

He tells Olivia they might be useful to one another:

> Our social system is very elastic, my dear Mrs. Sacret. It allows a good deal of scope for genteel adventurers, like you and I. It has no room and no pity for the weakling and the coward. Fortune, good or ill, befalls you, according to what you are. People are happy—or unhappy—because of what they are.... People even get murdered because of what they are [66].

He holds her with his gaze: "There was a quality in his agreeable face she had never seen in a human countenance before; she could not name it; to her it was a fascination not to be resisted, as if delights hitherto unknown were suddenly and richly offered to her" (56). By contrast, she saw herself as she would have been had she not visited Susan or had not met Bellis—as "a shriveled figure, daily withering, bent over a desk in a dim office, kneeling in a dim chapel, walking streets thronged with strangers, going home one dull evening and cutting her throat with the bread knife" (94).

Bellis's baleful influence grows stronger, and he orders Olivia to use her leverage over Susan to get her money and jewels—ostensibly, he hints, so they can get married and run off to Europe. All the while, Susan is half-aware of Olivia's duplicity. She tells Olivia: "I'm still afraid of you. I still could not endure to be disgraced. I don't any longer hope you will give up those letters. But I'll pay you, year by year, month by month, as you wish, to keep quiet about them" (167).

What, then to do about Susan's husband? Well, how convenient it is that the man is in the habit of pottering about his greenhouse, where all manner of exotic blooms flourish and intoxicate the air. "Martin Rue might die," reflects Olivia. "How easy that would make everything for Susan" (75). Utilizing her knowledge of a certain poison she had known about in Jamaica, she contrives to distill a potion from the greenhouse blooms. She cleverly maneuvers the unsuspecting Susan into administering the potion to him. The poor man dies after hours of suffering. There is an inquest. Olivia's hint that it is suicide successfully steers suspicion away from Susan. The death from antimony poison is declared administered under unknown circumstances.

But no one is satisfied. There is a second inquest. The deceased's mother suspects Olivia. This time Olivia comes perilously close to being implicated. But the verdict absolves both her and Susan of the deed. It is murder, "but by person or persons unknown."

Olivia is relieved and anxious to quit the place and run off with Mark Bellis. But Bellis has disappeared with the money and the valuables Olivia had gotten from Susan. Olivia realizes she has been duped all along. She considers her position: Maybe she had not really believed anything Bellis had told her; that he had never given her the slightest proof of his good faith. "She had *wanted* to be deceived, for she had supposed that he would continue to deceive her for a long while, because of her power to get money from Susan" (161).

In page after page of a relentlessly increasing intensity, the story swiftly comes to its inevitable close. The police want to open up a third inquest into the death. They set a trap for Bellis. "You deliver him to us," they tell Olivia, "and we will let you go—if you leave the country quickly.... Play your part a little longer, then make a tryst with him—and inform us" (251). And so it happens that, lured into the open by the promise of more money, Bellis arranges to meet with her. But suddenly, ahead of the scheduled meeting, he accosts her and whisks her into a waiting carriage. As it rattles along, the poor deluded woman still suffers the delusion that she and Bellis can get away together: "Why don't we go away now?" she asks him. "There are ships at the docks—we could get away." To *get away*... "She repeats it again and again, from the cathedral, from the town, down the river, to the sea..." (254). "How little any of it had availed," she thinks to herself, "—so much violence, so many lies, such intricate scheming, and she was where she had been, a poor missionary's poor widow. It was all the fault of her parents, who had brought her up so poorly, who had cheated her so cruelly, who had never given her a chance" (253).

But no, Bellis tells her he has discovered she has betrayed him to the police. He turns to her. She eagerly anticipates his embrace. But what he has in his hand "is clear for her to see ... and her cry is checked in her throat." (255).

Bellis steps away from the coach, wondering how "to get rid of the thing inside the cab" (256). But shadows close in on him. The coachman lifts the lamp and reveals that he is a policeman. Bellis is taken away.

The sergeant opens the carriage door and shines a light into the interior.

The closing sentences of the book are bathetic, yet horrifying: "The missionary's widow was on the floor with her face and throat hidden and some red shining among her mourning veil."

The sergeant understood the reason for her "grotesque silence" (256).

For Her to See was adapted in 1948 in a Paramount film. *New York Times* critic Bosley Crowther sniffed, "The talent of Joseph Shearing, the novelist, for communicating in words the measured but monstrous malevolence of Victorian ladies steeped in crime has again eluded the film-smiths who would get it onto the screen." (For more details, see the chapter on Adaptations.)

Blanche Fury

> "If I have no soul that is struggled for by angelic and infernal
> powers—of what importance am I? A speck of dust!"

Blanche Fury is Joseph Shearing's masterpiece. The very name commands our attention. As the title suggests, the whole sordid business is drenched in the destructive agencies of the Furies. At once the most complex, fine-grained, and deliberately paced of his narratives, it demands close attention on the part of the reader; yet it settles afterward into the mind like a canker lesion that cannot be removed. Blanche Fury herself is Shearing's ultimate manipulator. As the still point, the passive center, of a surrounding web of intrigue, betrayal, and violence, she deploys her wits and her sexual allure in the destruction of everyone around her. The price she pays is a withering solitude. Shunned by others, in the end she bears the awful stain of a guilt than can never be appeased

The facts in the actual case are these: On 28 November 1848 Isaac Jermy and his son were shot and killed on the porch and entryway of their mansion, Stanfield Hall, Norwich. The killer was disguised as a gypsy. Suspicion fell upon James Bloomfield Rush, their tenant farmer, who had been trying to defraud them of their property. He was arrested, convicted, and hanged at Norwich Castle on 21 April 1849. An alleged accomplice in the murder was Rush's mistress, Emily Sandford, the governess to his children. She was not convicted. Rush was buried on the grounds of Norwich Castle. The case was reported in detail in *The Stanfield Hall Assassinations! Authentic Report of the Trial, Conviction, and Extraordinary Defense of James Bloomfield Rush* (Cleave, London, 1849).

Blanche Fury draws extensively upon the circumstances, characters, and details of the case. One of Joseph Shearing's most complicated novels, its tangled weave of greed, intrigue, and murder is a modern-day Jacobean tragedy. Indeed, playwright John Webster's *The White Devil* provides Shearing with the template.[27] Its characters and events parallel and inform the action at every turn. Quotations appear at strategic places in the novel's text. And the stiffly upright, black-clad figure of Blanche Fury, Thisophone's agent, steps out of Webster's play to preside over it all. As if there's any doubt of the matter, we find this quotation from the play above the Prologue:

> You see, my lord, what goodly fruit she seems,
> Yet, like those apples travelers report
> To grow where Sodom and Gomorrah stood,
> I will but touch her, and you straight shall see
> She'll fall to soot and ashes (Act III, Scene 1)

And she is greeted at the outset by the man who will become her lover and accomplice in her bloody campaign to take over the Fury estate: "Blanche Fury, that's a pretty name. Isn't there an old play called *The White Devil*? I suppose you might say the same thing—Blanche Fury, the White Devil" (53).

"It's an exquisitely-told tale of horror," enthused a critic on the novel's appearance. "Mind you, this isn't everybody's dish, but it is the sort of thing which will appeal to those who like their crimes of fiction carried out right under their noses without any of the Ellery Queen or Agatha Christie clues littered around."[28]

Blanche Fury is a saga of the complicated family lineage that winds its torturous way through the number of competing claimants to the Fury name and the estate of Clere Hall. Greeting anyone who comes to the entrance of the hall is the image of a garlanded ape and the motto: *He that looks at Fury's Ape/ Fury's Ape shall look at him*. It is a warning against interlopers and pretenders to the Fury name. We have encountered this cautionary warning before in all of Shearing's novels. It's the Gothic trope predicting the nasty consequences of the quest for Forbidden Knowledge—or, in this case, the attempt to seize the Fury name and estates. Indeed, as presumptive claimants to the estate, Blanche and her lover find themselves locked in a symbiotic embrace of love, hate, and death. "Supposing it was Fury's ape itself," Blanche tells her lover, "come to throw out the intruders, eh?" (202). They have "looked at Fury's Ape," as it were, only to have the deadly gaze returned to them.

Yet, in their shared guilt is a momentary rapture, the unholy bond that erases the boundaries between good and evil, love and hate. It marks so many of the unholy alliances in archetypal Gothic narratives, from Hawthorne to James M. Cain.[29]

After the complicated Prologue sets out the backstory in 1740, in which the death of old Adam Fury leaves control of the family estate in the hands of two competing family lines, the Furys and the Fullers, the action moves forward a hundred years.

Blanche Fury arrives at Clere Hall, invited by her uncle, Simon Fury, the Recorder of Norwich, a widower, to come and be a governess to Simon's granddaughter. "She had come from penury and loneliness: she was going to loneliness and dependence, for she had no hope that among the Furies of Clere Hall she would find a friend.... [She] would be an interloper on this serene and happy scene" (23). She leaves behind an abject background, nursing an invalid father and mother, both now deceased. She is twenty-five years of age. Her sole possession, she knows, is her striking beauty. She is uncommonly tall, with a voluptuous body, belied by a severe, mask-like face:

> She wished to hide her feelings from the world. She had no emotions that she wished others to know; she was well aware that most of the passions that she hid behind that smooth exterior would be considered blameworthy by those who surrounded her and whom hitherto she had invariably deceived with her self-control [29].

Her first view of the Hall is a presentiment of what is to come:

> To the glance of the sensitive stranger, it had an oddly gloomy air hard to account for, perhaps the tall trees at the sides and back crowded too closely round the moat, which was too wide, deep, and dark; perhaps the oriel windows had too cold a glitter, for the place caught no sun save, in the spring, the last gleams from the west; perhaps the ivy rambled too heavily on the red brick, or the situation was too solitary, for there was no other house in sight. But certainly Clere Hall had no cheerful aspect, even now, in the prime of its prosperity and under the spring skies [15–16].

Perhaps, she muses to herself, "she might put in some claim of relationship and possibly force the consideration she would not be able to bring herself to beg" (24).

The Fury household consists of Simon, his wife Olivia, his son Laurence (Blanche's cousin), and Laurence's daughter, Lavinia. Simon Fury is really a Fuller who took on the name Fury after the death of his father, George Fuller. His son is likewise a Fury by appropriation. Lavinia will become the true heiress of Clere. And there is a steward to the estate, Philip Strangeways. He is a curious figure, a direct descendent through his father, Thomas Thorn, who was the son of Henry Thorn, who was the illegitimate son of Adam Fury and Rosa Spinelli (he picked up the name Strangeways through his mother's marriage). He is convinced that he is old Adam Fury's direct descendant. What Strangeways lacks, however, is the marriage documents that would validate Adam's marriage to Rosa. There are yet more complications to what is a Byzantine tangle of competing family lines ... but we will leave it here.

As Blanche is apprised of these connections, she sees opportunities for her schemes, not the least of which could involve eliminating Simon Fury from the equation: "They held a germ of storm and trouble and therefore began to please her, for her active, dominant nature was always looking out for a chance of an intrigue or drama or something in which she could use her hitherto dormant emotions." Strangeways, in particular, she regards as akin to herself—"slighted, cast-out, in a menial position, a paid dependent where he felt he ought to be a master" (40).

The rest of the novel is a kind of dance between Blanche and Strangeways. He attempts a bargain with Blanche: That they were "born to rule" and that they will live together while waiting for his wife and mother to die so they can gain the estate together. But there is the inconvenient presence of Simon Fury. She wavers:

> In a flash she had seen the proposal, the temptation, and almost succumbed to it. He and she together! Had not that been her ideal since she was a child? To meet a man who was her own equal in wits, daring and cunning? One who had a streak, like herself, of what she supposed the world called evil. One who would be unscrupulous, resolute, implacable, and stop for nothing ... [110].

Things are at a stalemate while three years pass. By now, she has lost all sense of a moral compass:

> The church would never be other than a charnel-house to her. . Once it had seemed to her a sign of intelligence not to believe in God or devil, now she felt that her incredulity heightened her anguish. For, she thought, if I have no soul that is struggled for by angelic and infernal powers—of what importance am I? A speck of dust! [117].

Further, she muses: "I want to believe, else all is void and nothing matters—yet I fear I have no faith, and yet again, if what I do is for mere convenience, I am base indeed, and that I won't allow" (119).

By this time, Simon Fury is convinced that in some indefinable way, the presence of Blanche Fury is poisoning Clere Hall and the family: "Since she had come to Clere there had been this sense of ill fortune over all of them.... Yes, it all revolved round her" (123).

Woman to man is either a god or a wolf. (The White Devil, IV, ii)

More time passes. Blanche is irresolute. Philip is making little attempt to raise the money on his debt to Simon. All is tedium. Philip's mother and wife aren't dead yet. And neither is Simon Fury. As the pace of the book's narrative slows and the tension increases, Blanche is torn between a wish for a conventional life at Clere Hall and the temptation to go away with Philip. At length, despite the warnings by Philip's mother to Blanche that her son is "an evil man," Blanche decides to cleave to Philip, even if it meant rejecting a conventional marriage: "He had ideas, plans, schemes, of that she was sure. And she, she was a born intriguer. And now she would throw aside all scruples. They had never been scruples of honesty, but prudence; and now they would go too" (132). As for Philip, he is so drawn to her that he becomes obsessed and feels himself bewitched: "He was drawn towards her by a fascination that sometimes seemed to him feverish, as if she were a witch who worked spells" (151).

Thus, at the end of that time a crisis is reached. Philip confides to Blanche that there is a way to get rid of Simon Fury. It involves poachers and gypsies who have allegedly been seen on the Fury property. "You seem to have started the story," says Blanche, falling in with his plan. He explains: "Wouldn't it be an end to all our troubles if an accident should happen to Mr. Simon and another accident to Mr. Laurence? Supposing they ran out after these poachers and were shot, and the poachers escaped in the dark! That would be very well, wouldn't it, for you and me? Such a deed would never be put down to me. Not when there're vagrants about—and thieves" (158). But, typically, Blanche has doubts, wondering how they will live, fearing what will happen when their passions cool. She muses: "And maybe his feeling for me is merely gross and sensual, and maybe mine for him is no better! Where shall we be when these passions are sated?" (164).

Philip on his own forges Simon Fury's name to a fake document declaring his debt has been paid. He persuades Blanche to sign it as a witness. She says: "We shall have to go, I suppose—millstones round one another's neck" (166).

Philip lays the groundwork for plan to shoot Simon Fury. He spreads rumors of marauding gypsies, roams the grounds at night discharging his pistol, and spreading rumors that an old gypsy woman is leading a pack of outlaw gypsies. As a defensive measure, Simon and his men patrol the grounds, to no results.

Finally, in an explosive scene of violence, Philip appears at Clere Hall disguised as a gypsy and bursts into the entryway, guns blazing. Simon and Olivia and Laurence are killed on the spot. Little Lavinia is mortally wounded. It is a horribly graphic tableau:

> [Blanche saw] the familiar drawing-room, Laurence getting out the piquet-table, Olivia in her frilled, slate-grey frock behind the tea equipage, and the child at her side with a book full of plates of shells open on her knee.... Blanche saw the scene as if by unexpected brilliance of lightning.... In the doorway of the dining-room that was faintly lit stood a tall dreadful figure, with long grey hair falling over the face, which was covered up to the eyes with a red cotton handkerchief. This person wore a ragged cloak and skirt and carried a double-barrelled gun; bright eyes glittered above the kerchief as the murderer stared at the murdered.... Blanche hardly knew what she saw or heard; it sounded like a blaze of musketry with the smoke slowly curling into the room; she snatched up the child and dragged her into the window-space behind the heavy curtains ... the air was tainted and dulled by acrid smoke.... The large lamp set at an angle of the wall showed Olivia on her hands and knees ... she looked ugly, inhuman; close to the open front door was the Recorder [Simon]. It was grotesque to see these two men sprawling on their backs. Simon Fury lay as he had fallen when shot after he had opened the door, flat on his back and still; Laurence was on his side and his limbs twitched; the smoke wreathed away over them and there was blood on the floor and on Olivia's slate-coloured dress; the child broke from Blanche again and threw herself into her mother's clutching embrace; Blanche dragged in vain at the demented woman's stiff shoulders.... Darkness laced with shadowy lights spun before Blanche's vision; she felt as if cloaked with lead and heaving with nausea.... The tea was still streaming in the silver kettle, the book with the pictures of shells lay open on the floor; through the folding-door could be seen the long dining-room. Smoke lingered there and the portrait of Adam Fury hung in tatters in the handsome frame. The murder had emptied the last shot in his piece into the picture [179–183].

Among the survivors, including the servants, only Blanche keeps presence of mind. Her testimony as a witness is confusing. The subsequent inquests are kept open. There were too many conflicting descriptions of the intruder, including those that described the old gypsy woman. There were suspicions about the new will in which Simon left everything to Blanche and the little girl. Regarding questions about the will signed by Simon attesting that Philip had paid off his debt for Saltash Farm—where had he found the money to do so? Blanche was already disliked in the neighborhood, but what might have been her complicity? She had been the only person who had kept her wits during the moments of the tragedy. On the other hand, she and Philip benefited from the deaths. Philip had his wife's alibi that he was nowhere near the scene of the crime. But rumors that Philip and Blanche had been lovers are rife.

Blanche and Philip maintain distance during all this time. She behaves oddly, the smile on her lips disturbing and cold, oddly detached from the crime: "She could think of them both [Simon and Laurence] lying in the entrance hall, the older man on his back, the younger on his side, without regret or even horror save for the ugly details" (213). So who is guilty of the murders? The killer might escape the law, she remarks prophetically, but he can't escape punishment. "Suppose it was Fury's Ape itself, come to throw out the intruders, eh?" (202) She ignores her lawyer's advice to burn the "accursed" house to the ground.

At last, they meet. She tells Philip that she recognizes him as the killer. He reminds her that what happened had been arranged between them. She's evasive: "I understood that there might be a poaching affray, that the Recorder and his son might be shot" (204). Philip says the rest of the slaughter was an "accident." He reminds her that her signature on the forged document makes her an accessory. And he further reminds her, "You've gained your ends, haven't you? You are mistress of the place, all the estates. You'll have the locks pulled and the curtsies dropped to you now—mistress of Clere…. Don't you see that we're free now? Free from them and their tyranny and their injustice? We were their slaves and now we're free! There's nothing wrong in a slave's killing his master! They asked for it, again and again-for their injustice and insolence!" (204–205). He adds that when they marry, he will take over the name Fury. Blanche protests that he's mad: "Do you really think that we could marry and live here *after that*?" (206). And yet, she still admits she loves him: "Yes, it's true I love you…. Hate's near love, don't they say, Philip? What brought you and me together, hate of them or love of one another?" (207) And a little later, she tells him: "Part of me loves you, Philip, The baser part, I think" (232)

And yet, she muses to herself, "I don't know what manner of creature I am" (206).

Blanche isolates herself. The servants, who hate her, have all left. People find excuses to stay away from Clere Hall. She rejects attempts by Philip to see her (while he runs wild in town with his gambling). She sits alone, at her meals, gazing at the empty place on the wall where Simon Fury's portrait had once hung. Her beauty has suffered a shocking alteration: "Her flesh seemed to have withered and shrunk so that the bony structure of her head showed in an unpleasant fashion. Her clothes hung loosely on a figure that had once been plum and trim" (222).

If the devil did ever take good shape, behold his picture. (*The White Devil*, III, ii)

Blanche reaches a turning point in her thoughts. She can't countenance Philip's shooting of little Lavinia. If the girl lives, how can she trust her to the care of a man who might have intended to kill her, thereby clearing the way for Blanche's title to Clere Hall? "Children die, and suffer too," he had said (228). She sits down and write out a "confession," of sorts, a document describing in detail Philip's culpability in the crimes. She omits any reference to her own complicity, only saying, at the end. "He does not know that I suspect him. I should have liked to have told him that in the event of the death of Lavinia Fury I should denounce him. If I had done so, he would have escaped; my own life would be in danger" (217).

She departs with a final "Good-bye."

She's turn'd Fury. [III, ii, 278].

Blanche goes to Inspector Wilkins and delivers her hand-written document. Her respectability as a woman of title now protects her: "Blanche seemed to him a fine, genteel young lady and he could hardly endure to believe that she had been mixed up in any intrigues with a low rogue and villain like Philip Strangeways" (239). But he decides not to accuse her as an accomplice and not to delve too deeply into her motivations: "He had no ability and no desire to investigate the darker and more subtle sides of human nature, the strange borderland of the mind and spirit where Blanche Fury and Philip Strangeways dwelt" (238). She's anxious that Philip be arrested and hanged.

Indeed, the evidence is produced, including the forged document. On the stand, she testifies in a steady, calm voice, subtly altering the facts in her favor and turning them against Philip. Philip fails to cross-examine her, as he had a right to do. Instead, he exchanges a look with Blanche: "They looked at each other—prisoner and witness—in silence.... Neither flinched before the level gaze of the other; the man even smiled" (249).

Philip speaks to the judge and jury: "I said and say, not guilty. I am a man deeply wronged, one who inherited wrongs and has ever been disposed...." His words are impassioned, incoherent, and violent, by turns, "full of desire for revenge and the lust for blood...." It provoked an uneasy dismay that such a noble and attractive quality should be possible in a murderer. He accuses Simon Fury for his utter ruin. He argues there is no proof of his guilt. He never mentions Blanche Fury. On her part, she remains immobile and neutral ... but "there were few who did not think she was at least as guilty as the man in the dock. She was the more hated as it was clearly seen that she would not pay the penalty that he was not able to escape" (253).

Philip is pronounced guilty and sentenced to be hanged. Blanche resolves to return to the mansion as sole owner. Few servants are willing to remain with her. She is more isolated than ever. The house's reputation for being haunted increases among the villagers.

Shortly thereafter the constable delivers to her a letter. These last lines of the novel deposit us with a chilling *thump* into the story's end. Philip Strangeways now pronounces himself a "Fury" after all:

"Welcome home, my bride, my dear! At last we have inherited Clere and we shall never leave it—you and I."
(signed) Philip Fury

And one last quote from *The White Devil* is appended:

And so I leave thee,
With all the furies hanging about thy neck [IV, iii, 124–125].

We conclude now reiterating that question—*Who is Joseph Shearing*? Yes, we've relinquished our little game and identified "him" as Marjorie Bowen, the true "Enchanting Brewer of Dread." Only Bowen could have been truly capable of rising to the challenge of Thomas De Quincey:

"Design, gentlemen, grouping, light and shade, poetry, sentiment, are now deemed indispensable to attempts of this nature."

Only she could empathize with those words:

"There was something in this case that no man could wholly understand, but that would be clear to all women without much trouble."

Thus, only she possesses the complicated soul best qualified to write of these horrors:

"As an artist human material must interest me. I might have to draw a murderer or his victim. I must assimilate their characters" [91].

The last word belongs to Bowen's most sympathetic commentator, Jessica Amanda Salmonson: "These extremes of passion are from the heart. They are real, for the heights and grisly lows in the author's life were every bit as intense as in her tales.... She was able to convey a calm demeanor to those around her while working through bursts of emotion and ideality via creative impulse."[30]

SIX

Marjorie Bowen: A Life Within

It is only when we know what were the conditions of the average woman's life—the number of her children, whether she had money of her own, if she had a room to herself, whether she had help in bringing up her family, if she had servants, whether part of the housework was her task—it is only when we can measure the way of life and the experience of life made possible to the ordinary woman that we can account for the success or failure of the extraordinary woman as a writer.—Virginia Woolf[1]

"Let me recommend," wrote Marjorie Bowen, "that you can see in the side of your teapot the history of every person and every thing reflected there."

We don't know when she wrote that, or where. But she wrote it. She left more notes like this, some of which follow here, curious, unpublished, random jottings scattered among her papers.[2] In their own modest way, along with her stories, they bring us close to the inner life of her imagination, to her life, to her identity as a writer: "I have never been conscious of inventing anything," she writes; "I describe something I have seen—a little scene here, something glimpsed there, and then all fitted together."

The world around her is a succession of "magic-lantern" views dissolving in and out of each other. Life is a picture book remembered from childhood: "One picture was of a lovely woman, richly dressed, I felt so happy to think that such a person had really existed, and though I knew nothing about her, I felt as if I could write her entire story." And write it she did—*This Shining Woman: Mary Wollstonecraft Godwin*. Life is a "peep show," disclosing wonders: "I found a peephole once, and it was in the door of an empty room. The Devil was as clear to me as if he had really there—he was seated on the dusty ground, wearing a red turban of monstrous size." He reappears in the story "Wrath." She sees faces peering through windows: "I could follow all their lives wherever I wished." She imagines the world can be "rolled up like a drop cloth, revealing

Marjorie Bowen, 1940 (courtesy Bowen Estate).

183

endless vistas and countless scenes?" Before such a painted flat appears "a monstrous Punch with a floured wig dancing to the music of an invisible orchestra." This tantalizes her for years—"and I can, so far, find no use for it." But she eventually does: Her pen twitches out a novel called *The Man with the Scales*. She peers into the depths of a mirror and grows fearful of "one's own double"—"probably most of our ghosts come from mirrors"—and she writes *The Veil'd Delight*. She discloses her fear of waxworks that "mock our mortality"—and she writes *The Shadow on Mockways*. She confesses that "puppets and marionettes always have some tragic story"—and she writes her play, "Homage to the Unknown." While in Italy she absorbs the "desolation of heat, wild fig trees, a narrow white house with yellow and scarlet fruits drying at the window" and writes *Stinging Nettles*. The "perfume of hay, the sickly bitter scent of hawthorn" and "the primrose that grew from a hedgerow" evokes pastoral scenes in *The Presence of the Power*. She populates "old houses, once splendid, long deserted" with the ghosts of *The Devil Snar'd* and "*Five Winds.*"

Hers is a world of the big and the small. The "largest landscape" that she ever saw was a miniature view painted on the back of a watch. Paradoxically, "that landscape filled my mind" with its "sense of boundless adventure." If her brush ever failed her, it was because, she admitted, she "could never draw angels."

But she does transmute her angels—and gargoyles—into her words: "A table, a bottle of ink and a pad of foolscap were sufficient."[3] Disappointed as a painter, she turns to that "pad of foolscap" that is her canvas, where the teapot's "dissolving views" come to life...

The images stir and change... A child is scribbling pictures on brown paper. In "Vessels of Gold," a little girl named Margaret (Bowen's own birth name) lives in poverty with a mostly absent mother, a shiftless, uncaring father, and the sense that she should never have been born.[4]

> She spends her time drawing pictures with a box of chalk from the few pennies her father gives her. Yet, despite her privations—or because of them—Margaret has developed a curious sense of self-sufficiency. She began to think that it was a secret austere pleasure to be able to sacrifice everything, to have nothing but what she could get from herself. She felt, vaguely, that she possessed a great power in this self-sufficiency, and the joy of the lovely, sunny afternoon returned to her; she glanced up at her mother, completely detached from that unhappy creature [66].

Contrast that with the grown woman who is no longer "Margaret" but "Marjorie," a professional writer satirizing the commercial realities of the literary business in the wickedly funny "The World's Gear"[5]:

> Adrian Quinn has just written a literary sensation called *The World's Gear*. This "ferocious and perfectly innocent attack on women" related, "with a wealth of scathing detail, how the fascinating hero escaped the wiles of various wholly respectable sirens and finally fled to the Welsh hills to write poetry in peace and live 'his own life in solitary grandeur'" (221). In retreat from angry female readers, Adrian takes to the hills. It is time, he decides, to write "something really worth while" that will rock the literary establishment off its foundations.
>
> He finds a lonely house reputed to be haunted. Previous occupants had either gone mad or hanged themselves. Perfect! It's isolated and dismal and rundown, all right, but the place is lousy and his own cooking a disaster. Meanwhile, the promised novel is still one solitary blank page in his typewriter.
>
> Just published is a novel called *Pearls for Tears*, "written by some fool of a woman to prove that the suffering in the world came through men." The authoress is, improbably, one "Dolly Diamond." She is reputed "to be lurking in the deep seclusion of a convent where she nurses a broken heart." (232).
>
> One day a smart and attractive young lady named Miss Damaris Oughtred invades Adrian's premises. No, she is no ghost haunting his house. But she will be haunting his life. Fresh and smart, she repairs

to his kitchen and cooks up his lunch. Uninvited, she rifles through the blank pages on his desk. "Have you been looking at my manuscripts?" he asks. "Well, I wanted something to light the fire with," she smirks (235).

You guessed it—this impertinent, bright young lady is indeed the "Dolly Diamond" of woeful reputation. He is astonished at her bright energy: "But you——she—Dolly—is supposed to have a broken heart—." And she replies, "And you are supposed to hate women!" She continues: "Father said you were trying to be St. Anthony and I had better be the Temptation so as not to disappoint you. I'm sure a decent meal is a temptation. You look like a wolf" (233).

She asks him for a donation for her father's church. "I don't care about the church, my dear lady." But she interrupts him: "But I do. I might be getting married there someday. I'm only twenty-eight and I've just come into a lot of money." Adrian stares: "Good idea; getting married. I might try it." Without missing a beat, Damaris responds, "Think what a stunt for your publisher: 'Famous misanthrope in love ... the great woman-hater pays homage to the divinest of her sex'" (235).

He agrees: "I say, shouldn't we make a thundering good thing of it if we went into partnership!" (236)

And so it happens that Adrian Quin returns to town with a beautiful young wife. Gossipy tongues say he had gone away on purpose for a secret marriage; others that it was just a new advertisement dodge. Whichever, everyone soon loses interest in him altogether. The swift succession of satiric novels written by "Dolly Diamond" excite the reading public. Her royalties are quite enough to allow Adrian to write the masterpieces that probably won't sell—even if he had wanted to. But, as it turns out, he doesn't [236].

A few confessions of the writer's life appear in the story collection, *Dark Ann*. In the title story she is recognized by a stranger as a writer of romances:

> Perhaps he had heard of me as a foolish trifler in dreams and visions, a writer of stories fantastical and strange [5].

Other stories in *Dark Ann* reveal the writer at work. In "Expiation," she takes trips to villages and hamlets, rambling around the shops and houses, observing the "red brick churches with fretted turreting, the wooden fronted houses" and finding scraps of stories in the "graveyards with monstrous rococo tombs and flamboyant monuments" (47).

> Coming across three gravestones together, she confronts the local doctor: "I'm trained to notice. It's my job. Tell me the story." When he replies the story is "most ordinary," she persists: "Look here, Dr. Conyers, what do you think 'stories' are? Something woven out of air? Stories are only just people's lives. Now, here are three people—something must have happened to them, good or bad or indifferent, they must have been stupid or clever or kind or mean—they weren't blanks, you know—now you tell me what you know of them, and I expect would make a full size novel" [53].

At length a story does emerge, very plangent and affecting, a village idyll about a man named James Trant, whose undying love and loyalty kept him from the life and success he would otherwise have enjoyed. In the wonderful conclusion, narrator/Bowen seems to recognize the story as her own, something long forgotten, lost, now freshly poignant:

> I wish I hadn't seen the little house behind the chestnut trees.... I wish I couldn't picture so vividly the superb man in the threadbare clothes passing from house to church, from church to village, glancing daily at his own grave space, undergoing isolation, poverty, contempt, complete frustration as an expiation for—what? Can you give it a name? I can't. I hate the place, it's like a trap, I shan't go there again" [71].

But then come her final words, soft, but like a hammer-blow, revealing her own secret, her own untold story: "*I wish I had had the honour to be the woman James Trant loved*" *(72).* [italics mine]

In three more stories from *Dark Ann*, "Nocturne," "The Truth about the Hobart Marriage," "Praeludium," we meet female writers who remain detached from their characters—at a price. In the first, Amy Dacre is a middle-aged writer vacationing in Lucca. Languishing in the hot Tuscan heat she develops a voyeuristic fascination with a man in a nearby villa who indulges in an adulterous liaison with a young woman.

> Their passionate embrace stings her: "Everything in her life that she had ignored seemed symbolized in that embrace; her flesh quivered in revolt.... She detested the villa, she loathed the [young] woman; she would like to have struck her, insulted her, shamed her, to have told her what an outrage she was." And then, the telling words: "She did not loathe this new world because it was wicked, *but because she was shut out of it*" [79–80].

The writer who narrates "The Truth of the Hobart Marriage" is another observer who must reject an involvement in an ongoing erotic ménage:

> She admits it is all some absurd melodrama, but adds, "We may be, as the novelists say, very hard, very wide awake, very contemptuous of passions and flourishes and hot impulses and fierce speaking, but we get 'caught out' now and then..." [189].

In "Praeludium" a writer is confronted by one of the women she frequently writes about, one of those predatory females driven by The Furies—

> the type the modern novelist would love to write about.... Thirty-seven, unmarried, dissatisfied—pages would go to my complexes, inhibitions and repressions—but I'm not conscious of feeling any of these things.... We women have such a reputation for spite and jealousy that I should like to put on record how often I have been touched and moved and made ashamed by the admiration of women who have had nothing ... [305–308].

The reflected images shift, and change... The scene is Italy. A young woman sits at a tiny table. Beside her is a bed upon which a man languishes in pain. Marjorie Bowen's novel, *Stinging Nettles* (1923) is a semi-autobiographical account of a writer struggling to retain her professional identity while facing an intolerable domestic responsibility. It is perhaps the single most revelatory account of Marjorie Bowen's life as a writer and a woman that she ever wrote. Lucie Uden follows her husband, an Italian, to Tuscany, where for a year he will languish in the throes of a terminal illness:

> Your work, your individuality, your chances went by the board, you were swept into another life.... And with this heavy blight over you, you must work—you'd been fool enough to marry a penniless, sickly man.... Fool, no doubt—but you thought you loved him, you wanted so desperately to be loved, you dreamed you could make it wonderful. And what else offered save bleak negation? That which was within you and too powerful for your poor control betrayed you [33].

But, somehow, against all odds, Lucie finds a way to write:

> Lucie would have her simple breakfast meal at "a little table at the foot of his bed, since he could not endure her out of his sight; when this was over, and he had been made comfortable and the room tidied again and the stove filled, she could count on about two hours while he slept.... In this interval, she wrote her articles, always using the table at the foot of the bed." When he woke, there was medicine to prepare, food to make, tea to be carried upstairs, and mending and washing to be done. At length, when he slept again, she had "another hour or so to herself to work again" (93). And so the days would pass in nightmarish regularity. "She stuck to her task doggedly with just this idea of doing things decently and performing her duty.... She felt herself utterly worn out, and her highest dream of what she would do when it was all over..." (108). Through it all, "she was writing short stories, as well as articles, and they were fairly successful, but it was hard keeping abreast of the expenses and so far from her market" [120].

Stinging Nettles is a harrowing narrative whose autobiographical identity was confirmed when Bowen wrote her memoir sixteen years later, *The Debate Continues*.

In the surface of the teapot, the images blur and refocus, the face of an infant appears. Marjorie Bowen is living in the 1920s with her three boys, Michael, Athelstan, and Hilary in the Kentish village of Wittersham, about seventy miles south east of London. Her writing studio is a short walk from her home. Nearby is the church at Stone-in-Oxney and the cemetery where her first-born, Giuseppina, is buried. The little girl had died of meningitis when she was just five months old. Bowen's short story, "The Blue Glove," conveys something of that private pain.[6] It is Bowen's most tender, most affecting ghost story:

> Mrs. Trevennick sits quietly in a church, near the tombs, quietly knitting. She muses that if her baby had lived, he would have been called "Tom," after her late husband:
>
> Her mind dwelt morosely on the past, the perpetually hidden sting of her thwarted maternity suddenly drove into her heart, sharp and bitter; her suffering made her young, the stupid, dirty old face became quite sharp and eager as she stared at the child's tomb [68].
>
> At that moment, "something pattered down the aisle ... a child came ... and stood by her knee. 'Will you knit me a pair of gloves, Mrs. Trevennick? I have no one to look after me now ... take me up for I am cold'" (68). So there, in the dim and shadowed church, "the child drew close to her knees and she saw his face like an aureole of light; she put down her knitting and took him up on her knee; pressing him to her dry withered body and her barren breast" (69). "This is what finding your baby means," muses Mrs. Trevennick. "Heaven it is, I suppose'" (69). But now the verger approaches with his candle, taking no notice of her. She rises and wonders what she had been thinking about and what she had been doing: "She remembered that she would be late and that this would make them cross at home..." (70). She reaches the door and, thrusting her knitting into her bag, realizes that she has made a baby's blue glove, "a clumsy little thing with no fingers." A waste of time, she thinks, and a waste of wool, too—"'ain't never the same since it has been unravelled'" [70].

Marjorie Bowen's home parlor, 1940 (courtesy Bowen Estate).

The pictures flicker and move forward in time ... London during wartime, a house interior in Chelsea. Photographs of three young men rest on the bookshelf. Her newest published book, *Lady in a Veil*, has just arrived from the publisher. It bears two dedications: The first reads: "For Athelstan Long, Captain, R.A., Malaya, 1940. Singapore, 1942." The second: "For Hilary Long, Captain 60th Rifles (K.R.R.C.) Africa (The Eighth Army), 1941. Tunisia, 1943." A second book is in preparation, *Nightcap and Plume* [as by George R. Preedy] which upon publication in 1945 will bear a "Foreword" thanking "Major Hilary Long" for "the help given in writing this novel."

Since the mid–1930s, the woman the world knows as "Marjorie Bowen" has left Wittersham and is living in London, 46 Markham Square, Chelsea. She remains there during the war years while her husband, Arthur, and her boys are away on active service. Tucked away in the Bowen Papers at Yale, a typed, unpublished poem bearing the title, "London, April 1945," attests to her concerns about her three absent sons:

> I watched him in his cradle,
> I held him at my heart.
> He looked at me and trusted me...
> He left me when the world was dark
> And he was fair and straight,
> Now I cannot find him
> Wherever he may wait.[7]

The war is in its third year. She bends to the letter she is writing... Now a cache of handwritten letters survives, written to her youngest son, Hilary. (Return letters are, unfortunately, missing.) They provide an intimate glimpse at life at home in London during the Nazi air raids:

> The cramped, irregular lines are frequently difficult to decipher. She signs them with the name, "Karl." [Why the name "Karl"? No one knows, least of all the people at the Bowen Estate. Another of the many Bowen mysteries.] There are hundreds of them, some separated only by a few days. They are very chatty and relate news of the air raids, blackouts, and rationing. Here are the daily routines of the household, the neighborhood gossip, anxious inquiries about the current whereabout of Hilary's brothers, Athelstan and Michael who are abroad on active service. Here are daily moods, postings of newspapers and books, birthday notes, some correspondence with people like William Roughead, comments on "hack" female writers, and a few notes on her novels.[8] They are a testament to a wartime mother's enduring love and concerns about her sons. In one letter, dated 3 August 1940, she expresses regret about writing her memoir, *The Debate Continues*: "I don't think you would care about it—I wrote it when I was very unhealthy ... when nothing seemed

Athelstan, Michael, and Hilary Long, 1930 (courtesy Bowen Estate).

to matter very much, and there were a few things I wanted to put von [the record]." In another, there is a telling admission that she is "seeking a tranquil mind" against the turmoil around her.⁹

She keeps writing. A letter, dated 11 November 1944: "Is the war coming to an end at last? The news is dazzling—I feel quite dazed—that all these horrors are really coming to an end? I have to keep concentrated on my own tasks, the only sane thing to do, but difficult."¹⁰

Her story, "Little Boys," from *The English Paragon,* is a cameo portrait of another woman whose sons have gone to war:

Hilary Long, 1941 (courtesy Bowen Estate).

> Queen Philippa has two sons, Edward Plantagenet and John of Lancaster, who are at war in Spain. She remembers happier days, "when she had played with her sons 'before they were taken from her and given to the knights to train'" (161). Now, as she observes two little boys at play in the courtyard, she fears they, too, will grow up as soldiers. She asks them what they want to do when they grow up. To the Queen's horror, they reply—
> "Soldiers!" [164].

She has gained a measure of acclaim as a writer and has even created several pseudonyms to accommodate the steady flow of her work. She usually works alone. She lacks a circle of helpful colleagues. She depends upon her capacity to work through the distractions around her. When she isn't researching at libraries, archives, and galleries, she spends eight-hour days at her desk, uninterrupted, save around Christmas. Despite her claim that "every word I have published has been written with my own hand," we know at this time she occasionally dictated into an early recording device. "Her method of working is interesting," reported a magazine article in 1932:

> She has an ediphone in the room where she works, and to it she tells her story aloud. The tale unfolds from her brain as steadily as though she were reading it from a written page. When the story is told, she

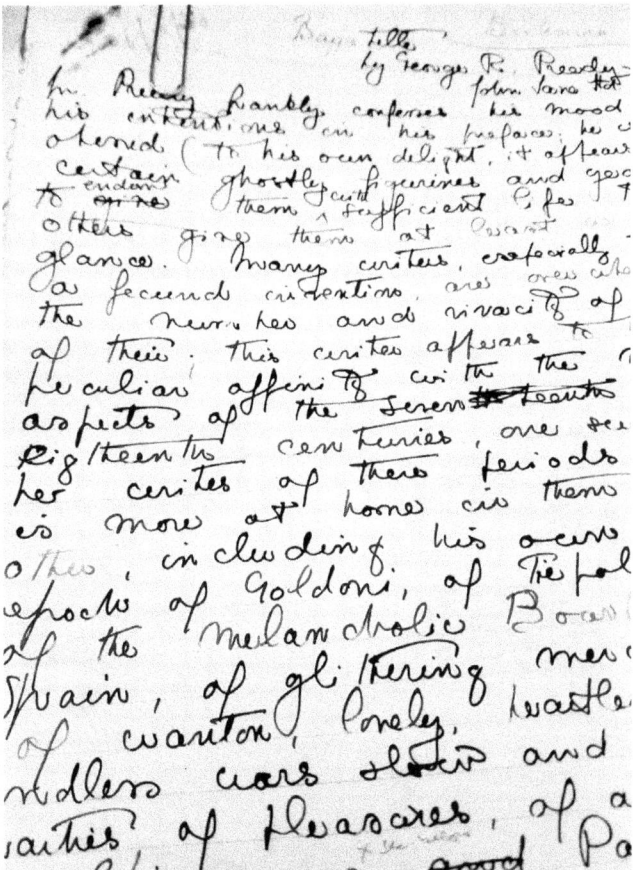

Sample handwriting of Marjorie Bowen (courtesy Bowen Estate).

transcribes it to paper, developing and colouring characters and scenes. She finds the ediphone an inspiring helper. Listening to music frees her mind, she says.[11]

This and a lack of editorial assistance, along with her own aversion to re-read her manuscripts, result in uncorrected idiosyncrasies in her prose style. We do indeed feel, at times, as if we are *hearing* a story, rather than *reading* it. Thus, run-on sentences sometimes pile headlong upon each other; descriptive adjectives repeat themselves; semicolons are used to a fault; and vividly detailed descriptions of costume, flora, and architecture occasionally overwhelm the narrative flow.

Another scene comes into view, a house interior, London, 34 Holland Park. December 23, 1952. It dissolves to a faraway place, a tropical setting, where a flag is flying at half-mast. Gabrielle Margaret Vere Campbell Long has died from a concussion from a fall in her bedroom. We know little about the precise circumstances. But a few letters that survive between her sons Athelstan and Hilary reveal their profound sense of loss and their enduring devotion to her. Writing to Hilary from Nigeria a few days later, on the 28th, Athelstan reveals a pet name for their mother—"Towser":

> I received my father's [Arthur Long] telegram this morning telling me that Towser died on the 23rd. I find it impossible to put my feelings adequately on paper. I have been away in the Tropics for 13 years with only short intervals at home, and yet the image of Towser and her personality have always been with me, and there are not many actions which have not been guided by her influence and standards.... [I feel] the awful sense of loss of a great and dear character who stands like an immense flame of the forest rising above the multitude of lesser trees.... She always said she had a natural sense of the stage and this last exit would bear her out.... I never knew I could feel so sad.... *I have one thing for her.... I am flying the Union Jack at half mast....* [italics added] With all my love and deepest sympathy.... Towser would wish me to say, "Keep Cracking."

In another letter to Hilary, dated January 6, 1953, Athelstan reveals his relief that "our mother's death was so painless and peaceful and that she had none of the dragging suffering outside her own environment which she would have hated.... I am happy that she went like this before her faculties were infirmed and as you say I think it is what she wished."[12]

In the more than sixty years since her death, the majority of her writings have fallen into an undeserved obscurity. In her story, "A Famous Woman," do we discern anxieties about her future?[13]

Marjorie Bowen with Athelstan and Hilary, 1928 (courtesy Bowen Estate).

> During a train stop in a little town on a wintry night, a traveler rambles through the empty streets. He pauses before a statue of a woman. On the base is etched only a simple inscription: "Gabrielle Buzot." Standing before it, he feels a curious, pricking

sense of chivalrous love. A few quick inquiries yield no information, save the remark that long-ago a forgotten scandal had been associated with the woman. Returning to the train station, he begins to think he had known her intimately for years; and he wonders if he should ask her pardon for leaving her alone in the colourless, chilly weather (144). As the train pulls out of the station, he sees a peasant woman sitting on the platform. The porter explains, offhandedly: "Would you believe that wretched as she is, she claims to be descended from a famous woman—Gabrielle Buzot?'" (148). Our traveler consults a guide book: "[The town is] worth visiting for the splendid fifteenth-century Gothic church. In the public gardens is a statue of the famous Gabrielle Buzot (1773–1793)." Only twenty years old when she died? Tellow wonders, how did somebody become so famous in so short a time? It's just a passing thought: "Who was she, left behind in the out-of-the-way town in the deserted gardens, under the snow? He would never know, and by to-morrow he would cease to care" [148].

Marjorie Bowen plaque (courtesy Bowen Estate).

Story's End?

The teapot *gleams*. Is this to be the end? Is Marjorie Bowen, as writer and woman, just another "famous woman" to be consigned hereafter to obscurity? We trust this may not be true. At least she seems to anticipate something that yet may come. She looks away from the teapot. She remembers once as a child finding an iris bud. She had picked it up. She suffered an epiphany: "It opened in my hand—I cannot forget the delight that it gave me. All at once I felt full of ardent confidence for the future, somehow as if I were going to be divinely protected all my life. I do not really think we are excluded from the Garden of Eden. There are many times when the flaming sword is lowered and we can enter in."

Marjorie Bowen signature (courtesy Bowen Estate).

Appendix I:
Biographical Timeline

1 November 1885 Gabrielle Margaret Vere Campbell born in Hayling Island, Hampshire, second daughter of Josephine Elisabeth Campbell and Vere Douglas Campbell. In the home is a nurse, Nana, and a sister.

31 August 1906 Marjorie Bowen's first novel is published, *The Viper of Milan: A Romance of Lombardy*.

10 May 1907 *The Glen O' Weeping* is dedicated to Mark Twain.

March 1909 *Black Magic: A Tale of the Rise and Fall of Antichrist* is published, Bowen's first historical novel with supernatural overtones.

1910–1911 Publication of Bowen's "William of Orange" trilogy (*I Will Maintain, God and the King, Defender of the Faith*).

11 October 1912 Bowen marries Zeffirino Emilio Costanza, a young Sicilian living in London.

21 November 1912 *God's Playthings* is published, Bowen's first collection of short stories.

June 1913 Bowen and her husband leave England to live in Lucca.

December 1914 Bowen's first child, a girl, Giuseppina, is born in Sicily, where she and her husband have relocated.

February 1915 Bowen and her husband and baby daughter return to London to live on a farm in Kent.

May 1915 Bowen's daughter, Giuseppina, dies of meningitis at the age of five months.

January 1916 Marjorie Bowen and Zefferino's second child, Athelstan, is born in Torquay, where she is living with Nana, the family nurse. Two more sons, Michael and Hilary, will be born; and all three survive into adulthood.

February 1916 Bowen leaves for Tuscany to nurse her terminally ill husband.

November 1916 Zefferino dies of tuberculosis at age thirty-three.

Christmas, 1916 Bowen returns to England, where she lives for the rest of her life.

4 December 1917 Bowen marries Arthur L. Long, a resident of Richmond, Surrey.

1923 Bowen's semi-autobiographical novel, *Stinging Nettles*, is published. She is living in the village of Wittersham, where she keeps nearby a studio. The baby Giuseppina is buried in the churchyard at Stone-in-Oxney.

July 1926 *Nell Gwyn* is the first motion picture adapted from a Bowen novel. Dorothy Gish appears in the title role. Bowen leaves Wittersham for London, where she lives the remainder of her life.

September 1928 Bowen publishes her first novel under the pseudonym "George R. Preedy," *General Crack*. It is adapted to the movies a year later, starring John Barrymore.

1930 Bowen publishes *Bagatelle*, a volume of short stories by "George R. Preedy."

November 1933 Bowen edits an anthology, *Great Tales of Horror*. A second anthology is published two years later.

1938 Bowen publishes *Orange Blossoms*, the only volume of short stories as by "Joseph Shearing."

1938 A Bowen memoir, "Margaret Campbell," is published in an anthology, *Myself When Young: By Famous Women of Today*, edited by Countess of Oxford and Asquith.

19 April 1939 Bowen delivers the Conway Memorial lecture, *Ethics in Modern Art*.

7 October 1939 Bowen issues under her own name, "Margaret Campbell," an autobiography, *The Debate Continues: Being the Autobiography of Marjorie Bowen*.

1945 Bowen publishes *The Church and Social Progress*.

1940–1945 Bowen remains at home in 46 Markham Square, Chelsea, during the wartime years.

1947–1948 Movie adaptations of novels by "Joseph Shearing" are released: *Moss Rose, Blanche Fury, Airing in a Closed Carriage, So Evil My Love* (novel title: *For Her to See*).

April 1949 Bowen publishes the *Bishop of Hell*, the last volume of short stories under her name during her lifetime.

17 September 1951 Bowen publishes *To Bed at Noon*, her last "Joseph Shearing" novel.

22 December 1952 Marjorie Bowen has a serious concussion from a fall in her home at 34 Holland Park. She later dies in the hospital.

25 January 1954 Bowen's *The Man with the Scales* is published posthumously.

1976 *Kecksies and Other Twilight Tales* is published by Arkham House, with a Preface by Marjorie Bowen that had been written before her death.

1997 *Twilight and Other Supernatural Romances* is a collection of Bowen's short stories, compiled and edited by Jessica Amanda Salmonson.

2002 Bowen's son, Hilary Long, deposits the Marjorie Bowen Papers in the Beinecke Library, Yale University.

Appendix II: "Too Much Posturing": Media Adaptations

In an address to the London National Liberal Club dinner, given in 1928, Marjorie Bowen expressed some frustration with the current state of the historical novel, a form she feared was becoming "out of date." It was to the movies, she predicted that historical matters might be best entrusted:

> Miss Bowen concluded by expressing her belief that the cinema, still in its infancy, provided a medium by which the moments of history could be portrayed with a vividness and movement that would give people a greater interest in history than books or pictures could do.[1]

We should bear in mind that these remarks came hard on the heels of the British screen adaptation of her novel, *Miss Nell Gwyn*, which, as we shall see, she admired. We should also bear in mind that just a year later she dismissed the American adaptation of *General Crack* out of hand. That's show biz.

It is disappointing that relatively few references can be found to movies and movie writing in her papers at Yale. In one handwritten note I found her contention that any British adaptation of her work should "be made entirely by British personnel, and not 'by foreigners who invade the British studios.'" It is undated, but it probably comes from the 1930s, when many Hollywood personnel were being transplanted to the U.K. In more undated notes about "Historical and Romantic Films," there are notes for a critique of Abel Gance's epic *Napoleon* as containing "too much symbolism, too many eagles, flags, crowds. Too much posturing." Many film critics today would subscribe to that opinion.[2]

In *Fond Fancy* there are references to motion pictures in two stories, "The Careful Youth," with its pungent depiction of a crowded movie theater, the site of a failed romance; and "Would You Believe It? A Film Close-up," a hilarious tale pitting crass moviemakers against the virtues of the local vicar's daughter, a country lass who outsmarts their attempts to make her into a glamorous movie star.

Several typed film treatments can be found in the files dated 1923–1937: "Courage: A Synopsis for a Film Story" purports to be set in 1881 and is about "the suitors of Selina Fullerton."[3] Another typescript is "Poor Man's Treasure: A Story of Today." This is significant, inasmuch as it reveals some of Bowen's attitudes towards writing scripts for the movies: "[They should possess] the peculiar rhythm of the film" and should "call for a large treatment, the use of types more than of individual characters, for wide instead of intimate backgrounds, and for the employment of all resources to express a given action or emotion in a way impossible in either novel or stage play." She notes that "sounds and actions" are to be preferred to "streams of dialogue, which soon weary and can be far better done in the stage play, which has far fewer resources." Moreover, "in a film every sentence should tell and not a single sound be wasted." (Box 24).

SELECT SHORT STORIES ADAPTED FOR TELEVISION

"Scoured Silk" (from the 1919 *Crimes of Old London*) was adapted for *Alfred Hitchcock Presents*, Season 7, Episode 13, 1961, by Halstead Welles and Norman Ginsbury. Directed by John Newland and starring Michael Rennie. The basic plot elements are intact, although the final disclosure is abruptly terminated and all the grisly details are only suggested. Attributed to "Joseph Shearing."

"The Avenging of Ann Leete" (from *The Last Bouquet*, 1933) was adapted for *Lux Video Theater* in 23 May 1955, starring Roger Moore. Attributed to "Joseph Shearing."

"A Flourish of Trumpets" (from *Bagatelle* by George Preedy, 1931) was a TV movie from 1962 under the title, "The Brockenstein Affair." Adapted by John Keir Cross. Attributed to "Joseph Shearing."

"They Found My Grave" (from *Orange Blossoms*, 1938) for *Shoestring Theatre*, 1961, starring Kay Tremblay as "Madame Destiny." Attributed to "Joseph Shearing."

FILM ADAPTATIONS OF THE 1920S

Nell Gwyn. British National/Paramount. 1926. Directed by Herbert Wilcox, starring Dorothy Gish in the title role and Randle Ayrton as Charles Stewart.

The 1926 edition of *Mistress Nell Gwyn* bears Marjorie Bowen's dedication:

> To Miss Dorothy Gish, whose characterization and portrayal
> of "Pretty Witty Nelly" will give delight to thousands throughout the world.

Bowen is acknowledging what is immediately apparent in viewing the film: It is indeed, an amusing showcase for Dorothy Gish's Chaplinesque performance.[4]

In the novel's Author's Note, Bowen observes; "though the narrative must be taken as fiction, it contains no fictitious characters, nor do they which appear there, say or do anything that does not tally with what they are known to have said or to have done.... None of the details ... outrage history or defy probability."

The movie begins with the title card, acknowledging "Marjorie Bowen," and subtitles the production as "A Character Study." What follows is a selection of scenes from the novel, beginning with Nell's initial appearance selling oranges outside the theater door, continuing with dinner at a nearby inn, her payment of the bill, the King's gift to Nell of a pair of slippers, the jealousy of Lady Castlemaine, Charles's promise to Nell to establish the Chelsea Hospital, and concluding with Nell's vigil at the King's deathbed, and his final words, "Don't let poor Nelly Starve!"

A preliminary title card announces: "What learned men call 'history,' the dull records of wars and treatises, often dies, while the simple stories of human love live on forever."

And Nell is introduced as: "A ragged, tender-hearted orange peddler, who loved and laughed her way through triumph and disaster."

Charles is introduced, without his wig: "The 'Merry Monarch,' loved for his quick wit, his ready laugh, and his human touch."

And several cutaways picture none other than Samuel Pepys, diary in hand:

The First Wholesaler of Gossip, in whose famous Diary we find much not written in history."

Nell's onscreen relationship with the King remains relatively chaste, excepting a charming scene when the two appear together in close-up, and the King extinguishes several candles, leaving their tryst in darkness and the viewer to his or her own imaginations.

There are amusing exchanges between the jealous Castlemaine, whom Nell dubs "a carrion crow" and Castlemaine, who describes Nell as "a gutter-bred hussy." One of the funniest moments in their rivalry transpires on stage, when Nell appears in a preposterous, outsized version of Lady Castlemain's hat and costume—

Nell Gwyn **poster**

> And when I find my charms fall flat/
> I simply wear a larger hat!

The film strips away the details in Bowen's narrative—the incidental characters, theater scenes, intrigues with the Duke of Monmouth—to a drama among the three characters of Nell, Charles, and Lady Castlemaine. The larger intrigues surrounding Charles, private and international, are omitted. There is no mention of Nell's son. Likewise omitted are Nell's saddened last days, fraught with unpaid bills and illness, which are among the most touching pages in the novel.

And how we miss in the last pages of Bowen's carefully nuanced, compassionate attitude toward Nell, who was, after all, a scandalous figure:

> "Nelly was eager to repent, but could not separate her sin from all the pleasure she had had in life.... How was she, brought up in the gutter, in rags, pushing an oyster barrow down the Lane or selling oranges at the door of the theater, to know the meaning of Honour and Virtue?" And we see her, near the end, declaring: "I do repent, of all I ever did wrong, but I cannot repent of having loved the King" [224].

In general, the film is well produced, with lavish costumes and sets. Critics were enthusiastic: "This is the first British production to reach these shores that will meet with the approval of American audiences."[5]

General Crack. 1929. Warner Bros. Directed by Alan Crosland and starring John Barrymore in the title role.

An American pre–Code talking picture produced in 1929, *General Crack* was released by Warner Bros. on 25 January 1930. The sound version of *General Crack* is lost. The silent version of this film, with Czech intertitles, survives, but does not have any of the original color sequences. Copies are located in the Czech archive and the Museum of Modern Art and are unavailable for screening. Although the complete soundtrack for the sound version survives on Vitaphone disks, the silent version was either a "B" negative or an alternate take with intertitles. So while this is a legitimate version of the film, it does not match up with the Vitaphone soundtrack.

General Crack was Bowen's first novel under the name "George R. Preedy." (The film's title card erroneously identifies the author as "George Preddy.") The publication of the novel in 1929 precipitated a minor flurry of commentary from those who discovered that Preedy was none other than Marjorie Bowen. One report greeted the discovery with enthusiasm: "Reviewers sat up and shouted (with their pens) paens of praise over a brilliant new writer, George Preedy—'a writer of genius,' they called him. His book, 'General Crack,' set the literary world talking, speculating, and asking where the young man was to be seen. The powerful writing showed the fresh vigour of young manhood. In its breadth of canvas and splendor of colouring 'General Crack' was compared with 'Jew Suss,' but, said the critics, "it is a finer work."[6] The discovery that "Preedy" was Bowen made critics squirm, because "George R. Preedy" had been accepted by the reviewers as a "new star on the firmament of literature."[7] When the book came to the attention of John Barrymore, as reported the *Sydney Morning Herald*, he declared: "I must act that part. It was made for me." Bowen reputedly disowned the results.[8]

The novel is a grand, sprawling story set in eighteenth-century Austria and Russia and features the conflicts, personal and political, between two men: There is the mercenary soldier whose name, "General Crack," was derived from the initials of his full name, Christian Rudolph Augustus Christopher Ketlar. Christian suffers from an inner "wound," that he was "'base born,' no aristocrat"; rather, the bastard child of his father, the result of a dalliance with a Italian *Commedia* dancer. Why, Christian wonders, did his father not marry this exotic, dark-eyed dancer, instead of leaving Christian merely a bastard with "a lifetime of secret shame"? (171). His father left him with wealth but not the throne of Kurland. Kurland had been annexed by Russia; the family of Ketlar was regarded as extinct. "I admire danger," declares Christian, "the perilous attempt, the difficult conquest, and power. All the power in the world would hardly satisfy me.... What I have gotten, I have gotten by selling my sword, fighting for other men'" (43).

Christian falls into an uneasy alliance with Prince Leopold, heir to the Imperialist throne. By contrast to Christian's indomitable figure and stern self-discipline we have Leopold, a selfish and indecisive heir to the Imperial Throne. He is the only son of the Elector of Bavaria, inheritor of the Hapsburg blood, and in a position to assume the title of Emperor. But he lacks the ruthless ambition of Christian: "He had not yet shown any violent emotion of any kind; he was a learned dilettante in the Arts and had acquitted himself with credit as a soldier if he had cut no grand figure as a general" (60).

Intervening in their relationship is the villainous Ferdinand Gabor, whose loyalties are only to himself. He will prove to both these power mongers that "he was their master, to snap his fingers at them and laugh in their faces at the end of this ironic little comedy" (180). His machinations will bring disaster to everyone.

The film adaptation's plot synopsis provided by the *AFI Catalogue of Feature Films, 1921–1930* is incomplete. But it does reveal that the novel's general outline of the contentious relationship between Prince Christian and Leopold II takes center stage. The story takes place in 18th century Austria where Prince Christian (John Barrymore), has been denied his Kurland Dukedom because he was the illegitimate offspring of his father's dalliance with a gypsy dancer. Now a notorious soldier of fortune, and known as "General Crack," he sells his services to the highest bidder. He is enlisted by Leopold II of Austria (Lowell Sherman) after demanding the hand of Leopold's sister, the Archduchess Maria Luisa (Marion Nixon), and half of the gold of the Empire. However, en route, he meets a gypsy dancer, Fidelia (Armida), and marries her instead. At the court, Leopold becomes infatuated with Fidelia. While General Crack is abroad on his military campaign, Leopold forces his attentions on her. The affair is exposed by the General's former aide, Gabor (Otto Matiesen). In a rage, General Crack executes him. Subsequently, during a climactic battle, Crack kills Leopold. After Fidelia's death, Crack accepts Maria Luisa's offer of marriage, and the film ends with him being elevated to his rightful title, the Archduke of Kurland.

FILM ADAPTATIONS OF THE 1940S

The following films, *Moss Rose, So Evil My Love, The Mark of Cain,* and *Blanche Fury*—have their problems, to be sure, not the least of which is the sanitization mandated by the prevailing censorship codes in America and England. But they do benefit from the *film noir* style and tone that was at its height in that decade. Of the bunch, *Blanche Fury* deserves at least the recognition that it comes within shouting distance of the intensity—dare I say, the *fury*—of Bowen's original.

Moss Rose (1947). 20th Century–Fox. Directed by Gregory Ratoff, adapted by Jules Furthman, starring Peggy Cummins as Belle Adair/Rose Lynton, Victor Mature as Michael Drego, and Ethel Barrymore as Lady Margaret Drego.

It's a pity that *Moss Rose* had to wait until the late 1940s to come to the screen. Had it appeared in the early thirties, as a pre–Code production, it might have benefited from more grim and sordid details of blackmail and betrayal it deserved. As it stands, it's quickly apparent that the restrictions of the Production Code in the late 1940s take their toll on Joseph Shearing's novel. Belle Adair in her ruthless scheming cannot survive the transfer to the big screen. The script tiptoes clumsily around the blackmailing tactics so nastily depicted in the novel. We first realize this when Belle (Peggy Cummins) stumbles upon the murdered body of Daisy Arrow and, instead of surreptitiously gathering up incriminating clues left behind by the killer, as described in the novel, she immediately cries the alarm, openly and innocently. Nothing to hide here. When it comes to that messy issue of blackmail, the script prefers that suspect Michael Drego (Victor Mature) be the one to first offer her some hush money, which she righteously refuses, demanding only two weeks of respectability in his country estate. Hey, a girl has got to have some fun. Belle thus comes across as more an innocent cockney wench yearning to be free than a sordid, conniving opportunist out to wreck the lives around her.

The real villainy will have to reside elsewhere… That's where Michael Drego comes in. He looks properly sinister in the opening scenes, set against the fog-filled backdrop of the London streets. When Belle comes to his estate to enjoy the good life, there are no more references to blackmail. She makes friends with Michael's fiancée, Audry Ashton (Patricia Medina), picnics with Michael, and earns the regard of his mother, the dowager Lady Margaret. Still no more references to any blackmail. Meanwhile, because the legendary dramatic actress, Ethel Barrymore, is portraying Lady Margaret, you can bet that the role will acquire more heft. A lot more heft. While the characters of Belle and Michael fade into the background, it is Lady Margaret who comes to the fore and gobbles up the scenery. Robbed of her son's upbringing when her husband had whisked him away to Canada, Lady Margaret has kept his room locked and his toys intact while zealously guarding it against any intruder. Now, possessive of her errant son newly returned home, she is decidedly cool toward Michael's loving fiancée and warms up to Belle only when she is assured the girl has no romantic interest in Michael. And so, when fiancée Audrey is found strangled, in a manner like the murder of Daisy Arrow at the film's beginning, we're not a little confused. Has Michael done it again? If not, who?

Moss Rose poster

Inevitably, when Lady Margaret learns that Belle is indeed falling in love with her son, we're not surprised when she corners the girl alone one night in her room, drugs her, and attempts to smother her with a pillow. The dirty deal is fortunately interrupted by the opportune arrival of Vincent Price (did I mention he's in the cast?) and the London police. Their clue to Lady Margaret's villainy?—the presence of a telltale moss rose.

In the epilogue, we find Belle on a train, headed to Toronto, where her lover, none other than Michael Drego, now presumably shorn of his sinister manner, awaits.

Regarding the "moss rose" of the title... Shearing's novel used it merely as a reference to a Music Hall turn by Belle Adair, who dances to a sweet little waltz that was once popular in Victorian England. The movie will not have any of that. Now a moss rose is found, tucked inside the bible left behind by Daisy Arrow's corpse. And another moss rose is found inside the bible next to the corpse of the fiancée. One of the investigating detectives knows a thing or two about moss roses and knows they are currently out of season. When he learns that Lady Margaret had recently purchased several bibles; and that she grows moss roses in her greenhouse, well, *voila!* Even though we never find out just why she chooses to place moss roses besides her victims, the device is not without interest. Especially, when a throw-away line reveals that "moss roses grow best in acid soil." Now, *that's* interesting!.

The real mystery of it all is why Victor Mature, who initially was on his way to being a sadistic killer in the opening scenes, is so cruelly emasculated and sanitized by the script. He emerges only a suitably insipid partner to the silly girl Belle Adair has become.

Hollywood columnist Louella O. Parsons read the script and commented, "Darryl Zanuck paid the impressive amount of $225,000 for the rights. Gene Markey, who is producing it, verifies the amount and says that this book is less sordid and grim than the other Shearing novels. Gregory Ratoff will direct Miss Cummins.... I have read a lot of the Shearing novels and they all end on an unhappy note. But Darryl tells me he has a great script for this one, and there's a note of comedy in it."[9]

So Evil My Love (1948). Hal Wallis Productions. Directed by Lewis Allen. Joseph Shearing's novel, *For Her to See*, adapted by Ronald Miller and Leonard Spigelgass. Starring Ray Milland, Ann Todd and Geraldine Fitzgerald.

We first meet Olivia Harwood (Ann Todd) and Mark Bellis (Ray Milland) on a ship bound to London from the West Indies. A widowed nurse, she restores the ailing stranger back to health. No sooner has she set up a boarding house in London than he shows up looking for a room. She doesn't know he's a rake and a scoundrel, an art thief and forger. He quickly casts his spell over the staid and conservative Olivia. Romance blossoms. When she is invited to stay as a companion in the home of an old friend, Susan Courtney (Geraldine Fitzgerald), Mark seizes the opportunity and tells her to steal her wealthy husband's bonds. Another opportunity to extort money comes in Olivia's discovery that she possesses letters from Susan's immoral past. Under Mark's malevolent influence, she agrees to blackmail Susan. Intrigues come to a head when the husband confronts Susan about the stolen bonds and the letters. At that moment, he suffers a heart attack. Olivia places a poisonous substance in a medicine bottle, which the unsuspecting Susan administers to him. Mark decides he and Olivia must escape London and sail to America. But before they can carry out their plan, she finds out he has been having on an affair with somebody else. She confronts him in a hansom cab and fatally stabs him. In a fit of remorse, she decides to save Susan from hanging. The film ends as Olivia turns herself in to the police.

Doubtless due to prevailing censorship codes, the character of Olivia is softened considerably from the book and atones for her crimes. No longer the scheming murderess pursuing her own malevolent ends, she is more the dupe of the seductive Mark. Mark himself is merely a petty thief and not the murderous, shape-shifting villain of the book. He is the victim of Olivia's outrage at his faithlessness.

New York Times critic Bosley Crowther sniffed, "The talent of Joseph Shearing, the novelist, for communicating in words the measured but monstrous malevolence of Victorian ladies steeped in crime has again eluded the film-smiths who would get it onto the screen."

The Mark of Cain. Great Britain. 1947. Directed by Brian Desmond Hurst and starring Eric Portman, Sally Gray, and Patrick Holt.

The film is unavailable for screening. Based on *Airing in a Closed Carriage*. English industrialist Richard Howard (*Eric Portman*) visits Bordeaux, France to buy cotton for his mills from Sarah Bonheur (Sally Gray), He becomes enamored by Sarah and spends much of his business trip sight-seeing. When his younger brother, John (Patrick Holt] arrives to close the deal, he also is attracted to Sarah, and after a whirlwind courtship, marries her.

When living out a lonely existence in John's grand house in Manchester, England, Sarah confides to Richard that she is depressed by her marriage. Richard encourages her to divorce John and run off with him. Sarah consults a lawyer, but finally ignores Richard's advice, and somehow reconciles with her husband. Seeking revenge, Richard then poisons his brother and attempts to frame Sarah for the murder.

Dr. White (James Hayter) is suspicious of the circumstances behind John's rapid decline, and after his death, Sarah's purchase of arsenic casts suspicion on her. In standing trial for murder, Richard defends Sarah thinking he will win her love, but she is found guilty. Another suitor,

So Evil My Love poster

Jerome Thorn (Dermot Walsh), is convinced he knows the identity of the poisoner, and comes to Sarah's aid.

Film critic Allan Essler Smith wrote, "This powerful drama is an interesting example of a strand of late 1940s British cinema, but has been long neglected and not shown on British TV for many years, if at all. Set in the late Victorian and early Edwardian eras, it has excellent period detail and the sets effectively highlight Sarah's alienation and despair in the Howards's suffocating and gloomy household."[10]

Blanche Fury. Great Britain. Screenplay by Audrey-Erskine Lindop and Cecil McGivern. Photography by Guy Green and Geoffrey Unsworth. Directed by Marc Allegret. Curiously, the Joseph Shearing novel is not credited.

The film version of *Blanche Fury*, apart from a conclusion that unfortunately radically departs from the book, is the best of the Bowen screen adaptations. The lush Technicolor photography of the estate's surrounding lands and the beautifully detailed interiors lends a stately melodrama of its own to the story. Their performances are nicely nuanced in their chilling, albeit at times compassionate qualities. The novel, one of Bowen's most complex, is followed in many particulars, including the recurring family motto of "Fury's Ape." Apparently, the censors dictated that *both* murderers, Blanche and Philip, must die for their sins. How much more affective was the novel's conclusion, when the stark, black-clad figure of Blanche lives on in the gloomy old mansion, accompanied only by the ghost of Philip. Instead, the film settles for the happier prospect of a child, conceived by Blanche and Philip, living on to inherit the estate.

At the film's open, Blanche is struggling in the throes of childbirth. The image wavers, the sound dims ... and a prolonged flashback begins...

Blanche Fury, née Fuller (Valerie Hobson) is in search of employment. She has already lost several positions of employment due to her independent temperament. She is given one last chance to be the hired companion

Blanche Fury **poster**

for a irritable rich old woman, Mrs. Hawkes (Margaret Withers). However, she receives a letter offering her another position and she leaves Mrs. Hawkes after having given her opinion of what she thinks of her.

Blanche, who is distantly related to the Fury name, has come to the Fury estate at the invitation of her Uncle Simon. She is to be the new governess at a generous salary. Upon her arrival, the first thing she sees is the curious emblem of "Fury's Ape" atop the doorway. "The legend has it," she is told, "that the Ape watches over the rights of the Fury's, hence the motto, 'Beware, Fury's Ape.'" Blanche's task is to teach and accompany young Lavinia (Suzanne Gibbs). But capturing her immediate attention in the household is the dashing, sardonic estate manager, Philip Thorn (Stewart Granger), who is seen, prophetically enough, cleaning his rifle. He's the illegitimate child of the late father of the family, and he's currently suing the family in an attempt to inherit what he protests is rightfully his. Standing in his way are the Fullers, who have usurped the family name of Fury.

There is a gypsy encampment near the village. Phillip enlists her aid in recovering some horses that were stolen by the gypsies. Under attack by some of them, she and Phillip fight their way free and escape with the horses. This angers the gypsies who vow revenge. Although Blanche is falling in love with Philip, it is to her advantage to marry the wealthy son of the family, Laurence (Michael Gough). When Philip is told by his lawyer that they couldn't find any proof of his mother having married secretly in Italy, he outraged and insists on his legitimate claim to the estate. When a beloved old horse is shot and killed, Philip seizes the opportunity and, disguised as a gypsy, murders the father and Blanche's husband. Blanche knows that he did it, because she saw him at the window that night. Indeed, she was complicit by not coming to the aid of the victims.

Philip impulsively behaves as if he were the master of the place, although Blanche tells him to be discreet. He tells her that the only thing which stands in his way from being master and commander is the little girl, Lavinia, but Blanche won't allow him to kill the innocent child, who in time will inherit everything. When Blanche witnesses Philip's attempt to lure the little girl into a dangerous jump while riding her pony, Blanche has a change of heart. She realizes his ambition to claim the estate exceeds his love for her. "I didn't think that any love could be as strong as ours," she tells him, "until I realized that your love for Clere is stronger than us both." She betrays Philip and accuses him of the murders. Philip is sent to jail awaiting a trial.

Philip insists on defending himself at the trial. Blanche gives her evidence and accuses him of plotting against Lavinia. However, Philip's skill in his defense throws doubt on Blanche's testimony. It is at this point that Philip receives a shock: Blanche reveals she is pregnant with his child. He now realizes the child will become the rightful inheritor of the Fury estate. Offering no further defense, Philip gives up his defense. He is convicted and imprisoned.

The day that Philip is executed, Lavinia is killed while attempting the dangerous jump. Consumed with guilt and grief, Blanche carries the little girl's dead body back to the estate.

At this point, the story moves back to the present. The trauma of childbirth results in the premature birth of Blanche's child. Blanche dies, but the boy lives and will become the sole heir of the estate. As images of the emblem of "Fury's Ape" is superimposed over the images, the doctor at Blanche's bedside says, "Philip Fury of Clere Hall. It has a good sound, doesn't it?"

The film failed at the boxoffice. Producer Anthony Havelock Allen is purported to have said,

> We took far too long over *Blanche Fury*, it cost too much money and it didn't "work" and never attracted any great audience. David and Ronnie didn't like what I was trying to do with *Blanche Fury*, which was along the lines of the very successful costume films from Gainsborough. I wanted to make a serious one with a better story and I thought it would make a lot of money. I found out what I was making was a 'hard" film, not a "soft" film which the others were. There was a real hatred in it as well as love, and the public didn't want it.[11]

Painting of Margaret Gabrielle Vere Long [Marjorie Bowen], date and provenance unknown (courtesy Bowen Estate).

Chapter Notes

Introduction

1. Handwritten, unpublished poem entitled "On the Scaffold," signed by "Gabrielle Margaret Brabant Vere Campbell," dated 1906–1907. The name "Marjorie Bowen" is written underneath. The Marjorie Bowen Papers, Beinecke Library, Yale University, Box 25, Folder 182.

2. The American scholars Edward Wagenknecht (1900–2004) and Jessica Amanda Salmonson have been Bowen's most enthusiastic and insightful champions. Professor Wagenknecht corresponded with Bowen in the 1940s and encouraged some of her publications. Three of his extended essays are quoted throughout my book. Ms. Salmonson collected and edited an important selection of her stories in 1997, *Twilight*, which included her valuable critical essay and an important biographical note from Bowen's then-living son, Hilary.

3. Walter Benjamin, "The Storyteller," in *Illuminations* (New York: Schocken Books, 1968), 91–92.

4. Marjorie Bowen, "Margaret Campbell," in Countess of Oxford and Asquith, ed., *Myself When Young* (London: Frederick Muller, Ltd, 1938), 41.

5. "Bowen" was her maternal great-grandfather's name, and "Marjorie" is a diminutive of Margaret.

6. In "A Precocious Author," the *New York Times* critic observed, "It would seem to such a reviewer simply incredible that a mere child could succeed … in transferring to the pages of a novel the spirit, the scenes, and the people of a long-past ago, and infusing them with the breath of life and reality" (17 November 1906, BR751, ProQuest Historical Newspapers). The two letters by Mark Twain are dated 25 March 1907 and 27 May 1907. He issues an invitation when he is next in England: "I think you will have to do as the American girls do: waive youth, sex, and the other conventions and call on me." The letter from Arthur Conan Doyle is dated 3 July 1916 and is in response to a later book, *Shadows of Yesterday*: "May I say how really splendid I think your new book … I don't like women's work as a rule, on account of a certain lack of substance, but here the detail, the atmosphere and the dramatic effect are all equally good." (Bowen Papers, Beinecke Library, Box 35, Folder 23).

7. Graham Greene, *The Lost Childhood and Other Essays* (New York: The Viking Press, 1951), 17.

8. Jessica Amanda Salmonson, Ed., *Twilight and Other Supernatural Romances* (Ashcroft, British Columbia: Ash-Tree Press, 1997), xix.

9. Michael Dirda, "Ghostly Women," *The Weekly Standard*, 6 March 2017, 38–41.

10. Edward Wagenknecht, "The Extraordinary Mrs. Long," *The New York Times Book Review*, 2 May 1943, 23.

11. This memorable epithet is by Sinclair Lewis in his Foreword to Bowen's novel, *The Golden Violet* (New York: The Readers Club, 1943), 6.

12. Quoted in Donna Heiland, *Gothic & Gender: An Introduction* (London: Blackwell, 2004), 57–58.

13. Patricia Murphy, *The New Woman Gothic* (Columbia: Missouri University Press, 2016), 1–30.

14. Sandra M. Gilbert and Susan Gubar, *The Madwoman in the Attic* (New Haven and London: Yale University Press, 1984), 3, 44. Virginia Woolf declared that before women can write, they must "kill" the "Angel in the House." See Gilbert and Gubar, 17.

15. "A writer needs her poisons," wrote Philip Roth appositely, "and the antidote is often a book" (quoted in "Roth Agonistes," by Nathaniel Rich, in NYRB, March 2018, 38).

16. Michael Dirda, *Readings: Essays and Literary Entertainments* (Bloomington and Indianapolis: Indiana University Press, 2000), 117.

17. Marjorie Bowen, *Black Magic*, 313.

18. Marjorie Bowen refers to the words of her hero, George Herbert (1593–1631), a seventeenth-century metaphysical poet whose poems were published only shortly after his death. Perhaps Bowen felt a kinship with Herbert in that the poet forsook a career at court for a more "commonplace" life as a cleric in a country church. His was an ordinary human ambivalence with regard to faith. It's unclear to me at this writing where Marjorie Bowen found this quotation. One source that could have been available to her was the *Dictionary of Burning Words by Brilliant Writers* (1895), edited by Josiah Hotchkiss Gilbert, where the quote appears on page 20. It seems to come originally from a letter or essay rather than from one of his poems. As for the quotation itself, it can be found on the internet in a review by Mark Jarman of John Drury's biography of Herbert, *Music at Midnight* (2014). Jarman's critique is titled "Writing for God: The Life and Work of George Herbert":

The story is that one night on his way to a gathering of musicians like himself [George Herbert] stopped to assist a man who was exasperated with his horse, who had fallen under its load. Herbert, after providing the man with help in getting the horse loaded again, and giving him some money to refresh himself and his animal—a typical gesture of his—proceeded to his rehearsal. Herbert, who was known for the care he took with his clothing and his cleanliness and neatness of dress, arrived soiled and in disarray. Asked about the reason, he shrugged it off and explained what had transpired and said that helping the man as he had—and advising him against beating his horse—would provide a solace for his own conscience that would be "music at midnight" in the future." See https://hudsonreview.com/2014/10/writing-for-god-the-life-and-work-of-george-herbert/#.WyrpoqdKiUk.

19. Marjorie Bowen, "An Initial Letter," *Harper's Monthly*, April 1910, 663–666.

20. Geoffrey Chaucer, *The Canterbury Tales* (New York: The Heritage Press, 1946), 1–2.

21. G.K. Chesterton, *Chaucer* (London: Faber and Faber, Ltd., 1937), 106.

22. G. K. Chesterton, "The Long Bow," in *G.K. Chesterton: The Collected Works*, Vol. XIV (San Francisco: Ignatius Press, 1993), 96.

Chapter One

1. Marjorie Bowen, *The Haunted Vintage*, 59–60.

2. The words of the corrupt monk, Thierry of Dendermonde in Marjorie Bowen's *Black Magic* (London: Gray's Inn Road, 1974), 273.

3. The three major occult systems in the 19th and 20th century were the ceremonial magic and writings of Eliphas Levi, the Theosophical Society of Madame Blavatsky, and the Hermetic Order of the Golden Dawn. Perhaps the most influential was the Theosophical Society, which was founded in New York in 1875. It attempted to inculcate the so-called "wisdom of the East" with Western philosophies. Blavatsky herself was discredited as a charlatan by the British Psychical Research Society. If nothing else, at least a sympathetic awareness of aspects of Eastern modes of thought surfaced in the West. For an overview of contemporary reactions to Theosophical thought and Blavatsky's writings, see Ruth Braddon, *The Spiritualists* (New York: Alfred A. Knopf, 1983), 235–254.

4. No better contemporary commentary can be found than in Henry Adams, *The Education of Henry Adams* (Boston: Houghton Mifflin Co., 1961).

5. Virginia Woolf, "The Supernatural in Fiction," in *Granite and Rainbow* (New York: Harcourt Brace Jovanovich, 1958), 64.

6. Derek Jarrett, *The Sleep of Reason* (New York: Harper and Row, 1989), 80. This is a useful overview of the intersections and contradictions of fantasy and reality during the years spanning the Victorian Age to World War On.

7. Saki's short story, "Music on the Hill," was included in his story collection, *The Chronicles of Clovis* (1911). When a young woman ventures into the "wild open savagery" of the woods surrounding her home—where purportedly the Nature-God Pan dwells—she hears a "low fitful piping as of some reedy flute" and is drawn to her gruesome death. See *The Short Stories of Saki* (New York: Modern Library, 1958), 179–185.

8. Charles Lamb, "Witches and Other Night Fears," from the *Essays of Elia*. In *The Works of Charles Lamb, Vol. 2* (London and New York: Dent and Dutton, 1903–1904), 68.

9. Hoffmann's writings on music are among many ecstatic expostulations on music from the early German Romantics, such as Novalis and Wackenroder. Hoffmann's essay on Beethoven profoundly influenced Baudelaire: "Music opens up to man a kingdom, a world which has nothing in common with the world of the senses which surrounds him." See Lois Boe Hyslop, *Baudelaire, Man of His Time* (New Haven: Yale University Press, 1980), 70–71.

10. Swinburne's public reputation as a pagan was based on *Poems and Ballads*, which he published in 1866. The most notorious poem in that volume was "Dolores," a hymn to the bloodthirsty pagan goddess, Dolores, whom he dubbed "Our Lady of Pain." An amusing contemporary riposte came from G. K. Chesterton whose poem,, "Dolores Replies to Swinburne," declaimed:

> I implore you to stop it and stow it,
> I adjure you, relent and refrain,
> Oh, pagan Priapean poet,
> You give me a pain.

11. I refer, specifically, to Schumann's great piano cycle, *Humoreske*, opus 20.

12. Vernon Lee, "Faustus and Helena," in *Hauntings* (Ashcroft, British Columbia: Ash-Tree Pres), 2002), 357–358). The pagan was always in flux. As Christian orthodoxy was called into question, people starved for a spiritual life in a desacralized age turned to cultic paganism. Spiritualities of any sort promised strong visceral experiences without accountability to God.

13. Marjorie Bowen (writing as "George R. Preedy), *Homage to the Unknown*, in *Bagatelle* (New York, Dodd, Mead, 1931).

14. These and other harrowing details of her childhood are related in the memoir, "Margaret Campbell," in Countess of Oxford and Asquith, ed., *Myself When Young* (London: Frederick Muller, Ltd., 1938), 45–46.

15. Margaret Campbell, *The Debate Continues: The Autobiography of Marjorie Bowen* (London: William Heinemann, 1939), 49.

16. Marjorie Bowen, *The Church and Social Progress* (London: Watts & Co., 1945), 23.

17. "Margaret Campbell," 61.

18. Alan Watts, "Western Mythology: Its Dissolution and Transformation," in Campbell, Joseph, Ed. *Myths, Dreams, and Religion* (New York: E.P. Dutton & Co., Inc., 1970), 22–23.

19. Marjorie Bowen, *The Church and Social Progress*, 86.

20. "Margaret Campbell," in *Myself When Young*, 56.

21. Marjorie Bowen, Preface to *Great Tales of Horror* (London: John Lane, 1933), xii.

22. Bowen admires these lines by the English poet, Edward Young, from *Night Thoughts*, and quotes them in her book of essays, *Worlds of Wonder* (London: Hutchinson & Co., 1937), 185–186.

23. In his "Farewell" to flowers, Herbert expresses a noble resignation to fate,

> I follow straight without complaint or grief,
> Since if my scent be good, I care not if
> If it be as short as yours.

See Bowen's comment in *Worlds of Wonder*, 179–180. Herbert joins the other Metaphysical poets of his generation, Henry Vaughan, Richard Crashaw, and Richard Baxter in Bowen's pantheon of favorite poets. They appear as characters in her novel, *Mr. Tyler's Saints* (London: Hutchinson & Co., 1939), which is set during the reign of Charles I and the Commonwealth. They share an ecstatic vision of heavenly serenity deriving from and transcending Nature. Vaughan's poetry is quoted extensively in Bowen's *God and the Wedding Dress*.

24. Margaret Campbell, *The Debate Continues*, 298.

25. According to the article, "Bowen's characterization of Herbert in this story seems to owe much to Izaak Walton. To Walton we may attribute the depiction of Herbert's sanctity, his love of nature, his courtly manner, and his commitment to clerical duties" (66). See *George Herbert Journal,* Vol. 28, Nos. 1–2 (Fall 2004/Spring 2005), 65–70. George Herbert (1593–1631) was a seventeenth-century metaphysical poet whose poems were published only shortly after his death. Perhaps Bowen felt a kinship with Herbert in that the poet forsook a career at court for a more "commonplace" life as a cleric in a country church. His was an ordinary human ambivalence with regard to faith. It's unclear to me at this writing where Marjorie Bowen found the words, "music at midnight." One source that could have been available to her was the *Dictionary of Burning Words by Brilliant Writers* (1895), edited by Josiah Hotchkiss Gilbert, where the quote appears on page 20. The quote seems to have been originally from a letter or essay rather than from one of his poems. As for the quotation itself, it can be found on the internet in a review by Mark Jarman of John Drury's biography of Herbert, *Music at Midnight* (2014). See https://hudsonreview.com/2014/10/writing-for-god-the-life-and-work-of-george-herbert/#.WyrpoqdKiUk.

26. Margaret Campbell, *The Debate Continues,* 267.

27. See Wright, John L., "Goodness in Chesterton and Lewis," in *The Chesterton Review,* Vol. XVII, Nos. 3 and 4 (August–November), 1991, 339–347. *Phantastes* was George MacDonald's direct response to Goethe's *Das Maerchen,* Novalis's *Heinrich von Ofterdingen,* and the so-called "literary fairy tales" of Hoffmann and Ludwig Tieck (particularly Tieck's "The Elves" and Hoffmann's "The Golden Pot"). In the opinion of cultural critic Gary Wolfe, "MacDonald produced some of the greatest literary fairy tales in the English language and in so doing helped to liberate the form from the ghetto of children's literature (Gary Wolfe, in "Fairy Tales, Maerchen, and Modern Fantasy," in Frank N. Magill, Ed., *Survey of Modern Fantasy Literature,* Vol. 5. Englewood Cliffs, New Jersey: Salem Press, 1983, 2278). See also the extended commentary on *Phantastes* in U.C. Knoepflmacher, *Venltures into Childhood* (University of Chicago Press, 1998), 117–120.

28. George MacDonald, *Phantastes* (New York: Ballantine Books, 1970), 212.

29. Ibid., 5.

30. Ibid., 211.

31. Jean-Antoine Watteau (1684–1721) executed two similar paintings by that name, the first in 1717 and the second two years later. "One might say that that *Cythera* was an allegory, not so much about love but about the power of erotic poetry and gallantry…. It represents a moment and is beyond time" (*Watteau,* 400). Cythera is an island in Greece. The painting of the guitar-playing Mezzetin, a character in the Commedia dell'arte, was executed by Watteau around the same time as *Cythera*. It is appropriate that Bowen would mention Watteau, since of all 18th-century painters, he perhaps understood best the music of his time.

32. Doubtless, Bowen is describing the kind of mythological frenzies depicted in the allegories of the vast ceilings of Venice and Wurzburg in the 1750s, such as *Apollo Bringing Beatrice of Burgundy to the Seat of the German Empire* and *The Allegory of the Four Continents*. See William L. Barcham, *Tiepolo* (New York: Harry N. Abrams, 1992, 104–109.

33. Finvarra is the King of the Shee in Irish folklore. He is a benevolent figure who ensures good harvests, a master at chess, strong *horses,* and great riches to those who will assist him. However, he also frequently kidnaps human women. The Shee, or Sidhe, are of two kinds, either tall and fair, or frightening, misshapen monsters like the Leprechaun, the Phooka, the Merrow and the Banshee.

34. Gwydion was a magician, a hero and trickster who appears most prominently in the Fourth Branch of the Mabinogian. Blodeuwedd was made from the flowers of broom, meadowsweet, and oak by the magicians Gwydion and Math. She is a central figure in the last of the Four Branches of the Mabinogian. Gwydion turns her into an owl, the creature hated by other birds.

35. Shiva is the brother of Brahma, god of creation, and Vishnu, god of preservation. Shiva has a third eye, which when opened portends the destruction of the universe.

36. "Yggdrasil," as attested in the Poetic *Edda,* compiled in the 13th century, is an enormous mythical ash tree that is the center of the cosmos and connects the nine worlds in Norse cosmology. Romilly's walled city—the "Sacked City" of the book's title—is the counterpart of Asgard, where Odin rules over the Aesir, a tribe of Norse deities. Klara's account of the sacking of the titular city by Valdemar Atterdag is a reference to the Danish King Valdemar Atterdag's pillaging of the city of Visby in 1361. He is commonly associated with the figure of the mythical Wild Huntsman. "Balder" is the son of Odin and beloved by the gods and goddesses.

37. In *Sexual Personae,* 423, Camille Paglia reminds us that Cythera is also the pagan site of sexual adventures and horrifying revelations, as in Baudelaire's poem, "A Voyage to Cythera," which is a "sardonic" revision of Watteau's painting.

38. "Margaret Campbell," in *Myself When Young,* 61. In the first of his 1641 Meditations on First Philosophy, Descartes purportedly imagined that an evil demon of power and cunning had beset him and told him that the world around him was a delusion and a deception.

39. *The Courtly Charlatan* is concerned only with St. Germain's years at the Court of Louis XV at the mid-eighteenth century, when he was an unofficial "advisor" to the King. His birth and background—not to mention his sorceries—are suitably obscure, although there seems to be at least one allegation accepted by many that he was the son of Prince Francis II Rákóczi of Transylvania. One wishes to have been present at his meeting in Paris with another celebrated adventurer and raconteur, Giacomo Casanova! Among the many storytellers who have since followed Bowen's example in chronicling Germain's exploits are Chelsea Quinn Yarbro and Diana Gabaldon.

40. Marjorie Bowen Papers, Beinecke Library, Yale, Box 22. 176–177.

41. Jessica Amanda Salmonson, "Rose Petals, Drops of Blood, n.p. www.violetbooks.com.

42. The Furies, or *Erinyes,* are female poisoners in Greek and Roman mythology. In the second play of Aeschylus's trilogy, *The Oresteia,* Orestes is assaulted by the vengeful Furies after murdering his mother, Clytemnestra. Orestes cries out:

"Look, see them, there! Like Gorgons, with grey cloaks and snakes coiled swarming around their bodies! I know them—avenging hounds incensed by a mother's blood…. And see—their dreadful eyes dripping with bloody pus! I know you do not see these beings, but I see them. I am lashed and driven! I can't bear it!"

"In her book, *Sexual Personae*, Camille Paglia presents an overview of the various incarnations of the Furies. Without fixed shape in Homer, they first gain substance in Aeschylus. Their servants are the Harpies, who are 'the Snatchers,' airborne pirates, befouling men with their droppings. Paglia goes on to describe them as "daemonic spirits of earth-cult, black as their mother night. They are ugly. They *offend the eye*. The Furies are snake-crowned hags, eyes dripping pus. Apollo and his priestess cannot stand to look at them: he banishes them to their home of beheadings, torn-out eyes, cut throats, castration, mutilation, stoning, and impalement... At the end of the *Oresteia* the Furies, cleansed of the chthonian, become Eumenides, "Kindly Ones,' Athens' benevolent guardians. See Paglia, *Sexual Personae* (New York: Vintage Books, 1991), 101–102).

43. See Joseph Shearing, *Airing in a Closed Carriage*, 289.

44. Marjorie Bowen, *Black Magic*, 313.

45. For example, in another story, "A Visit to Verona," from *Bagatelle*, a fable by Lucretius is a central metaphor in a story about illusion and reality. Lucretius talks of the effect of a silk canopy spangled with stars spread over the heads of a crowd of people: "The glare of common day being excluded, they came to believe themselves ... transported into Heaven, and in that rosy light, felt neither the defects of others nor their own disgraces." Thus, they are deluded into thinking they have left the earth and ascended into the heavens (281).

46. Stephen Goldblatt, *The Swerve: How the World Became Modern*. New York: W.W. Norton, 2011), 6–10. Its sensational opening "Hymn to Venus" influenced Botticelli's *Primavera* in the late 1470s. Novelist Philip Pullman adapted Lucretius's "atomistic" philosophy to his trilogy of novels, *His Dark Materials* (1995–2000).

47. The man who had recovered Lucretius's manuscript around 1417 was Poggio Bracciolini. Poggio had many friends in Florence and had allied himself in the mid-1450s with the interests of the Medicis, who were happy to claim him as one of their own." Poggio served as chancellor of Florence for five years. See Stephen Greenblatt, *The Swerve*, 43, 215.

48. In the "Author's Note" regarding her novelization of this alleged episode in history, *Pope Joan* (2009), Donna Woolfolk Cross declares, "Given the obscurity and confusion of the times, it is impossible to determine with certainty whether Joan existed or not" (417). She provides a measure of historical evidence, however, that reveals her own supposition about Pope Joan existed. See Cross, Donna Woolfolk, *Pope Joan* (New York: Broadway Books, 2009), 411–422.

49. Edward Wagenknecht, *Seven Masters of Supernatural Fiction* (Westport, CT: Greenwood Press, 1991), 155.

50. The setting has its American counterpart in the Hudson Valley, in the region of Sleepy Hollow. Washington Irving once described it "as under the sway of some witching power, that holds a spell over the minds of the good people, causing them to walk in a continual reverie." Residents were prone to trances and "the whole neighborhood abounds with local tales, haunted spots, and twilight superstitions."

51. Edward Wagenknecht, 156.

52. They have been interpreted as the Gospel writers who ushered Jesus's message into the world. William Blake thought the four animals were the divine aspects of both God and of human beings. A similar vision occurs in the book of *Revelation*.

53. The Agapemonites, or Community of the Son, was a Christian religious group in England. It was founded by the Rev. Henry Prince. It built a church in Upper Clapton, London. Its primary object was the spiritualization of the matrimonial state. Prince had been dismissed by the Church of England earlier in his career. It predicted the imminent return of Christ. Prince's successor was John Hugh Smyth-Pigott, who declared himself Jesus Christ reincarnate. Both Prince and Smyth-Pigott took many spiritual brides and produced illegitimate children.

54. See Amos N. Wilder's examination of "Myths and Dreams in Christian Scripture," in Joseph Campbell, Ed., *Myths, Dreams, and Religion* (New York: E.P. Dutton & Co., Inc., 1970). 68–90.

55. A comparison with a more recent account by historian Anne Somerset confirms that in most of the salient details, Bowen got her facts straight. Here is the historical record as recounted by Somerset. "Needing guile and ruthlessness, rather than strength, poison was a weapon in some respects ideally suited to a woman and was the more to be dreaded on that account" (7). Such a woman was Marie Madeleine d'Aubray (the Marquese de Brinvilliers), whose poisonings of members of her family began the investigations. "The condemned woman was no low-born wretch who had turned to crime to claw herself out of a desperate existence. She was, on the contrary, a person of 'birth and condition,' a marquise ... who was related to some of the most influential people in France" (7). Her key allies in the procuring of the poisonings were Gaudin de Sainte-Croix and his henchman, the Italian Egidio Exili. See Somerset, *The Affair of the Poisons: Murder, Infanticide and Satanism at the Court of Louis XIV* (London: Weidenfeld & Nicolson, 2003).

56. Anne Somerset, *The Affair of the Poisons*, 144.

57. *Ibid.* (42).

58. *Ibid.*, 11–12.

59. From 1937–1939, precisely the time spent by Bowen writing *The Poisoners*, Carr published six mystery novels foregrounding a strong atmosphere of the supernatural. *The Burning Court* is ranked by Carr specialist, S.T. Joshi, at the "highest" peak of Carr's works: "In its quiet intensity, lack of histrionics, careful characterization, vast ingenuity in producing a plausible natural explanation of the phenomena and stunning climax it perhaps Carr's greatest novel" (124). For the only time in all of Carr's books, the element of witchcraft is not ultimately explained away. Usually, the relationship between the natural and supernatural is much more ambiguous. S.T. Joshi makes a fine point of this in considering Carr's strategies—which works for Bowen, as well— that "the dispelling of the supernatural manifestation into a natural—or, more specifically, a human—agency serves another function in Carr's work: it underscores the pervasiveness of human evil" (115). See Joshi, *John Dickson John Dickson Carr: A Critical Study* (Bowling Green, OH: Bowling Green State University Popular Press, 1990). And we find frequent declarations to that effect in Bowen.

60. William Mompesson (1639–1709) was a clergyman in the Derbyshire parish of Eyam during the plague years of 1665–1667. In conjunction with the Puritan dissenter, Thomas Stanley, he isolated the community from the outside world, thinking it prudent to prevent the spread of the disease. Despite the quarantine, his children were permitted to leave the area. His wife, Catherine, remained behind and died. Mompesson survived

and settled as Rector at Eakring in Nottinghamshire in 1670.

61. Note the suggestion that this "visible miasma" was a cloud of mosquitoes and fleas, the true cause of the spread of the disease, was lost on him. The hazards of disease-ridden mosquitoes were unknown at the time.

62. Edward Wagenknecht, "The Extraordinary Mrs. Long," *The New York Times Book Review*, 2 May 1943, 22.

Chapter Two

1. Margaret Campbell, *The Debate Continues (Being the Autobiography of Marjorie Bowen)* (London: William Heinemann, Ltd, 1939), 32

2. Marjorie Bowen Papers, Beinecke Library, Yale University, Box 180. *Royal Pageantry, 12th May 1937* was published in London by Moss Bros. & Co. Ltd., 1937. The quote is on page 25.

3. Hal Orel, *The Historical Novel from Scott to Sabatini* (New York: St. Martin's Press, 1995).

4. *The Third Estate* is an historical novel about the author and politician, Comte de Mirabeau, and his involvement in the years leading up to the French Revolution. The novel was published in 1917.

5. Edward Wagenknecht, "Bowen, Preedy, Shearing & Co.: A Note in Memory and a Check List," *Boston University Studies in English*, Vol. III (Autumn 1957), 181-189. The quote is from page 181.

6. Marjorie Bowen, *Mary Queen of Scots*, 15.

7. Richard Holmes, *Footsteps* (New York: Vintage Books, 1985), 208.

8. *Ibid.*, 5-15.

9. Marjorie Bowen Papers, Beinecke Library, Yale University, Box 22.

10. Samuel C. Chew, *The Nineteenth Century and After (1789-1939)* (New York: Appleton-Century-Crofts, 1948), 1354). It is perhaps significant that it was also a favorite novel by Arthur Conan Doyle, a friend and contemporary of Marjorie Bowen, himself no mean writer of historical novels. Writing in 1893: "I do not know where I can find a book in which the highest qualities of head and heart go together as they do in this one.... It is from the struggle between the church and human love, the life of the home and that of the cloister, that the book takes its title. Such an indictment against celibacy of the clergy has never yet been penned. But the wonder of the book is the extraordinary clearness and power with which the middle ages, in many countries, in many countries and from many points of view, are laid before us." (see http://freeread.com.au/@RGLibrary/ArthurConanDoyle/Autobiographical/MyFavouriteNovelist.html,)

11. Marjorie Bowen Papers, Beinecke Library, Yale University, Boxes 24 (Folders 171 and 173); Box 25 (Folder 176 and 180); and Box 38.

12. "The Macedonian Groom, from Marjorie Bowen, *God's Playthings*.

13. James Cawthorn and Michael Moorcock, *Fantasy: The 100 Best Books* (New York: Carroll & Graf, 1988), 56.

14. Marjorie Bowen, "Margaret Campbell," in Countess of Oxford and Asquith, Ed., *Myself When Young* (London: Frederick Muller, Ltd., 1938), 42-43.

15. Margaret Campbell, *The Debate Continues*, 50-53.

16. Marjorie Bowen, "Margaret Campbell," 53-54.

17. Marjorie Bowen, *William Hogarth: The Cockney's Mirror* (New York: D Appleton-Century Company, 1937), 48. In his appreciative review of the book, William Benet wrote: "We see the available Hogarths through the eyes of a close and critical observer—not without acute comment on the manner of their preservation." See Benet, "Painter Pug," *The Saturday Review*, 23 January 1937, 12.

18. Marjorie Bowen, *William Hogarth*, 54.

19. Margaret Campbell, *The Debate Continues*, 20.

20. *Ibid.*, 55.

21. Chesterton's lines are inscribed on the opening page of an illustrated children's book by Randolph Caldecott, as presented to a young friend.

"A Piece of Chalk" was included in Chesterton's collection of essays, *Tremendous Trifles* (New York: Dodd, Mead and Company), 1909: "Brown paper represents the primal twilight of the first toil of creation, and with a bright-coloured chalk or two you can pick out points of fire in it, sparks of gold, and blood-red, and sea-green, like the first fierce stars that sprang out of divine darkness" (9-10).

My many references to G. K. Chesterton throughout the pages of my book on Marjorie Bowen suggest a profound kinship between these two contemporaries. Although there is no extant evidence they ever met, or even knew each other, their mutual interests in the romance of English history, their excursions into nightmare, and their fascination with myth and allegory are compelling. As indefatigable storytellers, their industry and output are yet to be adequately documented. And, of course, they both drew their pictures on brown paper.

22. Excavations in the ancient Greek city of Aphrodisias reveal traces of color in the statues of gods, heroes, and nymphs. "For centuries," reports Mark Abbe, Professor of Ancient Art in at the University of Georgia, "archaeologists and museum curators had been scrubbing away these traces of color before presenting statues and architectural reliefs to the public.... The idea that the ancients disdained bright color is the most common misconception about Western aesthetics in the history of Western art." The study of "polychromy" is a hot pursuit in the archaeology of art these days. The bias to equate whiteness with beauty, taste, and classical ideals, and to see color as alien, sensual, and garish is being questioned and overturned. See Margaret Talbot, "Color Blind," in *The New Yorker* 29 October 2018, 42-45.

23. Schama reports, for example, that in 1271 Marco Polo was intoxicated by the sight of lapis lazuli quarried from a mountain at Badakhshan, in what is now Afghanistan: "Laboriously prepared by removing impure specks of glinting iron pyrite, it became ultramarine—as expensive, ounce for ounce, as gold, and so precious that it was initially reserved for depictions of the costume of the Virgin." See Schama, "Blue As Can Be," *The New Yorker,* 3 September, 2018, 28-31. In another article, Schama writes that Van Gogh spent his last years in search of unadulterated color and was infatuated with chrome yellow. For him, reports Schama, "colour marked the presence of the divine. The unadulterated colour would have the innocently brilliant intensity of children's art.... The artist's own heightened perception would be translated for the spectator so that we might share in this universe of intense feeling and looking. Modern paintings would be acts of friendship, a visual embrace." See Simon Schama, *The Power of Art* (London: BBC Books, 2006), 299.

24. See Daniel Mendelsohn, "Is the Aeneid a Celebration

of Empire—or a Critique," *The New Yorker*, 15 October 2018, 87–93. Quote on page 92.

25. Edward Wagenknecht, "The Extraordinary Mrs. Long," *The New York Times Book Review*, 2 May 1943, 2.

26. Pamela Cleaver, "Marjorie Bowen," in *Romance and Historical Writers* (Chicago: St. James Press, 1990), 65-68.

27. G. K. Chesterton, *Chaucer* (New York: Sheed and Ward, 1956), 73.

28. Marjorie Bowen, Preface to *Mary Queen of Scots* (London: Endeavor Press, 2015), 5–6.

29. Historically, there really was a Gian Galeazzo Visconti (16 October 1351-3 September 1402). He was the first Duke of Milan and ruled the late-medieval city just before the dawn of the Renaissance. Soon after seizing Milan he took Verona, Vicenza, and Padua, establishing himself as *Signore* of each, and soon controlled almost the entire valley of the Po. In 1400, he appointed a host of clerks and departments entrusted with improving the public health. For the new system of administration and bookkeeping this established, he is credited with creating the first modern bureaucracy. Gian Galeazzo had dreams of uniting all of northern Italy into one kingdom, a revived Lombard empire. Galeazzo's dreams were to come to naught, however, as he succumbed to a fever at the castello of Melegnano on 10 August 1402. He died on 3 September. His empire fragmented as infighting among his successors wrecked Milan, partly through his division of his lands among both legitimate and illegitimate heirs.

30. Edward Wagenknecht, *"Marjorie Bowen,"* in *Seven Masters of Supernatural Fiction* (Westport, CT: Greenwood Press, 1991), 153.

31. "A Precocious Author," 17 November 1906. BR751. ProQuest Historical Newspapers.

32. "A Guide to the New Books, *The Literary Digest*, 5 January 1907, 25.

33. Fredric Taber Cooper, "The Value of Contrast," *The Bookman*, January 1907, 487.

34. "Current Fiction," *The Nation*, 13 December 1906, 518.

35. Bowen's son, Hilary Long, reports that Mark Twain's admiration for *The Viper of Milan* and *The Glen O'Weeping* led to his writing a letter to her in 1907, inviting her to a meeting. "Addressing her as Miss Marjorie ('The privilege of three score and eleven') he wrote, I will be in London for ten days—June 18–28—and I think you have to do as the American girls do: waive youth, sex and other conventions and call me.... They 'collided' over lunch.... It must have been an interesting sight to see the venerable Mark Twain, with his wonderful head of white hair, and the timid young girl talking together as colleagues in literature" (xiii–xiv). See Hilary Long's memoir, in Jessica Amanda Salmonson, Ed, *Twilight* ((Ashcroft, British Columbia, Ash-Tree Press, 1998), ix–xvi.

36. Graham Greene, "The Lost Childhood," in *The Lost Childhood and Other Essays* (New York: The Viking Press, 1962), 15–16.

37. Margaret Cambell, *The Debate Continues*, 92.

38. Ibid., 95–96, 111, 118.

39. Marjorie Bowen, *The Sword Decides* (New York: Endeavour, 2015), 5. Originally published in 1908. Quotation from the Preface to the 1924 edition. She adds, "It would be difficult for anyone to write of Italy, as it emerges from the Middle Ages, without catching something in the narrative itself, of that swift play of passion and impulse, of that tense, highly wright tendency to dramatic climax, which starts into life from the pages of the barest records of the period (5).

40. Christopher Hill, *God's Englishman* (New York: Penguin Books, 1970), 13–16.

41. Pamela Cleaver, "Marjorie Bowen," 67.

42. Marjorie Bowen, *World's Wonder* (London: Hutchinson & Co., 1937), 112. By the way, Bowen is not above viewing William with sardonic humor, witness this anecdote: During William's coronation the weather was so bad that it continued throughout his entire reign: "The adherents of James II laid the whole blame on His Majesty, so that a Highlander in March 1702 [the year of William's death] beholding, as he declared, the first gleam of sunshine he had seen for fourteen years, gave a Gaelic fling and exclaimed: 'King Wullie must be dead!'" (Bowen, *Royal Pageantry*, 15).

43. Marjorie Bowen, *William, Prince of Orange* (London: John Lane the Bodley Heat, Ltd, *1928*), xv. In his biography, *King William III* (London: The Rubicon Press, 1997), Bryan Bevan stresses that William, in the final analysis was a *European*, that he "had never been popular in England, and few people felt his loss.... William remained a passionate Dutchman to the end, largely a stranger to the island race he reigned over, but he had paved the way for England's greatness in the eighteenth century" (183). Bevan also quotes a telling remark by Daniel Defoe, who became a friend of William, who recognized that Englishmen regarded William "as a foreigner." Defoe reminded his nation of its own origins, "thereby to let them see what a banter is put upon themselves in it; since speaking of Englishmen *ab origine* we are really *all foreigners ourselves.*" (173).

44. Marjorie Bowen, *William, Prince of Orange*, xv. Bevan also emphasizes these qualities: "It is surprising that in the long notice devoted to William III, it is stated that he disliked learning and art. It is not true. He was indeed keenly interested in art and collected pictures.... Though no intellectual, he was interested in learning, education and social reform. And it was he who encouraged men of erudition such as Edmund Halley and Isaac Newton" (183).

45. Marjorie Bowen, *The Church and Social Progress* (London: Watts & Co., 1945), 32.

46. Ibid., 33.

47. Marjorie Bowen, *World's Wonder*, 80.

48. Ibid., 76.

49. All quotations come from Marjorie Bowen, *The Glen O' Weeping* (London: Endeavour Press, 2015).

50. Biographer Bevan admits that the Massacre was a great blot on William's record. But the historian is measured in his own assessment: "It was Sir John Dalrymple, Master of Stair, who was mainly responsible for the hideous massacre, but King William must share some of the blame for abetting him" (134).

51. Fredric Taber Cooper, "Heroines in Fiction," *The Bookman*, June 1907, 393.

52. "The Master of Stair," *The Sydney Mail*, 3 July 1907, n.p.

53. "Tries to Bleach Sir John's Name," *The Philadelphia Record*, 2 June 1907, n.p.

54. All quotes are from Marjorie Bowen, *I Will Maintain* (London: Metheun & Co., 1910).

55. Bryan Bevan, *King William III*, 140.

56. John M.S. Allison, "The Dutch Background," *The Saturday Review of Literature*, 3 August 1929, 21.

57. All quotations are from Marjorie Bowen, *Defender of the Faith* (Alberta, Canada: Inheritance Publications, 1994).

58. "The battle of Saint-Denis was a victory for the Dutch allies," reports biographer Bryan Bevan, "but one wonders whether it should have taken place at all. The Prince's critics maintained that he was aware of the signing of the Treaty of Nijmegen a few hours before the battle. It is possible that William had received news of the Treaty, but in the confusion of the battle had put the packet in his pocket unopened" (58).

59. Wilkinson Sherren, "Defender of the Faith," *The Bookman*, 11 March 1911, 284.

60. "Defender of the Faith," *The Nation*, 1 November 1917, 487.

61. All quotations are from Marjorie Bowen, *God and the King* (London: Methuen & Co., Ltd., 1924).

62. In his appreciative Preface to Marjorie Bowen's *Affairs of Men* (London: Heath Cranton, Ltd., 1922), Lieut.-Gen. F. de Bas (Director of the Military Historical Section General Staff of the Dutch Army) examines with expert approval Bowen's abilities to envisage her researches into battle tactics. The quotation is on page 11.

63. "The Prince of Orange Again," *The Boston Evening Transcript*, 19 March 1912, n.p.

64. "Marjorie Bowen's New Story," *The New York Times*, 10 March 1912, n.p.

65. All quotations are from *The English Paragon* (London: Hodder and Stoughton, 1929). Bowen does not use the sobriquet, "The Black Prince," because, she writes, "The first mention of it is in Grafton's *Chronicle*, written in 1563, nearly two hundred years after his death" (11). See also David Green, *The Hundred Years War: A People's History* (New Haven and London: Yale University Press, 2014), 104. Five English and five French kings—the House of Plantagenet and the French House of Valois—contested the Hundred Years War, roughly the years 1337–1453. Each side drew many allies into the war, resulting in one of the most notable conflicts of the Middle Ages. It was shaped by and in turn influenced "the increasing importance of state institutions, the growth of bureaucracies, representative assemblies, and the greater intricacy of local government, and, despite the emergence of gunpowder and a major restructuring of the social order." And "Just as kings shaped the outcome of the war, so the struggle reshaped many of the characteristics of kingship in England and France." The war marked both the height of chivalry and its subsequent decline, and the development of strong national identities in both countries.

66. Bowen treats of the death of Edward elsewhere in her story, "Defeat," in *God's Playthings* in 1913. This story appeared later, retitled as "Edward Plantagenet of Wales, Duke of Cornwall" in *Exits and Farewells*, in 1929.

67. David Green, *The Hundred Years War: A People's History* (New Haven and London: Yale University Press, 2014), 31.

68. Ibid., 23–32: "Chivalry was at the core of medieval aristocratic identity. Although subject to a variety of definitions, chivalry had dominated the thinking of the secular elite for three hundred years and it remained central to the self-image of the aristocracy in the Hundred Years War. Chivalry had become a cult, an ideology, little less than a 'secular religion,' and as such it influenced conduct during conflict; the struggle was shaped by demands of honour, demonstrations of prowess and exigencies of loyalty.... Chivalry was much more than a game, fantasy or a self-delusion: it exercised enormous influence over military and diplomatic conduct.... It is sometimes assumed that chivalry died as the Middle Ages waned, but chivalry was far from dead in the Hundred Years War" (23–24). "Nonetheless, chivalry did provide a justification for the actions of the ruling elite, and it served as a mechanism to protect the international, aristocratic, military caste on the battlefield.... Although chivalry encouraged restraint in some circumstance, without violence there was no chivalry" (32).

69. David Green, *The Hundred Years War*, 54.

70. All quotations are taken from Marjorie Bowen, *The Governor of England* (London: Endeavour Press, 2015).

71. In his biography of Cromwell, Christopher Hill observes that in the Calvinist scheme of conversion, which Oliver accepted, "grace always came from without after one's own works had failed and one had sunk to the depths" (44).

72. Also as "George R. Preedy," Bowen had previously published a short story, "Hurry! Hurray!" in *The Knot Garden* in 1933, about an unsuccessful assassination attempt during a masquerade ball against King Gustaf of Sweden. A few years earlier, in *Sundry Great Gentlemen* (1928), "Marjorie Bowen" returned to Swedish history in the essay, "Gustavus Adolphus II." Swedish nationality owed much to the great House of Vasa, she wrote, to which "this country, so long ignored by Europe, owed everything; under the guidance of Gustavus I, the Swedes had warmly embraced the tenets of the Reformation; following these, commerce, learning, the arts had flourished on the shores of the Baltic; the culture of Sweden, under the Vasa Kings, first equaled and then surpassed any culture of the north; the world began to hear of Sweden; these people, of Viking descent, cold, hardly, brave, and sane, seemed the fitting exponents of the era of common sense inaugurated by Martin Luther" (171).

73. Giuseppe Verdi composed his *Un ballo in maschera* in 1859, based on a libretto by Eugéne Scribe. Italian censorship changed the setting to Boston.

74. Marjorie Bowen, *Royal Pageantry*, 20.

Chapter Three

1. Marjorie Bowen, "Vigil," in Salmonson, Ed., *Twilight* (Ashcroft, BC: Ash-Tree Press, 1997), 188.

2. Margaret Campbell, *The Debate Continues: Being the Autobiography of Marjorie Bowen* (London: William Heinemann, Ltd., 1939), 27, 116–117.

3. "Margaret Campbell," in Countess of Oxford and Asquith, ed., *Myself When Young* (London: Frederick Muller, Ltd, 1938), 46.

4. Ibid., 45.

5. Ibid., 14, 22.

6. Ibid., 49.

7. Sam Johnson paid tribute to George Lyttelton (1709–1773) by including his work in the collection of English poets prefacing his *Lives of the Poets*. The Epworth Rectory of John Wesley was plagued by the sounds of an invisible horn, accompanied by strange running and bumpy sounds. The house was searched in vain. The sounds ceased in January 1717.

8. Marjorie Bowen, *Kecksies* (Sauk City WI: Arkham House, 1976), x–xi.

9. Ibid., x–xii.

10. Marjorie Bowen, "The Accursed Portrait," in *More Great Tales of Horror* (London: John Lane, 1933), 314.

11. Marjorie Bowen, Ed., *Great Tales of Horror* (London: John Lane, 1933), x–xi.

12. Marjorie Bowen, *Kecksies*, xi. Bowen continues that there is "more than a jest" about this kind of ghost, inasmuch "that centuries ago women were taught 'to glide' with tiny steps inside farthingale or crinoline so that they appeared 'to float,' that they were high wooden heels or pattens, and so, mincing in their wide skirts, tapped, tapped on polished boards, that their silks, stiff enough to stand alone, did rustle...," (xii).

13. Marjorie Bowen, Ed., *Great Tales of Horror*), ix.

14. Marjorie Bowen, Ed., *More Great Tales of Horror* (London: John Lane, 1935), x.

15. Marjorie Bowen, Ed., *Great Tales of Horror*, ix–xi.

16. Marjorie Bowen, *Kecksies*, iv–xiii.

17. Graham Greene, *The Lost Childhood and Other Essays* (New York: The Viking Press, 1951, 17.

18. Edward Wagenknecht, "Bowen, Preedy, Shearing & Co.: A Note in Memory and a Check List," *Boston University Studies in English*, Vol. III (Autumn 1957), 182.

19. Michael Sadleir, Introduction to *The Bishop of Hell* (London: Bodley Head, 1949), x.

20. Jessica Amanda Salmonson, *Twilight and Other Supernatural Romances* (Ashcroft, BC: Ash-Tree Press, 1997), xix.

21. Edward Wagenknecht, "Review of *Mignonette*," *New York Herald Tribune*, 18 July 1948, n.p. Marjorie Bowen Papers, Beinecke Library, Box 36, folder 246.

22. The motif of a "spectral bride" appeared in a short story, "The Dead Bride," that Bowen included in her anthology, *Great Tales of Horror*. In that tale is this anecdote:

> A woman had lived in the fourteenth or fifteenth century. She was a noble lady who had conducted herself towards her lover with such ingratitude and perfidy that he died of chagrin. In the conclusion, when she was about to be married to someone else he appeared on her wedding night and she died. The legend was that the spirit of this unhappy creature wandered on the earth as a penance and took all manner of forms, particularly those of charming creatures, to render lovers unfaithful. As it was not permitted to her to re-clothe herself in the appearance of a living person, she appeared under the disguise of girls lately deceased and if possible under the shape of one who resembled her the most. It was for this reason that her formless ghost haunted the chateau where she had once lived, and, if occasion offered, took on the likeness of a dead young girl of the house to which she had once belonged. She was also said to haunt galleries and museums in search of dead beauties whose charms she could assume for the undoing of some living, faithful lover. These dismal pilgrimages were to be repeated in punishment for her perfidy until she found the man so faithful that she was not able to induce him to forget his living betrothed. This has not yet occurred (219).

23. Kenelm Digby (1603–1665) was a seventeenth-century English courtier and philosopher who conducted alchemical experiments involving the manufacture of what he called a "powder of sympathy" as a curative balm.

24. Edward Wagenknecht, "Marjorie Bowen," in *Seven Masters of Supernatural Fiction* (Westport CT: Greenwood Press, 1991), 161.

25. "The Intruder" may have influenced Daphne du Maurier's *Rebecca*, which was published ten years later, in 1938. In brief, Bowen's story concerns newly married Ann Vereker who, upon entering her husband's estate for the first time, is rebuffed by the perceived presence of his late first wife, whose portrait still hangs in a locked room. "She is still here," says Ann, "in this room. In this house. In the church. How she must laugh at me!" (287). Feeling her inferior, an intruder, Ann departs, as "the painted figure seemed to step from the frame and dominate both of them" (288).

26. Sally Benson, "Mystery and Crime," *The New Yorker*, 10 May 1941, 89.

27. The resemblance between Laura's name and the name of the laurel leaves is not coincidental. Bowen makes it clear that she is referencing the poet Petrarch's great love for another Laura, Laura de Noves, the sight of whom impelled Petrarch to give up his vocation as a priest. There is little definite information in Petrarch's work concerning Laura, except that she is lovely to look at, fair-haired, with a modest, dignified bearing. Laura and Petrarch had little or no personal contact.

28. Bowen appends these lines to *The Devil Snar'd*.

29. Marjorie Bowen, Preface, *More Great Tales of Terror*, ix–x.

30. Jessica Amanda Salmonson, Ed., *Twilight*, xxxvi).

31. Bowen identifies this quotation as belonging to the *Memoirs of the Paris of St. James, London* (London: Corbie Pettigrew, 1830).

32. Ronald Taylor, *Hoffman* (New York: Hilary House, 1963), 32.

33. Jessica Amanda Salmonson, *Twilight* (Ashcroft, BC: Ash-Tree Press, 1997), xxxvi.

34. Michael Sadleir, Introduction to *The Bishop of Hell*, x.

35. "Margaret Campbell," *Myself When Young*, 63.

Chapter Four

1. All quotations from the short stories are from the volumes cited in the Bibliography.

2. Marjorie Bowen, Prologue to *Bagatelle*, v–vii.

3. "Accident" serves as a kind of preface to Marjorie Bowen's *Dark Ann and Other Stories* (1927).

4. "Sea Piece," in *The Gorgeous Lovers*, 278.

5. Virginia Woolf, *The Common Reader* (New York: Harvest Edition, 1984), 177.

6. The first stories for which we have a record began appearing in the years 1907–1909, concurrent with the publication of *The Viper of Milan*, *The Master of Stair* (*The Glen O' Weeping*), and *The Sword Decides*. For example, from 1907 came "A Moral Lesson" (*Cassell's Magazine*, June), "The Black Pearls" (*The Pall Mall Magazine*, December), "Huntly of Dunbar" (*The Story-teller*, April)," and "Clarinda" (*The Story-teller*, October); from 1908, "My Lady Played" (*Cassell's Magazine*, November), "The Yellow Ribbon and Giovanna" (*Short Stories*, May) "The Apple of Venus" (*Harper's Monthly Magazine*, February), "A Princess of Kent" (*Harper's Monthly Magazine*, April); and from 1909, "The Apple of Venus" (*Harper's Monthly Magazine*, February). With the exception of "My Lady Played" and "A Princess of Kent," both of which later appeared in her story collection, *The Pleasant Husband* (1921), none of these have been reprinted. The titles hint at their variety.

7. Marjorie Bowen, "The Luck of Madame de Maupret," in *The Gorgeous Husband*, 102.

8. The Epigraph to the volume of short stories, *Grace Latouche*.

9. Geoffrey Chaucer, *The Canterbury Tales* (New

York: The Heritage Press, 1946), 261–266. Note the resemblance to the classic B. Traven novel of 1927, *The Treasure of the Sierra Madre*, and the subsequent John Huston movie adaptation in 1948.

10. G.K. Chesterrton, *Chaucer* (London: Faber & Faber Ltd., 1932), 158.

11. In Edmund Wilson's essay, "Philoctetes: The Wound and the Bow," Wilson discusses the *Philoctetes* of Sophocles. The hero, Philoctetes, who possesses the enchanted bow of Herakles, suffers from an incurable wound from a snake bite. Not until Philoctetes returns to Troy with the bow can he be healed and Troy captured. His pain has "a dignity and an interest" for Sophocles. Philoctete's misfortune, writes Wilson, "has enabled him to perfect himself." Through that wound, says Philoctetes, "I come to know more of the secrets of life than my masters had ever revealed to me." Edmund Wilson, *The Wound and the Bow* (New York: Oxford University Press, 1947), 123.

12. Mel Gordon, *The Grand Guignol: Theater of Fear and Terror* (New York: Da Capo Press, 1997), 9–10. Historically, reports Gordon, the French theatrical *grand guignol* dates roughly from the late nineteenth century to the 1960s and was often based on real-life criminal stories from newspapers and laboratory reports: "The shocking stage display was a more truthful unveiling of the savage human soul than anything available elsewhere on stage or in the cinema. Only life matched the horror of the *grand guignol*" (2).

13. H. P. Lovecraft, "Supernatural Horror in Literature," in August Derleth and Donald Wandrei, Eds., *The Outsider and Others* (Sauk City, WI: Arkham House, 1939), 526.

14. Arnold Kellett, *The Dark Side of Guy de Maupassant* (New York: Carroll & Graf, 1989), xiv.

15. Christopher Morley, "Introduction," to *The Short Stories of Saki* (New York: The Modern Library, 1930), vi–vii.

16. David Cecil, *Max: A Biography* (Boston: Houghton Mifflin, 1965), 179–197.

17. S. T. Joshi, *Unutterable Horror: A History of Supernatural Fiction*, Vol. 2 (New York: Hippocampus Press, 2014), 386.

18. Tom Milne, "The Elusive John Collier," *Sight and Sound*, Vol. 45, No. 2 (Spring 1976), 104–108.

19. H. P. Lovecraft, "Supernatural Horror in Literature," in *The Outsider and Others*.

20. S. T. Joshi, Level, *Thirty Hours with a Corpse* (Mineola, NY: Dover, 2016), viii.

21. Joyce Carol Oates, "The Art of Vengeance," *The New York Review of Books*, 26 April 2007, 44.

22. Eugene Current-Garcia, *O. Henry* (New York: Twayne, 1965), 138.

23. Margaret Campbell, *The Debate Continues* (London: William Heinemann, 1939), 84.

24. Jessica Amanda Salmonson, "Rose Petals, Drops of Blood," addendum to Salmonson's Introduction to *Twilight and Other Supernatural Romances*. See https://web.archive.org/web/20130628075333/http://www.violetbooks.com:80/bowen.htmln.p.)

25. Edward Wagenknecht, *Seven Masters of Supernatural Fiction* (Westport, CT: Greenwood Press, 1991), 179.

26. Margaret Campbell, *The Debate Continues*, 16.

27. Jessica Amanda Salmonson, Introduction to Marjorie Bowen, *Twilight* (Ashcroft, BC, 1997), xxiii.

28. The pagination of "Decay," is from its inclusion in *Twilight*.

29. Note: Pagination from *The Last Bouquet*.

30. Note: Pagination from the *Kecksies* volume.

31. The imagery of an angry ape is a device that figures prominently as the family motto in the novel, *Blanche Fury*.

32. The pagination is from the story's inclusion in the Edward Wagenknecht anthology, *A Fireside Book of Yule-Tide Tales* (New York: Bobbs-Merril, 1948).

33. Marjorie Bowen, Ed., *Great Tales of Horror* (London: John Lane, 1933), x–xi.

34. Marjorie Bowen, Ed., *More Great Tales of Horror* (London: John Lane, 1935), ix.

35. August Derleth, Ed., *The Night Side* (New York: Rinehart & Company, 1947).

36. Marjorie Bowen, unpublished sheaf of notes under the title, "Through the Eyes of an Author," courtesy of the Bowen Estate.

37. Marjorie Bowen, Preface to *Bagatelle*, v–vii.

Chapter Five

1. Sinclair Lewis, Foreword to Joseph Shearing, *The Golden Violet* (New York: The Press of the Readers Club, 1943), 6.

2. Joseph Shearing, "Blood and Thunder," from *Orange Blossoms* (London: William Heinemann, 1938), 306–323.

3. De Quincey's fascination with the cast included several essays of gruesomely vivid reportage, beginning in 1823 with "On Knocking at the Gate of Macbeth," and continuing with "On Murder Considered as One of the Fine Arts" in 1827, "A Second Paper on Murder" and a "Postscript" in 1839.

4. Robert Morrison, *Thomas De Quincey: On Murder* (New York: Oxford University Press, 2009), vii.

5. Quoted in Robert Morrison, *Thomas De Quincey*, 253.

6. See Theodore Dalrymple *The Social Order*, Spring 2018 https://www.city-journal.org/html/quiet-evenings-reading-15844.html.

7. Quoted in Alexander Woollcott's Foreword to William Roughead, *The Murderer's Companion* (New York: The Readers Club, 1941), x.

8. Luc Sante, Ed,. *Classic Crimes: William Roughead* (New York Review of Books, 2000), ix.

9. Sally Benson, "Mystery and Crime," *The New Yorker*, 10 May 1941, 89.

10. James Sandoe, *Murder Plain and Fanciful* (New York: Sheridan House, 1948), 616.

11. William Charlton, "She of Many Names," *Wormwood Magazine*, 2007, 64.

12. Edward Wagenknecht, "The Extraordinary Mrs. Long," *New York Times Book Review*, 2 May 1943, 2.

13. Luc Sante, Ed., *Classic Crimes*, ix.

14. Mary S. Hartman, *Victorian Murderesses* (New York: Schocken Books, 1976), 1–3, 288–289.

15. It is worth noting, before proceeding further, that historian and cultural commentator, Jessica Amanda Salmonson, suggests that Shearing's *femmes fatales* have a source much closer to home. And that is the author's mother, Josephine Elisabeth Ellis Campbell: "They must, in part, reflect the darkest personal emotions and passing fantasies of redress" against her. We already have had glimpses earlier in these pages of the mother's neglectful treatment of the child to a degree that falls little short of domestic abuse. An attractive and charismatic woman, she was separated from an unhappy marriage

and led a bohemian life while "orchestrating continuous discord" at home." This is interesting as far as it goes, although hardly sufficient to explain the Furies that attend Shearing's women. See Salmonson, "Rose Petals, Drops of Blood," https://web.archive.org/web/20130628075333/http://www.violetbooks.com:80/bowen.html

16. Joseph Shearing, *The Lady and the Arsenic: The Life and Death of a Romantic* (New York: A.S. Barnes, 1944), 2.

17. Christopher Morley employs the memorable phrase, "angels of the darker drink," to some of the predatory females in the stories of Saki. See Christopher Morley, Introduction, *The Short Stories of Saki* (New York: The Modern Library, 1930), vi–vii.

18. Sally Benson, "Mystery and Crime," 89–90.

19. Marie-Fortunee Lafarge (nee Capelle, 15 January 1816–7 November 1852), was a Frenchwoman who was convicted of murdering her husband by arsenic poisoning in 1840. Her case was one of the first trials to reach the public through daily newspaper reports. The was first person to be convicted largely on direct forensic toxicological evidence. Questions about her guilt still persist. Orphaned at eighteen, she was adopted by a maternal aunt. Treated as a "poor relative" at school and envious of the young ladies who married wealthy noblemen, she used every means to pass as the daughter of a wealthy family. She eventually married in 1839 when she was twenty-three to Charles Lafarge and lived with him in a former Carthusian monastery in the hamlet of Le Glandier. She was quickly disillusioned with her new home, which was rat-infested, and with her new husband, who proved to have deceived her about his wealth. Within a year Charles began to complain of illnesses, at first thought to be cholera. Suspicions were raised that he was suffering from arsenic poisoning. She had fed him various kinds of foods thought to be poisoned. And she kept a small cabinet which contained arsenic, purportedly for the rats. She was seen taking white powders from the cabinet and stirring it into liquids, like eggnog. Marie called the powder "orange-blossom sugar." Her husband died in 1840. He left a will that, contrary to what he had told Marie, left his money to someone else. During the trial, which became a national sensation, several tests both confirmed and denied the presence of arsenic in Charles's exhumed body. A renowned toxicologist, Maathieu Orfila, was called into administer a new test, the "Marsh Test." This eventually became the means by which Marie was convicted and sentenced to life with hard labor in prison. King Louis-Philippe removed the "hard labor" from the sentence. George Sand was sympathetic to her. And so was a portion of the general public. In 1852, stricken with tuberculosis, Marie was released by Napoleon III. She died a few months later that same year. (In Joseph Shearing's investigation, there appears a shadowy character named "Denis Barbier," who may have been involved in the murder, although he was never brought to trial). In 1937 a French version of the case, *L'Affaire Lafarge*, was directed by Pierre Chenal.

20. Edward Wagenknecht, "The Extraordinary Mrs. Long," *New York Times Book Review*, 2 May 1943, 23.

21. "A Murder Mystery—and a Literary One," *The Age*, 10 April 1943, 3.

22. "The Roving Eye," *The Wilson Literary Bulletin*, October 1942, Vol. 17, 242.

23. Jane Steadman, "Joseph Shearing," *Twentieth-Century Crime and Mystery Writers* (Chicago; St. James Press, 1985), 960.

24. Marjorie Bowen Papers, Beinecke Library, Yale University, Box 37, Folder 254.

25. Sally Benson, "Mystery and Crime," 87–88.

26. "Moss Rose," *The Age*, 6 October 1934, 4.

27. John Webster's *The White Devil* (1612) is a five-act Jacobean revenge tragedy from 1612. It was first performed in London by the Queen Anne's Men. Based on events in Italy in the 1590s, the complicated plot involves two adulterous characters, Vittoria Corombona and the Duke Brancchiato, and their complicity in the murders of their respective marital partners. The play's version of events, explains scholar J. R. Mulryne, in his edition of the play, was intended to point up the political and moral corruption in contemporary England: "The moral anarchy shows itself everywhere in the play. As we watch or read, we enter a world of libertinism and unrestricted appetites" (xix). The term, "white devil," Mulryne adds, refers to hypocrisy, a condition inherent in virtually everyone in the play. All quotations from the play are taken from Mulryne's edition: *The White Devil* (Lincoln: University of Nebraska Press, 1969).

28. "Death Out of the Past," *Calgary Herald*, 21 February 1942, n.p.

29. For example, there is the scene in *The Marble Faun*, in which Donatello and Miriam have thrown their pursuer into a precipice to his death. They turn to each other in a conspiratorial embrace, a "dark sympathy, that is "closer than a marriage bond." So intimate is the connection that "it seemed as if their new sympathy annihilated all other ties, and that they were released from the chain of humanity, into a new sphere, a special law, had been created for them alone." Nathaniel Hawthorne, *The Marble Faun*, in Norman Holmes Pearson, *The Complete Novels and Selected Tales of Nathaniel Hawthorne* (New York: The Modern Library, 1937), 645.

30. Jessica Amanda Salmonson, "Introduction," to *Twilight* (Ashcroft, British Columbia: Ash-Tree Press, 1997), xix.

Chapter Six

1. Virginia Woolf, "Women and Fiction," in *Granite & Rainbow* (New York: Harcourt Brace Jovanovich, 1958), 77.

2. These notes are contained in a sheaf of unpublished writings bearing the collective title, "Through the Eyes of an Author," provided me by the kind folks at the Bowen Estate in Cornwall. What other writings, we wonder, reside somewhere, as yet unread, unpublished, and unremarked?

3. Margaret Campbell, *The Debate Continues: The Autobiography of Marjorie Bowen* (London: William Heinemann, 1939), 118).

4. See "Vessels of Gold," in Joseph Shearing, *Orange Blossoms*.

5. "The World's Gear" first appeared in the story collection *Seeing Life!* (London: Hurst & Blackett, Ltd., 1923). It was reprinted five years later in *Fond Fancy* under the title, "The Best Seller." These quotes taken from the 1923 edition.

6. "The Blue Glove" is in Joseph Shearing, *Orange Blossoms* (1938).

7. Marjorie Bowen Papers, Beinecke Library, Yale University, Box 25, Folder 183.

8. Athelstan Long was a Japanese prisoner of war, and later became governor of the Cayman Islands. He served as Cayman's last administrator from 1968 to 1971

and as the first governor from August 1971 to August 1972. At this writing, he has just celebrated his 100th birthday. His son, Charles Long, is a prominent Cayman painter. Michael was a prisoner of war in Germany. Later he held a senior position in the Civil Service. He died in 1999. Hilary was the youngest. During the War he was a Major in the Greenjackets and fought in North Africa. He wrote the Preface to the Salmonson collection of Bowen stories, *Twilight* and was in charge of depositing the Bowen Papers at the Beinecke Library at Yale University. He died at age 87 in 2007.

9. Marjorie Bowen Papers, Box 37, Folders 254, 256–257.

10. Marjorie Bowen Papers, Box 37, Folders 259, 263, 1943–1944.

11. Gertrude Mack, "Marjorie Bowen: A Triple Personality," *Sydney Morning Herald*, 27 August 1932, 5.

12. Correspondence provided by Sharon Eden of the Bowen Estate.

13. "A Famous Woman" appears in *Orange Blossoms*.

Appendix II

1. "London Letter," *The New York Times*, March 25, 1928, 69.

2. Yale Papers, Box 22.

3. The reference to the name "Fullerton" and the year given as 1881 suggests this might be an early treatment of the novel and film that later became *Blanche Fury*.

4. *The New York Times* noted Marjorie Bowen's evident research into the Restoration years of *Nell Gwyn* and praised the novel as "a readable story with sentiment.... It is a simple and pleasing tale of the love of Charles II for one of the most delightful ladies in the record of English history." "Nell Gwyn: Mistress Nell Gwyn," *The New York Times*, 26 December 1926, n.p.

5. James Quirk, "Nell Gwyn," *Photoplay*, April 1926, 56.

6. "Marjorie Bowen: A Triple Personality," *Sydney Morning Herald*, 27 August 1932, 5.

7. "Woman 'Creates' Pair of Authors to Fool Critics," *Prescott Evening Courier*, 20 March 1931, 4.

8. "Marjorie Bowen: A Triple Personality," 5.

9. Louella Parsons, "Moss Rose," *The Deseret News*, 21 Sept. 1946, p. 8.

10. Allan Essler Smith, "The Mark of Cain," *briandesmondhurst.org*. Retrieved: 27 August 2016.

11. See "The Pre-Raphaelite Sisterhood, http://pre-raphaelitesisterhood.com/blanche-fury/

Bibliography

Books and Articles About Marjorie Bowen

Adams, Henry. *The Education of Henry Adams.* Boston: Houghton Mifflin Co., 1961.

Arendt, Hannah. "Remembering W.H. Auden," *The New Yorker,* 3 December 2018, 68–70–71. (Originally published in *The New Yorker,* 30 January 1975).

Ashton, Mark. "Allegory, Fact, and Meaning in Gianbattista Tiepolo's Four Continents in Wurzburg," *The Art Bulletin,* Vol. 60, No. 1 (1978), 109–125.

Barcham, William L. *Tiepolo.* New York: Harry N. Abrams, 1992.

Beerbohm, Max. *And Even Now.* New York: E.P. Dutton & Company, 1921.

Beerbohm, Max. *Seven Men.* New York: Alfred A. Knopf, 1932.

Benet, William Rose. "The Phoenix Nest," *Saturday Review of Literature,* 3 August 1935, 19.

Benjamin, Walter. "Some Motifs in Baudelaire," in Walter Benjamin. *Illuminations* (New York: Shocken Books, 1968), 155–200.

Benjamin, Walter. "The Storyteller," in *Illuminations,* 83–109.

Benson, Sally. "Mystery and Crime," *The New Yorker,* 10 May 1941, 86–92.

Braddon, Ruth. *The Spiritualists.* New York: Alfred A. Knopf, 1983.

Campbell, Joseph, Ed. *Myths, Dreams, and Religion.* New York: E.P. Dutton & Co., Inc., 1970.

Carr, John Dickson. *The Burning Court.* New York: Harper & Brothers, 1959.

Carter, Lin. "Beyond the Gates of Dream." In *Phantastes.* New York: Ballantine, 1970, v–x.

Cawthorn, James, and Michael Moorcock, Eds. "Black Magic." In *Fantasy: The 100 Best Books.* New York: Carroll & Graf, 1988, 55–56.

Cecil, David. *Max: A Biography.* Boston: Houghton Mifflin, 1965.

Charlton, William. "She of Many Names," *Wormwood Magazine,* 2007.

Chaucer, Geoffrey. *The Canterbury Tales.* New York: The Heritage Press, 1946.

Chesterton, G.K. *Chaucer.* London: Faber & Faber, 1928.

Chesterton, G.K. "George MacDonald." In Fonseka, *G.K.C. as M.C.* London: Methuen and Co., 1929, 163–172.

Chesterton, G.K. "Utopias." In Fonseka, *G.K.C. as M.C.* London: Methuen and Co., 1929, 156–162.

Chew, Samuel C. *The Nineteenth Century and After (1789–1939).* New York: Appleton-Century-Crofts, 1948.

Cleaver, Pamela. "Marjorie Bowen." In Lesley Henderson, ed. *Romance and Historical Writers.* Chicago: St. James Press, 1990, 65–68.

Cohen, Morton. *Rider Haggard: His Life and Works.* London: Hutchinson & Company, 1960.

Countess of Oxford and Asquith, Ed. *Myself When Young: By Famous Women of Today.* London: Frederick Muller, Ltd., 1938.

Current-Garcia, Eugene. *O. Henry.* New York: Twayne, 1965.

Dalymple, Theodore. "A Quiet Evening's Reading," *The Social Order,* Spring 2018. https://www.city-journal.org/html/quiet-evenings-reading-15844.html.

Dirda, Michael. "Ghostly Women," *The Weekly Standard,* 6 March 2017, 38–41.

Dirda, Michael. *Readings.* Bloomington and Indianapolis: Indiana University Press, 2000.

Dunsany, Lord. *The Fourth Book of Jorkens.* Sauk City, WI: Arkham House, 1948.

Fonseka, J.P. de. *G.K.C. as M.C.* [a compilation of thirty-seven Introductions by G.K. Chesterton]. London: Methuen and Co., 1929.

Gilbert, Sandra M., and Susan Gubar. *The Madwoman in the Attic.* New Haven and London: Yale University Press, 1984.

Gordon, Mel. *The Grand Guignol: Theater of Fear and Terror.* New York: Da Capo Press, 1997.

Graham, Carla. "Phantastes." In Shippey, TA., Ed. *Magill's Guide to Science Fiction and Fantasy Literature,* Vol. 3. Englewood Cliffs, NJ: Salem Press, 1996, 737–738.

Graselli, Margaret Morgan, and Pierre Rosenberg, Eds. *Watteau.* Washington, D.C: National Gallery of Art, 1984.

Green, David. *The Hundred Years War: A People's History.* New Haven and London: Yale University Press, 2014.

Greenblatt, Stephen. *The Swerve: How the World Became Modern.* New York: W.W. Norton, 2011.

Greene, Douglas G. *John Dickson Carr: The Man Who Explained Miracles.* New York: Otto Penzler, 1995.

Greene, Graham. *The Lost Childhood and Other Essays.* New York: The Viking Press, 1951.

Heiland, Donna. *Gothic & Gender: An Introduction.* London: Blackwell, 2004.

Herman, Arthur. *The Cave and the Light*. New York: Random House, 2013.

Jarrett, Derek. *The Sleep of Reason*. New York: Harper & Row, 1989.

Joshi, S. T. *John Dickson Carr: A Critical Study*. Bowling Green, OH: Bowling Green State University Popular Press, 1990.

Joshi, S.T. *Unutterable Horror: A History of Supernatural Fiction*, Vol. 2. New York: Hippocampus Press, 2014.

Kellet, Arnold. *The Dark Side of Guy de Maupassant*. New York: Carroll & Graf Publishers, Inc., 1989.

Kenny, Dylan. "Between Me and My Real Self: On Vernon Lee. *The Paris Review*, 3 April 2018, n.p.

Knoepflmacher, U. C. *Ventures into Childhood: Victorians, Fairy Tales, and Femininity*. Chicago: University of Chicago Press, 1998.

Lanagguth, A.L. *Saki: A Life of Hector Hugh Munro*. London: Hamish Hamilton, 1981.

Lee, Vernon. "Faustus and Helena: The Supernatural in Art." In David G. Rowlands *Hauntings*. Ashcroft: Ash-Tree Press, 2002, 353–370.

Level, Maurice, trans. S.T. Joshi. *Thirty Hours with a Corpse*. Mineola, NY: Dover, 2016.

Lovecraft, H.P. *The Outsider and Others*. Sauk City, WI: Arkham House, 1939.

MacDonald, George. *Phantastes*. New York: Ballantine, 1970.

Maupassant, Guy de, trans. Arnold Kellett. *The Dark Side*. New York: Carroll & Graf, 1989.

Mendelsohn, Daniel. "Epic Family," *The New Yorker*, 15 October 2018, 87–93.

Milne, Tom. "The Elusive John Collier," *Sight and Sound*, Vol. 45, No. 2 (Spring 1976), 104–108.

Morley, Christopher. "Introduction," to *The Short Stories of Saki*. New York: The Modern Library, 1930.

Morrison, Robert. *The English Opium-Eater: A Biography of Thomas De Quincey*. New York: Pegasus Books, 2010.

Morrison, Robert. *Thomas De Quincey: On Murder*. New York: Oxford University Press, 2009.

Mulryne, J.R. "Introduction" to John Webster's *The White Devil*. Lincoln, NE: University of Nebraska Press, 1969, xi-xxviii.

Oates, Joyce Carol. "The Art of Vengeance," *The New York Review of Books*, 26 April 2007, 44–46.

Oates, Joyce Carol. *The Doll-Master*. New York: Mysterious Press, 2016.

O'Brien, Michael. "Chesterton and Paganism," *The Chesterton Review*, Vol. XVI, Nos. 3-4 (August–November), 1990, 181–181–201.

Paglia, Camille. *Sexual Personae*. New York: Vintage Books, 1991.

"A Precocious Author," *The New York Times*, 17 November 2006, BR751.

Prickett, Stephen. "Phantastes." In Magill, Frank N., Ed. *Survey of Modern Fantasy Literature*, Vol. 3. Englewood Cliffs, NJ: Salem Press, 1983, 1241–1245.

Richardson, Betty. *John Collier*. Boston: Twayne, 1983.

Roughead, William. *The Murder's Companion*. New York: The Readers Club, 1941. Foreword by Alexander Woollcott.

Salmonson, Jessica Amanda. "The Last Bouquet." In Jones, Stephen and Kim Newman, eds. *Horror 100 Best Books*. New York: Carrol & Graf, 1988, 88–89.

Salmonson, Jessica Amanda. *Rose Petals, Drops of Blood*," addendum to Salmonson's Introduction to *Twilight and Other Supernatural Romances*. See https://web.archive.org/web/20130628075333/http://www.violetbooks.com:80/bowen.html.

Sandoe, James. *Murder Plain and Fanciful*. New York: Sheridan House, 1948.

Schama, Simon. "Blue as Can Be," *The New Yorker*, 3 September 2018, 28–31.

Schama, Simon. *The Power of Art*. London: BBC Books, 2006.

Somerset, Anne. *The Affair of the Poisons: Murder, Infanticide and Satanism at the Court of Louis XIV*. London: Weidenfeld & Nicolson, 2003.

Stableford, Brian. "Haunted by the Pagan Past." sf@infinityplus.co.uk.

Steadman, Jane. "Joseph Shearing" [Marjorie Bowen]. *Twentieth-Century Crime and Mystery Writers*. Chicago: St. James Press, 1985, 957–960.

Talbot, Margaret. "Color Blind," *The New Yorker*, 29 October 2018, 42, 45–51.

Tibbetts, John C. "'An Enchanter Brewer of Dread': Marjorie Bowen and Her Ghosts," *Weird Fiction Review*, Centipede Press: No. 9 (Winter 2018), 296–320.

Tomalin, Clair. "At the Heart of the Onion," *The New York Review of Books*, 9 July 1994, 3737–38.

Treglown, Jeremy. *Roald Dahl: A Biography*. New York: Farrar Straus Giroux, 1994.

Veyne, Paul. *Did the Greeks Believe in Their Myths?* Chicago: University of Chicago Press, 1988.

Villiers de l'Isle-Adam. *The Scaffold*, trans. Brian Stableford. A Black Coat Press Book, 2004.

Villiers de l'Isle-Adam. *The Vampire Soul*, trans. Brian Stableford. A Black Coat Press Book, 2004.

Wagenknecht, Edward. "Bowen, Preedy, Shearing & Co.: A Note in Memory and a Check List," *Boston University Studies in English*, Vol. III, No. 3 (Autumn 1957), 181–189.

Wagenknecht, Edward. "The Extraordinary Mrs. Long," *New York Times Book Review*, 2 May 1943, 2, 22–23.

Wagenknecht, Edward. *Seven Masters of Supernatural Fiction*. Westport, CT: Greenwood Press, 1991.

Wagenknecht, Edward, Ed. *A Fireside Book of Yuletide Tales*. New York: Bobbs-Merrill, 1948.

Walbridge. "L'Affair Shearing," *Saturday Review of Literature*, 31 October 1942, 11.

Walbridge, Earle F.. "Shearingiana," *Saturday Review of Literature*, 12 July 1941, 11.

Webster, John. *The White Devil*, ed. J. R. Mulryne. Lincoln: University of Nebraska Press, 1969.

Wilson, Edmund. *The Wound and the Bow*. New York: Oxford University Press, 1947.

Wilson, Emily. "Myths Remixed," *The New York Times Book Review*, 5 August 2018, 18.

Wolfe, Gary K. "Fairy Tales. *Maerchen*, and Modern Fantasy." In Magill, Frank N., Ed. *Survey of Modern Fantasy Literature*, Vol. 5. Englewood Cliffs, NJ: 1983, 2267–2281.

Woolf, Virginia. *Granite & Rainbow*. New York: Harcourt Brace Jovanovich, 1958.

Wright, John L. "Goodness in Chesterton and Lewis," *The Chesterton Review*, Vol. XVII, Nos. 3 and 4 (August–November), 1991, 339–347.

Books, Articles and Edited Anthologies by Marjorie Bowen

[Note: Pagination throughout *The Furies of Marjorie Bowen* refers to these volumes.]

Abode of Love. London and New York: Hutchinson & Co., 1944 [as by Joseph Shearing].
Airing in a Closed Carriage. New York: Harper & Brothers, 1943 [as by Joseph Shearing].
Aunt Beardie. New York: Berkley, 1965.
Bagatelle. New York: Dodd Mead & Company, 1931 [as by George R. Preedy].
The Bishop of Hell. London: Bodley Head, 1949.
Blanche Fury. New York: 1965 [as by Joseph Shearing].
Boundless Water. London: Ward, Lock & Co., Ltd., 1928.
The Church and Social Progress. London: Watts & Co., 1945.
The Circle in the Water. London: Hutchinson & Co., 1939.
The Courtly Charlatan. London: Herbert Jenkins, 1942 [as by George R. Preedy].
The Crime of Laura Sarelle. New York: Berkeley, 1965 [as by Joseph Shearing].
Crimes of Old London. London: Odhams Ltd., 1919.
Curious Happenings. London: Mills & Boon, Ltd., 1917.
Dark Ann and Other Stories. London: John Lane the Bodley Head, Ltd., 1927.
The Debate Continues: Being the Autobiography of Marjorie Bowen [Margaret Campbell]. London: William Heinemann, Ltd., 1939.
Defender of the Faith. Alberta, Canada: Inheritance Publications, 1994.
The Devil Snar'd. London: Ernest Benn, Ltd., 1932 [as by George R. Preedy].
English Paragon. London: Hodder and Stoughton, 1930.
Ethics in Modern Art. London: Watts & Co., 1939.
Exits & Farewells. London: Selwyn & Blount, 1928.
"*Five Winds*." London: Hodder & Stoughton, 1927.
Fond Fancy and Other Stories. London: Selwyn & Blount, 1928.
For Her to See. London: Hutchinson & Co., n.d., 1947 [as by Joseph Shearing].
Forget-Me-Not (1942). London: Endeavour Press, 2015 [as by Joseph Shearing].
The Fourth Chamber. London: Hodder and Stoughton, 1944 [as by George R. Preedy].
General Crack. New York: Grosset & Dunlap, 1928.
Glen O' Weeping (1907). London: Endeavour Press, 2015. [American title: *The Master of Stair*].
God and the King. London: Methuen & Co., 1924.
God and the Wedding Dress. London: Endeavour Press, 2015.
God's Playthings. London: Smith and Elder, 1912.
The Golden Violet. New York: The Readers Club, 1941 [as by Joseph Shearing].
Gorgeous Lovers. London: John Lane, 1929.
Governor of England. London: Endeavor Press, 2015.
Grace Latouche and the Warringtons. London: Selwyn, 1931.
Great Tales of Horror (edited anthology). London: John Lane, 1933.
The Haunted Vintage. London: Odhams Press, Ltd., 1921.
I Dwelt in High Places. London: Collins, 1933.
I Will Maintain. London: Metheun & Co, 1910.
Julia Roseingrave. London: Ernest Benn, 1933 [as by Robert Paye].
Kecksies. Sauk City: Arkham House, 1976.
A Knight of Spain. London: Methuen & Co., Ltd., 1913.
Knot Garden. London: John Lane, 1933.
Lady and the Arsenic: The Life and Death of a Romantic. New York: A.S. Barnes and Company, 1944 [as by Joseph Shearing].
Last Bouquet: Some Twilight Tales. London: John Lane the Bodley Head, Ltd., 1933.
Lindley Waters. London: Hodder and Stoughton, 1942 [as by George R. Preedy].
Man with the Scales. London: Hutchinson, 1954.
"Margaret Campbell [Marjorie Bowen]," in Countess of Oxford and Asquith, ed. *Myself When Young*. London: Frederick Muller, Ltd., 1938.
Mary Queen of Scots. London: Endeavour Press, 2015.
Mignonette. New York: Harper & Brothers, 1948 [as by Joseph Shearing].
Mistress Nell Gwyn. New York: D. Appleton and Company, 1926.
More Great Tales of Horror (edited anthology). London: John Lane, 1935.
Moss Rose. New York: Harrison Smith and Robert Haas, 1934. New York: Berkeley, 1934 [as by Joseph Shearing].
Mr. Tyler's Saints. London: Hutchinson & Co., 1939.
Nightcap and Plume. London: Hodder and Stoughton, 1945 [as by George R. Preedy].
No Way Home. London: Hodder and Stoughton, 1947 [as by George R. Preedy].
Old Patch's Medley. London: Selwyn & Blount, 1928.
Orange Blossoms. London: William Heinemann Ltd., 1938 [as by Joseph Shearing].
Pleasant Husbands. London: Hurst and Blascett, 1921.
Poisoners. New York: Endeavour Press, 2017 [as by George R. Preedy].
Royal Pageantry: 12 May 1937. Covent Garden: Moss Bros. & Co. Ltd., 1937.
The Sacked City. London: Hodder Stoughton, 1949 [as by George R. Preedy].
Seeing Life. London: Hurst and Blascett, 1923.
Shadows of Yesterday: Stories from an Old Catalogue. London: Smith Elder & Co., 1916.
Sheep's Head & Babylon. London: John Lane, 1929.
The Spectral Bride. New York: Smith & Durrell, 1942 [as by Joseph Shearing].
Spider in the Cup. New York: Harrison Smith and Robert Haas, 1934.
Stinging Nettles: A Modern Story. London: Ward, Lock & Co., Ltd., 1923.
Sundry Great Gentlemen. London: John Lane the Bodley Head, Ltd., 1928.
The Sword Decides. London: Endeavour Press, 2015.
This Shining Woman: Mary Wollstonecraft Godwin. New York: D. Appleton-Century Company, 1937.
To Bed at Noon. New York: Berkley Publishing Corp, 1965 [as by Joseph Shearing].
Twilight and Other Supernatural Romances. Ashcroft, B.C: Ash-Tree Press, 1998 [as Marjorie Bowen]. Edited by Jessica Amanda Salmonson.
The Veil'd Delight. London: Odhams Press, Ltd., 1933.
Viper of Milan. London: Endeavour Press, 2015.
William Prince of Orange. London: John Lane the Bodley Head, 1928.
World's Wonder and Other Essays. London: Hutchinson & Co., 1937.
Wrestling Jacob: A Study of the Life of John Wesley. London: William Heinemann, 1937.

Index

Numbers in ***bold italics*** indicate pages with illustrations

The Aeneid (Virgil) 61
"Affair of the Poisons" 41, 210n55
Agapemonites 32–35, 210n53
All This and Heaven Too (movie) 170
Arkham House 1, 147
Ash-Tree Press 1

Barrymore, John 198
Baudelaire, Charles 14
Beinicke Library at Yale University ix–x, 5, 58, 188
Benjamin, Walter 6
Benson, Sally 162
Benson, Stella 55
Blanche Fury (film) 199–205, ***203***
"Bonfire of the Vanities" 25
Bouguereau, Adolph-William (cover painting) iv, 2, 3, 14
Bowen, Marjorie [Gabrielle Margaret Vere Campbell]: biographical timeline 193–194; childhood 14, 97–98, 183–184; children (Giuseppina, Athelstan, Michael, Hilary Long) 187–190, ***188***, ***189***, ***190***, 216n8; as on conte cruel 119–125; death 190–191; on "female gothic" 8, 160–161; on The Furies 6, 23–24, 161–164, 203–205, 209n42; on ghost stories 97–102, 214n12; on history and biography 53–62, 195–196, 215n3; as pagan 13–14, 17–52; painter 58–61, 211n22; parents 97–99, 215n15; personal "Journey to Cythera" 15–24; personal "Music on the Hill" 13, 24, 52; pseudonyms 2, 7, 159 (George R. Preedy 7, 141, 213n72; Joseph Shearing 7, 56, 157–161, 165; Marjorie Bowen 5, 6, 7, 9, 207n5; Robert Paye 7); spiritual identity 14–15, 52, 97–98; on television and motion picture adaptations 175, 195–205, ***197***, ***200***, ***202***, ***203***; on true-crime stories 157–164; on William of Orange 8, 70–72, 77–79, 212n42–44; on witchcraft and the occult 19–52, 208n3; on writing 183–189
Bowen, Marjorie, works: (as **George R. Preedy**)—*Bagatelle* (short stories) 14, 17, 138–141, ***139***; *The Courtly Charlatan* 19, 209n39; *The Fourth Chamber* 111–114; *General Crack* (book and movie) 198–199; *Homage to the Unknown* (play) 14, 16, 138–140, 184, 208n13; *The Knot Garden* (short stories) 141; *Lyndley Waters* 18; *Nightcap and Plume* 18–19, 59, 61, 94–96, 213n72; *No Way Home* 60–61, 116–117; *The Poisoners* 23, 40–47, 210n55; *The Sacked City* 18–19, 117–118; (as **Joseph Shearing**)—*The Abode of Love* 32–35, 210n53; *Airing in a Closed Carriage* 160, 163; *The Angel of the Assassination* 159; *Aunt Beardie* 160, 161; *Blanche Fury* 160, 176–182; *Blanche Fury* (movie) 203–205; *The Crime of Laura Sarelle* 108–110, 160, 214n27; *For Her to See* 23, 159, 173; *Forget-Me-Not* 159, 168–170; *The Golden Violet* 160, 165–168, ***166***; *The Lady and the Arsenic* 160, 56, 162, 219n19; *Mark of Cain* (movie version of *Airing in a Closed Carriage*) 202–203; *Moss Rose* 170–173; *Moss Rose* (movie) 160, 199–201, ***200***; *Orange Blossoms* (short stories) 21, 144–146; *So Evil My Love* (movie version of *For Her to See*) 201–202, ***202***; *The Spectral Bride* (*The Fetch*) 103–105, 160, 214n22; *The Spider in the Cup* (*Album Leaf*) 160–161; *To Bed at Noon* 160; (as **Margaret Campbell**)—*The Debate Continues* (autobiography) 7, 9; "Myself When Young" (memoir) 208n14; (as **Marjorie Bowen: novels and biographies and essays**)—*Affairs of Men* 213n62; *Black Magic* 2, 25–27, 58, 210n48; *Carnival of Florence* 24–25; *Church and Social Progress* (essays) 14–15, 71; *The Circle in the Water* 27–29; *Defender of the Faith* 77–79, 213n58; *Dickon* 61–62; *The English Paragon* 83–90, 135, 213n65, 213n68; "Five Winds" 50–52, 115–116; *Glen O' Weeping* (*Master of Stair*) 72–75, 212n50; *God and the King* 79–83; *God and the Wedding Dress* 47–50, 210n60; *The Governor of England* 62, 90–94; *The Haunted Vintage* 13, ***15***, 30–32; *I Dwelt in High Places* 35–40; *I Will Maintain* 75–77; *Lady in a Veil* 188; *Man with the Scales* 7, 118, 184; *Mary Queen of Scots* 56–57; *Nell Gwyn* (*Mistress Nell Gwyn*) (book and movie) 196–198, ***198***, 217n4; *Patriotic*

Lady 56; *Presence and the Power* 17–18; *Royal Pageantry* 53–55; *The Shadow on Mockways* 184; *Stinging Nettles* 186–187; *The Sword Decides* 212*n*39; *The Third Estate* 211*n*4; *This Shining Woman* 56–57, 183; "Through the Eyes..." 216*n*2; *The Veil'd Delight* 184; *The Viper of Milan* 7, 55, 62–69, **63**, 207*n*6, 212*n*24; *William Hogarth* 56, 59, 211*n*17; *World's Wonder* 70; *Wrestling Jacob* 20, 56; (as **Marjorie Bowen: short story collections**)—*Bishop of Hell* 146–147; *Crimes of Old London* 21, 126; *Curious Happenings* 125; *Dark Ann and Other Stories* 130, 185–186; *The English Paragon* 83–90, 135; *Exits and Farewells* 21, 130–131; *Fond Fancy* 17, 131–***132***, 195; *God's Playthings* 124; *Gorgeous Lovers and Other Tales* 133–135; *Grace Latouche and the Warringtons* 135–138; *Great Tales of Horror* (ed.) 99, 150–151; *Kecksies* 21, 101, 147–149; *Last Bouquet: Some Twilight Tales* 142–144; *Miscellaneous* (uncollected) 152–156; *More Great Tales of Horror* (ed.) 99, 150–151; *Old Patch's Medley* 131; *The Pleasant Husband* 18, 127–128; *Seeing Life! and Other Stories* 6, 17, 128–129; *Shadows of Yesterday* 6, 125; *Sheep's-Head and Babylon* 132–133; *Twilight and Other Supernatural Romances* 147, 194, 207*n*8, 214*n*20, 215*n*24, 217*n*8; (as **Robert Paye**)—*Julia Roseingrave* 1, 22
Beerbohm, Max 122
Bowen Estate (estate of Gabrielle Long) ix
Browning, Elizabeth Barrett 16
Browning, Robert 14

Canterbury Tales (Chaucer) 9–11, 121
Carr, John Dickson 1, 46–47, 210*n*59
Chaucer, Geoffrey 9–11, 55, 208, *intro.n* 20
Chesterton, G.K. 10, 60, 62, 118, 157, 211*n*21
Cleaver, Pamela 61–62
The Cloister and the Hearth see Reade, Charles
Collier, John 121, 122
Conan Doyle, Arthur 2, 7, 55, 207*n*6

Conte cruel 120–123, 215*n*11–12; see also Bowen, Marjorie
Costanzo, Zefferino Emilio (first husband) 193
Cromwell, Oliver 62, 69–70, 90–93, 213*n*71

Dahl, Roald 121, ***123***
Dalrymple, John 72–74, 158, 212*n*50
The Debate Continues ("Margaret Campbell" autobiography) 7, 9, 52, 98, 187–188, 194, 208*n*15, 208*n*24, 209*n*26, 211,*n*1, 211*n*15, 211*n*19, 212*n*37, 213*n*2, 215*n*23, 215*n*26, 216*n*3
Debussy, Claude 14
Dee, Jane 20, 24, 35–41, 127
Dee, John 20, 24, 35–41, 127
de la Mare, Walter 100
De Quincey, Thomas 157–158, 159
Derleth, August 147, 152
Dirda, Michael 1–3, 7, 9
Dunsany, Lord 122

Eden, Sharon 217*n*12
English Civil Wars 90

Farinelli (Carlo Broschi) 138
female gothic 8; see also Moers, Ellen
Feuillade, Louis 42
film noir 199
The Furies 6, 23, 161–163, 176, 209*n*42; see also Bowen, Marjorie; Webster, John

Gance, Abel 195
ghost stories see Bowen, Marjorie
Gish, Dorothy 196–198
Glencoe Massacre 72
Goldblatt, Stephen 5, 25, 210*n*46
Greene, Graham 2, 7, ***67***
Gustav Vasa, III 25, 59, 61, 94–96, 141

Handel, George Frideric 17, 43
Hecate 32
Herbert, George 16, 207*n*18, 208*n*23–25; see also "Music on the Hill"
Hoffmann, E.T.A. 14, 208*n*9
Hogarth, William 8, 59; see also William Hogarth

James, Henry 105, 115
James, M.R. 1, ***100***
Joshie, S.T. 123, 210*n*59
"Journey to Cythera" (painting) 16; see also Bowen, Marjorie

Kelley, Edward 20, 24, 35–37, 39

Lafarge, Marie 160, 162–163, 216*n*19
Lee, Vernon 7, 14, 208*n*12
Le Fanu, J. Sheridan 100
Level, Maurice 122–123
Lewis, Sinclair 157, 166
Limoges, Battle of 89
Long, Arthur (second husband) 7, 188, 190, 193
Louis XIV 23, 24, 41–42, 46, 62, 70–71, 75, 77, 124, 210*n*55
Lovecraft, H.P. 121–122
Lucretius: and *On the Nature of Things* 19, 24–25, 139, 210*n*45, 210*n*47

MacDonald, George: and *Phantastes* 16, 118, 209*n*27
Machen, Arthur 14, 100
"madwoman in the attic" 8, 163, 207
Mahler, Gustav 14
Mark of Cain (film) 199–205
Marston Moor, Battle of 90, 92
Maupassant, Guy de 121–122
Mezzetin 19, 139
Moers, Ellen 8
Morley, Christopher 122
Moss Rose (film) 199–205, ***200***
"music at midnight" 9, 16, 208, *intro.n*18, 209*n*25
"Music on the Hill" see Bowen, Marjorie
"Music on the Hill" (Saki short story) 13, 208*n*7
"Myself When Young" ("Margaret Campbell" memoir) see Bowen, Marjorie

Najera, Battle of 83, 87–88
Namur, Siege of 71, 75, 81–82, 124
Nell Gwyn (film) 196–198, ***197***
"New Canterbury Tales" (Bowen) 9–11
Nymuegen, Battle of 77

"O. Henry" (William Sydney Porter) 123
Oates, Joyce Carol 2
"On the Nature of Things" 25
Orel, Harold 55
Oresteia (Aeschylus) 209*n*42, 210*n*42

Paglia, Camille 23, 209*n*37, 210*n*42
Parlinganesia 104
Phantastes see MacDonald, George
"Piece of Chalk" see Chesterton, G.K.
Plantagenet, Edward 83, 84,

86, 88, 90, 109, 124, 135, 213n66
"Pope Joan" 2, 26, 210n48
Priest to the Temple see Herbert, George

Radcliffe, Ann 8
Reade, Charles 57
Roughead, William 56, 157–158, 165

"Saki" (Hector Hugh Munro) and "Music on the Hill" (story) 13, 52, 122
Salmonson, Jessica Amanda 1, 7, 100, 115, 207n2
Savonarola 24–25, 91, 124
Schama, Simon 60, 211n23
Schumann, Robert 14, 208n11
Shelley, Mary 8; see also *This Shining Woman*

So Evil My Love (film) 199–205, **202**
Stevenson, Robert Louis 55
Swinburne, Algernon 14, 208n10

Theodora see Handel, George Frideric
This Shining Woman 56, 183
Tibbetts, John C. *x*, 1–2
Tiepolo, Gianbattista 17, 59, 139, 207n32
true-crime stories 157–158; see also Bowen, Marjorie
Twain, Mark 2, 7, 67, **68**, 207n6, 212n35
Wagenknecht, Edward 8, 56, 61, 100, 117, 159, 163, 207n2
Watteau, Jean-Antoine 16, 59, 138, 209n31
Webster, John and *The White Devil* 176, 181; see also *Blanche Fury*
Wesley, John 20, 32, 56, 98, 213n7
West, Rebecca 7
Wharton, Edith 7
Wheatley, Dennis 2
The White Devil see Webster, John and *The White Devil*
William Hogarth 56, 59, 211n17, 211n18
William of Orange 70–72, 212n42–44; see also Bowen, Marjorie
Wollstonecraft, Mary 8, 57, 183; see also *This Shining Woman*
Woolf, Virginia 13, 55, 207n14

Yale University 5–6, 53, 57–58, 165, 188, 194–195

www.ingramcontent.com/pod-product-compliance
Ingram Content Group UK Ltd.
Pitfield, Milton Keynes, MK11 3LW, UK
UKHW050531150426
5217IPUK00026B/1882